MW01045224

My Life as a Colomb.

Revolutionary

In the series *Voices of Latin American Life,*

edited by Arthur Schmidt

Also in the series

Robert Gay, *Lucia*

Elena Poniatowska, *Nothing, Nobody: The Voices of the Mexico City Earthquake*

My Life as a Colombian Revolutionary

Reflections of a Former Guerrillera

María Eugenia Vásquez Perdomo

Translated by Lorena Terando
and with an Introduction by Arthur Schmidt

TEMPLE UNIVERSITY PRESS PHILADELPHIA

María Eugenia Vásquez Perdomo is currently coordinating an NGO project in conjunction with a UN organization, which serves women forcibly displaced by the armed conflict. The Spanish-language version of this book, published as *Escrito para no morir: Bitácora de una militancia*, was awarded the Colombian National Prize for Testimonial Literature in 1998.

Lorena Terando is Assistant Professor of Translation at the University of Wisconsin, Milwaukee.

Temple University Press
1601 North Broad Street
Philadelphia PA 19122
www.temple.edu/tempress

© 2005 by Lorena Terando
All rights reserved
Published 2005
Printed in the United States of America

Text design by Kate Nichols

♾ The paper used in this publication meets the requirements of the American
National Standard for Information Sciences—Permanence of Paper for Printed Library
Materials, ANSI Z39.48-1984

Library of Congress Cataloging-in-Publication Data

Vásquez Perdomo, María Eugenia.
[Escrito para no morir. English]
    My life as a Colombian revolutionary : reflections of a former guerrillera/
María Eugenia Vásquez Perdomo; translated by Lorena Terando and with
an introduction by Arthur Schmidt.
        p.   cm. — (Voices of Latin American life)
    Includes bibliographical references and index.
    ISBN 1-59213-100-X (cloth : alk. paper — ISBN 1-59213-101-8 (pbk. : alk. paper)
    1. Vásquez Perdomo, María Eugenia.   2. M-19 (Colombian guerrilla group).
3. Guerrillas—Colombia—History.   4. Colombia—History—1946–1974.
5. Colombia—History—1974–6.   Women guerrillas—Colombia—Biography.
I. Title.   II. Series.

F2279.22.A37A3 2004
986.106′32′092–dc22
    [B]   2004047983

2   4   6   8   9   7   5   3   1

Contents

Photograph gallery follows page 126

Acknowledgments

To my dead, who left but never gave up their dreams; and to those who still trust in life. To my mother, whose silent presence has been the most eloquent of testaments to love. To my son Juan, from whom I inherited this life of the now. And to my son José, I offer these pages as an inheritance with no regrets.

To life and the gamble to save it. To my professor, Luis Guillermo Vasco, because he always opened up paths for me. To Professor Jaime Arocha, who trusted in me more than I did; he guided my search and patiently suffered my process. To Alonso Salazar, with whom my past stopped being clandestine; he granted me the word and allowed me to feel proud of my stories. To Pilar Riaño, with whom I discovered the complexity and value of memory. To my *amigas*, the women with whom I undid and redid myself so many times... with whom I learned to cry without shame. To my friends, that legion of loving accomplices who read these pages over my shoulder, entered into them, and sustained my spirit. To the love that inspired every word.

And to all of you readers, who are the meaning and the magnetic attraction of this story, because I am sure that without the support of each one of you, I would not have begun the adventure of looking back on my life. Nor would I be who I am.

Introduction

Arthur Schmidt

MARÍA EUGENIA VÁSQUEZ PERDOMO's memoir recounts the compelling story of a highly unusual personal journey. Born in Cali, Colombia, the country's third-largest city, in 1951, Vásquez Perdomo came of age amid the radical student politics of the National University, where she gave up her previously "bourgeois" existence, exchanging, as she tells us, her makeup and miniskirts for jeans. For her, this would be no mere alteration in appearance but a deep submerging of self within the society of her revolutionary *compañeros* and their shared goal of liberating Colombia from poverty and oppression. Takeovers of academic buildings soon gave way to life as a revolutionary *guerrillera*, an existence that would define her identity for the next eighteen years.

An unstinting devotion to "the cause" sustained her clandestine and risky life, taking precedence over her personal self—over loves won and lost, over two sons given birth, and even over her own comprehension of what it meant to be a woman. Whether transporting hidden weapons, fronting for an urban safe house, holding foreign diplomats hostage, attempting a rural insurgency, going into exile, or doing time in jail, Vásquez Perdomo acted completely as the soldier that she was. Her identity as a revolutionary suppressed her identity as a woman, an experience not unknown to other female Latin American radicals of her generation. "The fact that I was a woman by biological definition didn't bother me," she recalls, "but I wasn't very aware of what it meant, either, in a world that made us all the same in ideology. Equality weighed more than difference."

Women and Guerrilla Movements in Latin America

Vásquez Perdomo lived through an era of revolutionary struggle in Latin America whose impulses for change directed themselves primarily against the oppressions of class and imperialism. Matters of gender occupied a distinctly secondary position in left-wing agendas. Revolutionary guerrilla insurgencies appeared in various parts of Latin America following the triumph of Fidel Castro's Cuban guerrilla fighters in 1959. In the words of the Mexican intellectual and former foreign minister Jorge G. Castañeda, an expert on Latin American radicalism, "The Cuban Revolution impacted the left in Latin America as nothing had ever done before. . . . Before Fidel entered Havana, the left in Latin America was reformist, gradualist, or resignedly pessimistic about the prospects of revolution. For the three decades that followed, revolution was at the top of its agenda."[1]

The sudden emergence of the Cuban revolutionary regime inspired the belief that a relatively small cadre of armed revolutionaries—the revolutionary *foco* so widely publicized in Latin America by the writings of Che Guevara and Régis Debray—could create the appropriate conditions for successful national revolution.[2] In the early 1960s, rural guerrilla insurgencies appeared in Colombia, Guatemala, Nicaragua, Peru, and Venezuela. Some Latin American insurgents have left widely read personal accounts of their exploits, among them Héctor Béjar's saga of lost causes on the Peruvian altiplano and Omar Cabezas's adventures in the Sandinista insurgency in Nicaragua.[3]

1. Jorge G. Castañeda, *Utopia Unarmed: The Latin American Left after the Cold War* (New York: Knopf, 1993), 67–68.
2. Ernesto Guevara, *Guerrilla Warfare*, with an introduction and case studies by Brian Loveman and Thomas M. Davies Jr. (Lincoln: University of Nebraska Press, 1985); Régis Debray, *Revolution in the Revolution? Armed Struggle and Political Struggle in Latin America*, trans. Bobbye Ortiz (New York: Monthly Review Press, 1967).
3. Héctor Béjar, *Peru 1965: Notes on a Guerrilla Experience,* trans. William Rose (New York: Monthly Review Press, 1970); Omar Cabezas, *Fire from the Mountain: The Making of a Sandinista*, foreword by Carlos Fuentes, trans. Kathleen Weaver (New York: Crown, 1985).

Vásquez Perdomo's story forms part of a new wave of testimonial literature in Latin America that seeks to heal the wounds left by a long generation
of revolutionary and counterrevolutionary conflict, recognizing, as one author put it, that "recovery begins with memory."[4] Nevertheless, her tale is
something of a rarity. For one thing, "women have generally been under- or
misrepresented in stories of war, and are most often seen as grief-stricken,
powerless victims."[5] Vásquez Perdomo was an active combatant who ultimately discovered that she was a victim as well. For another, most book-
length insurgent testimonies have derived from men's memories. Initially, relatively few women fought in guerrilla movements in Latin America, although
Che Guevara himself declared in *Guerrilla Warfare* that "the woman . . .
can work the same as a man and she can fight." Nevertheless, as Vásquez
Perdomo notes, politics and military affairs tended to remain "clearly in-
scribed in the man's universe. Men's things." War, by its very nature, has
tended to discourage gender equality. While open to women, Latin American guerrilla movements remained male-dominated organizations, and male
attitudes usually confined women to purely supporting roles in revolutionary warfare. Guevara's text revealed his clear preference for using women to
transport "objects, messages, or money," to teach revolutionary recruits, to
provide medical care, and to carry out their "habitual tasks of peacetime,"
such as cooking and sewing.[6]

This pattern held true in Colombia, even though the origins of its guerrilla insurgencies differed considerably from other areas of Latin America.
Left-wing guerrillas appeared during the last phase of the widespread political violence that convulsed Colombia between 1946 and 1966. Known as
la Violencia, this highly complex period is only partially understood by schol-
ars, although new research has tended to show that it remains "inextricably
intertwined" with the revolutionary and counterrevolutionary struggle and
the other forms of conflict that Colombia has experienced ever since Vásquez
Perdomo was a teenager.[7] While some women are known to have taken part
in combat during la Violencia and the early years of revolutionary insurgency
in Colombia, most remained active in the support networks that sustained

4. Alison Brysk, "Recovering from State Terror: The Morning After in Latin America," *Latin American Research Review* 38, no. 1 (2003): 239.
5. Olivia Bennett, Jo Bexley, and Kitty Warnode, "Introduction: Our Words," in *Arms to Fight, Arms to Protect: Women Speak Out about Conflict*, ed. Olivia Bennett, Jo Bexley, and Kitty Warnode (London: Panos, 1995), 2.
6. Guevara, *Guerrilla Warfare*, 132–34.
7. Mary Roldán, *Blood and Fire: La Violencia in Antioquia, Colombia, 1946–1953* (Durham: Duke University Press, 2002), 1.

armed combatants.[8] This gendered division of labor certainly reflected sexism, but at times it embodied good strategy as well, particularly in clandestine urban operations where a woman might attract less suspicion than a man.[9] As she acknowledges, Vásquez Perdomo could ferry weapons and messages through urban security zones more safely than could any male. On more than one occasion, she used her femininity to distract guards, disguise the presence of a guerrilla safe house, or escape a government "manhunt."

Many more women became involved in guerrilla activities during the "second wave" of insurgencies that washed over Latin America in the late 1960s. In Nicaragua women composed about one-quarter of the Sandinista combatants, including several well-known officers by the time of the successful overthrow of the Somoza dictatorship in 1979.[10] In more recent years, women such as Comandante Ramona and Comandante Ester have acted as prominent spokespersons for the Zapatista rebels in the southern Mexican state of Chiapas. Observers have remarked on the high visibility of female soldiers in the ranks of the guerrilla forces that still operate in Colombia today.[11] Second-wave movements during the 1970s–1980s, such as Vásquez Perdomo's own M-19 in Colombia, proved more attuned to local circumstances than did earlier guerrilla organizations, and more adept at incorporating women into their ranks. Vásquez Perdomo declares that "in Colombia you had to shoot to be heard," and shoot she did. She took part in key M-19 armed operations such as the capture of the embassy of the Dominican Republic in 1980 and the guerrilla landing on the Pacific coast near the Mira River in 1981. She worked closely with top figures in the M-19, among them Jaime (el Flaco) Bateman, Alvaro Fayad, Iván Marino Ospina, Lucho Otero, Rosemberg Pabón, and Carlos Toledo, all of whom appear in her narrative.

Yet, as women continue to discover, greater female participation in revolutionary action does not guarantee gender equality. Despite a "visibility never before seen in any political party in Peruvian history," women in the Shining Path found themselves manipulated by "patriarchal relations [that] were reproduced to benefit the party." The number of women did increase in combat ranks and in other important activities, such as intelligence, but

8. Gonzalo Sánchez and Donny Meertens, *Bandits, Peasants, and Politics: The Case of "La Violencia" in Colombia*, trans. Alan Hynds (Austin: University of Texas Press, 2001), 192.
9. Linda L. Reif, "Women in Latin American Guerrilla Movements: A Comparative Perspective," *Comparative Politics* 18, no. 1 (1986): 153–54.
10. Ibid., 157–61; Patricia M. Chuchryk, "Women in the Revolution," in *Revolution and Counterrevolution in Nicaragua*, ed. Thomas W. Walker (Boulder: Westview Press, 1991), 145.
11. Donny Meertens, *Ensayos sobre tierra, violencia y género: Hombres y mujeres en la historia rural de Colombia, 1930–1990* (Bogotá: Universidad Nacional de Colombia, 2000), 412.

the Sendero Luminoso never developed a serious women's agenda as part of either its program or its mode of operation. Similarly, female combatants in guerrilla forces in Colombia today rarely win top leadership positions.[12]

Even when revolutionary movements attained power, as in Nicaragua, a comprehensive attack on sexism and traditional gender roles proved elusive. The Sandinista Revolution was "reasonably successful in involving and integrating women" and brought about many institutional changes benefiting them. Nevertheless, women's share of the membership of the military and the Sandinista National Liberation Front (FSLN) dropped in the decade following the revolutionary triumph. No women held top FSLN leadership roles. While some see this as the result of security considerations or mistaken decisions, others have argued that men articulated Latin American revolutionary projects within a masculine narrative that inherently subordinated women.[13] Critics have faulted both Latin American radicalism and the post-conflict settlements for their failure to give women a central voice. As Paulina, the Chilean activist who survived torture without betraying her husband, tells him in Ariel Dorfman's play, *Death and the Maiden*: "Of course, I'm going to listen to you. Haven't I always listened to you?"[14]

Vásquez Perdomo's Experience

Readers of Vásquez Perdomo's story will quickly see how much she listened to the revolutionary cause and how long it took her to develop a woman's voice. Over many years, Vásquez Perdomo's female identity subordinated itself to her militancy. Only toward the end of her career as a revolutionary did issues of gender undermine her total devotion to guerrilla activity. At the start, this commitment drew upon her childhood fondness for drama— she imagined herself as Tania, the "heroic guerrilla warrior" immortalized in Cuba for having given her life in Che Guevara's failed attempt at revolution in Bolivia in 1966–67.[15] Fortunately, Vásquez Perdomo proved far more able than the ill-fated Tania. Overcoming the initial nervousness of her first revolutionary venture—helping to steal guns from the house of a friend—Vásquez

12. Isabel Coral Cordero, "Women in War: Impact and Responses," in *Shining and Other Paths: War and Society in Peru, 1980–1995*, ed. Steve J. Stern (Durham: Duke University Press, 1998), 349–53; Meertens, *Ensayos sobre tierra*, 412.

13. Chuchryk, "Women in the Revolution," 158–59; Ileana Rodríguez, *Women, Guerrillas and Love: Understanding War in Central America* (Minneapolis: University of Minnesota Press, 1996).

14. Ariel Dorfman, *Death and the Maiden* (New York: Penguin Books, 1992), 30.

15. Jorge G. Castañeda, *Compañero: The Life and Death of Che Guevara*, trans. Marina Castañeda (New York: Knopf, 1997), 362.

Perdomo promptly accustomed herself to the rigors of living a secret life. Her acting skills served her well as she eluded the government dragnets that characterized Colombia during the presidency of Julio César Turbay Ayala. Through her experiences, she discovered happily that government security forces expected any guerrillera to be "something like a tomboy." In employing her feminine charms to revolutionary advantage, Vásquez Perdomo remained acutely sensitive to her surroundings and capable of assuming the persona needed for survival in virtually any setting. Like Yolanda, the ballet dancer and Peruvian revolutionary in the Nicholas Shakespeare novel (and John Malkovich movie) *The Dancer Upstairs*, Vásquez Perdomo operated as the "woman no one suspected."

None of this could take place without a frightfully high cost. Unlike Yolanda, no detractor could say that Vásquez Perdomo benefited from her looks alone or lacked "the meat and gristle of character."[16] For years she lived a homeless "gypsy life" of false ID cards, transient loves, and constant insecurity. She often carried a cyanide pill with her with which to take her own life in case of capture. As time wore on she began to fear schizophrenia, discovering that "two diametrically opposed women lived inside me . . . pitted against each other." One woman executed the difficult tasks of a guerrillera with aplomb, the other sought the personal life that revolutionary militancy denied. Vásquez Perdomo's remarkable resiliency and her knack for drawing strength from friendships enabled her to navigate through the dangers of personal disintegration. At times her cohort of revolutionary compañeros filled the role of family, deadening the pain inflicted by her physical separation from her sons and by the constant anxiety of her clandestine existence.

The M-19 itself first separated Vásquez Perdomo from the guerrilla identity that had sustained so much personal sacrifice. Against her objection, it ordered her to Libya, where she arrived in April 1987 in the subordinated role of compañera to a male combatant. In the process of becoming more militaristic in character, the M-19 deprived Vásquez Perdomo of her customary levels of responsibility. The military training mission soon proved a farce. Even worse for Vásquez Perdomo, she found herself a female outsider in two male-dominated worlds, that of the local M-19 organization and that of Libyan society. No longer a functioning guerrillera but a dependent figure in a man's world, she could not withstand the devastating news of the death of her elder son, Juan Diego. His loss at age thirteen robbed Vásquez Perdomo of all sense of tomorrow, of a proximate future in which she could

16. Nicholas Shakespeare, *The Dancer Upstairs* (New York: Anchor, 2002), 265.

make up for years of lost motherhood and compensate for the aspects of herself she had negated in becoming a guerrillera. "I had no real referent," she writes. "All my sacrifice was unfounded, there was nothing more than an immense emptiness. . . . I began my existence as a ghost."

Leaving the M-19 involved more than just finding a new occupation. As Vásquez Perdomo put it: "The person I had been up to that moment had exploded into a million pieces. . . . For many years my identity had been formed by my politics, my belonging to the M-19, my ideals. . . . Now all of that was not enough." Throughout her time of armed struggle, exile, and prison, Vásquez Perdomo had never lost the support of her mother, an anchor in life who now helped with the difficult reconstruction of self following her return to Colombia. Slowly the "world populated by ghosts" began to recede. Vásquez Perdomo discovered that writing gradually wove the fibers of a life, bringing together the strands of old and new. Anthropology, the career she had long ago abandoned for life as a guerrillera, now beckoned once again. As she recalls, "I slowly discovered that it was nice to be outside the organization even though it hurt me, if only in the sense that I now felt in control of my own life. I no longer had to live for others." Ownership of her life entailed a retrospective understanding of how the inequalities of gender had operated as an unseen presence in her guerrillera world. This perception enabled her to open a new chapter in her life, embracing existence as a "draft idea that is invented every day."

The Colombian Past

María Eugenia Vásquez Perdomo's story reminds one of the title of playwright Lillian Hellman's autobiography, *An Unfinished Woman*.[17] Vásquez Perdomo recounts her experiences as a step forward in the project of constructing who she is. In doing so, she urges her readers to accept the unorthodox route toward selfhood that her life has taken. In a similar fashion, in his 1982 Nobel Prize acceptance speech, Colombian writer Gabriel García Márquez asked inhabitants of the North Atlantic world to avoid measuring Latin America "with the yardstick that they use for themselves, forgetting that the ravages of life are not the same for all, and that the quest of our own identity is just as arduous and bloody for us as it was for them."[18] Vásquez Perdomo's story is both an individual and a Latin American

17. Lillian Hellman, *An Unfinished Woman: A Memoir* (Boston: Little, Brown, 1969).
18. Gabriel García Márquez, "The Solitude of Latin America," 8 Dec. 1982, http://www.nobel.se/literature/laureates/1982/marquez-lecture.html.

story—in particular, a Colombian story. Few Latin American societies fit García Márquez's words as well as his native Colombia does when he spoke of how much "the immeasurable violence and pain of our history are the result of age-old inequities and untold bitterness." Nearly two centuries after independence, Colombia remains an unfinished nation-state characterized by widespread violence and severe social and political divisions. Seventeen years after Vásquez Perdomo's departure from the M-19, the country's condition appears critical. Colombians consider themselves "unprotected in life and property as at few times in the past. The indices of homicides, personal injuries, kidnappings, and forced displacement of families and neighborhoods are among the highest in the world. And they show no sign of declining."[19] Today Colombia's motto might well be the lament reputedly uttered by Simón Bolívar, the hero of its wars for independence, during his last months of life: "How will I ever get out of this labyrinth!"[20]

It is important to set Vásquez Perdomo's story in the context of the endemic violence—the "labyrinth"—in which Colombia has remained trapped since the end of World War II. Vásquez Perdomo credits her insurgent leaders with linking revolutionary activity to "youthful longings," making it "compatible with love, with *la rumba*, with theater, with laughter and studying. They didn't demand sacrifices of us, they offered us life alternatives." Ultimately, she discovered within herself the need to fulfill other dimensions of human existence. Nevertheless, her comments illustrate the point that structures of violence have come to offer different "life alternatives" for large numbers of Colombians. As one expert on the state of affairs in Colombia noted recently, "Many former combatants miss their old guerrilla lifestyle and are nostalgic about the collective feeling of security, power, and belonging that they experienced in their underground activities."[21] Violence has been a potent factor in shaping ways of life since 1946, when la Violencia commenced, the product of complex national and local political rivalries and unresolved social conflicts. During the past sixty years, national life in Colombia has evolved into a "war system" in which the commonality among the protagonists—and the protagonists in Colombia have multiplied over time—is the use of violence. Today violence links the leading actors—government

19. Frank Safford and Marco Palacios, *Colombia: Fragmented Land, Divided Society* (New York: Oxford University Press, 2002), 345.
20. Gabriel García Márquez, *The General in His Labyrinth*, trans. Edith Grossman (New York: Penguin Books, 1991), 267.
21. Gonzalo Sánchez, "Problems of Violence, Prospects for Peace," in *Violence in Colombia, 1990–2000: Waging War and Negotiating Peace*, ed. Charles Bergquist, Ricardo Peñaranda, and Gonzalo Sánchez (Wilmington, Del.: SR Books, 2001), 27.

officials, politicians, military, police, narcotics traffickers, guerrilla movements, paramilitaries, landowners, entrepreneurs, and agents of the United
States government—in a dynamic system characterized by three features: (1)
the failure of political institutions to resolve conflicts; (2) a political economy
that makes war "the best available option" for leading protagonists; and (3)
a relative impasse in the efforts to end armed conflict either by force or by
negotiation. One of the principal challenges to Colombians today is how to
make peace desirable to those in the "war system."[22]

The origin of this "war system" and its contemporary modes of operation constitute the primary concerns of research on Colombia today. Historians interpret nineteenth- and early twentieth-century trends as background
rather than as direct cause of the country's propensity for endemic violence
over the past six decades. They stress that Colombia entered the twentieth century with a relatively weak national state and a two-party political
system prone to extreme partisanship. The experiences of the nineteenth
century failed to overcome the obstacles to national unity that geography
and economy posed. At the time of independence in 1830, Colombia was a
relatively self-sufficient agrarian society. Even within the more heavily populated highlands, dispersed settlement was the norm. Colombia's commerce
proved too meager a force to generate economic and demographic concentration. As late as the 1850s, only the capital city of Bogotá approached a
population of 30,000. The remaining "urban" residents of Colombia lived
in 710 other municipalities, none of which possessed more than 15,000 people and 300 of which even had fewer than 2,000 inhabitants. Colombia
remained a rural country with rather small cities well into the twentieth
century.[23]

Throughout the nineteenth century, transportation proved a major bar-
rier to change. At the time of independence, in the words of one prominent
historian:

> The most obvious of all the obstacles to political and economic inte-
> gration and development of New Granada [Colombia] was the diffi-
> culty and cost of moving from one province to another, and sometimes
> even within provinces. Actual distances were not great: in a direct line,
> Bogotá was only about 200 kilometers from Medellín, or 600 from the
> Caribbean coast at Cartagena. The problem was, instead, that the na-
> tional territory was broken by a succession of mountains and valleys

22. Nazih Richani, *Systems of Violence: The Political Economy of War and Peace in Colombia*
(Albany: State University of New York Press, 2002), 3–4; Sánchez, "Problems of Violence," 30.
23. Safford and Palacios, *Colombia*, 9.

into isolated compartments, held together by a road network suited for draft animals and human carriers but not for wheeled vehicles, and by a system of river transportation that was also highly primitive for the most part.[24]

By mid-century, overland freight shipment in the dry season still cost ten to thirty times as much as in the United States, and that ratio doubled during periods of rain or civil strife. Transportation by water was easier and cheaper than by land, especially once steamboats began to ply the Magdalena River in 1847, but most Colombians did not live along riverbanks. Throughout the century, Colombia continued to suffer from weak export revenues, disconnected internal markets, and relatively low economic growth. After the mid-1840s, new exports in the form of tobacco and coffee did improve the situation somewhat, yet the pace of development remained exceedingly modest. Early in the twentieth century, Colombia possessed fewer than three hundred miles of rail lines, a population of only 4 million people, and per-capita export revenues less than one-third the Latin American average.[25]

Armed conflict was a prominent part of the political life of this physically divided and economically fragmented society throughout the nineteenth century, but most wars were skirmishes in which relatively few Colombians participated. Rather than indicating any peculiar Colombian proclivity for violence since independence, the nineteenth-century conflicts appear ordinary for their time, at least until the War of a Thousand Days between 1899 and 1902.[26] Worthy of note, however, are the profound and enduring loyalties engendered by Colombia's two elite parties, the Liberals and the Conservatives. Consolidated in the 1840s, the two parties established permanent nationwide organizations by the 1880s, leaving political affiliations—"hereditary hatreds"—deeply entrenched in Colombian society. Often faction ridden, the two parties varied little in social class composition and were anything but internally uniform in their political positions. Nevertheless, the Liberals and Conservatives did manifest—however unevenly and inconsistently—differences in their views on government organization, economic policy, and, especially, the role of the Roman Catholic Church in public life.

During the second half of the nineteenth century, the ascendancy of either the Liberals or the Conservatives depended considerably on the fate

24. David Bushnell, *The Making of Modern Colombia: A Nation in Spite of Itself* (Berkeley and Los Angeles: University of California Press, 1993), 74.
25. Safford and Palacios, *Colombia*, 5, 14, 235.
26. Roldán, *Blood and Fire*, 14.

of Colombia's export economy.[27] The Liberals dominated during the mid-century flourishing of tobacco shipments abroad but gave way to Conservative hegemony in 1885 after several years of depressed agricultural exports. Despite the high levels of partisanship that developed, Liberal and Conservative elites in the nineteenth century usually managed to limit political violence. As Gonzalo Sánchez put it, "These were, in the final analysis, conflicts between gentlemen of a single lineage."[28] Nevertheless, the potential of this "two-party system" for extended violence of a more modern sort was borne out during the War of a Thousand Days. The conflict began as a Liberal revolt in the midst of a severe plunge in world coffee prices. It ultimately degenerated into bloody guerrilla warfare in which elite party leaders could neither agree among themselves nor rein in the combatants. The length of the war undermined the country's ability to deal effectively with the United States over the issue of a canal through the Colombian province of Panama, contributing to yet another national disaster in 1903, when the United States engineered a Panamanian breakaway. In retrospect, the War of a Thousand Days offers some echoes of the present-day "labyrinth" in the weakness of Colombian political institutions, the inability of Liberal and Conservative leaders to end the violence of their partisans, and the brutality and prolonged character of the conflict.[29]

Once it ended, the War of a Thousand Days gave way to a long era of political cooperation and economic progress. Both the destruction caused by the war and the ignominious loss of Panama shocked the political elite into rejecting civil war as an acceptable mode of political competition. Internal divisions within the Conservative and Liberal Parties helped strengthen centrist elements on both sides, who found ways to cooperate in the interest of national stability and to guarantee minority party representation in Congress despite severe partisan disagreements over the outcome of elections. Between 1903 and 1946, Colombia's population nearly tripled, its economic output grew fivefold, and roads, rails, and airways combined to knit the country's diverse regions more tightly together. While bananas and petroleum gained important shares of Colombia's export trade, these were the years of the "coffee republic," and the rapid expansion of this crop became "the most decisive phenomenon in Colombian economic history in the twentieth

27. Charles Bergquist, *Coffee and Conflict in Colombia, 1886–1910* (Durham: Duke University Press, 1978), 7–8.
28. Gonzalo Sánchez, "*La Violencia* in Colombia: New Research, New Questions," *Hispanic American Historical Review* 65, no. 4 (1985): 790.
29. Charles Bergquist, "Waging War and Negotiating Peace: The Contemporary Crisis in Historical Perspective," in Bergquist et al., *Violence in Colombia, 1990–2000*, 198–99.

century."[30] By 1920, coffee generated more than 60 percent of Colombia's export earnings, a position that it would maintain or exceed for nearly half a century.

Still, not everything was harmonious, and the coffee republic's political handling of social questions ultimately gave rise, after 1946, to a period of uncontained strife. Colombian coffee grew on both large estates and smaller farms, and from the 1920s onward land struggles in coffee zones became an increasingly salient part of Colombian political life. Peasant smallholders, responsible for about three-quarters of Colombia's coffee production, endured miserable living conditions despite the crop's success as a source of national income. In the influential interpretation of historian Charles Bergquist:

> Accumulation of capital in the most important sector of the Colombian economy depended on relations of production and exchange that grossly exploited coffee workers and small and medium producers. Colombia's ability to expand coffee production and to capture a larger share of the depressed world market during the crisis of the 1930s—as well as its capacity to mount an impressive record of import-substituting industrialization during the same period—depended on the willingness of small producers and their families to subject themselves to an ever greater degree of exploitation.[31]

Coffee producers of all sorts—landless workers, sharecroppers, renters, and smallholders—"found themselves locked in constant combat with one another and with large landowners and merchants to improve their position and to avoid proletarianization."[32] Throughout the 1920s, 1930s, and 1940s, coffee production, smallholding ownership, and population all expanded amid an acute competition for survival. Land invasions, squatters' movements, and peasant leagues reflected serious agrarian unrest. Those who lacked land sought it in order to become small producers. Small producers, for their part, desperately needed more land in order to sustain themselves and provide a viable inheritance for their children.

Land struggles in coffee-growing areas occurred alongside other forms of social strife in Colombia during these decades, as a modern proletariat took shape in the nation's oil fields, banana plantations, textile factories, mines, and railways. At the same time, newly expanding lower- and middle-class

30. Safford and Palacios, *Colombia*, 272.
31. Charles Bergquist, *Labor in Latin America: Comparative Essays on Chile, Argentina, Venezuela, and Colombia* (Stanford: Stanford University Press, 1986), 277.
32. Ibid., 278.

urban populations sought services and opportunities. Efforts at popular or-ganization often met with repression from the Conservative governments that remained in charge of Colombia until 1930. In 1928 the military carried out a particularly notorious massacre at Ciénaga in the Caribbean banana enclaves of the United Fruit Company. The Liberals took over government in 1930 and engaged in social reforms in an effort to modernize Colombian socio-economic conditions. Particularly notable was the "Revolución en Marcha" of President Alfonso López Pumarejo (1934–38). Historians now interpret these efforts as one of the chief causes of la Violencia. Between 1930 and 1938 the liberal governments of Enrique Olaya Herrera and López Pumarejo abol-ished literacy requirements, thus allowing all males to vote; accorded workers the eight-hour day and the right to strike; allowed women to own and dis-pose of their own property; provided for stronger taxation; passed a modest land-reform bill; and generally asserted the power of the national state to mediate between socioeconomic groups in conflict. In 1936 Public Law 200 proclaimed that private property had a social function. Even more important than what López Pumarejo did is what he did not do—automatically take sides with the propertied elements in their disputes with labor.[33]

The biggest effect of the Liberal reforms was to alarm major segments of the elite in both parties, particularly an increasingly militant and authoritar-ian faction of Conservatives headed by Laureano Gómez. Fears of revolu-tion, communism, and popular self-assertion brought a backlash that sought to contain and roll back social change, thwarting López during his second presidency (1942–45) and provoking him to resign before his term was over. Despite the efforts of Communists and other radicals to provide leadership, the new popular forces were too diverse to create an independent vehicle of political expression outside the world of the traditional parties. The female textile workers in Medellín, for example, did not find Colombian unionism sufficiently sensitive to their needs as women to wean them away from Lib-eralism and Conservatism.[34] Many of the popular movements depended for their political representation on the left wing of the Liberal Party, cham-pioned by the charismatic populist Jorge Eliécer Gaitán. Some argue that Gaitanismo represented a coherent, unified, national movement of working- and middle-class interests that saw its struggle as that of a darker-hued people against a lighter-skinned, privileged oligarchy.[35] Others disagree, arguing, for

33. Bushnell, *Making of Modern Colombia*, 188.
34. Ann Farnsworth-Alvear, *Dulcinea in the Factory: Myths, Morals, Men, and Women in Colombia's Industrial Experiment, 1905–1960* (Durham: Duke University Press, 2000), 231.
35. W. John Green, *Gaitanismo, Left Liberalism, and Popular Mobilization in Colombia* (Gainesville: University Press of Florida, 2003), 2, 12, 266.

example, that the economic circumstances and cultural horizons of peasant coffee growers imbued them with smallholder individualism. In a world of individual, family, and small community, they pursued their interests through the partisan ranks of the Liberal and Conservative Parties, generating political tensions at the local level and undercutting "the power of an organized labor movement in which they were potentially the most important part."[36]

These differences of opinion form part of the larger unsettled question of whether Colombia was at the brink of revolutionary change. Whatever the case, many in the elite, particularly Conservatives, remained hostile to the reforms of the previous years and determined to reverse them. Increased partisan hostility between the two dominant parties generated opportunities for underlying local and regional antagonisms to boil over, a setting in which socially marginalized elements could pursue their aims more forcefully and their enemies could seek to repress or even to exterminate them. The state had lost its capacity to mediate social conflicts, one of the primary aims of the reforms enacted by the government of López Pumarejo. Conservatives recaptured the presidency in 1946 when Gaitán ran as an independent, splitting the Liberal ranks. Following their victory, Conservatives commenced "cleansing operations" against sources of popular activism throughout the country. Over the next twenty years, political violence cost the lives of an estimated 200,000 Colombians and obliged another 2 million to flee their homes. La Violencia was a traumatic blow from which Colombia is still reeling, an "extraordinarily heterogeneous and complex phenomenon" that still perplexes *violentólogos*. "Indeed," notes one analyst, "recent studies of *la Violencia* raise as many questions as they answer." Research has shown that "the notion of a single, blanket interpretation of violence" no longer remains tenable, and that la Violencia contains "many manifestations and meanings" in which local circumstances appear "the most significant factor in determining the nature of violence and its objectives."[37] From this wider perspective, observers now see strong elements of continuity threading together the social struggles of the 1920s–40s, la Violencia and the subsequent era of Vásquez Perdomo's guerrilla career, and Colombia's present-day "labyrinth." La Violencia marks the start of more than half a century during which Colombian elites have been able to influence, but not to contain, the proliferation of political violence, giving rise in recent years to the term las Violencias.[38]

36. Bergquist, *Labor in Latin America*, 312.
37. Roldán, *Blood and Fire*, 5, 23, 29.
38. Sánchez and Meertens, *Bandits, Peasants, and Politics*, 194–96.

La Violencia and las Violencias

Following the Conservative victory in 1946, Gaitán became the most prominent figure in the Liberal Party and its likely candidate in the 1950 presidential elections. His assassination in Bogotá on 9 April 1948 convulsed the
nation. A popular uprising, the Bogotazo, caused widespread damage in the
capital, while other protests, often violent, took place throughout Colombia.
A hasty power-sharing arrangement among Conservative and Liberal Party
leaders did not deter clashes at local levels, and in any case the agreement fell
apart in less than a year. During the latter part of 1949 the Conservatives nom-
inated the militant authoritarian Laureano Gómez for president, whereupon
the Liberals announced their intention to abstain from elections. Outgoing
president Mariano Ospina Pérez closed down Congress and declared a state
of siege. Congress did not meet again for another nine years.

   With the threat of social revolution quashed by government force, cycles
of conflict broke out at local levels around the country between 1948 and
1953, the most destructive years of la Violencia. Conservative repression of
Liberals, not just Gaitanistas, and armed Liberal responses reinforced old
partisan affiliations and the authority of local bosses. In Bergquist's words,

> With the breakdown in public authority and social control on the lo-
> cal level, the struggle for individual gain became a nightmare of land
> grabbing, robbery, and extortion. The means used to accomplish these
> material ends degenerated from polite and subtle persuasion to armed
> threats, house burnings, and brutal slayings. Once the Violence began in
> a region it fed on itself. Relatives, friends, and co-partisans avenged the
> crimes against victims by retaliating against their alleged authors, against
> those authors' families and friends, or simply against those identified
> with the opposite political party. In doing so they often simultaneously
> accomplished cherished material goals and settled old social debts and
> long-smoldering personal grudges.[39]

La Violencia meant selective, purposeful violence shaped by the diverse dimensions of local power struggles. Intense conflicts over land, for example,
took place in many of the coffee-growing regions where agrarian agitation
had been prominent during the previous generation. Liberals and Communists established autonomous guerrilla forces in the cattle-raising areas of the

39. Bergquist, *Labor in Latin America*, 361–62.

eastern plains. In Antioquia violence resulted from the hostility of centrally located inhabitants toward the Afro-Colombians who had settled in outlying regions.

Partisan Liberal-Conservative violence diminished substantially following the June 1953 coup of General Gustavo Rojas Pinilla. Yet the ambitious general, who modeled himself somewhat after Juan Perón of Argentina, succeeded neither at ending la Violencia nor at creating a new political system. La Violencia continued as a type of banditry under the aegis of local political bosses, landowners, and mafiosos, especially in coffee-growing areas. "The seasonality of the coffee harvest permitted exploitative armed bands to concentrate their extortions during a clearly delimited harvest period. By threatening to kill harvest workers or to drive them away, these rural mafiosos could bring landowners to their knees."[40] Those involved in *bandolerismo* rejected government amnesties. In addition, Communist rural self-defense forces continued to operate in several locales despite assaults upon them by the Colombian armed forces.

After initially supporting the initiatives of Rojas Pinilla, Liberal and Conservative leaders distanced themselves from his clumsy pretensions. The outcome was his overthrow in 1957 and the installation the following year of a joint Liberal-Conservative National Front that distributed power equally between the two parties. Under the provisions of the National Front, Liberals and Conservatives split all elective and appointed positions and alternated the presidency. The system continued until 1986 in accord with subsequent modifications that ended the presidential alternation in 1974 but required an "equitable" division of government posts. The National Front curbed Liberal-Conservative partisanship, extended government authority, and employed the armed forces in counterinsurgency operations against the *bandoleros*, thus bringing la Violencia to an end in the mid-1960s.

By then, however, a new form of political violence—revolutionary insurgency—had already broken out. Like so many of their peers throughout Latin America, Vásquez Perdomo and her compañeros acted from the conviction that "only a revolution would change the country." No alternative seemed possible to them in the face of Colombia's static governing system, monopolized by the National Front. When Vásquez Perdomo entered the National University in 1970, the share of those who bothered to vote had fallen from three-quarters of people over twenty-one in 1957 to less than one-fifth.[41] For those afflicted with what Vásquez Perdomo calls "revolutionary measles" or

40. Safford and Palacios, *Colombia*, 353.
41. Ibid., 330.

"militancy fever," only armed action held out the prospect of a fundamental solution to all of Colombia's problems.

Vásquez Perdomo began by painting walls at night with revolutionary slogans such as "ELN EPL FARC = VICTORY." As the multiple acronyms indicate, various groups have engaged in revolutionary insurgency in Colombia, each with its own origins, ideological perspectives, and tactics. The three most important guerrilla organizations have been the Ejército de Liberación Nacional (ELN, or Army of National Liberation), the Fuerzas Armadas Revolucionarias de Colombia (FARC, or Revolutionary Armed Forces of Colombia)— both of which still exist—and the Movimiento 19 de Abril (M-19, or 19th of April Movement), the organization to which Vásquez Perdomo devoted so many years of her life.

The ELN developed from efforts of youthful Colombians, many of them students, to carry out the *foquista* strategy that Che Guevara described in his account of the Cuban Revolution. They discovered that la Violencia had not left a viable foundation for a rural guerrilla campaign that could achieve national revolution. After several harrowing years of internal divisions, disappointed hopes, and costly defeats, the ELN entered a more stable period in the 1980s, aided by the revenues it could extort from oil producers in Arauca. The roots of the FARC ran much deeper than those of the ELN, going back to the self-defense organizations formed by the Communist Party in some rural areas as early as the 1920s. Longtime FARC leader Manuel Marulanda, known as *Tirofijo*, or Sureshot, was a veteran of guerrilla activities during la Violencia. Under the impact of Plan Lazo, an aggressive counterinsurgency campaign of the Colombian army, the defensive character of these communities shifted, leading to the formation of the FARC in 1966. By the 1980s, it had evolved into an independent guerrilla organization, separate from the Communist Party, with its own political and military doctrines.

Vásquez Perdomo's organization, the M-19, responded to the changing sociological conditions of Colombia. Despite the country's levels of violence, its economy grew rapidly after World War II, doubling in size by 1965. Conservative governments gave particular support to industry. Bogotá was one of the fastest-growing capital cities in Latin America. As Colombia urbanized, underemployed and underserved lower- and middle-class city dwellers found the National Front ill equipped to respond to their needs. Former general Rojas Pinilla returned to political life to organize a new populist party, the Alianza Nacional Popular (ANAPO, or National Popular Alliance). The ex-general came within two percentage points of defeating the official Conservative nominee for the presidency in 1970, leaving large numbers of people convinced that fraud had robbed him of victory. The M-19 emerged in 1973 as the armed wing of ANAPO, gathering in heterogeneous supporters on the left, including former elements of the FARC.

From its inception, the M-19 gained a broad following through eclectic tactics and a flair for the spectacular. In 1974 it "liberated" Simón Bolívar's sword from a museum; five years later it made off with a large quantity of weapons from a military installation in Bogotá. Vásquez Perdomo describes in detail the 1980 seizure of the embassy of the Dominican Republic during a diplomatic reception, after which the M-19 held officials from various countries hostage for two months as it negotiated with the government. The strengths of the M-19—its freedom from dogmatism and its inventiveness— also left it without clear direction. In the words of one commentator, the M-19 could act foolishly, "like adolescents on a joyride, ignorant of consequences."[42] Having started as an urban movement, like the Tupamaros of Uruguay, it capriciously took up guerrilla activity in the countryside. Vásquez Perdomo relates the dreary experience of her participation in a poorly planned and badly executed rural expedition in 1981 that landed her in prison. As she saw it, the M-19 contained everything "from dreamy poets and peace diplomats to men who wanted war. This was the M-19, a complex multiplicity of beings willing to think in the company of others, to deliberate publicly. . . . We tried to infect the excluded country with our dreams of power."

These "dreams of power" could prove costly. The M-19 suffered repression and torture during the presidency of Julio César Turbay Ayala (1978–82). The group's kidnapping of the family members of narcotraffickers cost it dearly in lost lives when the drug lords retaliated. The beleaguered M-19 responded to the peace overtures of President Belisario Betancourt (1982–86), even signing a truce. Negotiations for entry into the legal political process proved difficult, however, for distrust remained deep on both sides. Impatient and fearful, the M-19 foolishly seized the Palace of Justice in Bogotá in November 1985. The armed forces responded by attacking the building and setting it ablaze, leaving the M-19 commandos dead and killing many others, including eleven justices of the Supreme Court.[43]

Vásquez Perdomo was in Cuba when news of this disaster reached her. The sadness that it induced formed a link in the chain of events that pulled her away from the M-19 over the next two years. Her departure foreshadowed the guerrilla organization's fate. Militarily and politically weak, its popularity

---

42. Robin Kirk, *More Terrible Than Death: Massacres, Drugs, and America's War in Colombia* (New York: Public Affairs, 2003), 107.
43. Ana Carrigan's *The Palace of Justice: A Colombian Tragedy* (New York: Four Walls, Eight Windows, 1993) provides a vivid account of this episode.

seriously damaged by the attack on the Palace of Justice, the M-19 accepted a government amnesty in 1990, demobilizing, laying down its arms, and entering the legal political process. At first the M-19 fared well in the domain of electoral politics, despite the assassination of its former leader and 1990 presidential candidate, Carlos Pizarro. Stepping in with just a few weeks to campaign, Antonio Navarro Wolf won 13 percent of the vote for the M-19, a more than respectable showing. Optimism surged the following year with the publication of a new constitution for Colombia, one inclined toward a more pluralistic and decentralized system of government. Yet within a relatively short time, it became clear that the new document could not free Colombia from its system of violence. The initial electoral success of the M-19 rapidly faded and the organization virtually disappeared from the political landscape.

Las Violencias Continue

Although intermittent peace negotiations between the government and the guerrillas have gone on since the early 1980s, a considerable upsurge in violence has been the country's reality since then. Local and national political candidates of the FARC-supported Unión Patriótica suffered high rates of assassination between 1985 and 1990, effectively ending electoral participation as a possible mode of reintegration of that guerrilla group, regardless of the question of whether the FARC leadership ever seriously entertained the possibility of laying down arms. Like the rest of the apparatus of violence, the FARC found its situation profoundly affected by the expansion of narcotics trafficking in Colombia. Operating primarily in sparsely populated rural regions where the government was weak, the FARC provided protection to cocaine processing labs and to the peasant growers of marijuana and coca. Cultivation of the latter expanded as U.S.-sponsored eradication programs in Bolivia and Peru made coca growing in Colombia more advantageous. Mutual cooperation between narcotraffickers and the FARC proved lucrative for both. Meanwhile, the ELN also prospered, benefiting from its opportunities to extort revenue from expanding oil production in its regions of influence. While Vásquez Perdomo's M-19 stumbled, surrendered, and disintegrated, the FARC and the ELN have continued to grow in the last two decades of the twentieth century and the early years of the twenty-first. During the 1960s, Colombian insurgents never numbered more than 500, and in subsequent years they fell to even fewer. Over the past quarter-century, however, drugs, oil, and guerrilla control over local municipalities have amounted to a transformative difference. By 1986, the FARC had risen to 3,600 insurgents, reaching 7,000 in 1995 and 15,000 in 2000; over the same period, the ELN leapt from 800 to 3,000 to 5,000.[44] As the pieces of the "war system" fell into place, the increase in the number of guerrilla operatives brought an intensification of Colombian counterinsurgency programs, heavily supported by the United States through funds, advisers, and military equipment.[45]

Another crucial element in the "war system," the paramilitary forces, gained in importance as well, the product of three influences—local peasant community opposition to the FARC or the ELN; the efforts of the armed forces to use local civic-militia brigades against the guerrillas; and the desire of narcotraffickers (and, at least on one occasion, Texaco) to have their own armed brigades. Narcotraffickers and others of wealth had grown tired of guerrilla kidnappings for ransom, and death-squad organizations mushroomed after the model of Muerte a Secuestradores (MAS, or Death to Kidnappers), founded in Cali in 1981.[46] (Colombia remains the world leader in kidnappings, with about a third attributed to the guerrillas).[47] Bitter enmity arose between the drug lords and the leftist insurgents once the narcotraffickers began using their wealth to buy up land in guerrilla zones of operation. Narcotics kingpins used their armed networks against those deemed to be guerrilla supporters, such as rural peasant communities or political candidates of the Unión Patriótica. Throughout much of the 1980s, government officials were also targets of narcotics traffickers, as the latter fought a war to eliminate extradition to the United States. In addition, death squads "cleansed" neighborhoods of street people, prostitutes, addicts, and other urban "undesirables." Violence corroded the nation's institutions, producing widespread criminality and impunity. Colombia's murder rates rank among the highest in the world. "With violence an everyday affair for Colombians," notes Gonzalo Sánchez, "the time of the living has become the time of the dead."[48]

Even as the traffickers eased up in their offensive against the government once the 1991 constitution prohibited extradition, paramilitary organizations continued to flourish under the dual patronage of the drug world and the armed forces. They increased in size, developed systems of coordination,

44. Safford and Palacios, *Colombia*, 362. Alma Guillermoprieto provides excellent critical descriptions of life among the FARC in *Looking for History: Dispatches from Latin America* (New York: Vintage Books, 2002).
45. Information about U.S. counterinsurgency and counternarcotics efforts in Colombia can be found on the web site of the Center for International Policy at http://www.ciponline.org.
46. Gabriel García Márquez offers a compelling account of the kidnapping of a member of a prominent Colombian family in *News of a Kidnapping*, trans. Edith Grossman (New York: Knopf, 1997).
47. Sánchez, "Problems of Violence," 17.
48. Ibid., 9.

and took actions to gain legitimacy before the public. In 1997, a coalition of paramilitary groups formed the Autodefensas Unidas de Colombia (AUC, or United Self-Defense Forces of Colombia). At present the AUC may have as many as 12,000 members.[49] In its vertiginous growth, the AUC has successfully contested the guerrillas in a number of regions and has gained in political power. The AUC acts as a mechanism for privatizing counterinsurgency. Its existence permits the armed forces and the police to subcontract out, as it were, human rights abuses to the paramilitaries, allowing government to disavow responsibility for massacres, torture, and other inhumane actions that have become central counterinsurgency measures.

While neither the armed forces nor the guerrillas have been at all shy about committing serious human rights violations against civilians—killings, kidnappings, rape, wanton destruction—currently more than half of such actions, including large massacres, are attributed to the paramilitaries. Typically the paramilitaries attack vulnerable civilian populations rather than the guerrillas directly, killing large numbers and displacing even more from their homes and land. As in the days of la Violencia, these actions give the appearance of simple wanton brutality, but strategic calculations underlie them. Those victimized may be racial minorities, as in the case of Afro-Colombians in Urabá and the Chocó; as well they may occupy land coveted by others—landowners, merchants, foreign and domestic companies—for their own economic interests. Like the guerrillas, the paramilitaries are economic enterprises. The FARC derives its income from narcotics and kidnapping, the ELN from extorting oil companies, kidnapping, and drugs. The paramilitaries engage in drug trafficking and receive money from those whose economic concerns benefit from their armed actions. Thus, in the context of a weak state, peace makes no sense for either the paramilitaries or the guerrillas. Nor does peace serve the interests of the armed forces, whose expanding budgets, fueled heavily by U.S. government funds, depend on the "war system." Under President Andrés Pastrana (1998–2002), the government even ceded large territories to the FARC and the ELN for them to govern, yet peace talks still failed.

In recent years the "war system" has become increasingly globalized. Plan Colombia, largely financed by the United States, allegedly aims at building state institutions, strengthening civil society, and fostering economic development, but the heart of its program involves counterinsurgency and anti-narcotics activities. U.S. appropriations for the "war system" in Colombia now dwarf those of just a few years ago. At its current levels, conflict in Colombia kills about 3,500 people a year. It has displaced more than 2 million

49. Kirk, *More Terrible Than Death*, 218.

people in the past ten years, more of them women than men.[50] Colombia's new President, Alvaro Uribe, swept into office in 2002 on a pledge to defeat the guerrillas and has cultivated close relationships with Washington on the basis of "combatting terrorism." While nominally that rubric includes the paramilitaries, in practice the paramilitaries retain ties to the Colombian armed forces. Although the government signed an agreement in 2003 for the eventual demobilization of the AUC by the end of 2005, Amnesty International reports that paramilitary killings have "continued unabated." Efforts are under way to create "new legal paramilitary structures" and to grant immunity for past violence. Meanwhile, the guerrillas continue their abuses, engaging in "repeated and serious breaches of international humanitarian law, including hostage-taking and the abduction and killing of civilians."[51] At great personal risk human rights defenders and other elements of civil society have sought to hold offenders accountable and to restrain the "war system" from its expanding levels of conflict and victimization.[52]

Although she was an active revolutionary combatant, Vásquez Perdomo found herself oppressed by a war run by men. The traumas of a dead son, lost loves, and a rootless identity caused her to leave the M-19 and struggle to find herself. Her experience now stands as a fragment—albeit a well articulated one—against the large numbers of displaced Colombian rural women who suffer the traumas of violence and loss of family, home, and livelihood. Vásquez Perdomo was able to draw upon the resources of her education and her urban background in the painful task of reconstructing her identity. These other women cannot. Readers engaged by Vásquez Perdomo's moving experience need to remember the present-day war in Colombia, to which her account is an antecedent. They must understand the causes of the "war system" in the Colombian past and in the power exercised by the United States through its insatiable demand for drugs, its investments in oil and other facets of the Colombian economy, its counterinsurgency and counternarcotics programs, and its opportunistic new designation of the "labyrinth" as a war against terror.

---

50. Adam Isacson, "Washington's 'New War' in Colombia: The War on Drugs Meets the War on Terror," *NACLA Report on the Americas* (March–April 2003): 13–14; Gary M. Leech, *Killing Peace: Colombia's Conflict and the Failure of US Intervention* (New York: Information Network of the Americas, 2002), 53. For testimonies on the experiences of the displaced, see Constanza Ardila Galvis, *The Heart of the War in Colombia* (London: Latin America Bureau, 2000). Michael Taussig's *Law in a Lawless Land: Diary of a Limpieza in Colombia* (New York: New Press, 2003) describes the influence of violence in everyday life in Colombia.
51. Amnesty International, *Report 2004*, at http://web.amnesty.org/report2004/col-summary-eng.
52. See Kirk, *More Terrible Than Death*, for descriptions of the risks incurred by human rights defenders in Colombia.

Prologue

Memory, the Thread That Weaves Life

PERHAPS THIS AUTOBIOGRAPHY is an incantation against forgetting a political collectivity, or the ideas that gave meaning to the lives of many and are now lost in official memory and history. Or perhaps it is simply a way of locating myself for myself.

I tell the story of an anonymous life that links a period of time, a society perceived from within the world of the Universidad Nacional, a youthful choice, the customs and teachings of an urban guerrilla group, being a woman in a world that is predominantly masculine, like the world of armies, resistance in prison, and the uncertainties of return to civilian life. When a person narrates her life and another, or others, listen to or read it, the main character feels like she exists: she feels. This in itself is, for me, a good beginning.

I am a woman, and for more than eighteen years I was active in the insurgent group Movimiento 19 de Abril (M-19). My decision to renounce the militancy that was for so long the main reason for my existence left me facing a life that was a blank page. I had only my past as a source of experience; it was up to me to turn it into an anchor or a sail.

The personal process that led me to lay down my weapons came one year before the M-19's similar process, but we met again in the search for new directions in life and politics.

In January 1989 the M-19 signed an accord by which it renounced the armed struggle in favor of a new social pact that could serve as a basis for peace. This new pact was put into effect in the 1991 constitution. The time between the signing and the convocation of constitutional reform was a difficult one for the movement and its members. Neither the country nor the people in the groups that had until then been engaged in conflict could completely understand the implications of such a profound change. Mine was not a radical or precise decision; rather, it came to me as one possibility in my search for inner coherence, at a time when practicing armed politics was no longer enough to give my existence meaning. And so I began a gradual withdrawal from militancy. This meant seeking a different way of life and a new profession. At this crossroads I began to study anthropology again, as a way of locating myself within an analytical perspective in order to understand what I was up against in my return to civilian life.

At the beginning of 1989 I went to the office of my professor, Luis Guillermo Vasco, at the Universidad Nacional, with an idea of moving ahead with a project reflecting on my own experience, one that I hoped would contribute to our understanding of the violence of the previous decade. He referred me to Professor Jaime Arocha, who had taken part in the Commission for the Study of Violence, which published the 1987 report "Colombia, Violencia y Democracia." At that time Professor Arocha was working on a methodological proposal based on the use of the intensive journal—a practice of self-analysis developed by psychologist Ira Progoff and used as an ethnographic research tool. He proposed that I carry out an ethnographic study on myself, based on my memories. Thus began my process of reflection, one result of which is this autobiographical narrative. Within this methodology I found the first tools for exploring my past in search of several answers. Some of them referred directly to the ways the M-19 acted; others had to do with the particularities that made us different from other leftist sectors and from the larger society. Many pertained to the inner logic of my own actions, and to the agents of my initial socialization that would later facilitate my conspiratorial activities, and also to the breaks needed to transgress social norms to attain definitive change. All were useful in building the strategies necessary to diminish the anguish of change. Moreover, this academic exercise helped me to fully develop my memories and find new meaning in my life.

In order to begin my expedition into the past, I had to explore my memory to get the wheels turning. Any sensory or emotional trigger could activate old memories, which cropped up in the least expected places at the least expected moments. I was living in the delerium of my memories, and I began to write them on any paper I could get my hands on: index cards, notebooks, agendas, napkins, the backs of receipts or cigarette packs. I felt all the emotions again as they came rushing back on the tide of images from the past. This was a time of much exaltation but also of sadness, because along with the joy of reliving intense moments, I also felt longing and absence. Half of my memories ended in sobs; by 1989 many from the M-19 were dead or disappeared. My past was like my country's roads—a cross (or many crosses) at every bend marked death.

I couldn't recapture each specific event of my life because the human memory is capricious, but in time, after gathering memories, accessing absences, and confusing life and death, I found a way to organize my memory. Thus was born this autobiographical text.

Very slowly I began to put my story together, to weave my memories together and give them meaning, grant them nuances of gray and color. My story is not one homogenous whole; on the contrary, it presents empty spaces, ruptures, and discontinuities inherent in the dynamics of forgetting and remembering, in the textures of life, and in the contradictions within myself and within the purpose of the memories that I was elaborating.

Telling my life to others was like learning to bare myself in public. When I began to write about my life, I did it with a sort of shyness, both because I was unused to talking in the first person and, perhaps, because of the scant importance I granted the personal in relation to the political, not to mention the secrecy that had accompanied all my actions. But finally, when I began to find meaning in the telling, I learned to do it without shame. Meaning is granted by the purpose of narrated memory. In the autobiography a memory is unfurled for something or someone. In this respect there are no naïve memories. Memory has an end, a power, in that it rebuilds the past so that its voice, silenced by various circumstances, can be heard—for example, to demand reparations for exclusion.

Writing my life for others, examining it again and again as objectified in words, allowed me slowly to recognize my social condition, to reconcile past and present, to understand life as a process, and to refuse the imposition of the "ex," -militant or -*guerrillera,* that fragmented my identity. It allowed me to show the many women who inhabit me, to accept my fears and my weaknesses, and to learn to live with my cherished ghosts without its hurting so badly. As I simultaneously approached and retreated from my past, I could think about some concepts, practices, and habits learned in conspiratorial work and, as I did so, change those that made my immediate existence difficult. It was not at all easy to understand the nature of the changes I had to face. They were for the most part positive, but some were very difficult—like living without a project that subordinated all other activities, as did the revolutionary meaning that directed our militant activity. Without a clear mission, life seemed empty, pointless, and superficial.

As I wrote, tenuous traces of an identity appeared. The written words and I influenced each other, we affected each other always. Thanks to this exercise, I found meanings and explanations that had been invisible to me. I learned that life sometimes has reasons and sometimes doesn't, and that the point is not to judge but rather to understand. Most important, I found in my past the strength of an identity that pulled me out of nostalgia.

Assembling an autobiographical memory meant rethinking my identity and confronting a hostile present replete with contradictions between reality and the expectations implicit in the return to a law-abiding life. Here memory acted as a life force, because I was able to recover the positive in the midst of so much loss, to come out of the sadness and uncertainty in which I was submerged.

Memory had one initial demand of me: to stitch together an ethography by describing how people think and work in a group acting against the establishment. I believe that understanding myself as part of a history and as heir to a culture gave value to an activity, such as a socially demonized subversion, and at the same time gave my life value. Memory and identity were dynamically intertwined in my autobiographical narrative, in this process of empowerment that pushed me to seek a place in society without denying my past.

Standing inside my story, I felt I could appeal to the Colombian society that considered us insurgents undesirables. The force of identity is one of the most important referents of the individual or group seeking recognition within an order that has been denied them.

It is necessary to mention one aspect of this process at the outset. Cultural memory is not homogenous; it has fissures, and one of them relates to gender identity. Being a woman in a setting, like the army, that is obviously masculine fills one with inner conflicts. As I told my life story I began to question the power relations within an organization that, in spite of breaking many of the rules of mainstream society and even innovating some leftist political practices, maintained inequality with respect to women and, in the best of cases, emphasized or strengthened in us virtues identified with traditional feminine roles.

Official memory uses forgetting to hide people or social sectors and imposes its legitimizing version of events. But the excluded can also construct memories that summon the many forms of power. Nowadays sectors traditionally invisible to the mainstream—such as women, black people, indigenous people, youth, and the homeless—have begun to recover their stories as part of a process of identity-construction and the search for social recognition. Memory rescues from the past the traces of identity that one needs for the present; therein lies its potential for change. When I was writing my life story, I felt I was being reborn. It was as if I were doing a self-portrait for others.

There is one aspect of writing that is rarely spoken of: the interaction between the writer and her readers. This intangible yet ever-present audience plays a creative role in the story; with it, with you, the path of memory is negotiated. This is why from the beginning I have thought about who would read my story, about what I wanted to tell you and what could be useful from my experience, as we face a future of democratic coexistence where everyone fits in. This is why I wanted to show you that we are made of flesh and not merely armor, that we are closer to you than you thought, that we often have the same dreams, and that it happens that we stand on the same spot on the planet. It is time that we look each other in the face and discover each other.

A person's life story is a construction in which it is not vital to reproduce events exactly but rather to question the patterns that led to the distortion of those events, to find the meaning in memories as an area in constant renovation and construction controlled by human willpower. Memory is alive and is re-created in the present in a dynamic interaction between forgetting and remembering. Inconsistencies, distortions, inexact and false memories also say something in autobiographical memory: it is important to follow the trail they leave behind. Forgetting fulfills its work in memory. It can be a devastating, saving, or renovating force; it acts as a borderline for remembering; it is at once wise and cruel. This is why memory is a contradictory and creative space.

My greatest difficulty was pronouncing the text complete, setting a deadline, at the risk of spending the rest of my life like Aureliano Buendía in *One Hundred Years of Solitude*, when he found Melquíades's parchments, wherein his fate was written, and "began to decipher the instant that he was living, deciphering it as he lived it, prophesying himself in the act of deciphering the last page of the parchments, as if he were looking into a speaking mirror."[53] Because the text was alive, it interacted with me differently each time I approached it. I always touched it up, highlighted events, adding things and erasing others. It had become a never-ending story.

---

53. Gabriel García Márquez, *One Hundred Years of Solitude*, trans. Gregory Rabassa (New York: Harper and Row, 1970), 422.

When I placed the last period in my autobiographical story, ending the narrative with my decision to withdraw from the M-19 at the end of 1989, I felt a bit lighter, I think because I had fleshed out a good part of my past. I had reconstructed myself with some coherence in that past. Writing was like sketching myself out on a single page, like weaving life, finding the way to reconcile past and present. It helped me understand myself as a process, in my continuities and discontinuities, in my contradictions, in my changes and my consistencies. It was also a way of breaking the secrecy that half of my history was still steeped in, unveiling a memory that was encrypted in a code of silence, and accepting myself as I am. This sketch of the life of a woman is the testimonial I'm leaving in your hands today.

1
Family Portrait

I WAS BORN in Cali on 24 July 1951. I loved to say I shared my birthday with the liberator Simón Bolívar. Humberto, my older brother, picked out my name. He named me María Eugenia, maybe because it was popular. Papá and Mamá had separated before my birth, because Mamá understood that marriage was not her cross to bear, and she had no reason to bear it with the resignation everyone counseled her to have. My father took her son from her, and since she was pregnant, Mamá went to live with my grandparents.

I met my father and brother in the pictures Mamá kept in her album. To this day I associate them with the photo of the last family outing: the '48 Chevrolet pickup and the black cocker spaniel, Blackie, my mother, smiling, hugging a *moreno*[1] boy with big eyes. Beside her, a thin, tall man, also moreno, watching them. I didn't know much more than what the photo said; my mother didn't talk much about her story. I grew up longing for a brother, for a life-long accomplice, and Daniel Vásquez—that was what they called him—was a portrait father, always absent.

---

1. *Moreno* (m.)/-*a* (f.) denotes a nonwhite, nonnegro *mestizaje* (person of mixed race); it may describe many shades of brown complexion, with direct reference to skin or, sometimes, hair color.

In my grandparents' home I had all their affection to myself. Tiny, morena, with dark, shiny eyes like *chambimbe* seeds,[2] and straight Indian-like hair with bangs, I was almost always dressed in white, the lace of my panties peeking out from under my dress. I ran happily through the patios and yards.

Since we *negros*[3] were few on my mother's side of the family, the first songs and poems I learned attempted to reconcile me with the color of my skin.

> *I am morenita, señores,*
> *I don't deny my color.*
> *Among lilies and irises*
> *there's me, negrita; I'm better.*

> *I was born in a forest of coconut palms*
> *one July morn*
> *and they rocked me in a cradle*
> *of hummingbird feathers.*
> *My father was negrito*
> *my mother Carabalí* [4]
> *and me, a little black fugitive*
> *since the day I was born.*

I was surrounded by calm, loving people like my grandma, Mamá María, a marvelous accomplice to my doll games who walked as if she were swinging, as if the movement of the cradle were still inside her. There was no lap more comfortable at bedtime, no better place for calming childhood fears.

While my grandpa, Papá Marcos, was a serious man, he was always willing to talk to me. He worked on the farm during the week and came home on Saturdays with milk, plantains, *yucas*,[5] and *arracachas*[6] from the harvest. He loved watching me crawl and gobble up the fresh cheese he made for me, quick as a flash.

2. The *chambimbe*, or *sapodilla*, is an evergreen tree of the *Sapindaceous* family. Its seeds are large and black.
3. In Spanish the word is not necessarily discriminatory, nor does it always denote African descent. It can be used as a term of endearment, as can words such as *gordo* (chubby) or *flaco* (skinny); yet it also suggests, perhaps unconsciously, *mestizaje* and a lack of "purity." While it can also be discriminatory, it is not used that way here or anywhere else in this text.
4. From "Calabar," it applies to a region in Africa or people from that region. When applied to people it carries connotations of being untamed or incapable of being subdued.
5. Manioc, an edible root similar to a potato in shape and consistency.
6. From the Quechua word *racacha*, an edible root.

Ruth, my mamá, was so pretty with her sad eyes. At that time she worked in public relations with the Hoteles Unidos chain, to which the Aristi Hotel of Cali belonged. That's why I spent my days with my grandma.

Then there was *Tía*[7] Myriam. I remember her combing out her freshly washed hair in the sun. It was very long and smelled like Reuter soap. Entangled in that hair were the dreams of many a suitor who sang to her at night. I was Tía's secret accomplice. I spied on her suitors from the window while they offered up their serenades and enjoyed them with such emotion you'd have thought they were meant for me.

My great uncle lived in the same house. Napo was a bachelor who told stories from the War of a Thousand Days[8] as if it were yesterday. He had unimaginable treasures, which he kept in wooden trunks. For the band of nieces and nephews who visited, opening them was like going into Ali Baba's cave. There were tops, multicolored marbles, prints of saints, straight pins with glass heads, blue glass flasks, knives, wooden yo-yos, beads, whole and dismembered dolls, string, colored paper, ribbons, shiny stones, crucifixes, photographs, rosaries, and as many trinkets as the old man could find on his outings. If he caught us looking into those trunks, he blew up. We would scramble out of his way like terrified mice and listen to the old man yelling while we clung to Grandma's skirts in the kitchen.

Ramón, the youngest of the tíos, was still a bachelor and lived at home. I loved to see him dressed in white, his hair freshly coiffed with gel, ready to go out with his girlfriend. My older cousins preferred to watch him while he lifted weights on the terrace, and they invented any excuse to show up around five o'clock in the afternoon so they wouldn't miss the show.

Relatives and friends of all ages came by my grandparents' house every day to talk, have a *cafecito*,[9] tell their troubles, or swap recipes. I entertained myself by playing, sometimes by myself and sometimes with my cousins who dropped by for a visit.

7. Aunt or auntie. *Tío* means uncle.
8. The War of a Thousand Days was Colombia's longest and most destructive in a long line of civil wars fought since the country's independence from Spain. Lasting from 1899 to 1902, the war arose out of economic and regional crises, political intrigue, and clientelism. One rebel group surrendered and signed the Treaty of Neerlandia on 24 October; the signing of the Wisconsin Treaty on 21 November 1902 ended the war. See Arthur Schmidt's Introduction and Alvaro Tirado Mejía, "El estado y la política en el siglo XIX," in *Manual de Historia de Colombia*, vol. 2, ed. Jaime Posada (Bogotá: Tercer Mundo Editores, 1994), 373.
9. Coffee, a major crop, permeates Colombian culture. Here it is used in the general sense of "a little coffee." It will appear throughout the text as *tinto*, meaning strong and black, no sugar, and as *café con leche* (coffee with milk), and in other guises.

When I remember my childhood, what comes to me most forcefully are the emotions I had while vacationing with my grandparents in the country. It was as if I found myself growing up again outdoors.

Cominal was the name of their farm in the mountains, close to the Cerro Pico de Loro, among forests of maples and *comino* trees,[10] *yarumos*,[11] moss, ferns, *anturio* plants with red, white, and black flowers, and orchids, with ravines and trenches to take the water in aqueducts to the house of wood and *bahareque*[12] Papá Marcos had built. There I grew up around cows, horses, pigs, chickens, and dogs. When I was in Cominal, the city below was a patch of lights, which in the dark of night reminded me of where my mamá was.

Papá Marcos was a *huilense*[13] settler who came to the Valle del Cauca to establish his family and property. He and Grandma had seven daughters and one son. After administrating land owned by the Eder family, Papá Marcos staked out his own and dedicated himself to building it up with blows of his machete. He was able to establish a nice farm for himself, but he sold a part of it when the family had to move to Cali because the kids sought their futures in the expanding city. The farm contributed to the family economy with food and money from selling wood. This kept Papá Marcos in the country most of the time.

Vacations were times of freedom in the open air. I looked forward eagerly to July and December, when I would go with Mamá María to join Papá Marcos. Sometimes two or three of my cousins, or some other relative, came with us. We went to Jamundí and from there to San Vicente, a tiny municipality at the foot of the Western Cordillera, and from there to Cominal we rode up on horseback for a few hours. The house was on a hill and you could see it from a distance, its veranda overflowing with flowers.

Shortly after arriving we had hot food on the wood-burning stove and we kids roasted ripe plantains in the coals. All of us had domestic chores to do, some helping Grandma and others helping Papá Marcos. We helped her cook corn in ashes, then peel it in a sieve; and when there were boys around, they ground it. They taught us girls how to make *arepas*,[14] *pandebono*,[15]

---

10. Latin: *Aniba perutilis*; this tree is of the *Lamaceas* family and is valued for its aromatic, resistant wood. It grows in both warm and cold climates.
11. Latin: *Cecropia*; of the *Moraceas* family, it is has broad, open, palm-like foliage and small flowers. It grows to twenty meters in height; its wood is used in crafts.
12. Wattle and daub.
13. Someone from the department of Huila.
14. Small cornmeal patties, similar to pancakes in shape, a staple of the Colombian diet.
15. Small oblong bread made with a mild cheese worked into the yuca starch dough.

panderitos,[16] and bread in the clay stove Papá Marcos had made on the patio off the kitchen. We all swept the halls with brooms made from twigs we gathered in the pasture, and we carried dried brushwood for the stove.

When we were with Papá Marcos we cleaned the leaves from the aqueducts that carried water to the house, separated the calves from the cows at five o'clock in the afternoon, and brought in yuca from the garden. He liked to go for walks, especially with me. He didn't take my other cousins because he said they were lazy when it came to walking. We left early in the morning to walk around the mountain. Along with breakfast, Mamá María made us a lunch of dried beef, arepas, hard-boiled eggs, *bocadillo*,[17] and sweet *guarapo*.[18]

Papá Marcos cut branches that we used as staffs and we walked the trails that penetrated into the mountains and up to the sawmills. The path was full of surprises for me. I must have been around four or five years old, and Papá Marcos patiently explained the mysteries of the mountain to me.

"What's this?" I asked.

"They're cocoons. Butterflies come out of them."

"They look like gold . . ."

"They are all different colors. Inside they have a little caterpillar that changes into a butterfly, and when it's ready it breaks the cocoon and comes out to fly. Let's take one so you can see it when it breaks."

And he put it in his backpack.

"These purple seeds are *mortiños* and you can eat them," he said. "But you can't eat these over here, they're poison . . . snake food."

"And the ones hanging in bunches from the tree?" I asked.

"They're good for dying *cabuya*,[19] or cloth. We're coming up on the ravine," Papá Marcos said. "Can you smell it?"

I breathed in as deeply as I could to smell the scent of moss, dampness, and wood that I can still evoke when I close my eyes.

When we got to the ravine, Papá Marcos took some leaves from the smooth, shiny surface, rolled them up, made a funnel to hold water and give me a drink. Sweet, cold water—it tasted like herbs. Papá Marcos guided my

16. Round sweet bread of egg and yuca flour, so named because of its shape, similar to a tambourine, a *pandereta*.
17. A candy made of guava, shaped in a hard bar or squares and wrapped in paper.
18. A juice made from sugar cane, fermented a short period of time. When fermented longer it becomes *chicha*, used by the indigenous population.
19. Yellow pita fiber used to make cords, string, or rope.

steps, my sense of smell, my sight; he trained my sensitivity. We walked all day long and returned as evening fell.

When night fell, after we had eaten and prayed the rosary with more laziness than devotion, Mamá María told stories of the *paisa*[20] who went to heaven, the emperor's new clothes, the ugly duckling, and others that I don't remember. Every once in a while she told us scary stories, like the one about the elf who fell in love with Papá Marcos's younger sister and bugged her so much that she died very young, tired of putting up with the scares he gave her. Through her we met la Patasola and la Llorona,[21] and we discovered elves with children's faces and huge hats. We loved it when Grandma sang Julio Flórez's *Las flores negras*, because the words made our hair stand on end. There were also songs when we had nighttime gatherings, and our grandparents would remember the melodies that had accompanied their romance.

Fear of sleeping alone united the band of grandkids at Grandma's feet and made us negotiate in whispers among ourselves. We took turns going to the bathroom before we went to bed. To chase away the fear I remembered my mamá and sang to keep myself company in the dark of the night. Showing fear would make me look stupid in front of the others, so it was better to hide my feelings.

I felt happy and free on the farm. I wasn't spanked the way most kids were. When they thought my answers were snotty or my disobedience went overboard, a knock on the head from Grandma or a scolding from Papá Marcos was sufficient. The only punishment I remember—and a very unjust one, by the way—was when Grandma cut my shoulder-length hair because her sister-in-law had accused me of tormenting a piglet. But I was only chasing it with a stick to try to wrap the curl of its tail around it.

In Cali life was a little less exciting, but my memories of it are also associated with playing. I had a live-in sitter named Rosalba who appeared at the house one afternoon. My mother and grandparents had brought her from Huila. She had on a red dress with white polka dots. Her skin was the same color as mine, and her haircut was like mine, too. She was a young girl, about ten or eleven years old, and it was her job to entertain and take care of me. We played house, we dressed up in clothes Grandma lent us, and we made ourselves long blond braids with silk stockings. All

20. Someone from the department of Antioquia.
21. Women's tales from the region of Tolima Grande about suffering souls who frighten drunken and love-besotted men. La Patasola is a one-footed woman who appears on the path when young men travel from town to town. La Llorona is a woman who wanders around crying for her lost children.

dressed up like señoras, we got ready to go shopping, but before we left Rosalba always took the dolls that were our pretend children, put one on top of the other, and invariably said, "Let's go shopping and leave the kids fucking."

We left with our high heels clicking, swinging our blond braids. One day I was the one who repeated the routine phrase; Grandma was walking by the patio and stopped cold.

"What did you say?" she asked sternly.

I repeated the chorus slowly.

"Never ever say that again!"

My play continued, but they sent Rosalba home. She was teaching me bad habits—that was their response when I asked why she was leaving.

After Rosalba left I spent most of my time alone with toys and animals. When I was born I had been given a rag doll with a rubber face, a cute cowboy. When I was about four I fell in love with that doll, and from then on he was no longer my son but my husband, because that was the only way I could sleep with him. I took my Mauricio—that was his name—and when we went out, I talked to him all the time. We sat in the shade, and when I hugged him, caressed him, or gave him kisses, I felt a warm sensation inside. That was my first taste of love.

I also entertained myself by watching animals. I could spend hours spying on an anthill, putting up obstacles for the ants. I imaginined I was a giant, or that I was itty bitty and went into the queen's chambers, ran through secret passages, and had wild adventures underground. At other times I made things out of clay and dried them in the sun, then buried them so that years later someone would find them and think they were indigenous *guacas*, or burial mounds. It was a fantasy triggered by my grandma's dreams, because sometimes she thought she had received news from the beyond of a burial ground near the house.

Once, when Papá Marcos was away on a trip, Grandma and I, with the overseer as our accomplice, dug up the guaca she had dreamed about. She had chosen a hill that ended in a concave indentation; it looked like the one she saw in her dreams. We began to dig out the dirt and sift through it for signs of a guaca. Any variation in the texture seemed to confirm our suspicion that the dirt had been removed for a burial. This made us dig enthusiastically until we had dug about two or three meters straight down and then to the left, hoping to find a bigger cavity, and then the doors of the guaca. In addition to skeletons, we hoped to find gold and pottery, for Grandma said the dead buried all their possessions with them so they wouldn't lack for anything in the beyond. She knew all of this because in her land, Huila, a lot of people had taken part in *guaquería*[22] in the archeological zone of Tierradentro, looking for treasures. They wove many legends about it. They even drew maps and gave each other formulas to invoke the spirits of the dead without awakening their ire.

This adventure granted us marvelous hours, with moments of intense anxiety as we waited to see something appear, a piece of earthenware, a bone, anything. The dig ended the day a calf broke its leg in our excavation. Then Papá Marcos, who until then had ignored our delirium, got really angry and ended Grandma's dreams, forbidding her to dig holes to look for burial grounds.

When we didn't go to Cominal on vacation, we went to Caloto in Cauca, where Tía Rosa's family had a coffee business and a plantation called Casas Viejas, with a huge stream of water that fell into a tub and made a delightful bath for young and old alike.

Vacation was a time to share with *primos* and *primas*.[23] We were a large group—almost twenty boys and girls between four and sixteen years old. We grouped off by age to play, but there were activities all of us participated in, such as making *tamales*,[24] pandebono, or *desamargados*[25] for Christmas. Both boys and girls had their tasks. The boys cut wood, prepared the stove, cut the meat, ground the corn. We girls peeled the potatoes, crushed the garlic, cut the onion, while the older women mixed the dough, prepared the dishes, or made the syrup.

We also put on plays, directed by Arturo, one of the older cousins. We made the costumes ourselves and built the set, and we practiced a lot so we could put them on for the rest of the family and some guests.

I hung out with four primos and two primas. The boys had accepted us girls in their games after we begged them and accepted their conditions. Beto, who at ten was two years our senior, almost always initiated the activities. With him we made movies by casting shadows on the wall, made strange weapons that we used to kill spiders, collected butterflies, performed surgery on dolls, and went on trips to the woods to live the adventures of Tarzan and Jane or of princes and princesses. We girls always had to play the part of the wives or slaves. If we wanted to do something different, we had to win the privilege by accepting all sorts of challenges.

22. Raiding of Indian burial mounds.
23. Cousins. *Primo* is masculine in gender and *prima* is feminine.
24. Corn-based dough wrapped around filling of potatoes, carrots, vegetables, and perhaps chicken, wrapped in banana tree leaves and boiled.
25. Traditional candies made from lemon, orange, grapefruit, or lime peel, cooked in sugar syrup.

"I bet you can't turn like this . . ."

"Let's see if you can climb that tree."

"Grab this worm with your hand. Or are you scared?"

Once they killed a sparrow and took out its heart. I had to eat it while it was still warm because, according to Beto, warriors needed the blood of their victims to be courageous, and I wanted to demonstrate my courage.

During those games our first loves were sketched out, or at least we tried out new sensations of attraction to the opposite sex. There were plenty of serenades, poems with handwritten dedications stuck between the pages of a book, and lots of holding hands under our *ruanas*.[26] I liked Beto, who was two years older than I, but I confess I was a little afraid of him because he was a know-it-all and rambunctious. He was never my boyfriend, but he stole my first kiss in a game of spin-the-bottle.

A *Papá* for *Christmas*

It was Christmas 1957; I was six and we were in Cominal. Mamá arrived on Christmas Eve loaded down with gifts and brought with her a señor who the others said was going to marry her. I studied him carefully during dinner, while he devoured the duck cooked with tender palm shoots Grandma had made. He had a round nose like Father Christmas, and he had brought me presents. He spoke little and looked at my mamá all the time. I liked el Pato,[27] as they called him; it wasn't bad to have him as a papá.

Shortly afterward they legalized their union to appease Papá Marcos. They had a civil wedding out of the country, because they had both been married previously in the Church.

El Pato, a police captain, was almost immediately named military mayor of Sevilla in El Valle, a town that had been besieged by partisan violence since Gaitán's assassination.[28] When General Rojas Pinilla led the 1953 coup d'état, regions where the conflict had been sharpest were militarized, with the goal of restoring peace.

Mamá and I went to Sevilla on weekends. You could feel the fear; you lived in constant danger. You could hear gunshots at any time, day or night.

26. A woollen poncho-like wrap, typical in Colombia.
27. The Duck.
28. Jorge Eliécer Gaitán was the Liberal Party candidate for president who presented many plans for social change and political reform. He was assassinated on 9 April 1948, triggering the infamous *Bogotazo* and the resulting period known as la Violencia.

Along Sevilla's streets were pools of blood, evidence of death. Both sides sang publicly of their killed and wounded. The people talked as if it were normal that the *pájaros*[29] had killed what's-his-face last night, or that the *chusma*[30] had gotten what's-his-name. My stepfather had a bodyguard; he slept with his revolver under his pillow and was always half-drunk so he could shake off the death threats. You can imagine how bad things were—he gave my mamá a revolver with a mother-of-pearl handle to keep in her purse.

One night, because of the cold or because of my fear, I wet the bed in the hotel where we were staying. After that I didn't want to go back to Sevilla, I was so ashamed. What would people say if they knew the mayor's daughter wet the bed?

El Pato was eventually promoted to major and named transportation commander of the police in Bogotá, so we moved to the capital. It was my first plane ride, and Mamá and I wore special clothes. She had a black hat that looked like a lamp shade, a black coat, and kidskin gloves. I wore a yellow wool dress, a beige jacket, a beret, and white gloves that made my fingers feel like they'd been starched.

We checked into a hotel in the Teusaquillo neighborhood, and my adaptation to my new life began. I learned that in Bogotá café con leche was *perico*, *suspiros* were called *merengue*,[31] *sandía* was *patilla*,[32] and *zapallo* was *ahuyama*.[33] I didn't like the cold weather at all—it made getting up the feat of a martyr and undressing most uncomfortable. A bath was a veritable danger. The cold meant wearing more clothes, which limited movement. I understood that I was not made for Bogotá weather; I belonged in the tropics.

Some days later el Pato, Mamá, and I moved to an apartment near the Universidad Javeriana. That night, when we had finished putting things in place, my mother made vegetable soup. I had never seen her in the kitchen before; it was my grandma's domain. I don't know if it was the appetite the aroma of the soup awoke in me, or the warmth of the apartment as compared to the hotel, or the presence of a papá, but that day I felt as though I was trying on my very own family for the first time.

Mamá stopped working and started taking classes on how to start a business. First she set up a poultry farm outside the city, then a beauty salon. We were like any other family: my parents worked, I studied, and we went

29. Literally "birds," this term refers to the paramilitary-like assassins sponsored by the Conservative Party.
30. Literally "mob," or "scum," *chusma* were Liberal Party supporters.
31. A cookie-like sweet made of meringue.
32. Watermelon.
33. Pumpkin.

out on weekends. Since el Pato was a hunting enthusiast, he took us with a group of his friends to a place where they could hunt. My mother shared his enthusiasm for hunting and learned how to use the guns. She even became a better shot than he was. I loved to go along with them on their long walks; it was like a continuation of the walks with Papá Marcos.

But the hunting was a contradiction for me; it tore my heart to see a wounded animal. I preferred that they be killed with a single shot. I took on the hopeless task of saving the wounded. I bandaged them up, wrapped them in my kerchief, and tried to give them water, but they almost always died on the way home. My mamá tried to console me while I cried silently.

In time el Pato convinced me that it was better for the animals to die than to suffer, and so I learned how to mercy-kill. When the dog brought the prey back, I made sure it was completely dead, even though breaking the necks of the pigeons tore me apart.

I was the only girl in the group of hunters. Almost all of them were active or retired military men. They didn't bring their wives or children on hunting days; Mamá and I were the exceptions. The other families waited for us at the camping club.

I started out as a hunter by helping them clean the muskets. Then I trained the dogs to bring back the prey, and finally one day I shot and killed a bird that was resting on a tree branch. The group considered me ready for apprenticeship. I was about ten years old. From that time on there was always a moment for training on the outings. My papá lent me a double-barreled gun.

We hunters got up very early. We left before dawn, had a tinto along the way, and walked over nearly deserted plains, seeking myrtle trees or harvested sesame fields, the preferred foods of pigeons. The best time to hunt them was between six and nine in the morning or at five in the afternoon. You had to catch the ducks by six in the morning, and if we wanted to hunt rabbit we had to wait until nightfall to walk along the trails with a lantern, ready to pull it out in front of the animal, which, blinded by the light, froze until the shot pierced its body.

I can still remember the exhaustion, the thirst, and the beating sun that seemed to melt me from the head downward. I never complained, afraid to lose the respect of the hunters, because I felt immensely proud to be able to bear so much that even the tough ones accepted me.

Riding horses was another love that brought me closer to el Pato. From a very early age, Papá Marcos had put me on a tame chestnut. He made sure I was okay and that I wouldn't fall out of the saddle, and he let me wander the fields until I decided to come back home. It was almost always the horse who decided to go back. My stepfather fed this pleasure of mine. He taught me riding techniques and how to control the horse, and even how to make it stand on its hind legs. The man felt fulfilled with me, he compared me to favorably to his friends' sons, of whom he made fun.

Mamá and I shared el Pato's world effortlessly. Only school came between the endless yearning to travel, ride horses, and hunt.

From Park to Convent

I started school in Cali when I was four. It was a small coeducational school led by Señorita Mercedes Ayanegui, a Basque woman exiled from Spain because of her anti-Falangist activities. I liked it there because they treated me with affection, and two of my older cousins went there too.

We little ones were happy. The teachers were very special women who made all of us feel like special little people, even Isabelita Garza, who was mentally retarded and lifted up her dress in class to show us her panties. Manual activities, games, and arts and crafts were fundamental during the first years. We spent hours kneading modeling clay to make figures we would exchange. We took music and ballet lessons, put on plays, and some afternoons our señorita would read to us. We learned natural science on imaginary walks, math by playing store, geometry by cutting out figures on colored paper, and we learned to read. I don't remember how we learned it all, but it seemed effortless. Everything was easy to do there, and most of all it was fun. At recess we played with the director and sang children's rounds. We loved the Castilian way she pronounced her z's and c's, and the whistle of air when an "s"[34] appeared in the sentence.

Love was a game. The teachers laughed when the Italian twins chased us girls to give us a kiss. I fell in love in kindergarten, with a friend of my cousin's, and I learned how to write his initials in my notebooks: J.P.N., for Juan Pablo Negret. I swooned when I danced with him in ballet class, but my love ended because I was afraid of getting pregnant. I had always heard that children were the fruit of love, and I thought my love for J.P.N. might make me pregnant. I was afraid of motherhood at such a tender age.

I went to kindergarten and first grade in the Hispano-Colombiano School. When we moved to Bogotá I was enrolled in an all-girls school

---

34. In Castilian Spanish, the "z" and "c" are pronounced much like the English "th," while in Latin American Spanish they are pronounced like the English "s." The Castilian "s" is pronounced with the tongue lightly touching the gum behind the upper teeth; it whistles.

led by nuns, the Alvernia. My tía, a Franciscan nun, taught there, and that entitled us to a 50 percent discount on tuition.

The change was like going from a park to a convent. This was a school with hundreds of girls. All of us wore dark blue suits with very long pleated skirts, white blouses and bowties, laced-up black shoes, and brown socks. We had to line up two-by-two to go into the classroom, with our hands clasped behind our backs. No one spoke. Every nun stood at the front of her classroom, and we took turns marching into the room.

I felt lost among so many women. *Madre* Agapita, my teacher, had a furrowed brow and always looked angry. My first morning there I asked to go to the bathroom and was told to wait until recess. When we went out to recess I asked again, and the nun monitoring the playground told me to go to Belencito. I couldn't ask her where Belencito was. When I finally found the bathroom, I had already wet my pants. I closed myself in there to cry for a while, then I washed my panties and kept them in my pocket.

The second day was no better. Suddenly, without warning, Madre Agapita asked me a question in Sacred History class.

"Talk to us about our parents, Adam and Eve."

Adam and Eve? No idea, never heard of that couple.

"I don't know," I responded.

"Madre."

"I don't know, Madre."

"What do you mean, you don't know? Isn't your family Catholic? You must have forgotten. Who wants to remind this little girl who Adam and Eve were? Let's see . . . María Teresa."

So the smartest girl in the class told us the famous story I had never heard.

That afternoon when I went home, I was furious with my mamá. Why hadn't she ever told me about Adam and Eve? She had never thought that it would be important for my schooling, she said, but I still can't forget the shame I felt.

Until then my grandma or my mamá had taken care of my diet, and it was never a problem for me to eat. But with the nuns it became torturous. The lunch menu was dangerously changeable and they made me eat everything. It didn't matter whether I liked it or not, whether they gave me too much, whether I begged them not to make me eat something, whether I pretended I was sick; the nuns were inflexible. The nicest ones advised me to dedicate the sacrifice of eating what I didn't like to God, for the salvation of my soul. After every lunch, I felt worthy of going to heaven, shoes and all.

In the dining room we prayed before we ate. We ate in silence and no one got up from the table until everyone had finished. Meat gristle always made my lunch last ages. I tried to swallow it all at once, to take my stomach by surprise, but that damned thing was alert and sent those pieces of fat back to me in the form of greasy saliva. I insisted, with a glass of water, but the struggle between stomach and will seemed to last forever. When the critical point was finally passed, a mix of tears and snot ran down my face, and the other girls at the table looked up to the ceiling so they wouldn't be sick. All this beneath the implacable stare of the nun.

In time I learned tricks—to switch food, to hide what I didn't like, to throw the fat away discreetly, and, finally, to eat everything on my plate.

The best thing about school was always the girlfriends. Today these, tomorrow others, because at that age affections change on a whim. In primary school we had a Bugs Bunny—the Lucky Bunny—fan club. Six girls from my class were members. We made up a hymn, ID cards, and a slogan. We held meetings at every recess and traded our admired character's comics. I was elected president almost unanimously because of my bunny teeth. We named María Teresa, the smart one, treasurer, and Yolanda was secretary, because she wrote well.

When I was around thirteen, I had another group of friends, and three of us fell in love with a priest who conducted mass in the Divino Salvador Church. Every night we went to the seven o'clock mass to see our platonic love and receive communion from his hands.

My tía Pola, the nun, spoiled me when she had a little time during recess. She took me to the school's museum and to the nuns' dining room—part of the inner sanctum, where the students couldn't go. She gave me Swiss chocolates and apples, but she also scolded me when the class director complained to her about my disobedience. That blessed disobedience became my biggest problem in primary school. I couldn't keep my mouth shut in class, in line, or in the dining hall, nor could I keep my hands behind my back and my back straight. This wasn't part of who I was. The nuns always scolded me for the same reasons, but since I was a good student we got used to the ritual: the nuns punished me and I took the punishment. I was rumored to be honest, and since the nuns valued that, it sometimes mitigated the intensity of the discipline.

Around that time I got hepatitis and had to stay in bed for about a month. El Pato didn't want the nuns to admit me to the hospital, so he hired a nurse to take care of me at home. I asked him and Mamá to bring me comics. Mamá didn't want me to read that "garbage," but el Pato convinced her that it was the only way to keep me quiet. The nurse and I avidly read everything that was published around that time—mountains of stories that el Pato's driver traded in at the magazine stands whenever we finished a series.

From then on, the superheroes were my favorites. I loved Superman, Wonder Woman, Batman, and the Green Lantern. I knew where their powers came from, I learned who their enemies were, I shared the secret of their double personalities, and I had the most incredible adventures with them from my sick bed. I never lost my love for superheroes, and when the nuns took us on spiritual retreats, I camouflaged Superman comics under the cover of *Vidas ejemplares*.[35] But it wasn't always possible to avoid the obligatory sacred readings. My favorites among them were the stories of the martyrs who had suffered tortures, like being skinned alive, without renouncing their Christian faith.

At home, religious activity hadn't gone beyond praying to the Guardian Angel and responding to Grandma's rosary. But in school we prayed at the beginning and at the end of every class and before and after lunch. We prayed the Rosary before recess, the Angelus at six in the afternoon. We went to mass twice a week, took communion on the first Friday of every month in honor of the Sacred Heart, and worshipped the Santísimo expuesto.[36] Ah, and we went on spiritual retreats for Holy Week. Our program of study was Sacred History, Religion, and the Moral and Social Doctrine of the Church.

I made my first communion at the Alvernia. The hardest thing was understanding all that stuff about sin, especially accepting that at my age I had committed mortal sins. Only after lectures about the origin and condition of sin did I know that having watched, without modesty, when Adolfo Garzo showed Manuelita Sellarés and me his dinky and his bottom—we must have been about four years old—it was nothing less than breaking the sixth commandment: Thou shalt not fornicate. My shame was such that I didn't dare tell the priest what had happened. I was very young to have committed such a serious sin. The whole thing kept me up nights, so I decided to cover up the damned sin so it wouldn't be noticed. If at the time of my confession something sounded scandalous, the old chaplain would surely come out of the confessional to scold me publicly. The thing was that I had to be forgiven no matter what. Without absolution there would be no first communion.

Finally, after a lot of thought, I found a way to confess my sin in disguise, and when it came time I told the priest, "Bless me, Father, for I have sinned. I have had bad thoughts, words, and deeds."

I waited, terrified, my sweaty hands interlaced, for the priest to give me his blessing. It didn't matter if he made me climb up Monserrate barefoot as

35. *Exemplary Lives*, biographies of saints, including St. Francis of Assisi, María Goretty, and others.
36. This is said when the host is displayed in church the first Friday of every month. In some places, with special permission, it remains on display and special ceremonies are held daily.

penance or pray for a whole month. I only wanted him to absolve me so that I could be good from that moment on. I would never again look curiously upon a dinky, I promised God.

To my surprise, the confessor only made me pray three Our Fathers and three Ave Marías, and he absolved me. Finally I could go in peace, even though I couldn't stop worrying about whether God would charge me interest in hell for the details I had omitted from my confession.

After my first communion, I joined Christian groups organized by the school. First I was a member of the Corazones Valientes and then of the Cruzados.[37] Each group had its own emblem, weekly meetings, songs, and individual and collective activities that emphasized the exercise of virtue and sacrifice to win indulgences and contribute to the salvation of the world. On the first Friday of every month we offered communion to the Sacred Heart, and I liked to attend that mass because they put the group's coat-of-arms on our jacket collars and a band of silk on our chests, and we sang a hymn and swore to defend the faith.

In the Alvernia it was very important to keep up appearances. In a way, each of us competed to win points on the social scale and to look better than the rest—to be from a good family, have good connections, belong to some club, take a vacation overseas or at least on the coast in Colombia. My close friends were simple girls, but even so, I often didn't go to parties so I wouldn't have to ask Mamá for a new dress. But what complicated my life the most was keeping up the family façade: I had to hide the fact that I had a stepfather, and I was put on the spot when asked why my last name wasn't the same as el Pato's. Plus, his last name, Cabeza, didn't sound elegant. I had to make up a story in which Daniel Vásquez had died in an accident on the Cali-Palmira highway. It was the only way I could bring a stepfather into my story without going into details that would put my mamá in a bad light.

Every afternoon el Pato's driver picked me up at the school gate. If for some reason the police department's plain black Ford wasn't available, I begged the driver to park around the corner, because nothing caused me more shame than getting into a police car.

I was in my mid-teens when el Pato retired from the police force because he was sick with kidney trouble. The doctors told him he didn't have much time left and recommended that he move to the country to live out the rest of his days in peace. So he bought a country home with his retirement money, in El Valle de Sibundoy in Putumayo, and we moved. Since there was no

37. The Courageous Hearts and Of the Cross.

high school in town, I had to go to a boarding school in Pasto run by the same Franciscan nuns who were at the Alvernia.

Staging

I entered the third year of high school at this boarding school, called Maridíaz. It had three times as many students as the one in Bogotá, but the social composition was more diverse. Rich and poor alike went there for grade school, *bachillerato, comercial,* and *normal.*[38]

I liked it from the start. I didn't feel odd. There were some *compañeras*[39] from the Alvernia, teachers whom I knew, and a lot of *vallunas.*[40] But I really had to work at adapting to boarding school life. During the day I had a great time, but when the day was over and the day students had gone home, I was overcome with a feeling of being orphaned. The routine after five o'clock was monotonous. At five-thirty we went to chapel to receive the blessing from the Holy Father. Then we ate and went out to recess. From seven till eight-thirty we studied and did homework. Immediately after that we went up to our rooms. We had fifteen minutes to get ready for bed, ten minutes to pray before going to sleep, and a bell announced quiet time at nine sharp.

I slept very little because I couldn't get used to the light in the room being on. I was homesick and I cried, trying to stifle my sobs under the covers.

The routine varied on weekends, but our time was always planned. At Maridíaz, Christian activities were very different from the ones at Alvernia, where the nuns were content with our giving money to help the poor and praying for them. The nuns at Maridíaz had us visit the city's poor neighborhoods on Saturday morning, hand out food, and prepare children for their first communion or teach adults how to read.

On Sunday recess and mass were both longer, and we set aside some time to clean our rooms. Once a month we were allowed to go home for a visit, and once a month the nuns took us out to play volleyball on the Bombaná Batallion's courts.

To break the monotony, we boarders tried to dodge the rules by doing things like stealing bread and jam from the nuns' dining room, sneaking out in the wee hours of the morning to take hot baths in the nuns' tub, or showering

38. High school is divided into three different tracks: *bachillerato* is a six-year college preparatory school; *comercial* is a four-year vocational school, and *normal* is a six-year teacher school.
39. This word, and its masculine form *compañeros,* can denote many levels of relationship. It can mean companions or friends in school, comrades in arms, or romantic partners.
40. Girls from the Valle del Cauca; the masculine form is *vallunos.*

nude against regulations, which required us to shower in our *chingues.*[41] We also liked to put on cultural shows on Sunday afternoons to show off our artistic abilities. Elsa sang tangos, Sara recited "El seminarista de los ojos negros," Alba Lucía sang *rancheras,*[42] and Blanca played the piano.

Going home to Sibundoy every month, or for vacations, made me feel free. From the plateau you had the first panoramic view of the valley, gazing over the ancient *frailejón* plants. Then the highway curled and uncurled like a snake, alternately hiding and revealing the countryside at every turn. At the very end the Sibundoy Valley appeared, splendidly mirrored in the water of the lagoons. The beauty of it went straight from your eyes right down into your heart.

We lived in a house in the town, but el Pato had a small ranch with livestock not far from there. He gave me a beautiful mulberry-colored mare so I could ride. I disappeared on Sunday mornings and only surfaced again at dusk. I took the road to Planada, which went to where the indigenous people lived. I admired the landscape and watched the people who went down the road to church and to market. The men with their straight black hair in a bowl-shaped cut wore the striped *capisayos*[43] with mountains of *chaquiras*[44] around their necks. The women, with braids, wore red, blue, or fuschia *rebozo* shawls and colored *chumbes*[45] around their waists to hold up their black skirts. Almost all of them had a baby on their back.

In Sibundoy I learned of another reality through my mother. She had become good friends with the Camsá in spite of the fact that not all of the settler class approved of such intimacy. Mercedes Jacanamijoy taught her how to weave chumbes on a loom, Pedro Juajibioy taught her how to speak a little Camsá, and María Chindoy taught her to cook *guasimba,*[46] potatoes, and *kuna*[47] like they did. I went with Mamá on many of her visits, and I began to learn the customs of these people. Sometimes Aideé Seijas, an anthropologist, came with us. She researched indigenous medicine and explained some things about the Camsá culture to us.

My feelings toward the indigenous people of Colombia were of curiosity and respect. As an intermediary my mother was able to achieve a relationship

41. A light cotton smock worn to preserve modesty when showering.
42. A type of music and song typical in Mexico.
43. A type of striped poncho with a white or dark blue background worn by men of the Inga and Camsá ethnicities.
44. Colored glass beads used on necklaces, originally brought by the Spanish to sell to the indigenous population.
45. A woven belt worn by Inga and Camsá women.
46. An edible root similar to the arracacha.
47. A bulbous vegetable similar to an onion.

of trust and affection that was not very common between the indigenous and the whites. This made our trips around Planada unforgettable.

In 1963 Capuchin missionaries still lived in the Valle de Sibundoy. They had been coming since the beginning of the century to catholicize the region. Fray Bartolomé was legendary. He rode about the town square on his horse in his tan cassock and an extremely long gray beard that rested on his belly. White people greeted him by nodding their heads and the indigenous people kissed his hand. Nothing in the valley, or around it, moved without his consent. Fray Bartolomé married, baptized, punished, and in a way even elected the authorities of the town council.

El Pato didn't go to mass, and he didn't like priests or pious ladies either. He used to say, "If you pray and you sin, then you're even." He only believed in the Virgin of Carmen, and only so that she would grant him an easy death. He thought that investing in cathedrals, like they did in Sibundoy, was a waste of money; the people needed a sewage system and electricity. Because of this, and because he observed the military custom of not voting and of putting down politicians whenever he could, they said he was a Communist or belonged to the INCORA,[48] which meant almost the same thing to the priests.

Around that time the state was fighting with the Capuchins over the vast possessions of the missionaries in the area. Rumors of agrarian reform were sweeping through the country, and the INCORA, created for that purpose, proposed expropriation—with indemnities—of Capuchin land, which they proposed to divide among the landless indigenous people. Father Bartolomé shot out sermons like darts against the INCORA, as if it were the devil incarnate. Victor Daniel Bonilla's book *Servants of God or Masters of Men: The Story of a Capuchin Mission in Amazonia*[49] had just been published, and it recounted the conquest of souls and lands at the hands of the Capuchins. Those who felt that ecclesiastic power had been used to accumulate land could consider themselves enemies of the Church. The community was divided, and in this dispute my father was on the side of the bad guys.

We lived in Sibundoy for a year and a half, and it was the best time my family had together. I was in the fifth year of bachillerato when el Pato died, and with his death our stay in Sibundoy and our family life both came to an end. I experienced my first deep pain—the pain of being orphaned and of watching my mother's battle to make it on her own.

48. Instituto Colombiano para Reforma Agraria (Colombian Institute for Agrarian Reform), a government institution established at the time of the abortive 1961 agrarian reform.
49. Translated by Rosemary Sheed (Harmondsworth: Penguin Books, 1972).

We had nothing left but memories of the old man. His brother, a lawyer and a senator of the republic, swooped down like a vulture on el Pato's property. When my mamá dried her tears, she had nothing left. The brother had even taken his dogs and hunting weapons. So we moved to Pasto, my mother got a job as a secretary in the Nariño lottery office, and I continued my studies.

Life in Pasto consisted of school, the occasional party, and the frivolity of dodging suitors. The ritual was repeated every Sunday: go to ten o'clock mass, go out with the guys to see the band at the Gobernación,[50] and there, beneath the watchful eyes of the entire congregation, insinuate a promise, let slip a tender word, and allow the Don Juans' fantasies to soar until the next week.

Around that time I became a fan of the theater. One day Armando Guerrero came to school; he was a law student at the Universidad de Nariño. He suggested we form a theater group, and we were excited about the idea. Shortly afterward, some eight girls got together as the Las Euménides theater group. Armando was our director, aided by Alvaro Velasco, both of them members of the Partido Comunista Marxista-Leninista, the PCCML.[51] We put on García Lorca's play *La casa de Bernarda Alba*. This was the key that opened the door to another world for me. The social sensitivity my mother cultivated and the nuns had affirmed, an adolescent rebelliousness that had no outlet, reading about the Spanish Civil War, and the *Frente unido* newspaper, founded by Camilo Torres,[52] new options for social action—all of these things together changed my life.

Revolutionary idealism, activism, debates with university students about the existence of God, and the study of theater scripts occupied the after-school time left us and began to introduce us to the youthful world confronting the traditional *pastusa*[53] society.

Our play was presented at the First Student Theater Festival in Pasto and was an absolute scandal. *La casa de Bernarda Alba* questioned traditional family structure, authoritarianism, and the sanctity of virginity in women, criticized the hypocrisy of a closed society, and lauded the right to rebellion.

50. The capitol building.
51. Marxist-Leninist Communist Party, begun around 1964–65 as the political branch of the EPL (Ejército Popular de Liberación, or Popular Liberation Army, formed in 1964).
52. Camilo Torres was a priest who, convinced that it was the best way to serve the people of Colombia, joined the Ejercito de Liberación Nacionale (National Liberation Army or ELN) in 1965. Before joining he was active in organizing in urban areas and had begun the *Frente unido* (United Front) newspaper and political organization. Torres was killed in combat in 1966, a few months after joining the guerrilla movement, and his urban organization was seriously weakened. See Carlos Medina Gallego, *ELN: Una historia contada a dos voces* (Bogotá: Rodríguez Quito Editores, 1996).
53. Someone or something from Pasto.

The bishop and the nuns who attended the plays in the festival had a lot to bemoan. The last straw in our affront to their sensibility came the day that el Loco (the Madman) Bedoya read his poems. Mingled with el Loco's incomprehensible metaphors were more concrete words describing his love as a shipwreck on the waves of his lover's menstruation. The bishop and nuns stormed out indignantly.

Thus was the school's sanctioning of our theater group revoked. The school authorities forbade us to continue the group and to put on our play again during the festival. From that point on, my rebellion had direction. I began to get bad grades in religion, wouldn't go to any more spiritual retreats, and was the only one in my class who didn't take communion at my graduation mass. Of the eight members of the theater group, six of us became active in Marxist groups.

The role of Adela in *La casa de Bernarda Alba* changed my life. I finished the bachillerato with a college boyfriend, Rodrigo Apráez, one of the leaders of a leftist youth movement that was beginning to form in Pasto. I began to participate in a Maoist study group, declared myself an atheist with little protest from my mother, and changed my major from veterinary medicine to anthropology.

2

Turmoil at the Nacional

GIVEN MY MOTHER'S financial situation and my good performance as a student, the Franciscans offered me a scholarship in social sciences at the Instituto Mariano. I accepted.

There was nothing new in the Instituto. I had the same compañeras I'd had since school and the same teachers from bachillerato, and the classes merely reviewed what I'd done the year before. The chaplain was the same, as were the Thursday masses and the eternal scolding of those of us who wore miniskirts. My rebellion began to find expression in my refusal to attend mass and the shortness of my skirts.

Between classes I took part in discussions with the Maoist study group organized by a student nicknamed el Diablo (the devil). The members were students from the Maridíaz and we held meetings at my house because my mother didn't freak out when she heard us talking about revolution. At these meetings we read and discussed the "Four Essays on Philosophy" of the "illustrious comrade Mao" and went over each paragraph of the Communist Party Manifesto with a fine-tooth comb.

These discussions fed my desire to break the rules and kick over the traces of Franciscan piety. My refusal to attend mass every Thursday or abide by the conservative dress code led the director of the Instituto to put me into psychotherapy for treatment of my atheism.

I felt more and more cloistered and increasingly limited. I knew I couldn't stay there, especially after the psychotherapy sessions with Madre Matilde began. Every Monday at five o'clock she shut me in an office that was more like a nun's cell and read me entire paragraphs from Apocalypse, her heavy arm, smelling of holiness, draped around my shoulders. She would poke her Cyrano nose in my face while warning me of the dangers of alienation from the divine hand. I left these sessions drained and spent the rest of the week worrying. Maybe I was more afraid of Madre Matilde than of God himself.

My way out of the Instituto presented itself one day when the social studies teacher explained the origin of the human race in the first couple—Adam and Eve. I asked her indignantly to present the many other theories, especially now that the Catholic Church had acknowledged that the story of the Garden of Eden was metaphorical. She responded confidently, "If Adam and Eve were not the first ones to live in the world, then who committed original sin?"

I said nothing more and left the classroom with my mind made up leave the Instituto. Interestingly, it was the story of Adam and Eve that marked the beginning and the end of my education with the nuns. My ignorance that first day at the Alvernia had made me look like a fool in front of my compañeras, and my stubbornness years later at the Instituto put me decidedly out of the Franciscan world. I refused the scholarship and enrolled in the Universidad Nacional to fulfill a longstanding desire, despite Madre Matilde's warning that I would find eternal damnation in that cave of Communists.

Fortunately Mamá supported my desire to study in Bogotá; after all, she said, the direction of my life was at stake. I passed the entrance exams and was admitted to the anthropology department, but there was no money to pay for it. My mother's salary as a secretary was barely enough for us to live on.

I decided to find Daniel Vásquez, my father, and ask him for financial help. That was how I met him, just after I turned eighteen. He paid my enrollment fees and the first semester's tuition without batting an eye. But, in an effort to exercise some sort of supervision over his daughter, whom he didn't know at all, he named his childhood friend, Guillermo Ponce de León, my counselor. Coincidentally, Guillermo's son, Juan Manuel, was also enrolled in his first semester of anthropology. My friendship with Juan seemed fated to be.

In July 1970 I bade farewell to Pasto. I knew I was leaving the nest, and conflicting emotions accompanied me to the plane. I was afraid to face the new on my own and sad to leave my mamá, but at the same time I had an unquenchable desire to experience other things. When the plane took off I let my thoughts take off as well. During the hour-long flight I was in limbo. I didn't want to think of anything at all.

Jaime Apráez and Benjamín Yepes, a couple of pastuso friends who were studying in the Nacional, met me at the Bogotá airport. The next day they took me to the university and showed me the ropes of registration and paying fees; they gave me a map and directions for the bus routes that took me from my place to campus.

The first thing that captured my attention was the amount of graffiti scrawled on the walls of the university. All the slogans talked of struggle and revolution. The words provided a stark contrast to the vast green field, trees, and blue sky that separated the various colleges. The university was the opposite of the nuns' school, with its tall adobe walls. I liked it, and I liked the people, too. They were all dressed so casually that you couldn't tell the professors from the students.

The second day, I ventured out on my own and got lost in spite of the map. I spent hours waiting in lines to get a stamp here, a seal there, a signature over there. My pilgrimage through offices and buildings seemed endless; each of them had an incomprehensible name, and when I dared to ask directions there was no end of jokers who sent me the wrong way. It was enough to drive you crazy. In the end, exhausted, I got the bulletin of course offerings. Now I had only to fill in my schedule with the codes for each class I wanted to take and hand them in at the registration window. When I opened the bulletin I saw a series of five or six numbers for each subject. Other numbers identified the colleges and still others were for majors—there was a number for everything. Even I was already coded—with the number 470–218.

I felt so confused that I left the campus and sat down on the front lawn. My strength was sapped, I was hungry, my feet hurt, and I was lost in a web of numbers and errands that were too much for me. When tears threatened to drip onto my papers, a *muchacho*[1] came out of the house and asked to borrow the bulletin I was holding. His name was Bernardo Younes, and he turned out to be my guardian angel. He was in his eighth semester of veterinary school, and with his help I was able to enroll in classes in one afternoon. He knew all the shortcuts to avoid all the red tape.

---

1. Young man (f. *muchacha*).

My first week was a marathon of trying to find the right classrooms in the different buildings, with nothing to go on but codes and my map. When I finally found the right room, class was almost over.

After about a month of classes my request for university housing was approved. My papá wanted to set me up in student housing run by nuns, but I persuaded him to save money and let me live in the women's dorms at the Nacional. Nuns again? No way!

My father made a thousand pesos a month and I needed only seventy a semester, plus ten pesos for health services. So altogether school cost about 240 pesos a year. I never went off campus; I had everything I needed right there. I shared a room that first semester with a girl named Margarita Aristizábal and one of her sisters. There were six Aristizábals studying in the Nacional, and their father was a guard at the campus Banco Popular.[2] Soon I was one more daughter to Papá Ramón, who looked after me with the same tenderness he did his own children.

Student social life was concentrated in cafés. The ones near the university, among them the Hechizada, el Viejo, or the Super Chisme, were frequented by groups of school friends and townies. Flirting and gossip abounded. By contrast, in the Cafetín, the Central Cafeteria, and the chess room, people talked politics. The long line to get in "the Central" at lunch and dinnertime was also a point of convergence and in moments of revolutionary effervescence we took advantage of it for demonstrations.

When I got to the Nacional they were still telling stories about the protests of 1970, which had called for the reopening of the university and reverberated all the way to Medellín, Cali, and Bucaramanga. Everyone who had participated in these protests was a revolutionary as far as the university was concerned.

Those of us from outside the city who lived at the university lived between politics and academics: maybe that's why we were the activists of the student movement. They could count on us to agitate, demonstrate, and participate in sit-ins or any kind of protest. We called ourselves foundational compañeros to differentiate ourselves from leftist groups that had distanced themselves from the people. We could be identified by our radical critique of the social and economic structure and of the political life of the country. Almost all of us belonged, or had belonged, to some leftist group, and we participated in one way or another in the frequent stone-throwing protests.

As a resident, I was part of the team that worked with Cooperación, a student work-study program that provided some services in the Central café

2. Popular Bank is a common bank in Colombia.

and got free food in exchange. In those days almost every one of the 5,000 students at the Nacional went through that café at one time or another. The "old-timers" initiated us newcomers, whispering in our ears:

"That guy is Germán Liévano, from the ELN. He just got out of prison. They accused him of stealing arms. He's in medicine."

"That one is Sergio Pulgarín, leader of the *Camilistas*."[3]

"She's Bertha Quintero, a *berraca*[4] woman who stands up to the police."

"That other guy is Guido Gómez. They accused him of throwing a Molotov cocktail in a muchacha's face. He was arrested."

"That one wearing the *maxi-ruana* is Jaime Caicedo. *Mamerto*."[5]

"The morenito is Marcelo Torres from the JUPA."[6]

"The *mono*[7] is Esaú Vásquez. He joined the Cabeza de Turco Committee."[8]

This was how I began to get to know the leftist world at the university, in all its diversity. I had arrived with only the information el Diablo, our group leader, had given me on the trip from Pasto: "In the Universidad Nacional, compañera . . . you're going to find other political groups. The JUCO[9] members are mamertos for the Communist Party and revisionists. The Camilistas are close to the ELN and far left. And the petit bourgeoisie are followers of the traitor Trotsky. But don't worry, there are also Maoist study groups there. I'll give you the contact."

Of course, the reality exceeded el Diablo's description.

That same semester, la Negra Puyana, a compañera from the theater group in Pasto, began to study economics. The *nariñense*[10] colony was numerous, and almost all its members were active in the JUPA—people said the letters really stood for Juventudes Pastusas—led by *costeño*[11] Marcelo Torres. They offered us membership, but la Negra and I said we wanted to get to know the group first. They still included us in a study group, the first

---

3. See Chapter 1, note 52, on Camilo Torres and the *Frente Unido*. *Camilistas* were the followers of Torres.

4. *Berraco/-a*, a very common Colombianism, can mean tough, wonderful, courageous, capable, difficult, painful, and other things, depending on the context.

5. A *maxi-ruana* is a long, heavy, woolen poncho. The term *mamerto* was coined in the 1960s, after names of some Communist Party leaders that ended in -erto, for example, Gilberto Vieira. It refers to members of the Communist Party, or leftist groups in general, who had become less radical and more conciliatory. It can also mean idiot or fool.

6. Juventud Patriótica, or Patriotic Youth.

7. Of fair hair or complexion.

8. A student committee organized before the 1970s student movement at the Nacional.

9. Juventud Comunista, or Communist Youth.

10. From the department of Nariño on the west coast of Colombia, bordering Ecuador.

11. From the Coast.

discussion topic of which was Mao's *New Democracy*, written as a political program for revolutionary China. Our task was to show, using data from our own national reality, the similarities that justified using Mao's program in Colombia.

This wasn't difficult when you looked at regions like Nariño, where in 1970 customs of servitude still prevailed on the large haciendas: there were arranged marriages to avoid dividing property, land that was sold or inherited included *aparceros*,[12] who were required to lend one day of service to the hacienda. On *fincas*[13] such as Guachucal and Tasnaque, along the Guáitara River, workers were paid sixty centavos a day, well below what was paid in industrialized regions like the Valle del Cauca or in the coffee zones. If Nariño was our prototype, the country could be categorized as semi-feudal. U.S. studies of our economy characterized it as semi-colonial. In this light, Mao's program, which counted the nationalist bourgeoisie an ally in the revolutionary struggle against economic dependency and vestiges of feudalism, was as appropriate for Colombia as it had been for China.

By contrast, the Camilistas, who opted for socialism as a way out of the capitalist crisis, took into account the relations of the free wage labor of the proletarian farmers in the coffee region and the Valle del Cauca. That was where one could find the best examples of the free labor market that typified the capitalist system, according to Marx. The analyses that came from this viewpoint saw a predominantly capitalist Colombia that needed a socialist revolution. It should be noted that almost all of the socialist leaders came from the Valle del Cauca and the coffee zone.

Until then, efforts to characterize Colombian society were plagued by sectarian considerations. Rather than look at studies on national reality, we read popular authors like Indalecio Liévano, Nieto Arteta, and Mario Arrubla for arguments to justify our revolutionary schemas, almost all of which were inspired by experiences in other countries.

The university community of that era saw in Camilo Torres, the priest-guerrillero, a model of commitment and a call to direct political practice rather than theoretical debates. At the same time, the popularity of armed groups in Latin America reinforced the idea of participating directly in insurrection with the masses. The most radical positions differed from those of the

---

12. Similar to sharecroppers, except that those who worked the land were also required to serve the owners one day a week (or a month, depending on the number of workers) in or around the hacienda, without pay. Landowners were often godparents of the children of the aparceros, which was supposed to keep the family dependent, obedient, and submissive. Aparceros could work off the land for pay but received no remuneration for work on the hacienda.
13. Large farms or ranches.

so-called conciliators in that they completely rejected electoral participation and change from within existing institutions. The radical left preached the destruction of the system and held that the university must play the role of intellectual vanguard in the formation of revolutionary cadres.

Other university students were into the hippy culture of rock 'n' roll, marijuana, and free love, but even they fell under the sway of the revolutionary consciousness sweeping the campus. Being revolutionary, believing in change, going against the established order, struggling for freedom, giving your life for the interests of the people—all of these ideas were interwoven, both in and outside the classroom. The theoretical epicenter was located in the College of Humanities, where students from different departments who shared these concerns converged.

The Nacional was splattered with graffiti urging people to make love, not war in Vietnam, declaring that the revolution must be socialist if it were to have any meaning, demanding liberty or death. Street art featured el Che, who looked at us from above with his sad, seductive gaze, Camilo, and Ho Chi Minh, with his heroic maxims, while comrade Mao walked on the waters of the Yang-Tsé and Enver Hoxa smiled from the rice paper pages of the latest publication. We sold *Voz proletaria* and *Tribuna roja* and handed out *Crítica marxista, Barricada*, and *Sol rojo y fusil*[14] for free. Uplifting revolutionary ballads filled the air, mixing with strains of salsa and tangos. We liked Violeta Parra, Carlos Puebla, Víctor Jara, and Ana y Jaime, and we sighed along with Neruda, De Greiff, and Benedetti. We attended the plays of groups like la Candelaria, the TEC,[15] and the *Teatro libre*,[16] and we gathered in the little Cafetín or in the chess room, or stretched out in the Freud Gardens. Men wore beards, jeans, pastusa boots,[17] and colored chaquiras.

For anthropology students it was the time of the Doñas:[18] Doña Ligia de Ferrufino in administration, Doña Gloria Triana in coordination, and Doña Blanquita de Molina in teaching. I attended class enthusiastically, but I had trouble taking notes. It wasn't like taking dictation at school. If I paid attention to what the professor was saying, I didn't write, and vice versa. We didn't have homework, but we read a lot. That was what the central library was for, but each college also had a reading section. The readings each professor recommended were copied, but they had been copied so

14. Voice of the Proletariat; Red Tribune; the Marxist Critique; Barricade; and Red Sun and Rifle.
15. The *Teatro libre de Cali*, a famous theater group directed by Enrique Buenaventura, an innovator in Colombian theater and forceful political critic.
16. Free Theater.
17. Lace-up boots made of raw, untanned leather, almost yellow because undyed, ankle height, rubber soled, hand sewn, good for hiking, and aesthetically military.
18. Ladies.

many times that we often had to guess at the meaning of the smudged and blurry text.

In the 1970s, Marxism as a tool for analysis and research was the order of the day. In the humanities we basically learned Marxist theory. We began in the first semester with Professor Vasco's course on historical materialism, in which we read Lenin's *State and Revolution*, Marx and Engel's *Three Sources and Three Component Parts of Marxism*,[19] *The Communist Manifesto*, *The German Ideology*, and *Pre-capitalist Economic Formations*, Stalin's writings on national minorities, and Mao's *Four Essays on Philosophy*.

The most admired professors were the ones we pegged as Marxists, among them Darío Mesa in sociology, Luis Guillermo Vasco and Guillermo Páramo in anthropology, and Jorge Orlando Melo, Salomón Kalmanovitz, Humberto Puyana, and Humberto Molina in economics.

I thought Vasco was the best of them all. He had the patience of an Eastern philosopher as he taught me how to study, but he was also unrelenting in his demands. He gave me the time I needed; he explained, asked questions; we read together, he reviewed my notes. But he didn't cut me any slack. I had to be both good at my academic studies and committed in my daily practice. He watched every detail of my behavior and lectured me harshly when he thought petit bourgeois weaknesses were corrupting me. At the same time there was a tenderness in his tutelage that very few of us enjoyed. Vasco was a hard man in his words, and not very expressive in his affections, but on more than one occasion, while I cried over my lack of commitment, he caressed my hair in silence. I not only studied historical materialism with my professor, I studied my first anthropology texts with him and read his drafts on the Chamí. The world of ethnographic research captivated me. In literature, he drew me to the classics of the Russian Revolution. He opened up his library to me and gave me the keys to his apartment so that I could go there to read whenever I wanted. In the first semester I made the honor roll, which was both an academic distinction and a practical benefit, for it meant I didn't have to pay enrollment fees.

Professor Vasco introduced me not only to academic life but also to a new revolutionary ethics. He and his compañera, Graciela, were a fundamental source of support for my first period of university life.

Vasco taught general anthropology in the first semester, and his critical vision and his stance on active social commitment influenced us deeply. La Nana, a compañera from the Colegio Andino, wanted to get closer to Vasco but had been unsuccessful in spite of the intelligent questions she asked in

19. The author of this work is actually Lenin. —Transl.

class. One day she got a copy of Mao's *Basic Tactics* in German and sat down to read it where Vasco could see her. The effect could not have been better. From that day on she had no trouble communicating with him.

Always critical of leftist groups, Vasco couldn't find one that came close to his expectations, but almost all of them consulted him. His view of them was unusual. You didn't talk to him about the Colombian Communist Party—he didn't even consider it leftist. He couldn't forgive the JUPA the idiocy of the disastrous Patriotic National Strike in 1970. To his mind, the ELN suffered from revolutionary volunteerism and vanguardism, and the Trotskyites espoused a petit bourgeois ideology.

Vasco was a Maoist by conviction. Rumor had it that the backdrop at his first wedding was an image of Comrade Mao. Mere proximity to Vasco turned his students into a band, and others called us *vasquistas*. At the Nacional in those days, either you affiliated yourself or you were affiliated. Almost everyone belonged to a group, and the majority were militant leftists or leftist sympathizers. Belonging to an armed group gave you a special aura and increased the respect of others. Of course this was never quite spoken out loud. Yet, though relegated to the realm of secrecy, it was murmured in huddled groups.

When I first arrived at the university, I still practiced the flirtatiousness of adolescence, and this desire to please made me spend half an hour every morning applying black liner and three shades of eyeshadow. Then I deliberated over which miniskirt and chaquira necklace to wear. I was always late to class. One day someone asked me sarcastically, "Compañera, did you come here to get a husband or to make a revolution?"

This question hit a nerve, and I decided to make my revolutionary vocation very clear. I stopped wearing makeup, traded my miniskirt for tight-fitting, well-worn, boot-cut jeans, and gave up my black leather, knee-high *mosquetera* boots for some lace-up pastusas. I kept only my chaquira necklaces.

I buried in the past my Beatles music, Woodstock album, Joan Baez songs, and the rock rhythms that possessed my body in endless rumbas beneath the black light of the '70s discos. Instead of tuning in to Radio 15 to hear "Boca de Chicle," "Yesterday," and "Gotas de lluvia," I became a fan of the morning news on Noticiero Todelar because I needed to be well informed. At night, with the other resident muchachos, we tuned the short-wave radio to Radio Habana, "from Cuba, America's free territory."

I ate less and less and drank more and more tinto. I went from puffing on an occasional filtered Parliament to smoking black tobacco, and I had no more time for parties. The last one I went to was held at the College of Arts.

Also in attendance were Guillermo Sáenz,[20] recently arrived from Germany, and his anthropologist girlfriend; the cream of the JUCO, represented by Jaime Caicedo; Marilú Posso and Ana Marta Rodríguez; a few anthropologists and some seniors in sociology; some Communist professors, students of the arts, and the ever-present costeños who never missed a *baile*.[21] No residents were there. Afterward I was told that the far left students looked down on social activities organized by the JUCO because they were bourgeois. So I decided to march to the beat of the leftists and dance only on vacation.

My relationship with my first-semester compañeros was uncomplicated. We used studying as a pretext to get together and chat and joke around. We almost always ended up turning some study session or group work into a *parranda*[22] with Ana Marta dancing flamenco on a table. In Juan Manuel Ponce's house we had the best get-togethers because the poet Carrillo and his old law friends in the Externado, Arnulfo Julio, Raúl Gómez Jattin, and Santiago Aristizábal, came to read their poems and stories. Juan's study and room were separated from the rest of the house, so we could drink wine until dawn and no one would bother us.

We compañeros came from diverse backgrounds; most had studied other fields or professions before. Juan Manuel Ponce had done nine semesters of law, Benjamín Yepes was a livestock artificial inseminator, and el Negro Valdés, who at thirty-three was the oldest, had gone from theater work to *arriero*[23] before he found his vocation in anthropology. La Nana, Vera Grabe, and Consuelo Mariño had studied in the Colegio Andino, the German immersion school; Marta Zambrano y Cloro from the Anglo-Colombiano, or English school. Margarita and I came from country schools. María Consuelo Mejía and Ana Marta Rodríguez had joined the group, and they were further advanced in their studies but took classes with us; both of them belonged to the Juventud Comunista.

Our group stayed intact for two semesters. We baptized ourselves the Punalúa Family[24] after reading Engels's *Origin of the Family, Private Property and the State*. Our favorite spot was the Freud Gardens, in front of the

20. He later became a member of the Central Command of the Revolutionary Armed Forces of Colombia—FARC.
21. Dance.
22. Huge blast.
23. One who drives carts pulled by mules, to bring food to market, collect garbage, etc. Feminine is *arriera*.
24. Engels took this name from Morgan. It refers to a type of primitive family in which incest began to be regulated. Men and women of reproductive age formed reciprocal groups or communities of husbands and wives who called each other *punalúa*, or partner, and blood brothers were excluded from the family for marriage.

anthropology building. There I learned that *la locha* was not only the antonym of *la lucha*[25] but also a time between classes to hang out on the grass, look up to the sky, close your eyes, and not think of anything. We were no longer teenagers but we played like kids on the newly mown lawn, and we ran in the rain until we were sopping wet. We loved each other well until we went our own ways.

The Takeover

We began our second semester of anthropology in February 1971, in the midst of student assemblies where we refused the so-called Basic Plan, the political stance of the public university derived from the Atcon Report for Latin America, which we considered the beginning of the privatization of the university. The Universidad del Valle led the protest. The murder of a student in street demonstrations in Cali led to disturbances throughout the country. The student movement took over the universities: the Valle, the Atlántico, the Palmira, the Antioquia, and the Nariño.

At the Nacional in Bogotá we marched to the College of Medicine, took over the administration building, stormed the dean's office and demanded that he leave the university. He tried to resist but was pushed out of the building onto Calle 45. Someone stopped a bus that was going to La Picota;[26] the dean got in and they paid his fare. It was said they even pinched his butt. We expelled him in the midst of public derision, just as we had read university students had done in Mao's China with reactionary professors.

Afterward, during a big assembly, we declared that the Universidad Nacional de Colombia was in the hands of the revolutionary student body. If the takeover was done with the help of all the university's leftist groups, the defense of the buildings was left in the hands of a smaller group of residents led by the Camilistas. We stayed in the administrative building for twenty-one days.

At the time of the takeover I was not directly attached to any group. I was thrown out of the JUPA for three infractions. One, I was Vasco's friend; two, I distributed a newspaper called *Crítica revolucionaria* in which the MOIR[27] was censured because of the failure of the Patriotic National Strike; and

---

25. Struggle.
26. La Picota Prison, in the south of Bogotá.
27. Movimiento Obrero Independiente y Revolucionario, the Independent and Revolutionary Workers' Movement. This Maoist group was begun at the end of the 1960s after the Sino-Soviet split.

three, I didn't applaud after Marcelo Torres's speech at an assemby (instead
I stood up and shouted "bravo!" when Ricardo Sánchez spoke about the
need for a student movement that would radically change the university).
The orator I had applauded was a Trotskyite.

The next day Marcelo Torres called me in. Maybe because I was a close
friend of la Negra Puyana, his girlfriend at the time, he warned me personally.
The scolding reminded me of Madre Matilde and her threats of hell, and I
told Marcelo I was leaving the group. From then on, no member of the JUPA
would greet me.

So I was an Independent. The Camilista commandos, the Valle Trotskyites, the Marxist leagues, and the Independents refused the co-
government proposed by the JUPA and the JUCO. We recognized as leaders Moncayito,[28] Sergio Pulgarín, Ricardo Mosquera, Lisandro Navia, and
Cristina de la Torre. They were the agitators, the speechmakers. Others led
behind the scenes. They were linked to armed groups; they were "serious
people." I remember some of them: Rogelio, Elías, and el Pato.

We fought for several days to keep the university, fought against the police
with stones. All day long there were skirmishes in the entrances off of Calles
26 and 45, with the outstanding performance of the so-called "Camilista
dogs"—three huge guys who coordinated the burning of cars.

I took part in all the uprisings The first time I tried to throw a stone,
I almost knocked out the compañero in front of me. My role was more to
provide moral support for the muchachos. I shouted at the police, whistled,
made noise, and pulled the wounded out of the area, and the rest of the
time I ran around, advancing or retreating according to the success or failure
on the battle field. I loved it. Throwing stones was like emotional venting.
Several times I lagged behind and was about to be caught by the police, but
a guardian angel always seemed to swoop down and rescue me.

Once the takeover was consolidated, there were meetings every day to
analyze the character of the student movement. We discussed endlessly the
different tendencies of the left with respect to any concept; we debated the
wording of every press release. Those of us who were less attached to any
particular theory came in and out of the meetings on the pretext of making
sure that everything was okay.

A group of Camilistas was in charge of security; among them were el
Mono, el Negro Vellojín, Pebles, and the Tarazonas. I had my hand in com-
munications; I answered the phone and issued statements about the takeover.
We had long phone conferences with other universities that had been taken

28. Héctor Moncayo, student leader from the College of Economics.

over by students and with the foreign press. We even called Cuba's *Prensa
Latina* to give our version of events.

We imagined that the dean got direct instructions from the Pentagon,
and from the first day we searched his office for proof of the "handing over of
the university to imperialism." What we found were letters from politicians
recommending their protégés for admission to the Nacional; among them
was one from Misael Pastrana Borrero, the president of Colombia.

When night fell, only the residents were left. We stayed alert, afraid the
police might decide to launch a nighttime assault to take back the university.
We drank a lot of tinto and thought about what we'd do in an emergency.
We took turns on watch and rested for two short hours on mattresses laid
out on the floor. I waited for as long as I had to to sleep next to el Mono,
Pebles, or Rogelio, the men I trusted most.

We barely ate. We looted the cellar of the cafeteria and got enough
food to last about ten days. After that even bread was scarce. Someone had
the great idea to sacrifice a calf they had seen in the College of Veterinary
Medicine. About a hundred students went for it, but none of them knew what
to do with the animal. It dragged Pebles around, wouldn't let Tolima kill it,
and stepped on el Paisa, until they finally decided to hold a checkpoint on
Calle 26 and raise the money to pay for a butcher. There was so much meat.
El Negro Vellojín made us a special soup from the blood.

The next day Pebles came in with the newspaper *El Espacio*. Its headline
read, "Hundreds of Students from the Universidad Nacional in Danger."
The story explained that the calf we had butchered was the subject of an
experiment in the veterinary lab. It had been injected with aphthous. More
than one of us went pale and left to vomit. Of course we wondered if this
rumor was part of a psychological warfare plan, but we all waited at our
combat posts for the symptoms to appear, like the crew of a ship in a storm.
In the end, nothing happened.

Fatigue and poor nutrition took their toll. At one point I was talking in
my sleep about the student movement with my eyes open, unaware of what
I was saying. My friends sent me to rest in the women's dorms, and I slept
for twenty-four hours.

We left campus to attend the National Student Encounter in Palmira,
Valle. The fields of the Nacional seemed bigger to me, the sky was much
higher up. I had been closed up in the administration building for so long.

During the event we met compañeros from all over the country who had
participated in the movement. They came from the Coast, Cauca, Tolima,
Santander, the Valle, Antioquia, Nariño, and Caldas. All the various factions
were represented: JUPAs, JUCOs, Trotskyites, Camilistas, Testimonios,

MLs, Ligas,[29] and Independents. Students from private universities attended, too. The Javeriana, los Andes, la Santo Tomás, la Libre, and el Externado had joined the movement.

The máximo and mínimo[30] programs resulted from this encounter, each representing a different political tendency. After months of protest and mobilization, the student movement in 1971 was a disparate collection of islands that slowly drifted away from the possibility of a unified student organization.

For the rest of the year we argued about the co-government until we came up on the elections for student representation. La Plaga promoted its own candidate, a man known as el Brother, from the College of Odontology. He had the highest grades, was a well-known, toothless pothead with shoulder-length blond hair, and campaigned in a *zorra*[31] crowned with flowers, from which he blew kisses in the manner of beauty queens in a parade. Those of us who opposed the participation of the student movement in the co-government joined up with this irreverent candidate.

The promotion of el Brother consolidated la Plaga as a group. La Plaga was not an organization but the name for a broad student sector made up mostly of people from the provinces with no political commitment to leftist groups, whose common denominator was belligerence and love of demonstrations. Throwing stones and fighting was its passion. One of the most hard-core *combos* (groups) of la Plaga was made up of Salsa, Cuero, Rata, el Chato, Papapicha, and el Camello—lawless men. Most students were afraid of them, and the muchachas wouldn't even go near them. They enjoyed the fame of the evil. They were tight with the far left. They were always very special to me, for they considered me part of their combo and took care of me.

The Betrayal

Moritz Ackerman, the most talented agitator of the student movement, arrived in Bogotá after he was expelled from the Universidad del Valle. His passionate speech the day our compañero in Cali was killed mobilized a thousand students at the Nacional. He was one of the stars of the Valle Trotskyites. More than one girl pined over his sad eyes and fiery rhetoric. He and other student leaders, among them Sergio Pulgarín, Ricardo Sánchez,

29. Testimonios were a Maoist political group; MLs were members of the PCCML, the Colombia Marxist-Leninist Communist Party; and Ligas were a socialist league.
30. Programs for students named for reforms that had yet to be made.
31. A horse- or mule-drawn wooden cart still used in Colombia for collecting garbage, selling fruits and vegetables, etc.

el Mono Luna, Cristina de la Torre, and Marcelo Torres, sat on the commission that negotiated the end of the takeovers with the minister of education,
Luis Carlos Galán Sarmiento.[32] They also chose me; I don't know why. But
I met Luis Carlos Galán, the youngest minister Colombia has ever had, and
the meetings in his office had the feeling of a belligerent student assembly.

At that time the Tendencia Socialista, another socialist group, was strong
throughout the country because of the quality of its student cadres in public
debate. When we least expected it, Moritz turned mamerto. Many say the
change came about after a night of passion with Marilú Posso, the famous
JUCO diva. What is certain is that he left a meeting in which we had agreed
that he would speak as representative of the Tendencia Socialista in a student
assembly in the College of Sociology. We got to the building and he launched
into his speech about adhering to the rank and file of the Communist Party,
denying Trotskyism. At first we didn't understand what was happening,
but as it sank in, Moncayo, Luna, and I cried in each other's arms, feeling
Moritz's betrayal like a knife in our hearts. The students in the assembly
began to whistle. Soon everyone was shouting. The audience was divided in
two, with the JUCO on one side and everyone else on the other. The speeches
were over with. I don't know where la Plaga came from, but they couldn't
stand mamertos, and they started throwing stones. The JUCOs were ready.
Rods, chains, and sticks appeared. Pebles lashed out with his belt buckle
and Moritz's bodyguard ended up wounded, his shirt stained with blood.
He lifted his face, which was extremely pale, and protected Moritz Ackerman.
This bodyguard belonged to the JUCO; his name was Carlos Pizarro, and
he had already asked to join the FARC. When someone flashed a revolver,
the Communists ran out the exit to Calle 45. Ackerman could never return
to the Nacional again.

It was a time of intense sectarianism. Each political group declared itself
the possessor of the absolute truth. Ideological discourse was enthroned, but
there was no discussion, only fighting. Everyone tried to finish the opposition
off. To do so they resorted to McCarthyism, satire, distorting arguments,
anything to discredit the other, even whistling and hissing. There was so
much division among the student groups that on more than one occasion,
in the middle of a stone fight against the police, two groups with different
agendas wound up fighting with each other.

The political differences mirrored Colombia's society and its forms of
struggle for power. If Colombia was semi-colonial and semi-feudal, we

---

32. Galán was a Liberal Party presidential candidate who was assassinated before the elections
(allegedly by narcotraffickers) in July 1989.

needed a Maoist revolution. This would require either an army of the people or elections, the war could be long or short, and we could work openly with the masses or go underground. If, on the other hand, Colombia was a dependent capitalist society, then we needed a socialist revolution. But for this we had to resort to either armed struggle or legal struggle, and, if legal, then we had to work with unions or with the peasants in the countryside. Was it better to combine all forms of struggle? But how could we do that? With a revolutionary party made up of cadres or made up of the masses?

It was endless. Everything was summed up in initials; every set of initials was an abbreviation, and every abbreviation was a different political group that didn't get along with the others. The student left of the 1970s was divided into tiny pieces. Still, we acquired at the university the ideological grounding that would direct our first revolutionary tasks.

3

A Criolla Guerrilla

THE WINDS OF revolution had descended on the university, stirring the embers and reigniting the fires. The triumph of the Cuban guerrilla and the experiences of May 1968 in Paris influenced the Colombian youth in the seventies. My generation wanted both to end the war in Vietnam and to change the world by revolutionary war; practice free love and build utopias in South America; break political continuity and propose other ideologies; and create a more egalitarian society. We were attracted to collective projects and played at imitating the idols of the time. We read the *Selected Works* of el Che, Fidel's famous speech (known as "The Historic Second Declaration of Havana"), María Ester Gilio's *Tupamaro guerrillas*, Carlos Marighella's *Minimanual of the Urban Guerrilla*, and Mao's *Basic Tactics.* We also read novels and epics like Ostrovsky's *How the Steel Was Tempered*, Gorki's *Mother,* Pomeroy's *The Forest,* Rojas's *Tania la guerrillera*, and *The Secret Papers of a Revolutionary: The Diary of Che Guevara.*

In this atmosphere my fervor for the cause grew. I found theoretical sustenance in the classics of Marxism that appeared in the shadow of my academic studies. Once I understood historical materialism, I understood that violence played the role of midwife in class struggle. I was eager to participate more directly in revolution. We young people saw limited possibilities for change within established social structures. The hippie movement of the 1960s transgressed the norms of social behavior, reaching toward greater individual liberty. Some hippies formed communes, a new way of life that radically questioned capitalist society, but we didn't find in them a vision of social justice appropriate for our developing countries. The politics guiding the traditional parties offered no possibilities for social transformation either. We put our hopes into revolutionary war as a means to radical change that would leave power in the hands of the people.

El Pato, or Jaime Sánchez, an ex-leftist militant, had told me that the guerrilla was like God: it was everywhere and watched carefully to choose the best for its members. I decided to strengthen myself in being a good revolutionary so they would pick me. I followed my counselor's instructions to a T. I climbed Monserrate for exercise, I practiced target shooting in the Parque Nacional, at one of those fair stands where you got a pack of *Pielroja* cigarettes if you could hit the target with a cork-shooting musket, and I practiced solidarity, which was easy among the residents of the Nacional; we were all still so wet behind the ears.

I learned to be serious whenever the subject of the revolution came up. The only piece of el Pato's advice I disobeyed had to do with wearing miniskirts, in spite of the fact that he assured me it was the best way to fool the enemy.

Indeed, the far left had its eyes on me. I moved in the most radical student circles; I was a tireless activist, and some of the men of the far left still enjoyed the memory of the miniskirts I wore in my first semester. Several had made the first step to recruit me. El Pato invested time because he wanted to recruit me for the ELN; el Prócer gave me some Camilo Torres documents and a Fabio Vásquez interview and suggested I join his study group. Elías talked a lot with me and began to hint at possible assignments. But Rogelio was the early bird, and without any readings or talks he hooked me up with Iván Marino Ospina. It was a coincidence, because Rogelio collaborated equally with the ELN and with the FARC.

Rogelio was a hotfooted *pereirano*[1]; they called him the roadrunner. He talked as fast as he walked. Seriousness and laughter tripped over each other in his facial expressions. For him, the university was nothing but a temporary shelter. He was enrolled in anthropology but was seldom seen in class. He was the typical conspirator; he made any subject a mystery by omitting first names and names of places, pluralizing pronouns, and basing his identity on concepts like "the organization," "serious work," and

---

1. Someone from Pereira.

"compartmentalization."[2] He was skillful at changing the subject when someone approached us during a conversation about our work. He must have been
about thirty-two, and had met Iván Marino in elementary school.

Rogelio's behavior captivated me. His mystery awakened respect, and
I committed myself to his direction unconditionally. I trusted him. I never
asked a question that could be construed as obvious. Nor did I know who
"we" were, or what organization he was talking about, or what the serious
work was. I simply let myself be led.

For quite a while I didn't know what group I belonged to. I had a feeling
it was the ELN, but it turned out that I was part of a new project of Jaime
Bateman's, before he was expelled from the FARC, to bring the war into the
cities. My involvement with FARC was a stroke of luck.

Mine was an unceremonious recruitment. I was brought into the fold
almost without realizing it. One morning Rogelio appeared and took me to
the language department. Changing buildings was a way of talking in private,
far away from curious acquaintances. Once we were there, he told me that
I had been chosen for serious work. I only needed to bring a change of
clothes, because we would be going out of the city. Was I willing? I said yes
and asked no questions. I had read somewhere that, for reasons of security,
no one should know more than what was necessary.

We would leave the next day. Neither Rogelio's mysteries nor my expectations mitigated the pleasure of the trip. Plus, my companion was especially
happy, and at every stop he got out to get me some sweets.

We arrived in Pereira. I didn't know our destination and I didn't ask. We
left our bags at a house and set off to see the city. We drank cold beer in the
Parque del Lago, walked along the business district, ate *almojábanas* with
avena[3] and ended up drinking tinto at nine at night at Rogelio's family home,
which was empty. He made my bed himself, and only then did he say that the
next day he would introduce me to a man who had been in the FARC and in
Douglas Bravo's guerrilla in Venezuela. Since we had to get up early, he set
the alarm and said good night. I could hardly get to sleep, I was so excited.
A grand event was approaching: I would meet a guerrillero in the flesh.

We got to the appointment a few minutes before seven. It was at a neighborhood diner where taxi drivers savored their coffee before heading off to
work. We ordered ours. I was anxious, my eyes glued to the door, when a man

2. Compartmentalization means keeping one's revolutionary activities completely separate from
other activities and secret from others. Members of the same organization do not necessarily know
their fellow members' assignments, even if they are close friends or lovers.
3. *Almojábanas* are cheese breads; *avena*, a cold or hot drink made of milk, oatmeal, some sugar,
and cinnamon.

came in and without hesitation headed to our table. He had just showered; droplets of water quivered in his curly black hair. He wore a light blue shirt, and as he approached he half-winked at us mischievously. A spontaneous laugh burst from his lips as he greeted us happily. He hugged Rogelio and slapped him on the back, and held out one hand to me while he took my arm with the other and squeezed it effusively. He spoke with a paisa accent and an easy fluency, wrapped up in a smile that dissolved his harshness, because there was no doubt that this was a strong man.

I watched him curiously. I looked for scars from life in the mountains on his arms. Maybe I expected to see him covered with wounds, as if he had fought a tiger in every battle. What I saw was a man about thirty years old who spoke enthusiastically, used a direct sort of language, made jokes, and laughed heartily. He proposed nothing mysterious to us; we simply agreed to meet two days later in a neighboring town. When we had finished our tinto he put his hand on my shoulder, looked at me with tender care, and smacked Rogelio in farewell, then got up and left before we did.

My image of the first guerrillero I met is etched like a photograph in my memory. Iván Marino, his smile and blue shirt. That was my meeting with the guerrilla, the initial ceremony, the approach. Shortly afterward, he came to Bogotá to stay and we began to act as a commando unit.

At nineteen years old I knew one or two things about the direction my life would take. But I didn't know where to start, so I decided to explore different paths. At that time the strength of weapons attracted me, and I entered the world of Tania la Guerrillera, like Alice in Wonderland, sliding along on a sled, curious and fascinated.

I had had time to build an image to which I wanted to adapt my actions. A model of honor, self-surrender, willpower, courage, and heroism. This wanting-to-be, much like a patchwork quilt, was made up of parts of people whom I had admired since I was a little girl, all woven together to create this imaginary model. It included saints like Francis of Assisi and Joan of Arc, superheroes like Batman, and loved ones like my mamá and my grandpa. But it was also built on values taken from el Che, Tania la Guerrillera, Carlos Mariguella, and Raúl Sendic, and on aspects of people from the Nacional such as Vasco, Norma Enriquez, and Berta Quintero.

Curiously, life passes by with us wanting to be something. At five I wanted to be a boy because it was easier to urinate standing up. At nine my dream was to be a dancer or an actress, and I spent hours acting for an imaginary camera. When I was a teenager I wanted to be a veterinarian or a doctor, and when I finished bachillerato I wanted to be an anthropologist. Now, in college, I wanted most of all to be a guerrillera.

But now this dream could be my reality. My first serious job was to transport the dynamite Iván Marino had given me and Rogelio from Risaralda to Bogotá. We filled a carry-on suitcase with about ten kilos of the stuff, covered it up with a tee-shirt, and took a *colectivo*.[4] Rogelio told me to pretend I was asleep, so I did, lying over the case. When we got to a checkpoint, the guard looked at me and didn't want to bother me, so he continued searching the other passengers. Meanwhile, I tried to breathe slowly so I could silence the beating of my heart, which I was afraid could be heard all the way to the guard's booth.

Later, thanks again to Rogelio, I hooked up with a study group with people from the Nacional. We read and discussed Lenin's *What Is to Be Done?* but our discipline was short lived. Most of us preferred other types of activities.

When Iván got to Bogotá, he brought his compañera, Adiela. Three people we all knew attended the first meeting: el Mono, Pebles, and me. Instead of starting with the study plan, as is customary among the university left, our compañero took out a Madsen submachine gun and began to instruct us in its use. I had seen one of these guns once before, in Sevilla, Valle, the one my stepfather's bodyguard used.

Thus I began my service in the regular militancy as part of an urban commando unit led by Iván Marino. We met at least once a week and went for walks on Sundays. It doesn't seem like much, but these activities became the most important ones in my life, because they linked me to the revolutionary dream. Iván Marino had come to work in Bogotá to create an urban guerrilla force to draw the war into the centers of the country's economic and political decisions, and to communicate the revolutionary message to the masses of workers and people. The idea was to support the insurgent struggle that up until then had been waged only in the countryside; we would raise the funds to finance this work, and we would link the disparate forces in a unified cause.

In one of our first meetings Iván told us to use pseudonyms to protect our legal identity. Adopting a pseudonym didn't seem odd to me. My mother had nicknamed me Ñaña when I was little; now, at the university, they called me la Negra. They called my tía María Mercedes Policarpa when she became a nun. Clark Kent was also Superman. Besides, having an alias is common in Colombia; our generation knew of famous outlaws like Chispas, Charro Negro, and Veneno. For revolutionaries, however, there is an ethical

---

4. This is a small van that follows a predetermined route and picks up passengers along the way. It is cheaper and thus more used than an individual taxi.

difference between a pseudonym and an alias. While an alias is like a nick-name, the pseudonym means protection and it represents who you want to be—the ideal image, the projection of the life that you want to realize.

It took our group only minutes to choose pseudonyms. We liked "Alvaro" for Iván, but he had used that name ever since he'd been in the FARC and thought he needed a new one, so I gave him the name "Felipe." He chose "Claudia" for me. Adiela said she wanted to be called "Ana María." El Mono chose "Pedro," and Pebles decided on "Kiko." We baptized ourselves by repeating all the names, mixed with laughs: Felipe, Ana María, Pedro, Kiko, and Claudia. There was no special ritual, but I will always remember my first pseudo, as we called it for short.

The name change was one step toward the world of secrecy, where you hid your true identity and "disappeared" your personal history. In this atmo-sphere of covering up, the conspirator becomes anonymous and can assume multiple fictitious identities. With the pseudo a new stage was begun. Hence-forth we made an effort not to talk about our past, not to mention the names of family members or loved ones, not to give information about what we did, where we lived, where we went. Each of us helped the other omit details, and we watched over the others' meticulousness.

I practiced constantly. If a person I didn't know wanted to talk, I took advantage of it to build on my fiction. I gave Claudia life. I filled her with content, acted her as I had acted the part of Adela in *La casa de Bernarda Alba*. Her last name was Montenegro; I made her part of a large family, a psychol-ogy student in a private university. I said she was born in Bogotá. Claudia was flirtatious and empty, she wasn't interested in politics and avoided any ref-erence to the guerrillas. I didn't have to work too hard to eradicate all traces of my radical politics. I drew on my acquaintance with Batman, Superman, and Wonder Woman, and on TV series like "Zorro." These heroes hid be-hind eyeglasses and other accouterments that suggested fragility, shyness, and timidity.

Under the pseudo I discerned three different personalities in myself. There was the everyday student who went to class, had a circle of friends, and maintained family ties. The other one, the new one, met secretly with her comrades to learn how to carry arms and make revolution. And then there was Claudia, the mask that protected the conspirator from the curiosity of strangers.

Whenever I traveled or did an assignment, if anyone asked me where I was going or what I was doing, the answer had to come quickly, and it had to hide my true destination and the point of the assignment. Maintaining secrecy was fundamental, and so I put my imagination to work for that. Later on it became habit, because my life and the security of others depended on it. Covering up, hiding, camouflaging, always throwing people off your trail, even those closest to you, was one of the first rules of being a revolutionary.

Target Shooting at the Fair

The hills of Bogotá were our commando's Sierra Maestra. During the training sessions we ran along its topography again and again, hoping to emulate Cuba's revolutionary history. We got up early on Sundays and by seven we were ready for training. We walked along the hills, and as we ascended a scent of damp ground, moss, and dead leaves filled our nostrils. We had to climb about 3,200 meters, and it wasn't easy. The first time I went up, my breath burned in my lungs, my heart wanted to jump out of my mouth, my throat was parched, and my legs trembled from the effort. I stopped, claiming I wanted to look down on the city. Everything went blurry and I collapsed. My head was spinning. I had a terrible urge to vomit. I went pale. I thought of el Che with his asthma in the Bolivian heights, and I felt like a failure. I almost started to cry.

Iván's voice brought me back to life: "Breathe! Breathe deep . . . that's it . . . breathe in lots of air and let it out slowly . . . put your arms up and fill up your lungs . . . there you go." El Mono and Pebles helped me get up. Little by little I got better; I could see more clearly. There below, enveloped in fog, lay Bogotá.

There was no way around it: those climbs were brutal. El Mono and Iván were in front, Pebles followed, then me, and finally Adiela. Iván came back with us for a while and then went back up front. Adiela was tired, but she didn't say anything; if I looked at her she smiled at me. Sometimes we heard instructions:

Maintain your breathing rhythm. Don't open your mouths, your throat will get dry. It's best not to talk. Don't stop. A little more . . . you can always go a little more . . . slowly but without stopping. First put all your weight on one leg. Go up on the right one, then when it hurts, use the left one. Don't ever look at the trip as a whole, because it seems like a long way. You have to set goals, points of reference. Concentrate on getting to that point, a hilltop, a tree. When you get there, set another one.

We walked six hours or more. Iván chose the stopping place. Under trees and close to water. We sat down to share a sandwich; Ana María divided it up.

Iván Marino always wanted to get his ration last. We ate bread and bocadillo or pieces of *panela*;[5] sometimes we had sardines with crackers, other times a thermos of hot coffee. We drank water from the natural springs. Resting was the best part; that's when we tightened our comraderie.

When lunch was over, the conversation started. We didn't have predetermined subjects, everything was brought up informally and interwoven with life stories. That's how we discovered different national geographies and people who were part of the hidden history of the country, people from the countryside, the pueblo, who became legendary in a region because of their exploits against the enemy.

Iván and Ana María narrated their experiences in the rural guerrilla or on urban assignments. They didn't talk only about successes but also made fun of their failures, and Adiela's peals of laughter sounded like pagan music. They told us what happened the day they went into a house where, according to their information, there were U.S. dollars to be had. When they subdued the man of the house under the threat of Flaco Bateman's weapon, his wife began to scream hysterically and that made them nervous, until el Flaco decided to stuff a handkerchief into her mouth, as he had seen done in the movies. They searched the house but found no money or anything of use. To make matters worse, the handkerchief they had stuffed into the señora's mouth was embroidered with the name Alvaro Fayad. It was a special gift from his tía. Batemen had been staying in Fayad's apartment since Fayad had gone to the FARC, and he used what he could of his compañero's clothes without paying attention to details. The news of the embroidered kerchief came out in the press.

They also talked about falling in love. They were part of the same group, and they were covering while the other compañeros went in for an attack. It was dark and they were in a jeep. Two policemen went by, and so Iván immediately kissed Ana María. The ruse worked, and the police continued on. But he didn't let her go. He took advantage of the situation to kiss her for real. Hearing their stories was like watching a movie, they told them so vividly.

We shared our dreams about the Colombia we wanted, but without the theoretical controversies of the university. We were united by a deep respect for armed groups and the conviction that change in the country needed armed support. Up until then the socialist project had been the clearest option for radical change from a country led by the privileged few to one in which social justice prevailed. We didn't distract ourselves with the state's proposal or

5. Unrefined sugar in round slabs, cut in pieces and eaten, or dissolved in water, for a hot or cold drink called *aguapanela*.

with social order, for we believed that the most important thing was to take power for the pueblo. In this first stage of our education I had never heard a critique of a leftist group, not even of the FARC, from which Iván had been expelled.

After lunch, we made a polygon. We found a tree and hung the target there. Sometimes it was a paper with a bull's-eye drawn on it, other times simply something that stood out. We started by learning the proper positions for shooting: standing, kneeling on the ground, and lying down. I already knew something from hunting. Afterward we took turns shooting with el Mono's rifle, a .22 caliber revolver, or a U-caliber revolver.[6] Sometimes Felipe brought us a pistol or a heavier .38 caliber revolver. This exercise familiarized us with weapons, with the sound of the shot, with its mechanisms, and helped us lose our fear and learn to carry them naturally.

In time we got better. We covered more ground with less effort, knew the paths and trails like the palms of our hands, and found new places for target practice. We liked nothing better than these outings. They took the place of movies, love, and rumbas. The hills were a place of total experience. Without the pressure of public places, where everyone could see us, without having to whisper, without being tailed, we gave our attention wholly to the training. Shared physical effort, the mystique, the enthusiasm, the comraderie, our will power and secrecy proved step by step—all of this made us closer compañeros and increased our conviction that only a revolution would change the country. We had a responsibility, and we prepared ourselves for it meticulously.

Now? Yes! A Guerrillera

At night we snuck out to paint signs: ELN EPL FARC = VICTORY and LONG LIVE GUERRILLA UNITY. We carried small revolvers so we could get used to carrying them. Someone with good writing and acceptable spelling spraypainted the sign, while the rest of us went off in couples, like compañeros, so the police wouldn't catch the painter with his hands in the cookie jar. The couples were usually made up of one experienced person and one novice, and it was better if they were a man and a woman because then they could pretend to be going together. If we saw the cops, we whistled to sound the alarm.

As part of our training we got pamphlets from other guerrilla groups throughout the country and writings from the Argentines, Uruguayans, and

6. A small, slim weapon used for sport shooting.

Chileans. These consisted of revolutionary proclamations, material on security measures, and instructions for conspiratorial practices. I remember Víctor Serge's book, *What Everyone Should Know about Repression*,[7] and a novel that Iván Marino gave me, *In the Name of the People*,[8] by Mitka Gravcheva; it talked about the heroism of a woman during revolutionary war.

In the second semester of 1971 *Battle of Algiers* was playing in movie theaters, and I saw it three times. I was moved by the story of the Algerian people's resistance against the French colonialism that had imposed a sort of apartheid. Each time I cried at the scene in which the army discovers a resistance commando unit. The army soldiers surround the commandos and demand their surrender. Two men and a boy decide to blow themselves up rather than turn themselves in. A pregnant woman, the compañera of one of the heroes, watches the scene from the street, along with people from the town. The camera pauses on her face, and only the sadness of her gaze and one tear rolling down her cheek betray her profound grief.

I had revolutionary measles, or militancy fever. I pursued my academic studies half-heartedly, while dedicating my heart and soul to practicing conspiracy with el Mono and Pebles. We decided to learn cryptography with Marighella's manual, and we spent hours encrypting messages we left in preestablished hideouts such as mailboxes, holes in trees, under rocks, or the hollow legs of cafeteria tables, so the others in the commando would pick them up. Rarely could we decipher them.

We were into something big. Talking in the first-person plural, of "us," of the "organization," created a sense of community, of belonging, of a collective. Although I knew no one outside our group, I had the feeling we were many.

We learned by doing. If we went out to walk along the streets, Iván would suddenly ask, "Did you see that *guacharaca*?"[9] "Did you see what time the armored car stops here?" He seemed to have a special radar to detect possible operations: "There must be money here." "Weapons are here."

We beginners missed these details, but we started learning, little by little. First we thought about what the organization needed to support the revolution: money, weapons, logistical materials like military uniforms, binoculars, medicine, and information on possible financial targets. Then we sharpened our observation skills in order to learn how to obtain these things. We reached

---

7. Victor Serge, *What Everyone Should Know about Repression*, trans. Judith White (New York: New Park, 1979).
8. My translation of the Spanish title, *En el nombre del pueblo.*
9. Five-shot automatic rifle with a short barrel used by guards in armored cars for transporting valuables.

the point where every time we met someone, our first thought was: Who does this person hang out with? What type of information does he or she have access to?

We constantly accumulated data and, when necessary, we put them together and initiatives were born. Once we were wondering how to get a musket. Immediately I remembered the guard at a building we had gone to with a classmate to study. Later we verified the information and we specified details and routines to plan the operation.

When Iván Marino mentioned the organization's need for weapons, I thought of the collection in my friend Juan Manuel's house. Immediately we started the labor of intelligence, the information-gathering stage. The leaders gave us assignments: I would take care of the internal data because I had access to the house and the inhabitants; the others would take care of the external routines.

When I was alone the contradictions hounded me. I loved Juano like a brother, and he wasn't reactionary; quite the contrary, he sympathized with the left. That made my situation more difficult. I was facilitating the robbery of my friend and of his father, Daniel Vásquez's friend, and in addition he was my counselor. I talked to Iván Marino about my doubts. He told me not to worry, that nothing was going to happen to Juan. For him the arms were mere decoration, while they could be of great help to us.

My doubts dispelled and my revolutionary convictions strengthened, I made a map of the first floor of the house from memory, using the conventions that Iván Marino had taught me. I indicated the doors with a blank space between two little vertical lines, the windows with very thin rectangles, and the stairs with horizontal lines. The next time I visited the house, I remembered details and corrected my first drawing. Later on I described internal routines and family schedules down to the last detail. I did whatever was necessary. The other compañeros drew the outside maps and confirmed watch routines, because the zone and the house had guards.

We pulled off the operation early when we learned that Juan's parents were away and that only he, the two maids, and the guard would be home. We recruited more compañeros from the organization and then all that remained was a detailed plan for how to get in the house. If we could guarantee that Juan would be there, we could go in as students, friends of his, and ask him to get into the study, where the weapons were. I thought that if we formed a study group we would know beforehand how many people would be there, and we could count on one more—me—for any type of emergency. The truth is that I would have burst had they not let me be close. I felt responsible for my friend. I had to be with him.

We had two weeks to act. Our first attempt failed. On the appointed day, when I got to Juan's house, Lucho Otero and another man were approaching, pushing a jeep that had quit on them. The two men sent me signals to suspend the operation. I breathed a deep sigh of relief. The next attempt was successful. An anthropology exam was coming up and Juan, his girlfriend, el Negro Yepes, and I decided to meet at Juan's house to study. When I arrived el Negro was already there, and his girlfriend had called to say she wasn't coming, which made me very happy because that meant one less.

The attack was scheduled for three in the afternoon. At three Iván Marino came into the study with a weapon in his hand and said in a very loud voice, "Everyone stay calm! We're the urban guerrilla force. We've taken over the house."

Behind him an incredibly tall man with a huge nose in a three-quarter-length raincoat and dark glasses with a pistol in his hand said, very softly, "Nothing is going to happen to you. Stay calm, we only came for the weapons." Ana María came in too. I almost didn't recognize her, for she wore a cap that covered her chestnut hair with a visor that hid half her face. She came in smiling, greeting everyone kindly.

Iván Marino's sentence sounded in my head like an echo; I was included in the plural "we." I was an urban guerrillera, too. His firm voice had given the attack an air of seriousness, but the other man gave the scene a hint of the surreal, talking nonstop with ease. My attention was fixed on him. The Walther pistol in his hand was cocked and it accompanied his gestures almost as if he weren't aware it could shoot bullets.

Where did Iván pick up this beginner? was the first thing that entered my head. Having the pistol cocked seemed insane to me. As judge and part of the action, I felt a mixture of rage and frustration toward the new guy.

Suddenly I realized that the back yard door was open. If Juan's German Shepherd were alerted, he would put us in a tight spot. I took my role of support seriously, and I threw myself toward the door to shut it, as fast as fear would allow, but I heard a shout: "Don't move, or you're dead!" I stopped cold. The tall guy was pointing at me with his Walther. I looked at Iván Marino anxiously and he made a sign to the other, who stopped threatening me. Finally I was able to point to the yard and sputter, "The dog . . . the dog's coming in." Iván Marino shut the door. I relaxed but felt a frightful rage toward the tall man in the raincoat, the sleeves of which were too short for his long arms. Of course, he could kill me—he doesn't know me, I thought.

Just then the man asked Juan if he liked any gun in particular; if so we would leave it for him. Juan pointed to a Colt revolver of the kind used by

North American cowboys. Ana María put the rest of the guns in her bag. There were about forty-five old weapons—collector's items.

Iván Marino tied our hands behind our backs. Then he took a roll of tape out of his jacket pocket and gagged us. It didn't work very well for el Negro Yepes because it stuck to his moustache.

From then on, you'd have thought the guerrillas were there visiting. Using the information I had provided about my friend, the tall guy addressed him as if he knew him. He asked about his family by name, about the university and the student situation, and about his brother, who was studying in the United States. He asked to borrow a book he found in the library and promised to return it soon. I was beside myself with amazement. So much kindness, so much eloquence, with the host, also tied up and beside himself, muttering his responses.

They finished packing and said good-bye, warning us not to move for ten minutes because the entire house was surrounded and there could be problems. As soon as they left I started to cry uncontrollably. I wasn't pretending, I was really upset. I couldn't figure out if it was fear or relief that everything had gone so well, or whether I felt guilt about what I had done to Juano.

We untied ourselves as best we could and went down to get help, thinking that we would find the others in the same situation. But they didn't even know anything was going on. The señoras in the kitchen were going about their duties, and the guard was in his spot. We told them what had happened. They looked at us incredulously. For them, nothing out of the ordinary had happened. The señoras had let the attackers in because they were there for the study group. When the attackers had left, they were very courteous and so aroused no suspicion.

We didn't know what to do. Should we file a report? Should we call the police? Juan and el Negro Yepes were worried; I was terrified. In the end I think we waited a few days, until Juan's parents came home and filed the report. Don Guillermo Ponce de León could think only about protecting his friend Daniel Vásquez's daughter from a bothersome situation with the authorities.

We had to make statements before a captain of the Institutos Militares Brigade. My description of the attackers didn't come close to reality. I said they were all about 1.65 meters tall, that one of them had glasses and another was fat, and that I didn't know if the third person was a man or a woman.

They followed Juan, el Negro, and me for some time. I had to stop going to my meetings with the group, and I took advantage of that to practice what spy novels said about how to behave when you're being followed. I went to class as usual, and I talked to more people than I normally did. In the afternoon, around five o'clock, I went downtown with el Mono to go window shopping and drink avena with almojábanas in the Sultana, a café on Seventh Avenue. It was good practice for all of us. I went out with el Mono to exhaust the tail, and Pebles went out with Ana María to practice following the three of us.

Every once and a while el Mono and I checked to see if the tail was following by going around in circles or making a senseless turn. When we went into a café we sat in the back, where we could see people coming and going, to confirm the presence of our tail. In any case, when we saw that a man in a dark wool suit walked at a safe distance from us and sat at a table nearby, craning his neck to hear our conversation, the noise of my heart pounding drowned out everything else, and a cold, painful feeling filled my stomach. If not for the feeling of security I got from el Mono's presence, I'd have lit out of there but quick.

Much later, when Ana María and Pebles confirmed that no one was following me, I had my first meeting with the group. Then I got the complete story of the attack. Another compañero, who didn't go into the study because Juan and el Negro might have recognized him, was on one of the stairwells with a knife. His mission was to stop anyone who went up, but no one saw him or mentioned him in the reports. Ana María's purse strap broke from the weight, and the weapons almost fell out on the floor right under the guard's nose as she was leaving the house. A getaway car was waiting a little way from the house.

That day the group asked me for a written report about the interrogation and a description of the captain who did the interrogating. Iván Marino assured me that it was a routine investigation, and that it was better to make an official report to the authorities. With this action, and Iván Marino's statement identifying us as an urban guerrilla group, I felt like I was really entering guerrilla life.

Iván Marino congratulated me in the name of the commanders because the success of the job was largely due to the intelligence I had gathered. As a reward, they assigned me a handgun, a U-caliber revolver. I had to take responsibility for keeping it clean and in a safe place. If there were operations, this gun was my defense.

I was happy—not only because they recognized my work, but also because the weapon meant that I had passed the first stage, from pre-militant to militant, and with that I gained status. A weapon and a pseudonym were two key symbolic elements in the initiation.

I took the weapon, put it in my bag, and went to my room at the university. No one was there. I cleaned it with genuine love. When I was done I put the bullets in the chamber and cocked the trigger. I knew that this was the position immediately before shooting. It still made me a little afraid to carry a loaded gun. Suddenly someone knocked on the door. My blood froze. I realized that I didn't know how to uncock the trigger without shooting the gun. The knocking continued. I couldn't think of anything to do except put my index finger between the hammer and the firing pin to muffle the sound. I shut my eyes and pulled the trigger. The hammer broke my fingernail. The pain from the slamming left a feeling like my heart pulsating in my finger. I hid the gun in a drawer under my clothes. I opened the door. It was a compañera asking me if I wanted to go eat lunch. I wanted to vomit.

Nothing Stops Love

Pebles, who was finishing his degree, almost never went out with us anymore; writing his thesis took time. El Mono and I were inseparable. It was common to see us together at the university. As residents, we both belonged to the same leftist social circles. After the takeover of the administration building, el Mono changed majors from geology to anthropology, and so we took some classes together. He was also a good friend of Ramiro, my boyfriend.

On top of all this, Iván Marino brought us together for assignments. He harbored a fantasy that we would fall in love and be a couple. Sometimes he resorted to tricks like passing himself off as a messenger of supposed declarations of love to me from el Mono, or vice versa, but since we were such good friends, his matchmaking schemes never worked.

I felt comfortable with el Mono, not because he had more experience than I but because it looked like he did. After one semester at the university he had gone beyond the freshman stereotype. Plus, his participation in student protests had given him a certain status on the left and, since he read a lot, he had enough information to back up his opinions. He knew a little about everything without being arrogant; in fact, he often doubled as a consultant.

El Mono could have been about my age, but he looked older; he even dressed like an old man. Not only that—he was different inside and out. He wore jeans that were too big so he'd feel more comfortable, his Grulla shoes[10] were one size too big (so he wouldn't get callouses), and his ruana folded lengthwise over his left shoulder. With his hair combed back

10. A brand of boots or shoes for workers, made with resistant leather and rubber soles, and used by the proletariat.

Gardel-style,[11] he shaved with a blade and cut his nails with a pocket knife. He always carried his transistor radio so he could listen to tangos, and his pocket knife was on his belt. You'd often see him whittling wood or making any little thing with the patience of an artisan, while he whistled or sang. He wasn't a man who'd laugh out loud, but when he laughed his whole body participated, and he said some hilarious, irreverant things that got the best of more than one of us. Even when he was insulting someone's mother he maintained his composure. He was gentle with me, but not overprotective, a true compañero, just like in the novels from revolutionary times. I completed all practices with him, from marches in the hills to gathering information for operations. And he didn't have that urgent need, so common among other muchachos, to compete, or to prove himself superior, or to pressure, much less to impress. He cared only about doing things as best he could, and he was very creative, as if the vocation of craftsman extended to everything he did. He always came up with variations for operations or suggested new ideas.

On two or three occasions our flesh betrayed us, and the teens we carried inside our uniforms emerged to play at exploring sensations. But we stopped there, in the very hands of desire. We loved each other with our fingertips, and our lips barely touched when the soldiers for the cause awoke. Reason overcame us and we abandoned the thought of falling in love because of the break we made between the political and the personal. I admired el Mono, but above all I loved him, to the point that if they had made me choose between him and my compañero, whom I loved with all the force of a first love, I wouldn't have hesitated an instant in declaring el Mono more important than Ramiro. After all, I believed that the revolution came before affairs of the heart. My heart was opening up a path amid the ideological brambles, trying to justify its rhythm and its feeling with theories.

I had had suitors among the compañeros from the cause ever since I got to the university. First there was Jairo Corredor, who was in charge of my group in the JUPA. When he declared his revolutionary love to me, I wanted to tell him that I simply didn't like him, but I thought I should find a less superficial argument. I told la Negra Puyana about it, but she only recommended Jairo's virtues. It was Lenin who came to my rescue, with his theories about organization and the incompatibility of militancy with love, and Jairo accepted that I didn't want to mix romantic feelings with revolutionary responsibility.

11. Carlos Gardel, of uncertain origin but generally considered Argentine, was a singer-songwriter and actor famous for his interpretation of the tango. He wore his hair slicked back with gel.

Then there was Sergio Pulgarín. During a get-together he stroked my hand and dedicated to me a popular song that went:

He seguido tus pasos, tu caminar
como un lobo en celo desde mi hogar
con la puerta abierta de par en par
de par en par . . .[12]

I eluded him by promising that we would talk when he was sober, and I sought refuge in el Mono so that no one else would bother me.

The biggest scare was Alfonso Molano, a student who had almost finished his studies in anthropology. One day he invited me to eat *dulce de guayaba*[13] in his apartment in the university dorms, and without skipping a beat he suggested I spend the night with him. I must have had a terrified look on my face, because Alfonso cracked up and said, "Relax, I'm not going to rape you. I'm only suggesting something." I babbled out something about not being in love with him. I was surprised by this proposal from someone who had no relationship with me but considered my position idealistic. What was truly materialist, he said, was going to bed and then waiting to see if feelings developed. I left him and went to cry on el Negro Valdés's shoulder. I told him what had happened, and in exchange I got the best advice ever: "Don't let them see you're new at this. Reject them as if you were a veteran."

I was starting to believe that I had a petit-bourgeois, idealistic heart and that there was no Prince Charming in the revolution, when suddenly Ramiro appeared like Don Quijote, a brick in his hand, ready to knock out a mounted police officer who was closing on me in the thick of a student stone-throwing demonstration. I succumbed to his heroism.

With a man like this, feelings could be supported in theory. Ramiro studied economics, which was a Marxist thing to do, with no help from his family, so he was more on the side of the proletariat than of the petit bourgeois. He spoke a radical Marxist language yet didn't belong to any student political group. This meant that he was probably involved in something serious. And if that weren't enough, he wrote love poems. When he took my hand under the table, I forgot all about political arguments. I was enchanted by this muchacho. I don't know if it was his hair or his big, padded hands. I don't

---

12. "I've followed your steps, your walk/like a wolf in heat from my home/with the door wide open/wide open." From "Quiero abrazarte tanto," arr. José Chova, sung by Víctor Manuel. Polygram Iberica, S.A. 1971, Madrid.
13. A sweet paste made from the guava.

know if I loved him because he was skinny or because he was mysterious. The only sure thing is that I fell in love, deliciously in love, with him.

Soon we went from talking to sighing, to silence and kisses. I was convinced that only love would open the doors of my sexuality and I entered into it with pleasure. More than losing my virginity, I gained in feelings of tenderness. When you know love, nothing can stop it. We loved each other in the moonlight of the fields of the Nacional, in the Hotel Italia in the center of the city when we had eighty pesos, or in the Chapinero[14] dorms when we only had fifty.

When the university was closed temporarily at the end of 1972 in an effort to discourage the growth of political resistance groups, Ramiro was living with el Mono and another classmate from economics in a room they rented in a house in the Santa Sofía neighborhood. Rather than go home, I went to live with Ramiro.

I idealized love between compañeros, and I assumed our coupleness in an odd confusion between the traditional woman who had lived in me from three generations hence and the modern one who demanded equal commitment in the political and in the private. There was no lack of love; I felt as if I had been transported to paradise in spite of financial difficulties, because I was sure that Ramiro and I could overcome anything.

That is why, when I got pregnant a few months later and he chased my fear away with a hug, everything about starting a family, going to school, and being politically militant seemed so easy to me. I understood quickly that any one of these things would by itself take up all my time, let alone doing them all at once. Being twenty years old helped—for a while.

Household Routine

In January 1973 our commando unit was given the mission to prepare to host a national meeting. We divided up the responsibilities, and Lucho Otero, whom I knew from the anthropology department, el Mono, and I were responsible for security. We went to a ranch house that belonged to the family of a compañera, close to Sasaima.

We first did reconnaissance work around the area, which for me involved no more than taking a walk and observing carefully. Then we made a map of the place and located roads going in, other ranches, and the railroad. Of the three of us, Lucho had the most experience; el Mono and I learned from him.

---

14. A neighborhood in Bogotá.

Afterward he sat down and marked on the map the observation points from which we could see any car that approached the house, and then he marked the places where we would stand guard. By dusk he had already designed a security plan with possible exits in case of an emergency. We spent the night at the ranch; we had a revolver and took turns keeping watch, more for training than out of necessity. The next day the other compañeros came in groups.

Compartmentalizing, or hiding, was an obssession, so the guests to the unique outing came wearing all sorts of hats, ski masks, glasses, and scarves. It was like a costume party; the only ones who came with their faces uncovered were el Flaco Bateman, Iván Marino, and Boris.

The tasks of cleaning and maintaining the house, security, and making food were distributed among those present, and someone was responsible for each task. The last people arrived at night, just as dinner—spaghetti with a thick sauce that had an undiscernible flavor—was being served. Then we made introductions all around (pseudonyms only, of course) and spent five minutes concocting a plausible story about why we were there together. We then reviewed the emergency plan so that everyone would know what to do if our meeting were discovered. There were only three women—Ana María, Slendy, and me—among about sixteen men.

The next day we got up early to do our exercise routine, used in martial arts. Boris led the group, and I did every movement enthusiastically, until he noticed my presence and asked, "Compañera, aren't you pregnant?"

"Yes."

"How far along?"

"Three months, why?"

"Because these exercises aren't good for you. You can sit these out."

I felt the limitations of my pregnancy for the first time. All those months I had gone up in the hills like I always had, and I got a bit more tired, but I was in perfect physical condition. I cannot deny that I was bothered by the exclusion, because I wasn't even showing.

The meeting lasted three days. Representatives came from Cali, Pereira, and Bogotá; they were part of a project led by Jaime Bateman to organize an urban guerrilla force that would bring the revolutionary war to the cities and serve as support for guerrilla unity. In this, our First National Conference, the political proposal for a new armed group was begun. We decided to call ourselves comuneros,[15] elect a central command, and work for unity in the actions of guerrilla organizations of that time: the ELN, the EPL, and

---

15. This name comes from the 1781 rebellion that channeled the socioeconomic tensions of the pre-Independence masses, in anti-tax protests and aspirations to join in the political arena. This

the FARC. Our politics was guided by three anti's: anti-imperialism, anti-oligarchy, and anti-sectarianism. El Flaco Bateman, the man in the raincoat and dark glasses from the attack on Juan Manuel's house, was one of those who promoted the political proposal that questioned actions taken up to now by a sectarian left.

After this first conference we continued our work and also published three editions of a magazine. It talked about the new political project and gave instructions on the use of some weapons. The fact that we called ourselves comuneros introduced an element that from then on characterized the movement: its recovery of the national at a time when the left in Colombia still looked primarily to China, the USSR, and Cuba more than to our own national situation.

I must have been about six months pregnant, because I was showing, when we decided to attack the police station on 40th Street in Bogotá. Because the police wouldn't suspect a pregnant woman, I was part of the group that facilitated the entrance. I went from one end of the city to the other, and carried the guns. When I got to the established meeting place, it was pouring rain and there was no place to take cover. I was afraid that if I went somewhere else to take shelter the contact would be lost, so I stood there in the rain. Passersby stared at me and I tried to look nonchalant, but time went by and no one showed. We were told not to wait more than fifteen minutes for anyone, but I waited about forty-five because I knew that without me the operation would not come off.

I wanted to cry. I was soaked right down to my soul, and growing more and more worried, when—finally—a huge, balding man approached me and uttered the secret phrase. I responded, half distrustful, half relieved. I didn't know him. He led me along the street to a café where we joined up with a skinny, tall muchacho whom I had met at the First National Conference. Manuel, the man who had contacted me, looked at me tenderly and gave me his handkerchief so I could dry my face and sponge my drenched hair. They had taken cover from the rain here and had hoped I would do the same. They never imagined that I'd brave the downpour.

"How far along are you?" asked Manuel.

"Six months."

"And you are going to participate like that?"

"Yes, why?"

---

rebellion was one of the significant "incubating" events of the war for independence. See *Manual de Historia de Colombia*, 2:23–24. See also John Leddy Phelan, *The People and the King: The Comunero Revolution in Colombia, 1781* (Madison: University of Wisconsin Press, 1978).

"I won't go with you. Understand me, we're going to worry more about you than the police; in your condition we have to take care of you."

He said all of this with affection while he helped me dry off. The other man was looking at the pipe he was smoking when Boris came to tell us the operation had been postponed. Manuel let out a peal of delight followed by a deep sigh. "Let's go, we'll take you home. Or rather, close to it. Poor thing. You're drenched."

We got in the car and the skinny muchacho drove, but since it was a loaner he couldn't figure out how to turn on the lights or the windshield wipers and had to drive without them. Everything from then on was laughter and jokes.

They didn't take me on any more operations and barely asked me to transport propaganda or keep weapons. By this time the university had been closed for almost a year, and I was working as a clerk in a stationery store so that I could pay the hospital bill when it came time to deliver my child. In spite of this involuntary recess, Ana María, Iván Marino, and el Flaco Bateman came to visit me rather often, as did el Mono, who also helped Ramiro with the carpentry preparations for baby's arrival.

My son was born one minute before midnight on 13 August 1973, after an incredibly long and complicated labor for which no one had prepared me. I spent one helpless night, forgotten by the doctors and nurses, in a room in a clinic. They paid attention to me only when the pain surpassed my limits and I began to cuss them out loud and long. Then they gave me a strong painkiller, so that the delivery, when it finally happened, was almost a surprise.

I knew he was a boy before anyone told me. Ramiro and I had considered several names and had decided on Juan Diego. With the baby, I felt like I had a family. My mother had come to be with me during the birth, and she stayed on for a week. She even gave me some advice on how to take care of him, but she did most of the caretaking in the first days. Ramiro was very taken with the muchacho; he changed his diapers and brought him to me so I could nurse him at any time of night. Ramiro had to work, of course, so when Mamá went home I was left with my son, and I didn't know what to do.

Lactating was torture. I had enough milk to feed a whole nursery, but I didn't know how to let it down and I wound up with mastitis. The first day I bathed my little one I almost drowned him. I ended up weeping with my baby in my arms.

I had to take care of him, wash his diapers, cook and clean the house like any of the neighbor women. I established a routine that allowed for no variation. Juan Diego woke at six. I changed him, fed him, and played with him until about seven while listening to the news on the radio. Ramiro made breakfast and went to work; I was on maternity leave from the stationery store. While the baby slept I cleaned the house while listening to the soap operas on the radio. At ten I gave him some juice, bathed him, and nursed him again. When he slept again I rushed to make lunch and wash diapers. At twelve-thirty Ramiro came home and we ate lunch. In the afternoons I listened to more soap operas, which were better company than nothing, and ironed or arranged the baby's things. Then we'd take a walk and I'd buy some food. By seven in the evening, when I put the baby in his pyjamas, I wanted to go to bed and never get up again.

This daily routine was varied only by Juan's doctor's appointments or an occasional visit to his paternal grandmother. I was submerged in a lethargy that I thought was matrimonial bliss, but it left me terribly irritated. My relationship with Ramiro was more and more distant; the entire weight of the household fell on me. He was the intellectual, the one who worked, the one who was involved in politics, and I was his wife, the one who raised the baby and took care of the house. This division of labor was no different from the one my grandma had followed at the beginning of the century.

The university reopened when Juan was two months old. I decided not to go back to classes that semester, not until he was a bit bigger. I couldn't leave him in day care just yet.

I was very isolated from everything that had mattered to me. We lived in the Caja de Vivienda Militar neighborhood in the northwestern part of the city, pretty far out. The neighborhood was made up largely of the families of police officers and subofficials. I talked to everyone, but I didn't have friends. The compañeros from the organization came to visit me once in a while, but they didn't say anything about my going back to work. They only left weapons, money, and propaganda for me to hold. Ana María and Iván were like family. Iván entertained himself by playing with the baby while Ana María and I talked about being housewives. In addition to working as a secretary at the Ministry of Health and participating in operation groups, Ana María took care of the house like all paisa women did, even if she had to get up at four in the morning. She had enough time to cook, wash, and iron, and take care of the plants and her compañero. But she didn't seem angry about it; she was always smiling, and she sang while she worked. I, on the other hand, was increasingly neurotic, so much so that when someone came to visit I was irritated by the tracks their shoes left on the shining floor of my house.

This reality began to become suffocating. One day I asked Iván Marino why they had isolated me from work.

"You aren't isolated," he said, "You are raising a child."

"But I want to be active again."

He accepted this. Now the meetings were held at my house. By this time el Mono had left for Medellín and Pebles for Cali. So I was hooked up with another commando unit, coordinated by a woman, the first feminist I had ever met.

Nineteen seventy-three was drawing to a close, and we were talking about the idea of focusing our work on the Anapista masses, who were indignant about the 19 April 1970 election fraud. We wanted to give a new twist to our group as the armed branch of the ANAPO.[16]

We Stole Bolívar's Sword

One Sunday I was told to be under the clock in the Parque Nacional at seven-thirty in the morning. Someone would pick me up, identifying himself with a signal. I was to bring a copy of *Cromos* magazine with me.

"Are you going to Tolima?" he would ask.

"No, I'm going to the coast," I would respond.

I was very punctual and had to wait about half an hour. Eventually a man with a maxi-ruana approached me. He had an afro and high cheekbones and an effeminate face. It couldn't be a compañero, I thought. But the man came closer and asked, "Are you going to Tolima?"

"No, to the coast," I answered with mistrust.

"Come this way," the character told me. His voice was sure and serious. I laughed at the first impression it gave me.

16. *Alianza Nacional Popular*, or the Popular National Alliance, the party led by General Gustavo Rojas Pinilla. The general took power after a coup d'état supported by the traditional parties in June 1953 to "pacify the country" and deactivate the Liberal guerrillas after the violence unleashed by the 1948 Gaítan assassination. As president, he attempted to organize a popular movement based on the binomial people and armed forces in which both would play a leading role. Hence the two traditional political parties opposed him. In 1957 the very Liberal and Conservative leaders who had put him in power unseated him and condemned him to exile. Now a victim of the oligarchy, the ex-dictator gathered around him those excluded from both parties, as well as a large sector of popular masses. He got the majority of the votes in the 1970 elections against Misael Pastrana Borrero, yet Pastrana was declared the winner. Rojas Pinilla did not mobilize his thousands of followers after the fraud, spurring some ANAPO members and others in armed leftist groups to organize an army to guarantee that this kind of blatant injustice would never happen again. Together with the comuneros, ex-ELN members, and others, they formed the Movimiento 19 de Abril, the April 19 Movement or M-19, at the end of 1973. It was a strategic step to strengthen the legal front and empower a military front. See Darío Villamizar, *Sueños de abril: Imágenes en la historia del M-19* (Bogotá: Planeta, 1997), and David Bushnell, *The Making of Modern Colombia: A Nation in Spite of Itself* (Berkeley and Los Angeles: University of California Press, 1993).

Further on there were more men and women. When we arrived, the meeting started.

"This will be an armed propaganda operation with a highly symbolical content," said a thin muchacho with lively eyes whom they called el Turco (the Turk), or David.

The man with the afro who had picked me up described the place to us in detail, with a map. The group immediately went on to operational details. The purpose of the operation was to influence public opinion and officially launch our organization. A press release would spread the news about who we were and what we were about. As a symbol of our struggle, we would take the Liberator's sword out of the encasement in which it rested in the Quinta de Bolívar. In our hands the sword of the Liberator would be wielded for new battles for freedom and democracy. It would not rest until the Bolivarian dream came true.

I had already taken part in previous attempts to steal Bolivar's sword, so the idea wasn't foreign to me. Besides, I knew the Quinta. I waited patiently to learn what my role would be. The specific instructions were doled out by groups. I wound up with a very quiet *pelada*[17] and a tall, husky muchacho who had come up from Pereira for the operation. From his nervousness I concluded that he was a first-timer. I thought it was better to make him feel confident, even if I myself felt lost. It was the first time I was going to act without my old buddies.

"How many operations have you been in?" the muchacho asked anxiously.

"Oh, quite a few."

"Good, because this is my first. You just look so young."

I smiled. Now I was the one, with all my insecurities, who was responsible for this freshman.

They assigned us to external patrol. We three would be at the entrance door to make sure that those inside wouldn't have problems. We would be the first to arrive and the last to leave. They gave us some grenades and, since I had never used them, I felt naked. I trusted handguns. But I said nothing.

On 17 January 1974 we arrived at the Quinta de Bolívar at 5:30 P.M. Two groups of compañeros had gone in half an hour before. When the guides were hurrying the visitors out at closing time, they lagged behind, and once the place was emptied of tourists they immobilized the guides and the door guard at the same time. Seeing the man trying to shout when nothing would

---

17. *Pelado* (m.)/*pelada* (f.): Kid, youngun, sapling.

come out of his mouth, trying to defend himself, made me very sad. But I concentrated on what I had to do.

A group of paisa tourists came up. The other compañero and I went out to meet them and tell them the Quinta was closed and they'd have to come back another day before five. They argued a little but then left. We were there for a while in silence. You could have heard a pin drop.

Suddenly el Turco appeared; I saw him put the sword in the neck of his maxi-ruana. He walked to the car that was waiting for him. The others left the place after him, some on foot and others in a second car. A group gave us the handguns. We waited for everyone to leave and started down the path, relieved. A patrol car was approaching, and the compañero at my side jumped.

We women grabbed his arms and kept walking slowly, acting like we were talking animatedly. My heart was beating in my throat. I was imagining myself pulling the grenade pin out with my teeth, like in the movies, and running down the street. The police car passed by.

I boarded a bus on Germania. The weapons I was carrying in my purse clattered with the bumpy movement of the bus, but fortunately the driver was listening to rancheras turned up loud. It was about six-thirty and there was a lot of traffic. Around seven, half way home, the radio interrupted the music to inform us that a group that called itself the Movimiento 19 de Abril—M-19—had just stolen Simón Bolívar's sword, and at the same time had taken the Council of Bogotá. The announcer read excerpts from our press release. "Shoot!" I thought. What if I couldn't get home? The trip was taking forever.

When I finally got home night had fallen. I called out a greeting to Ramiro, put the guns away in the closet, and picked up my baby; I hugged him close to my chest. I shut my eyes and fought back tears. The news was on, and Ramiro was glued to the radio.

"Were you in on that?"

"Me? No, no way. I just came from the university." He didn't even look at me. I was happy.

Our partnership had been exhausted by the daily routine and was drowning in contradictions. The discourse about relationships between compañeros was a far cry from the reality. In spite of the fact that we had both been involved in militant activity since before we lived together, now his work came first. He could do as he would with his time; I had the domestic chores and the baby. At most, Ramiro "helped" with some things, and according to a lot of compañero couples, I should have thanked him for his help. I myself thought his work justified his many absences. When he didn't come home to sleep, I couldn't sleep all night thinking that something had happened to him, waiting for a raid. When day broke, I would take the baby and all the propaganda from his organization and mine, his weapons and ours, and look for somewhere to stash them. It happened several times, but I wasn't jealous and always thought that revolutionary work excused him. I didn't even ask for explanations.

My son was eight months old when I discovered by chance that Ramiro had a *gringa*[18] girlfriend. I wasn't hurt so much because he had a girlfriend but because she was a gringa, and most of all because he wasn't able to tell me himself. I ran away from home for two days to cry alone, and when I got back I helped him pack up so he could go.

I was extremely depressed. My sadness actually made me sick. It was my first real heartbreak. I cried all the time and felt like the most unfortunate being on earth—a woman who couldn't maintain her love. The baby got sick, too; maybe my grief was contagious. Instead of decreasing, my depression got worse. At first I tried to keep myself busy so I wouldn't think, but sadness, like a windmill, dragged me down and exhausted my strength. I spent days waiting for footsteps to stop at my door. Someone, anyone, to keep me company. The silence was making me crazy. I needed to communicate my pain and no one appeared. One day Ramiro's superior came by, the one they called el Prócer, and to console me he suggested we make love.

I decided to seek support in my compañeros, and when I told them what had happened, they surrounded me in solidarity, with no big debates or questions. Iván Marino came over almost every afternoon to play with the baby, Ana María came after work and we made dinner for everyone. They left around ten at night. El Flaco Bateman brought his compañera—a psychologist—to the apartment to help me confront my sadness. Esmeralda was one of the sweetest women I have ever met. We talked for hour upon hour; I wasn't ashamed to cry with her, and she was able to dissipate that stupid feeling of guilt that invades us women when our relationships fall apart, as if this were our fault. Men abandon us, and on top of that we feel responsible. When she left, a minty fresh feeling lingered in my heart, right where the emptiness of love had been.

My mother lived far away, but I always felt her support, even in her silence, because she never judged me for the separation; she simply helped me with money in spite of her own shaky financial situation, and she called

18. Here, a woman from the United States. This can also denote someone who is unfamiliar with territory, customs, or who has no close family or friends in the area, or, even more broadly, a person of non-Hispanic but white origin.

me often or wrote loving letters. Affection of this kind is the best medicine for a broken heart. At the side of my people, my wounds slowly began to heal.

I went back to school but had to work twice as hard as before. I took care of everything in the house in the morning and left bottles, baby food, and clean diapers for the teenage neighbor, a bachillerato student, who took care of the baby in the afternoon, when I was in class. In addition I made a few pesos at a part-time job in the DANE[19] doing surveys. Sometimes I felt like I was going to explode with so many demands on me, but I was thankful that my sadness was reined in.

Ramiro came back after about four months, said he was sorry, swore his love, and insisted that the baby needed a family. What had happened was that his girlfriend had gone back to the United States. I accepted the offer, because I still believed that family was important, but I never could forgive him completely.

At the time Ramiro had brought together a group of friends around studies and political work. His compañeros were always in our house studying and talking, even on weekends. Sometimes I joined them briefly to listen or offer an opinion, but they didn't even look at me. I served them food and coffee. Never once was I thanked. After all, I was just Ramiro's wife. They knew of my militancy, but they looked down on our organization's activities, for they considered us a group of irresponsible adventure seekers.

Our work continued. After stealing the sword I was assigned to a new group and I didn't see my feminist compañera again. There were three women and one man in the new group. We studied works by Colombian writers such as Mario Arrubla, Gerardo Molina, and Estanislao Zuleta, and we discussed the situation of the nation, but we didn't act as an operational commando. I had a little more experience than the others, though, and the leadership sought me out for assignments. I participated with Iván Marino and Ana María, or with Elmer Marín, and sometimes with Pizarro, who had just left the FARC.

Between operations Elmer sought me out. He wooed me, was tender with me, and I could see a sort of mischievousness in his expression when he looked at me. His attention made me feel so good that I actually thanked him for noticing me. When I learned of Ramiro's girlfriend, I felt ugly and stupid, and I thought that no man would ever look at me again. With Elmer's flirting my soul came back into my body. His closeness, his light manner of seducing, his open laughter, with which he celebrated everything, restored me.

19. Departamento Administrativo Nacional de Estadística (National Administrative Department of Statistics).

But this was light flirtation. I was really afraid the day he took me to his apartment on the pretext of watching a soccer game. He asked me to keep my eyes closed along the way, so as to keep things compartmentalized, and he took my hand like a guide leading a blind woman. Both of us were married, even though my marriage was by now only a formality. We watched the game, but I couldn't relax. He, on the other hand, was so fresh, so unconventional. He began to play slowly with my hair, I felt his laugh in my ear, he kissed me slowly . . . and with the same gentleness he started to undress me.

I closed my eyes and felt only the heat of his body next to mine, and his hands roaming over me slowly. I abandoned my fear and myself, I let myself go. When I opened my eyes his chocolate-colored skin was naked before me, and I dove in, hungering for pleasure.

Elmer Marín, my first lover, recovered my body for me. I discovered with him that it was possible to make love to someone other than Ramiro, and it was just as delightful. But with him I also learned how to remove the seriousness from this pleasurable act. We didn't set dates, we saw each other in operations, and then, under any pretext, we would escape to savor each other in hiding. We made no promises but enjoyed the time life gave us. We were united happily and lightly in a mutual complicity. Our sexual relationship was even more clandestine than our militancy.

Ramiro was a good man, but I was disenchanted and increasingly indifferent to him. Living together was more and more difficult, yet even so we stayed together for a year, trying to keep the family together. One fine day, on the tiniest of pretexts, I decided to leave him. I did it abruptly, and I was serious.

In the morning I got in touch with a compañero who needed a house and told him he could sublet ours. I talked with my mamá in Cali, and she was delighted that I was going to leave the baby with her. In the afternoon I took my few belongings to a cousin's house, and that night, when Ramiro got home, the new renters were already moving in. That same night I went to Cali. My little boy lived for a while in this city with his grandma and great-grandpa. I went back to Bogotá and stayed with my cousin and her husband.

At the beginning of 1975 I ran into el Flaco Bateman in an operation and told him I wanted to get to know the masses that were the reason for our armed action. He told me to talk to Andrés Almarales, the director of the ANAPO newspaper, *Mayorías*, and to tell him about my interest in work with the masses, but he warned me that I couldn't work in both areas, the legal and the illegal. I had to choose one or the other.

In February I went from militant operations to legal work, where I was paid a meager salary that I sent to my family in Cali. I had left my role as housewife and felt as if I had come out of a cocoon. I was twenty-three.

During the four previous years I had learned to be professional in conspiracy assignments. From the time I joined my first group, in a family nucleus in which Iván Marino doubled as father and teacher, I received the mystical theology and foundation of knowledge of security, selective observation, constant state of alertness, and operations techniques. I also developed my ability to dissemble, in which I was helped by my theater experience, and of course I had the knowledge of arms taught me by my stepfather. My instructors in all of this were experienced people who taught us in daily practice. We learned by doing. Respect, affection, and trust in our leaders played a fundamental role in our learning. Their example taught, and their caring cemented the knowledge. Play, games, jokes, and the pleasure we found in our jobs made training a vital practice and gave us motivation. We were a group of friends who shared a common dream, with very strong ties of solidarity and affection. In following commandos, my discipline increased, my militancy matured, and I assumed responsibilities. Later I acquired more technical knowledge, but in those early years my body and my heart were strengthened for the obligations of conspiracy. It was not a burden but a choice I made freely. I believe that our leaders desacralized revolutionary activity. They brought it closer to the youthful longings of the time, they made it compatible with love, with la rumba, with theater, with laughter and studying. They didn't demand sacrifices of us, they offered us life alternatives. Dangerous? Yes. But exploring new paths always brings risk.

4
The Alliance with ANAPO

WHILE WE COMUNEROS took form as a group, the ANAPO broke the monopoly of the two traditional parties and consolidated itself as a third party with widespread popular support. People of all political persuasions had a place in ANAPO, from the most conservative to the followers of Antonio García, who were clearly socialist.

At midnight on 19 April 1970 the votes pointed to a victory by a wide margin for General Rojas, but at dawn the next day the winner was declared to be Misael Pastrana, the Frente Nacional's Conservative candidate.[1] The ANAPO masses took to the streets to denounce the fraud, but the party leaders were not there. Perhaps the government's house arrest of the general's family took them by surprise, or maybe there was an agreement to avoid bloodshed, as some think. What is certain is that by ignoring popular opinion,

1. The governing system that led the country from 1957 to 1977 was called the Frente Nacional. Its fundamental characteristics were alternating power and the equal division of government positions. The presidential seat had to be shared by the Conservative and Liberal Parties, which had tradition-ally disputed power. The Frente Nacional began with the Benidorm Pact, signed by Conservatives and Liberals in July 1956, to defeat General Rojas Pinilla and name a military junta to guarantee transition to the Frente Nacional system. Laureano Gómez and Alberto Lleras Camargo signed the accords as representatives of their parties.

the path was paved for the formation of armed groups. The tendency to defend the next election from this kind of swindle by force of arms began to gestate. Thus was born the idea of joining the force of the masses with the comuneros to form a broad political-military movement that would guarantee respect for the will of the masses and also give the armed apparatus we had formed a true sense of unity with the people. This was the raison d'être of the M-19, born as the armed branch of the ANAPO on 17 January 1974 when we stole Bolívar's sword. Our slogan: *With the people, with weapons, to power!*

I joined the ANAPO in February 1975. The general had just died and his daughter, María Eugenia, whom we called la capitana (the captain), had assumed party leadership. The power struggle was glaringly evident. Samuel Moreno, María Eugenia's husband, wanted greater rapprochement with the Conservative Party; the radical wing would not permit it. Carlos Toledo, Andrés Almarales, Israel Santamaría, Jaime Jaramillo Panesso, Julio César Pernía, José Roberto Vélez, Everth Bustamante, José Cortés, Fabio Hincapié, and Iván Jaramillo made up the board of directors of the *Mayorías* newspaper. They declared themselves against Samuel Moreno's decisions and used the newspaper to organize, to proclaim a socialist ideology inspired by class struggle, and to encourage popular participation in the fate of the country.

Some of the Eme[2] compañeros took over the Center for Socio-economic Studies (CISE). We participated in political tours, in ANAPO commando meetings, and in leadership schools. We learned to shout ¡*Viva la ANAPO! ¡Viva mi general! ¡Viva la capitana!*[3] overcoming our shy leftist nature. We ended up believing that General Rojas Pinilla had become a victim of the oligarchies when his dictatorship went for the populist option.

We were active participants in the JUAN,[4] mostly made up of muchachos from popular neighborhoods. The most famous youth commando was the Salvador Allende, who brought hundreds of youths together. Their politics was a mixture of leftism and belligerant nationalism. We recruited the best so that they would continue with that front, but directed by the clandestine structure of the M-19. We dedicated ourselves to building grassroots groups, drawing on the Leninist principles for organizing a populist party. We thought that within the ANAPO spectrum there was a possibility for ideological change that would give the party a revolutionary turn.

2. "Eme" (em-ay) is the pronunciation of the Spanish "m" and is used to designate the M-19.
3. Long live the ANAPO! Long live the General! Long live la capitana!
4. Juventud Anapista (ANAPO Youth).

The national meeting of grassroots groups in Bogotá in 1975 was a great challenge to the clientelist style that had characterized the ANAPO. After the general's death, about 900 people met to deliberate on the fate of the party. All of them recognized the leadership María Eugenia had inherited, but they did not all agree that we should form alliances with the traditional parties, as proposed by the rest of the leadership, feeling that this would be a giant step backward.

María Eugenia did not recognize the legitimacy of the meeting and expelled Andrés Almarales, Carlos Toledo, and Israel Santamaría. The Socialist ANAPO was formed as a wing that attempted to gather up the party's bases to create a new broad movement. Not all of the leaders belonged to the M-19, but the relationship between the legal and the clandestine fronts of our movement were increasingly obvious on the political line and less differentiated within the organizational structure, which was dangerous.

The M-19, which positioned itself as the armed branch of the ANAPO, was really a political-military organization that acted within the ANAPO through a management team called the Buró, which made decisions by consensus and was divided into two branches: the political, which included ANAPO leaders like Toledo, Almarales, Santamaría, and Bustamante, and the operatational, which included el Flaco Bateman, Iván Marino, Elmer, el Turco Fayad, and Boris. The armed activities of the clandestine group were to finance the newspaper and support the grassroots work.

In 1976 the M-19 kidnapped union leader José Raquel Mercado and, in an attempt to attract working-class support for the organization, tried him and found him guilty of surrendering the workers' interests in strikes. At this time security organizations were already convinced that the investigation to uncover the kidnappers had to begin with the leaders of the Socialist ANAPO, and particularly with those involved in *Mayorías*.

The detentions and interrogations began in DAS installations.[5] Some were conducted personally by DAS director General José Joaquín Matallana. Working legally and belonging to an armed group was truly dangerous. Every day the DAS picked up one or two compañeros who were leaders, in spite of their parlimentary immunity.

The hour of our arrest was looming. They hadn't tortured Toledo, Almarales, or Santamaría, but we were afraid they would not have the same consideration with us. I was terrified by the idea that they could raid the

---

5. Departamento Administrativo de Seguridad (Administrative Department of Security), similar to the FBI in the United States.

house when my son was there. I could take any risk, but the baby didn't have to. We decided to hide out for a while and went to a country house on the savannah, taking advantage of Holy Week.

The organization had arranged a national plebiscite on whether Mercado should be sentenced to death for betraying the working class and being an agent of North American imperialism. People wrote YES or NO on walls, bathroom doors, in the universities, on peso bills, and on bus tickets. The M-19 announced that it would commute the union leader's sentence if López Michelsen's administration favorably settled the Rio Paila sugar plantation strike before 19 April, election day. The administration said it could not give in to armed pressure, and José Raquel Mercado showed up dead on 20 April 1976 in a traffic circle near El Salitre park.

We heard the news on the radio, and none of us wanted to go back to the capital. We imagined that the repression would increase. We stayed another week, but we couldn't stay at the country house indefinitely, so we were forced to go back.

Mounting Pressure

The witch hunt was on. Many of the popular leaders were interrogated, and the security organizations aimed all energies against the commandos of the Socialist ANAPO. There was a period of infiltration. Dozens of new "militants" appeared, passing themselves off as students who wanted to join us. We gave them the hardest jobs: distributing the newspaper, visiting popular neighborhoods on foot, anything that meant a lot of work. The DAS infiltrators participated in political activism for about two months. The ANAPO muchachos detected several women tails and decided to seduce them so as to teach them a lesson. The avalanche of spies was financed by the 3 million pesos the leaders of two labor unions, the CTC and the UTC,[6] paid whomever gave information that could lead to Mercado's killers.

The Socialist ANAPO survived this stage and became less and less linked to the rest of the party and closer to worker and radical student sectors. The team that came together around the newspaper included not only militants in the M-19 but also people who had belonged to other leftist groups, including some of the founders of *La Alternativa* magazine, which had just split.

---

6. La Confederación de Trabajadores de Colombia (Federation of Workers of Colombia) and la Unión de Trabajadores de Colombia (Union of Colombian Workers).

In the seventies all of us Anapistas, leftists, Socialists, and Marxists dreamed of repeating the triumph of the guerrillas of the Sierra Maestra in Latin America. Lessons learned from Che's death, the struggle of the people of Vietnam, Pinochet's coup d'état against Allende's government, the death of Father Camilo Torres, and the ANAPO's electoral fraud were all combined in our imaginations, and we were clear about the fact that only a popular army could guarantee revolutionary change. But, along with this army, we needed to develop organizations for the masses; it was the only possibility for triumph. The debate was over the kind of army or organization of the masses, and how to join the two: should it be a vanguard army or a popular army? Should it be organized as a party or as a movement? The respective weights of the political and the military were defined by the conception of the revolution.

We in the M-19 built a political-military alternative by less than orthodox means. The work in the ANAPO taught us a lot. *Mayorías* was not the *Rude Pravda* Lenin talked to us about in *What Is to Be Done?* and the Leninist structuring of groups didn't work inside a populist party. One could not appeal to broad segments of the population with leftist radicalism.

Debates at the heart of the team that worked legally polarized us into two groups: those who believed in the need to keep the newspaper as an instrument of political education and those who wanted to liquidate it and put our resources into military action. Pressure came from many directions. The security organizations were on to us to get to the M-19, the ANAPO right wing threatened us, and the leftist forces didn't trust us.

Mayorías folded in mid-1977. My marriage to Sebitas crumbled with the demise of the newspaper. We lost both the battle and the relationship.

I met Sebastián Arias when I started to work at *Mayorías*, where he was editor-in-chief. Sebas, as we called him, was an extroverted leftist trained at the Universidad del Valle. He was one of the founders of *La Alternativa*. Within a month of my working there Sebas was treating me with special gallantry. I was flattered, but my recent separation from Ramiro made me distrustful. Sebas knew how to approach me. Almost without my noticing, he became part of my everyday life. He won my heart very subtly, and his was a delicious tenderness.

We had about four months of romance, at the end of which we decided to build a nest. Living together wasn't a tough decision; after all, our work brought us together for more than twelve hours a day. And since we had also begun sleeping together, it seemed best to formalize the arrangement. Everyone thought it was great.

It wasn't long before we had formed a true family; Juan Diego was with me again, and we made a family in every sense of the word. Our love was a calm one. We were a team at work, and Sebastián happily assumed the same tasks as I did in our daily routine. He cooked well, took loving care of the baby, went grocery shopping, and on top of all that he spoiled me. But the best part for me was that I felt valued.

Our financial situation became increasingly tight. I made very little money, and *Mayorías* didn't pay Sebas on a contractor basis anymore but as a militant. Toward the end we couldn't even pay the rent, and we had to move into the office and live with the dangers that implied. Once there was a shoot-out at our door, because the guard thought the party's right wing was going to attack us. We lived in the midst of what seemed an all-out war, and our nerves were frayed. But love could overcome all of it—for a while.

We had two years of near perfection together. Then the newspaper folded, and Sebas's disenchantment led him to drink. Along with the drinking and the parties came jealousy and arguments that had never before marred our relationship. The redirection of our work decided the rest. I wanted to go back to the military operations group, and Sebitas had nothing to do there. He was a reporter, a legal man, necessary in public tasks. We separated. It hurt me, but not as much as the first time. The one who suffered most from the dissolution of the family was Juan Diego, who adored Sebitas.

During my time working on the legal front I got closer to popular work, which was, after all, the motive behind our military action. Marxism emphasized the role of the proletariat in the revolutionary process, and we believed that ordinary working Colombians would play a principal role in our revolution. This is why we got closer to the ANAPO, and through it to the neighborhoods and the youth. This practice gave us another vision of reality; it helped break down some of our own orthodox theory. We didn't idealize the people but tried to understand them. The people were real; they were in the neighborhoods; they attended political meetings; they were part of clientelist networks and they strengthened rule by caudillos. We worked with them; we got impatient; we argued; we wanted to turn them into revolutionary cadres. They made us more realistic people. There were moments of bliss and moments of tedium.

The M-19 learned from this experience; we all learned. For one thing, our concept of secrecy changed. We had our own faces for work with the masses. We began to move among the people like fish in water, with greater ease and less mistrust. We found that we could submerge ourselves and go unnoticed if we could count on the kindness of those who surrounded us. And the kindness was won if we participated in their daily lives, if they felt us close to their customs. Bateman talked about winning the hearts of the people, of awakening a passion for politics, and we appealed to their affections as a basis for trust. Many people supported us because they believed in our project, but more than anything because they came to trust us.

Here among Ourselves

In September 1977 a civil strike reverberated throughout the country. Waves of people demonstrated their discontent with the government's policies. Government forces also took to the streets, their fear so palpable it seemed to spill out of their uniforms. Confrontations were to be expected, but they were more the fruit of the imprudence of those in uniform than of the organization of the masses. López Michelsen's administration was marked by the many assassinations the military committed in the streets that month.

We in the M-19 awaited our orders, but the organization had arranged to hand over Hugo Ferreira Neira, manager of INDUPALMA,[7] who had been kidnapped to force strike negotiations at that company in favor of the workers the same day that a general strike had been planned. It was feared that, when faced with the success of armed pressure on labor accords, the army itself would kill Ferreira to damage our credibility. Therefore we handed him over to journalists, in a church. The M-19's attentions were centered on the preparations for this handover. Those of us who participated in the strike acted independently, supporting the neighborhoods. I was in the southern part of the capital, where the confrontations were particularly harsh.

My life began to take on a different hue. There was a short recess in organizational work. My mother had just returned from Panama, and she was with me when I separated from Sebastián. I suggested that she stay a while, and she accepted. We hadn't lived together for about seven years, and her presence was a fundamental emotional support for me and Juan Diego.

I wasn't given any assignments for a while and had some free time. I had met el Indio (the Indian) at the first comuneros meeting, and I saw him again when *Mayorías* was in its final days. He had left the M-19 and gone to study economics at the Nacional. We invited him to work for the newspaper and he stayed on as photographer for a while. Sometimes he slept over at our place, and since it was a small apartment we put him in our room. The pervert would tease Sebas, telling him that there were no ownership rights in couples, and that he had to share love. And when we were sleeping, he'd

7. Industria de Palma Africana, a private company.

stretch out his hand to my bed and caress my face. I was scared to death and dying in a fit of laughter at the same time. It seemed a gutsy risk, and I told him so, but he couldn't have cared less.

El Indio was a very intelligent man, among el Flaco Bateman's favorites, but it was impossible to keep him in the organization's structure because of his anarchist concepts and his taste for pot. This didn't worry el Flaco too much, but it went against the daily discipline and the other concepts of militancy. Bateman had already tried in vain to keep el Indio with us. When I told him he was working at the newspaper and had gone a week without smoking pot, el Flaco laughed and said, "Hermana, see how long that lasts." But it didn't. About ten days later el Indio disappeared and didn't come back to work.

About a year later, after I had broken up with Sebas, el Indio was living in a country house in Chía where I sometimes visited him. He led a country life, picking fresh vegetables from the garden, getting water from the well, and cooking on the wood stove. His offer of love without exclusivity attracted me. I was excited about learning other ways of loving, outside of marriage. I was twenty-six years old, and six of those years I had lived as part of a couple. Ours was a calm friendship, but when I went back to operational work I couldn't see him again.

I had no friends outside the M-19, and I wanted to mingle with different people. I became a frequent visitor of La Mamá Theater and met the director of one of the company's first plays. The others were *chévere*[8] people who didn't belong to any movement. With them I returned to the endless nights of dancing and went to all the theaters in the city. Those were happy times, but I still couldn't find what I was looking for.

What *was* I looking for? I don't know, but I was only completely happy with my compañeros. After all, with them I shared my reason for living: politics. And I felt safe among people like me. The world of secrecy made me mistrustful toward those I didn't know. Anyone could be a potential enemy, or at the very least a danger. We had learned from classics like Serge's *What Everyone Should Know about Repression* that "the carelessness on the part of revolutionaries has always been the best aid the police have. . . . But good 'tails' can adapt to any variety of jobs. The most ordinary passer-by, the worker in over-alls, the street-hawker, driver or soldier may be a policeman. Be aware that women, youth, even children may be used for following people. We know of a Russian police circular recommending the use of school children on missions the police could not carry out without being noticed."[9]

8. Cool, great, very good.

In war you have to protect your own forces, and the circle of people you can trust must be tightly knit.

And to love, you must first trust. El Flaco Bateman had tugged on my sleeve even before I had separated from Ramiro, but I had avoided an entanglement with him, arguing that we both were involved and that, besides, I really respected his wife. He chortled and remarked that he loved her a lot more than I respected her. But he never pushed me.

At first Bateman and I met on operations and I saw him as one of us; to me, Iván Marino was the boss. In time, however, I started to know the human and political qualities of this extremely tall and jovial man. He was a great friend, in spite of his duties. He was always close by if you needed him. When *Mayorías* was agonizing over the debate between the two opposing political views, he sought a way to see me and Sebas, to hear us out. It was great to have him close again, for I missed my former compañeros. There wasn't so much controversy with them; we did things. He stayed at our place all night once, talking, and when he left in the morning I hugged him and told him I wanted to see him more often. He came back several times, late at night. We drank tea and talked about everything. The relationship with Sebas was ending, but until it was over, el Flaco never tried to court me.

Later, after Sebas and I had parted company, we became lovers. I loved el Flaco a lot but enjoyed his company more than his body. We met once in a while for a movie and then went to one of the motels on the way to the airport. He made love in a rush but then gave himself up to the pleasure of rest. We went to the sauna, talked about his life; he remembered things that made him double over with laughter: loves lost, difficult stages of his militancy. Above all he liked to talk about his dreams for a future broad-based movement that would conquer the hearts of all Colombians. We ended up singing ballads or boleros.

El Flaco relaxed with me, as if there were no other moment of rest besides this one, after making love. I loved to see him like that; I gave him massages, or tenderly caressed the great length of his damp body. I found happiness in giving him this time to think of himself, for him to enjoy what he deserved. With this man I felt safe, any threat disappeared when I was in his arms—so much so that, with him, I thought I could do anything. We did not talk of love, and we made no promises. Going to bed was simply an act of pleasure, a communicative ritual, as if sexual closeness opened the doors to our souls. Yet nothing passed beyond that room. A pact of silence protected those

9. Serge, *What Everyone Should Know about Repression*, trans. Judith White (London: New Park, 1979), 52.

meetings. For us, love was part of the great political stakes; it was not a life project in itself. We fell in love with our brothers in arms, with those who risked their lives at our side; we loved each other with the intensity that comes from the uncertainty of tomorrow and the trust of being among equals. We lived for the moment; we came together and separated without drama, because love was simply part of our mission for change. It lost, in a way, its exclusiveness, its possessiveness. Perhaps we felt no commitment to the responsibilities of building relationships that were stable over time. Our loyalties were first and foremost to compañerismo. Thus conceived, love and sexual relations lost the importance that society gives them and became an expression of closeness between people who shared a common ideal. What is called promiscuity—and is applied almost exclusively to women—is only a narrow way of conceiving relationships between men and women who operate with a freedom that contradicts social norms and conventional morality.

For many of us women, accepting the challenge of social change also meant assuming more active and participatory roles in our private lives. Making political decisions that put our lives in danger led us, in spite of the contradictions, to take control of our bodies with respect to sexuality and maternity. This made us a target for social censure, both in and outside the organization.

5

The Face Behind the Mask

AT THE END of 1977 I returned to the operations group. The leadership asked whom I wanted to work with; I could choose between Pizarro's or Afranio's team. The truth is that a man as good-looking as Pizarro scared me. I was afraid I'd fall in love with him. I liked Afranio; he was a calm compañero. I started to work with him in a structure that was directly linked to central command. We had nothing to do with the rest of the militancy, and we performed special security measures. The leadership warned me that I couldn't hang out with leftists or go back to places where people would know me. My only contact would be Afranio.

El Flaco gave me a brand-new Magnum revolver with full metal jacket bullets. It is an extremely powerful short range weapon, almost like a hand canon.

"It's your personal weapon," he said. "Take care of it!"

I planted a noisy kiss on his cheek. I was ecstatic. It was a marvelous gift for my new job. From then on I saw el Flaco only on rare occasions.

Iván also had a gift for me: a citizen's band radio with which to get local communications.

Everything was ready. I only had to talk to my mother, who lived with me at the time. She had gotten used to the comings and goings of the compañeros, the meetings at home, and my outings. She didn't ask any questions and happily accepted the muchachos, because they were all very loving to her. Of course she knew what the organization was, but she was quiet about it. My decision didn't take her by surprise. She wanted to be close to Juan Diego, and she accepted the risks. My vieja was always there! Her acceptance made me a little frighened for her. After all, mine was a deliberate choice; hers was pure love and solidarity. But I didn't want to think any more about it, or I might change my mind.

I saw Afranio almost every day and we established "automatics"—regularly scheduled appointments—so we wouldn't lose touch. I received instructions to go to an office in Finca Raíz, an urban real estate company, and fill out a form to rent a house, the address of which I was given beforehand. Then I had to visit the owner of the house and persuade him to rent it to me by offering to pay three months' rent up front.

I dressed up like a lady, acted like a lady, and worked my powers of persuasion. I told the owner about my traveling husband—I had been warned that landlords did not trust single women. I told him that I preferred a place with lots of room because I had so much furniture that I didn't know where to put it all, and I told him about my dream of having more kids and my concept of the home as a comfortable space. All this was to justify my interest in a huge house: three floors, two living rooms, six bedrooms, three bathrooms, two kitchens, an internal garden, a terrace, and a garage. The man was charmed and promised to let me know what he decided. When he asked for my personal information to confirm the deal, I told him that my phone hadn't been working for about two weeks, and I was in a drawn-out dispute with the phone company Empresa de Teléfonos de Bogotá. I'd better call him in two days. His answer was affirmative; I signed papers, paid three months' rent, and was given the keys. Now the problem was: how would I fill the house?

The mansion was strategically situated. From the roof terrace and large picture windows one had a clear view of the streets running both east to west and north to south. It had two separate apartments. I put my mother and the baby on the second floor. My mamá filled it with plants, put up curtains, and otherwise made it comfortable and homey, in spite of the sparse furnishings; she's a wizard with those things.

The two floors were not connected; each had a separate entrance. The one downstairs was empty. I put up heavy curtains so it would looked lived in and waited for instructions. Only Afranio and I knew that this was one of the town's house-jails,[1] but we didn't know where the hidden entrance was.

---

1. A house with a basement that has a secret entrance. Designed to hide people, house-jails were first used by the Tupamaros in Uruguay to hide people detained for exchanges or kidnappings.

One day we set out to find it as if we were on a treasure hunt. We concluded that it had to be on the first floor, in the bathroom under the stairwell, but that bathroom only had a bidet. It was absurd. Still, we couldn't find any way to open the cover, in spite of having read all the books on the Tupamaros and safehouses used as house-jails.

Days later, Afranio gave me a map that explained how to open the bidet. We had to clean the underground apartment and see what it looked like after a year of disuse. He also introduced me to the muchacho who would live on the first floor; we just had to find him a wife. The group already had a husband for me; Afranio gave me his name and the address of an office. When I met this man I was to tell him that I was interested in the deal on an estate in Santander; this was how my "husband" would know me.

The day I brought the downstairs tenant, el Flaquito, home, he compartmentalized himself out of habit; that is to say, he didn't see where I was taking him. But when we got there I said, "Hermano, take a good look at where this is, because you are part of the cover and you have to go in and out of the house."

The muchacho went outside and looked around, and paled.

"It can't be!" he exclaimed.

"What can't be?" I responded, alarmed.

"Compañera, I grew up in this neighborhood. Just around the corner."

Carajo! Just what we needed—for el Flaquito to blow his cover. The next day I went to the meeting with Afranio very worried.

"He should stay," he said. "After all, he knows where it is now, and he knows what it is; it's better for him not to be out of the picture."

And that's what we did. And we set to work getting the safehouse ready. We opened the bathroom door, turned the bidet a little to the right, and pushed the floor from outside the bathroom. As we moved the cover, we could see an iron stairway. It was like going into Aladdin's cave. I was excited; it was one thing to read about such things, another to see it with my own eyes. Below we found a cellar with electricity, water, two chambers, each with a bathroom and a cement slab jutting out of the wall for a bed, bookshelves, lanterns, a fan, and a coffee thermos. It smelled damp and the floor was several centimeters deep in water. We cleaned up, mopped up the water, and left the door open for several days so it could air out, because although it had ventilation passages, they weren't enough.

Soon thereafter I met my "husband." I went to the address I'd been given and asked for Dr. Aguilar, a lawyer. While I waited I amused myself by imagining what he would look like. I saw him as bald and with a gut, or tall and strong with gray hair peppering his sideburns.

"Come in," a voice said.

I went into his office. A pleasant-looking man of about thirty-two years with dark, wavy hair, about medium height, and wearing a suit and tie, held out his hand to me. "Mucho gusto, compañera. They've told me about you. Wait just a minute and we'll leave."

He drove a red Simca about the size of a go-cart. We went to a drive-in cream parlor at the park on Calle 32 and talked about the assignments we had to do together.

Since he couldn't leave his profession or go underground, as I had, we would play the part of a separated couple. He would visit his son rather frequently in order to maintain the cover, but he would have nothing to do with the internal assignments in the house, nor would he know anything about what went on there.

I took him to see the house, and I explained to my mother and son that this señor would double as papá, in case anyone asked.

"Is he going to stay with us?" my son asked.

"No, but he will come to see us," I answered.

We ate together, and that night we made up the rules of the game. The father would be known as "Pi"—Juan Diego picked out the name because of how much he liked cars—we would call my mamá *abuela* (grandmother). Juan was Panchito and I was Mamí. In front of the neighbors my mamá and I would call ourselves Marujas (a diminutive of María). El Flaquito was a relative renting the first floor.

"If anyone asks you our names, you tell them the names we just agreed on. You got that?" I warned my son, who was no more than six. "If they keep on you about it, tell them to ask one of us."

"We're going to pretend to be a family. No one should know who we really are. You already know that's dangerous," I kept telling him.

We made it clear that my mother was not at all linked to our work, and as such, she would know nothing, for her own safety. Neither she nor Juan Diego would go down to the first floor; they would never know about the safehouse. If anything happened, I would assume all responsibility.

A car came with the house, and I needed to learn how to drive as soon as possible, so Pi gave me my first lesson that very night. Two days later Afranio introduced me to la Gorda and her eight-month-old baby girl. She was about twenty-four, white, with rosy cheeks, light chestnut hair, and no front teeth. She was from the country but had lived in the city for years. She had just separated from her husband, and though she wasn't a militant she had worked with Afranio on other assignments and was trustworthy. She was to play the role of el Flaquito's wife.

The cover was complete. The first thing we did was send la Gorda to the dentist so she could get a bridge. She was adorable afterward. We did the shopping needed to completely set up house. The furniture came from someone who knew somebody in the organization. It took us a month to get everything ready. By that time we were working together like a real family. El Flaquito and la Gorda were like a couple and spent the day arguing like husband and wife over stupid things. The eight-month-old girl had taken to my son.

We decided to keep the kids on the second floor. La Gorda's "husband" went to work every day as a school teacher. I taught evening classes twice a week at the UNDESCO[2] University. The house could never be left empty, so we took turns going out.

We tried to make sure my mom and the kids lived a normal life. I put my son in a kindergarten directed by a psychologist friend of mine from the Nacional. A school bus picked him up every morning and brought him back at two in the afternoon. We even had pets, a little cat and dog that rounded out the image of a harmonious, stable home. We got groceries and went shopping for the house in different chain stores. My mother helped me keep records of all our expenses. She didn't ask any questions.

One day one of the compañeros from the operations team came. Pi brought him in on the floor of a jeep that was driven straight into the garage. It was Raúl; I already knew him. He was to get rid of the humidity in the hidden underground apartment and leave it ready for use. He stayed in the bedroom that was a sort of anteroom to the hole and came out only to use the bathroom. The rest of the house was off limits to him and all future guests. That way they couldn't figure out where they were.

The compartmentalization measures were severe. We used hoods with holes for our eyes and mouths; they were made of a light colored cloth so that if the kids saw us they wouldn't be terrified. Since Raúl and I knew each other, we didn't have to use them, but la Gorda and el Flaquito couldn't show their faces. It felt like a game of the mad. The hoods were for individual use and we had to keep them on hand, but all in one spot in case we had to get rid of them in a hurry. We kept them on a hook in the hallway inside the entrance of the hidden room. They weren't to be removed from the first floor. We soon learned how to handle them; we used them when we went into the room and took them off as we exited; it became automatic. Even so, once I left the room so quickly that I forgot to take off my mask, and when I opened the door to the street a gust of air blew the hood and molded

2. Instituto de Desarrollo Cooperativo (Institute of Cooperative Development).

it onto my face. I froze, one foot outside the house and the other inside. Fortunately no one happened to be walking down the street at the moment. But my carelessness frightened me.

Raúl worked tirelessly for about a month, and not only did he get rid of the dampness, he also took it upon himself to paint a mural on the walls. Raúl was a special compañero, very easy to get along with. He said a dream inspired the mural, and I spent hours talking to him while he painted the figures and helped him with the background color. Once, after we had spent two hours painting with paint diluted with thinner, the figures in the painting began to get bigger. I looked at Raúl, surprised, and saw him looking at the figures with the same silly, confused expression.

"Let's get out of here quick—fast!" he said.

I went up the stairs, still dizzy. Once outside we sat down on the bed.

"Breathe deep, compañera, like this, let the air out slowly. The thinner messed us up."

We both cracked up. Later on la Gorda brought us some milk, which was supposed to get rid of the high.

Raúl was very creative; he installed a bell between the first and second floors, a manual lift for sending small packages between the two floors so that movement wouldn't be noticeable from outside, an alarm system with lights that lit up the guard house to warn the basement of any emergency, a lock that could be activated from the inside and seal off the entrance, a new ventilation system in addition to the fan that we used to get fresh air, and amplifiers to bring music to the chambers. We transformed the bathroom with only a bidet into a less suspicious broom closet.

With the assignments and the mural finished, Raúl left, just as compartmentalized as when he'd arrived. Other visitors came to inspect the work. Pi brought them in the jeep and I never knew who they were.

One day they told me that Pi wasn't coming back, that it was better for him to keep a distance because of the kind of job he had. I was left without a husband and with a car I didn't know how to drive. I decided to learn to move the car no matter what. I started it up in the garage every morning. A boy from the house across the street—he must have been about twelve—stood at the door to watch what I was doing.

"You don't move it?" he asked one day.

"No, I don't know how to drive."

"It's easy."

"You know how to drive?"

"I watch my papá. He drives a truck, so now I know how."

That's how we started. The little boy gave me instructions.

"Step on the clutch. Put it in first, let the clutch out slowly, and step on the gas. Slow!"

I took the car out and went around the block. Later on, holding up my end of the bargain, I let the boy drive. We practiced up to four times in one day. I got a driver's licence before I knew how to drive very well. I couldn't risk getting any tickets. My mother went with me. She had driven before and she always encouraged me to go further out.

After two weeks I convinced myself that I drove well enough, and I tooled around the whole city. When Afranio rode with me he grabbed onto the handle above the glove compartment and wouldn't let go until we reached our destination. He was scared to death but congratulated me on my progress. It was fun. Sometimes we got stuck going around and around in a traffic circle because I couldn't muster enough nerve to pass to the exit lane.

I went out, against security norms, to do errands for as long as I could. I trusted in the fact that my actions were sporadic and irregular and so would not put our assignment at risk. These escapes were personal. I went to the university to talk to Professor Vasco and to see William. I visited friends like la Nana and Cloro. And I went out with a secret lover, an anarchist agitator at the Nacional. He had a seductive power with words and a Colgate smile. When he asked for my phone number, I told him I lived with my old man, and he was really jealous. He didn't believe me, but he didn't ask anything else either.

At one of our meetings, Afranio told me what I had to do to bring the new guests to the house. On the agreed-upon day, I got up early with el Flaquito to pick them up. I was extremely nervous, most of all because of my lack of confidence as a driver. What if there were an emergency while I was behind the wheel? I tried to shake it off, but my legs shook when I depressed the pedals. I drove the route slowly so that I could be counter-checked by the compañeros and throw off any tails. I stopped at the agreed-upon time in the agreed-upon place. El Flaquito opened the back door of the car and I felt several people get in. I could hear their rapid breathing. They lay down on the floor, the door was shut, and someone said, "Let's move!"

When I put the jeep in gear my fear dissipated. I entered into a different state of being, as if I were someone else acting a part. I started to hum. No one talked along the way. I drove along, and we made it home. I beeped the agreed-upon signal half a block before we got there, and la Gorda opened the garage door so that I wouldn't even have to slow down. Once we were inside the garage, the guests got out and el Flaquito gave them their hoods.

The hotel was full. The guests got settled in, and a bit later I went down to bring them up to date on the conditions. I found two tall, husky men, Juan and José. From what I could tell from the hair on their arms, one was blond and the other was dark. A tiny woman was with them. She had long hair that escaped from under her hood; they called her René. We said hello and I noted her foreign accent, which I found exciting. Now we were internationalists!

The operation was a Tupamaro kidnapping come to Colombia because of the repression of the Uruguayan dictatorship. For some reason the operation almost fell through, and they asked for help from our organization. The coordination for the internal work would be done by their leader and me. We would agree on the logistical necessities. From the hole in, they were the bosses, but from the door out I was in charge. Another commando with no links to us took care of the financial negotiations. I brought them up to date about the security measures. Later on we had coffee and talked. I was really happy to meet members of an organization like the Tupamaros; it was a myth in those times.

The external home routine didn't vary, but grocery costs doubled because the giants ate more meat than lions. After about a month the first problem sprang up. One of the tupas was complaining about being tired of being cooped up. They took turns keeping watch for six hours each, and rested for twelve. They had been told they would be relieved after a month, but it didn't happen. I promised Juan I would check it out, but I could do nothing more.

The answer took some time and Juan was becoming excessively irritable; he even threatened to flee. Then he encountered my strength of will. I let him know that I was the one who was responsible for safety on this assignment. If he went outside the permitted area, I would shoot him myself. I was furious when I left the room, convinced that the Tupamaros weren't as tough as the books said they were.

Andrés, a compañero from the M-19 who arrived with a case full of cassettes, eventually took Juan's place. René and José spent almost another month, but we lived easily with them. René knitted the whole time. During one of our talks I found out that she had a son who had been disappeared in Argentina. She must have been about forty-three and could have spent the rest of her life cooped up; she seemed to have infinite patience. José was very quiet, and when he did talk, he spoke so slowly that you couldn't understand him very well. They called him Murmullo (mumbler).

Seeing people only in hoods becomes quite funny, because you start to invent features for them. We were very disciplined and never saw each other. Curiosity is endless, but for security reasons, the sharing of unnecessary information is avoided.

René and José left and Simón and Carlos came. By this time Andrés was quite neurotic, and every once in a while he had a run-in with la Gorda and el Flaquito. I dealt with him as a bullfighter does a bull. During breaks he told me he was getting over a broken heart, because his compañera had suddenly ended their relationship. His sadness hurt me, and so I kept him company when he wept, while we listened to boleros. When he was in a bad mood, I went down to eat with him. I massaged his neck to ease his tension, gave him pills for the headaches he frequently suffered, and we listened to music until he started to tell jokes again. Then I knew he was cured.

The problems with the *compas*[3] were quickly solved; the hardest thing was accommodating the kidnapped man, whom we called "the patient." He only wanted to listen to Bach, read literary classics, and eat T-bone steak, fresh fruit, nuts, and yogurt. I spent hours hunting in music stores, bookstores, and supermarkets for what he wanted, always trying to please him. After all, it was one way of making his captivity less difficult.

One day I wanted to clear away any doubts the neighbors might have had about our house by inviting them over. I warned the team that I would be setting off the alarms. Everything had to run as if it were an emergency. It was a drill. When I entered the house with the neighbor couple, la Gorda would turn on the light alarm and everyone would go to their designated positions. The door would shut as we entered the garage, and by the time we got to the bedroom, no one would be there. They shut off the lights downstairs and made sure the "patient" was calm and completely quiet. The neighbors didn't stay too long, they went all around the first floor with no reservations. Everything went like clockwork, except that I forgot to let Simón, Carlos, and Andrés know that the drill was over. The poor compañeros and the "patient" were in a horrible state of alarm for almost an hour. When I finally remembered and shut off the light alarm, signalling that it was okay for them to open the cover to the basement, which was locked from underneath, they came out with great alarm showing on their faces.

Andrés explained that the air had become very heavy without the fan and they had started to feel the pressure of being locked up, and the weight of the darkness. It felt like a tomb.

Being locked up is a nightmare. No attention we gave the "patient" was enough; he suffered moments of acute depression. The poor man lost weight fast, and could barely muster enough interest to play chess, one of his favorite things. He didn't sleep, and he didn't want to exercise. He got sick, and we had to bring a doctor to look him over, but more than the mild tranquillizers

---

3. Diminuitive of compañeros.

he was prescribed he needed his guards to treat him with affection. The ties that are created between the victim and the victimizers are very conflicted, but very real. The tension also affected the compañeros; forced cohabitation made daily relations difficult. I was often surprised by the pettiness of their arguments.

The kidnapping lasted longer than expected, but it was successful. When it was over, we all breathed easy. We didn't know who was happier, the "patient" or us.

Afterward I took a short vacation, some time off with no operation responsibilites. I went to the movies; we went out with the abuela, the kids, and Afranio and his family. My friendship with Afranio flourished. We liked the countryside, people, and colors; we maintained the ability to be surprised by the little things nature gave us. He wrote stories and poems that we read together; he made necklaces and painted watercolors for me. As in childhood, we ran after the fog or climbed up rocks to get a flower. When we couldn't go out together, he painted what he thought was most beautiful to share with me. We also harmonized rancheras—his favorite music—when we went into the hills close to Bogotá to test some weapons. I never hesitated to go along with any idea of Afranio's, because I felt that with him there was no danger we couldn't get out of.

This new stage in my operations work meant a qualitative leap, because I had successfully put into practice the things I had learned in my first years. I was able to fulfill the missions assigned to me with no problems, and go in and out of the structure without the enemy knowing my identity. This time I followed my intuition, and I took the danger signals into account, which prevented us from landing in prison. I made quick decisions at the right time, and improvised a theatrical presentation better than when I played Adela in *La casa de Bernarda Alba*. I used my acting skills to the fullest to maintain my cover. My artistic creativity developed along with my delegated responsibility. It was a test I happily passed.

At the end of 1978 I worked with M-19's high command, but I cultivated my friendship with Afranio on the side. We continued to meet, to chat, and to go to movies. One day as we said good-bye, I felt a sharp emptiness in my chest. I walked a few steps, and when I turned around to look at him, a bad feeling suddenly came over me, and I started to cry. Days later the press published the news of his arrest. Nineteen seventy-nine had begun.

6

Operation Colombia: Weapons for the War

IN 1978 WE HELD our Sixth National Conference. At these conferences we mapped out strategies and lines of action that were critical to the next period. At this one we adopted a hierarchical organizational structure to take on the new tasks of forming an army, and we began the rural work related to what we called mobiles.

The mobiles were conceived of as structures for political-military action in rural and semi-rural zones; they were formed by taking advantage of the work done by peasant organizations and, according to us, they would also function as embryos of the popular army. In the cities the work was to strengthen the front—a broad legal structure working to link diverse sectors of the population, other social organizations, and political groups or parties.

After the sixth conference el Flaco Bateman put me at the head of a new mission: supporting the formation of mobiles. I had to go to different departments where these groups were beginning to form. I loved this job. I used the same Jeep I had learned to drive with; it had a false floor, which made it particularly useful. I loved it like a compañero and called it Jacobo, and I learned something about auto maintenance so I could keep it in good working order. Jacobo and I got along very well.

In December 1978 my mother and Juan were in Cali on vacation. El Flaco set up a meeting with me for the morning of the 31st. We met in a café in Chapinero and he introduced me to José, a muchacho who would accompany me as a relief driver. El Flaco insisted that he preferred a woman at the wheel—not only because women were more careful but because we aroused fewer suspicions. He asked me to pick up the Jeep around seven that night in the same spot.

We met that evening at the appointed time, and el Flaco warned us that the false floor was full of weapons. We were to drive to Ibagué that same night and stay in a hotel. The next day we were to go to Cajamarca to hand over the load at six in the morning. A compañero with a copy of *Condorito* magazine would take the car. I was to approach him and ask if he was related to Señor Tabares; he would answer that his last name was Meneses.

We left Bogotá with José at the wheel. Suddenly a muchacho got off a bus in the middle of the street and ran to the sidewalk; the light had just turned green, and we hit the boy. Fortunately we weren't going fast, but the kid was knocked down. I got out to check on him. I told José that while I took the muchacho to the hospital he had better take off. The Jeep could not fall into the hands of the cops. As it turned out, however, the boy had taken only a light tap to the leg, so we took him home and went on our way. I took over the driving.

There was not one checkpoint on the road. At twelve midnight we went through a police checkpoint at the entrance to Ibagué. We beeped and beeped and waved at the guards.

"Happy New Year, señooores! ¡¡Feliz Añoooo!!"

They made not the slightest attempt to stop the car but answered our greeting by waving cheerfully. Thus we pulled off the first leg of the trip.

In Ibagué we looked for a hotel with a garage, but they were all full. We found a cheap motel of the kind used for romantic rendezvous. We parked the Jeep and got a room. I wanted to celebrate the new year, so I suggested we go to a disco for a little dance therapy and a drink, but José didn't want to let the Jeep out of his sight. I convinced him that nothing would happen and he finally gave in, though not very enthusiastically.

We went into the first dive from which we heard danceable music blaring. The fashionable rhythms were pulsating, alternated with New Year's classics like *La mula rusia, El palo de caimito,* and *Feliz Año pa' tí.* I ordered a brandy and toasted the success of the assignment. We danced one dance, but José was a terrible partner, so we went home early.

Sleeping next to a compañero was no problem for me. I took off my jeans and got in bed, and José did the same. The walls were perforated toward the ceiling for ventilation, so we could hear the whispers and moans of our neighbors as if they were in our room. I fell asleep right away, but after a while José's tossing and turning woke me up.

"Hermano, you can't sleep?"

"No, qué va. With all that noise and you in the same bed."

He put his arm around me, to see if he'd get any response.

"Look, hermano, maybe you should go take a shower so you can sleep," I told him calmly but firmly.

José took a shower at three in the morning. I don't know whether he ever slept, but at least he stopped moving.

At five we were on the road. We got to the meeting place right on time. I got out of the car, ordered a coffee, and sat down at a table where I could see the door. Not five minutes had passed when a motorcycle appeared and a muchacho with a magazine in his hands got off. When he went up to the counter I saw that the magazine was *Condorito*. I looked at the man. I still hadn't seen his face yet I already knew it was Andrés, my *llavería*[1] from the assignment in the house-jail. He must have recognized me immediately as well. As soon as he took off his helmet he cracked up. We embraced like old friends. We had never seen each other face to face during the job, but we knew each other's height, build, clothes, arms, walk, and even smell. It was great to see him again!

He took the car and brought it back in about two hours. Meanwhile, José and I had breakfast. When Andrés came back, we didn't have a lot of time to talk, but he gave me a post office box number so we wouldn't lose touch, now that we had found each other. José and I departed immediately, arriving in Bogotá around noon.

Only la Gorda, el Flaquito, and I were now left in the house-jail. We decided to go out to the early evening show of *New York, New York* with Liza Minelli. Bogotá was empty and quiet, perfect for walking around in. We left the Jeep in a parking garage and walked around the Chapinero, enjoying the abandoned city on the first day of the year.

On 3 January, the papers ran the story on the M-19's robbery of the army in Bogotá. The group took 5,000 weapons from a warehouse in El Cantón Norte, through a tunnel. The theft was accomplished without the firing of a single shot, and the army didn't even know it for twenty-four hours. This was Operation Colombia, and it deeply wounded the heart of the army.

We almost had a fit from the excitement. Five thousand weapons! What would the organization do with them? Was war close now? But on 4 January

1. Good friend, from *llave* (key).

the first compañeros were taken prisoner. The army raided homes throughout the country. Things became unstrung. They found a hideout with a lot of weapons. They tortured the detained. Military installations filled up with people accused of being members of the M-19. The civil and political rights of the accused were abused. President Turbay turned a blind eye, and the minister of Defense, Camacho Leyva, turned a deaf ear.

Every day the headlines announced new arrests. The organization entered a time of great uncertainty. The authorities already knew the names of the M-19's high command—Jaime Bateman Cayón, Iván Marino Ospina, and Carlos Toledo Plata—who had signed the press release claiming responsibility for the arms theft.

I began to feel the need to get out of the house-jail. I can't explain why, but I smelled danger. But there was no one to authorize our move; the central command was busy with other, more urgent issues. So I listened to my intuition, got a truck, and packed up all our belongings. Since I had nowhere to take our things, I rented a cellar in some friends' house. La Gorda, el Flaquito, and I went our separate ways and set up automatics so we could meet every week at a different time and place. We had to act with extreme caution, given the situation. A countrywide hunt was on, and things were hottest in the capital.

Not ten days passed before the house was raided. I began to fear for my safety. I didn't know what trails the state intelligence organizations might be on. But then my compañero Manuel contacted me for a new assignment. The rush to save the remaining stolen weapons and put them in safe places was on. We came and went, transporting arms in two cars. Since the false floors didn't hold very many, we risked carrying arms in cabuya bags without even covering them up. The risk was the same, whether we were carrying one pistol or a hundred rifles.

One of those nights, the car brimming with guns, we suddenly happened upon a mobile army unit checkpoint on the Sur Highway. We only realized they were there when we were about eighty meters away. My heart dropped into the pit of my stomach. Manuel cursed everyone's mother. He doused the lights, spun the car around, and we hightailed it out of there. I was mute, but I immediately felt my way to the cyanide pill in my pocket.

Influenced by spy novels, I always thought I would choose suicide if I were captured, to make sure the enemy would get no information. Few compañeros shared my view, since they considered it a weakness to opt for suicide when threatened with torture. But I had made the decision without much dispute. After all, it was my skin I was risking. All I know is that the cyanide gave me a unique feeling of safety. I got it from my best friend, who said it was very effective; he had tried it out on a dog.

We went down side streets, heading north to avoid the police. After midnight the city was silent. My heart clanged against my ribcage. Manuel suddenly started laughing, and I relaxed a little.

"We got out of that one!" he said.

It wasn't altogether true. We hadn't taken the precaution of leaving one weapon at hand to defend ourselves in an emergency. We had about fifty unloaded guns packed in the sides of the car, and not one in our hands. The cyanide pill melted in my sweaty palm. It took us more than three hours to cross the city because at every crossroad we had to see if there was a checkpoint and keep off the avenues and main streets. We got lost several times, and it took us a long time to find the way again. Finally we got to the other side of the city.

"Bueno, compañera, get out here, I'll take the car to the safe house. There's no danger now."

Manuel left me on the Norte Highway at four in the morning, alone and without so much as a needle to defend myself. I felt like Little Red Riding Hood lost in the woods. I was exhausted. An intercity bus was going by and I signaled for it to stop. I boarded the bus and settled into a seat; my whole body throbbed, as if I had been walking all night. I had nowhere to go at that time in the morning. I would have liked to go to some friendly place and rest, but I had to stay in some sleazy motel. I couldn't even sleep; I was too tired and keyed up at once from the events of the night.

After we'd moved out of the house, my family had dissolved. I left my son and his cat at his father's. My mamá stayed with the dog at the home of one of her nieces. I began my gypsy life, moving from friend's house to friend's house, never spending more than two nights in one place.

A Woman No One Suspected

This was true secrecy. I had a fake ID card and went by the name Blanca Reina, a twenty-five-year-old woman from Girardot. I took great pains to emphasize my womanhood, because people expected a guerrillera to be something of a tomboy, and I wanted to avoid arousing suspicion. I carried my Walther 7.65 in my belt, with one bullet in the chamber ready to go. I kept some underwear in my purse, along with a toothbrush. I had no agenda, no addresses, no notes. I made do with my memory. I made meetings and automatics and took care to check the place out before I went in. I never waited more than ten minutes. My natural radar told me what to do in any given situation. The pressure of danger sharpened my perception and I was always poised for self-defense. I'd feel a slight crawling sensation when someone watched me; a face seen for a second time alerted me to a possible tail. I also felt tension or nervousness in other bodies. I saw situations in slow motion and could therefore make decisions just in time.

We all acquired a special skill in picking up any abnormality in the surroundings: the smallest of signals between intelligence agents, an unusual vendor, or a car strategically positioned for observation. I learned to see the way flies do, with peripheral vision. You keep your eyes fixed in front of you and over your shoulder at the same time, so you can take in everything that's happening around you without turning your head. I think that I even got used to sleeping with one ear open.

It was difficult to conspire during these dangerous times. Many of the detained were tortured and wound up giving away the locations of our meeting places. The B-2, F-2,[2] DAS, or any other state security organization grabbed the first person they thought looked suspicious. They captured and tortured first and investigated later. Hundreds of innocent people suffered from the arbitrary nature of the interrogations and military trials.

Manuel and I became an effective duo in these circumstances. Danger was like a rope that bound us tightly together. We communicated with the subtlest of facial expressions. A simple look, a barely perceptible signal, was enough to convey a message.

Manuel was a *bacán*.[3] He was born in Girardot, a Magdalena River port where the Communist Party was flourishing at the time by forming unions with laborers and craftsmen. He joined the Juventud Comunista because there was space for his rebellious spirit there. His friends were in the same political game, and so was Ester Morón—the tallest, prettiest, and most revolutionary muchacha in town. By virtue of her mere presence, Ester recruited more members than the JUCO secretary for organization.

Manuel didn't inherit his father's French last name because he was the monsieur's illegitimate son. But he did inherit his outer package: he was big and strong. He remembered with more disgust than nostalgia the Sundays he had to go to the Frenchman's shop to get the weekly money for him and his brothers, and he left with a few coins that jingled in the bottom of his pocket. Perhaps he owed his stubbornness, his refusal to be beaten by life,

2. The B-2 and F-2 are part of the police intelligence service.
3. From *bacano* (cool).

to his mother. Manuel had an unstoppable—even irresponsible—optimism. He knew from childhood what it was like to go without because his mamá didn't make enough money to support them in her job as a cook in the town's hotels. From a very early age he did odd jobs to make a few pesos and help out at home. He dodged no task. He cooked for his brothers and sisters, ran errands, and still had time to go bird hunting with his friends. He went to the public school, as did almost all the muchachos, at a time when the best teachers taught there. He learned to barter in the streets, and this helped him in door-to-door sales.

Manuel met el Flaco in 1962, but it was through the FARC that they got to be good friends. Batemen knew he could trust Manuel with anything and that he would make sure it got done. No job was too much for him, and he was effectively practical; he didn't get all tangled up in rhetoric. His adrenal glands worked overtime, for Manuel's operative creativity was often at odds with his instinct for self preservation. I tried to maintain the balance of the team. I took care of the security measures and reined in his insatiable hunger for action a bit. I was his grounding pole.

I met Estela in the midst of this state of emergency. She was a compañera from Zipaquirá who snuck out of her house through a window to go to our meetings. The story of the furtive escape struck me as funny. No one suspected her subversive activities, and her family still considered her a good daughter, in spite of the fact that she was an M-19 professional in the public sector.

You could see great dedication to the cause in this tiny woman with the serious face. She was a classic revolutionary. She let only a brief, occasional laugh escape in the midst of our usual joking around. Laughing at everything was a way to lighten up life-and-death issues, and to make the load lighter for Manuel and me.

One night we went with Estela to get some weapons out of a safe house and pack them up for a move. It was up to her to find a place to put them. There were so many that we split them up in two cars. I don't remember why, but we both ended up alone and lost in a tiny village at midnight looking for the ranch where the safe house was.

The people who opened their houses to weapons storage took an enormous risk. Almost all the collaborators I met during this time were very cool people. It's too bad our relationships were so fleeting.

Manuel and I remained a team in 1979. I was not aware of the blows to the structure of the organization, thanks to the feverish activity we were involved in and the indomitable spirit of my teammate. As everything was falling apart around us, we kept rescuing people and weapons. At moments like this, one's commitment takes on a renewed sense of love and urgency. There is neither a sense of personal sacrifice nor time for despair.

Luck and intuition saved me on more than one occasion. Waiting for contacts was dangerous because you never knew who had fallen and could give up information. Sometimes, as I approached a meeting place, I felt the pressure of danger and proceeded with exaggerated calm to see if there was anyone watching the place. I went to a pay phone and pretended to call someone so I could look around the place naturally, or I stopped to buy some golosina at the candy stand so I could watch the people's movements. If I saw something weird, I heeded my gut feeling and walked on by. Sometimes I was followed, but I got away by taking several buses or a taxi or going down a pedestrian walkway. I was inspired in these operational tactics by novels and texts like *Tania la Guerrillera*, *The Red Orchestra*, and *The House on Garibaldi Street*. The rest I owed to *criollo*[4] ingenuity.

In March 1979 the first Forum for Human Rights was held. People took this as a sign of progress, but the repression didn't decrease. By mid-1979 the country was still in upheaval. Stories about armed propaganda operations and detentions filled the papers. Osuna did caricatures in *El Espectador* about what was going on in the army stables.[5] With every trip overseas, President Turbay denied human rights organization accusations of torture and arbitrary military trials. Left-wing intellectuals were persecuted and entire families went into exile in embassies. Meanwhile, the few of us who hadn't been captured kept moving to prove they hadn't exterminated us.

"¡THE M-19 WON'T GO INTO EXILE OR SURRENDER!" We wrote this and other slogans on the walls of the city to keep our spirits up. El Flaco Bateman said that as long as one of us was alive, the organization was active.

Which One Is Me?

El Flaco always talked about Fayad—el Turco—with admiration. He said he was the one with new ideas, the one who developed the political theory. I only remember the fuzzy image of a small man with the Liberator's sword in his hands. When I saw him again in mid-1978, I scrutinized him, looking

4. Originally *criollo/-a* meant a child of European parents born anywhere outside Europe. It now applies also to descendants of the Spanish-born in Spanish America and to things of Spanish America in general.
5. Héctor Osuna Gil, famous political cartoonist, whose cartoons criticized the Turbay administration's torture policy. He drew horses in the stables as witnesses to the torture sessions held there by the Cantón Norte in Usaquén, the Military Institute Brigade headquarters.

for evidence to bear out Bateman's assessment. I wanted to see if the reality lived up to the propaganda about him.

At the end of 1979 Manuel and I had a meeting with el Turco, the high official who replaced el Flaco while the latter was overseas opening up paths for the organization. Central America burned in a revolutionary fervor with the triumph of two insurgent movements: Grenada's Nueva Joya and the Sandinistas in Nicaragua.

We went out of the city for the meeting. Fayad asked us to be the link between the high command and the mobiles, or regionals. He needed people he could trust absolutely, people who could transmit political orientations and interpret them in practice. And people with the judgment to make quick decisions. The apparatus of logistics and communications was inaugurated with us.

I felt honored, but the responsibility was overwhelming. The compañeros in the high command who were still free were the country's most wanted, and we were the only contact between them and the regional organizational structures. We had to move with extreme caution. I had my cyanide just in case. But why think about the risks? Now I could be near Fayad, see him often, and feel his presence in my work. I loved this man above any inconvenience. At our meeting in 1978 we had found an indelible point of convergence: we had the same birthday.

"I was born on the same day as Bolívar," he said.

"Me too," I responded.

We looked at each other incredulously and then burst into laughter. We agreed to meet to celebrate our birthdays together, even if we couldn't manage to be together on the day itself. We met in a good restaurant, had some wine, and talked for hours. El Turco had the command over words of a magician. I was unable to disengage myself from his words for even a second, because he wove them with such passion and precision that it was impossible not to be caught up in his story. The feeling he wanted to get across—it didn't matter what it was—came to me through his tone of voice and penetrated me to my core. He possessed me; I trembled with him. I took flight and came back down to brush against reality. I couldn't pay attention to anyone else. I wasn't aware of the door; I didn't remember anything about our cover. I gave myself up to him.

When they closed the restaurant, we went to a dance bar to listen to some music. I was still seduced by his words, his vehement gestures, the depth of his gaze. This man had magic, but there was something even stronger: his passion. From that night on I knew I would love him forever, with a kind of love that seemed to belong to him like a birthmark.

Fayad became my strength, my reason, my reference point in life. I knew, even when I was possessing him physically, that I didn't want him "for me." He was beyond desire, beyond time. He was the "ideal being" of politics and life incarnate. That is why I could see him or not see him and love him just the same. I could love others without its affecting how I felt about him. We could make love or not; that was marvelous, but it was irrelevant with respect to the whole feeling he inaugurated. Working with el Turco, even though it was very dangerous, was also the best thing that could have happened to me.

After the meeting at which he gave Manuel and me the link assignment, the three of us went to Melgar. I established myself in a summer house and stayed alone. My only contact would be with one of them.

Living in Melgar put me right in the wolf's mouth. It was a town that lived off tourism and two military bases: the FAC Air Base[6] and the army's X Brigade, headquarters of the lanceros school, a counter-guerrilla unit.[7] The women in the town were divided between the two bases: they were girlfriends or friends of either the army men or the air men. Since it wasn't a good idea for me to arouse the interest of the army, I got close to the muchachos in the air force through my neighbor.

I made up a life history. My ID was under the name of Maricela López, from Tolima. I decided that Maricela was recently separated and very traumatized by the the breakup of her marriage; she wanted to get away from it all and start a new life. She had studied social communication and had written a few freelance articles. She traveled to Bogotá or Ibagué once in a while to spend a few weeks with her family. Manuel was her closest uncle, and that's why he visited a lot.

I also organized my activities. I got up early and exercised. I ate breakfast and read till around noon. Then I ate lunch and took a nap. In the afternoon I walked around, sometimes with the muchachos from the FAC, who worked straight through till three. Then I went to the pool till seven. It was a quiet, routine life, with after-dinner get-togethers with the neighbors, with whom I sat and talked and enjoyed the fresh evening breeze. I shared the banal talk of the townswomen enthusiastically—the eight o'clock soap opera, the chats the FAC muchachos had about motorcycles and girlfriends. Doña Carmenza, the widow who owned the house I lived in, walked me to my door at night so as to prevent gossip. That's how Maricela's life went.

6. Fuerza Aérea de Colombia (Colombian Air Force).
7. Lanceros refer to Simón Bolívar's liberating troops, almost all from the eastern plains of the country and skilled in long-range lance throwing, which they often used in battle. They were famous for their courage and were responsible for winning many a battle in the war for independence from Spain (1810–19).

Emilia, as I had decided to call myself after El Cantón, did other things under the table. She got all the information she could about the movements of the military men. Through new friends she got to know the air force installations and their equipment little by little, and she made friends to make my cover stronger.

When Manuel came, we went out to the mobiles to supply them with ammunition, weapons, or money. Before departing we met with Fayad for new instructions. The trips took ten days to two weeks, sometimes less. We went from the Atlantic Coast to Caquetá. The mobiles were located in Córdoba, Santander, Quindío, Tolima, Cauca, and Caquetá. There were always risks, surprise checkpoints, minute inspections, false papers, burned cars. But we got out of everything with flying colors, thanks to Manuel's quick responses and my ability to entertain the soldiers. A captivating smile, a piece of fruit in my hand, and my Walther ready under my leg. A pair of suggestive shorts, a loose blouse, and my pistol at my belt while I talked to a soldier. Manuel and I, arm in arm like a couple in love, while they inspected a car full of groceries, the false floor filled with ammunition. My cyanide in my pocket, weapons ready, the decision not to be taken alive, our hearts pounding, mouths dry, but on the surface calm, with a kind word, a timely smile. That was Emilia.

Two diametrically opposed women lived inside me, one delicate and fragile, the other tough as nails. When I got back from the trips and went into the house, the characters were pitted against each other. I felt dizzy, unreal. I knew from reading some of Franz Fanon's *Wretched of the Earth* that the impact of a clandestine lifestyle affects the personality of combatants, and from several talks with William in anthropology class I knew that schizophrenia was a real possibility for people who lead double lives. I was aware that radical behavioral changes could affect my personality. And I felt alone; I needed my compañeros. They were my universe. Family I no longer had; I had lost track of my son because his father had decided to hide him to be safe. It hurt so much to separate so abruptly from my boy that I would think I saw him in the street and run up to see. But I always found myself in front of a complete stranger, an anxious smile on my face. I felt utterly uprooted. I had left the city, my friends, my relatives, the familiar buildings and landmarks, to live another life with no more contact with my things than the trips with Manuel provided.

A talk with William saved me. In the past we never made plans to meet but were brought together by chance. But this time I sought him out. Only someone like him, who had wandered the dark labyrinths of madness, could understand what was happening to me and help me cope with it.

We met in a park away from the city to go rowing, and we stopped in the middle of the lagoon, where no one could spy on us, to talk. I could cry and tell him my fears, my worries, my anguish. He listened to me in silence. Then he explained with perfect clarity what I needed to do. I lived my aliases too completely, he said. I needed to keep them sharply separate from my real self. I couldn't take on other personalities with so much realism. I had to put up limits, create a border, and take care not to cross it.

We also talked about fear of death, its proximity and inevitability, and he left me Castañeda's book *Journey to Ixtlan*, about Don Juan's teachings. I kept the book with me from then on. "Death Is an Adviser" and "The Last Battle on Earth" exorcised the tiniest hint of fear of death and opened up the limitless possibility to enjoy the little things. Two paragraphs became etched in my mind:

> Death is the only wise adviser that we have. Whenever you feel, as you always do, that everything is going wrong and you're about to be annihilated, turn to your death and ask if that is so. Your death will tell you that you're wrong; that nothing really matters outside its touch. Your death will tell you, "I haven't touched you yet."

> Acts have power . . . there is a strange consuming happiness in acting with the full knowledge that whatever one is doing may very well be one's last act on earth.[8]

I said good-bye to my friend, feeling relieved. Once before William had given me the cyanide, and with it, insurance against uncertainty. With it I was given a contingency plan for tackling life.

I went back to my operations base in Melgar not only more at peace but actually euphoric. Some weeks later the M-19 assigned us the mission of hiding Carlos Toledo in Melgar. Toledo was one of the most wanted men in the country and would come to us from Barrancabermeja. Some rail workers brought him in the middle of a huge security operation the M-19 had prepared. He came through more than seven military checkpoints, at which they were looking for him, photo in hand, and wasn't discovered. No one could tell that it was he, the doctor, the ex-member of parliament, and leader of the guerrilla organization that had stolen thousands of weapons from the army.

We went to La Dorada, and the train got in on time. All the passengers got off, but we didn't see Toledo, which worried us. What if they had gotten him?

8. Carlos Castañeda, *Journey to Ixtlan* (New York: Simon & Schuster, 1972), 55, 110.

How could we ask? *Whom* would we ask? We walked along the platform looking at everyone, and he was nowhere to be seen. We started a third walkthrough, when an old peasant man approached us, walking with great difficulty on a cane, leaning on a little girl.

"Good afternoon, are you looking for me?" said this old man.

We couldn't believe it. This hunched old man in a striped suit, wearing a hat as old as he was and lace-up hemp sandals, walking on the arm of his granddaughter, was Carlos Toledo. The little girl handed us a small basket with eggs in it.

"There are two grenades in there, compañeros. Hasta luego, I leave him in your hands. Adiós, tío."

¡Carajo! That's how he got through the checkpoints—he really was unrecognizable.

Manuel and I had concocted an operation that was just as strange. We decided to take a family drive with Manuel's wife, the two kids (about eight and ten years old), and their dog. We split up and went in two cars. Manuel went in the first one with one of the kids and the dog. He had a CB radio with which to communicate with us. About a kilometer behind were Toledo, Manuel's compañera, the younger of the two children, and me. The leaders let us know if there were army checkpoints. The kids pretended to play with the CBs, sending messages back and forth. We took only side roads and got to Melgar at dusk.

I had to justify the presence of the old man to my neighbors. I told them that a bachelor uncle was visiting me and almost never left of the house because he was a tired, grouchy old neurotic. Still, Doña Carmenza saw him once in sweatpants doing exercises on the patio, and she was captivated. She insisted on inviting my uncle to her house for dinner. I teased Toledo about the widow's interest in him.

Living with the old man was nice and calm. He liked to cook and did it very well. When I was home, we talked a lot. Sometimes he put on a straw hat and, with his cane in hand, we took a walk when the sun was setting. We went to the Seventh National Conference together. This was the meeting at which the M-19 encouraged the struggle for democracy, emphasizing the need to carry out a political-military mission aimed at the masses. This was a new direction for the left, one that distanced us from the ideology of the traditional left.

Manuel and I were in charge of moving all the assistants and their security. Only I remained outside the meeting as a link, which was a huge responsibility. I was never more careful with any assignment; I almost never left the house. When the meeting was over, once again it was up to us to drop each person off safely. They had put me in charge of the documents on the conference's conclusions.

On one of the trips something unexpected happened. Manuel and I were following each other in different vehicles. His Jeep was leading the way. Suddenly we came to a recently set up checkpoint, and there was no way to avoid it. We were both armed and carrying false papers. I had the conference papers in my vehicle. There was no way we would pass an inspection. Manuel signaled that I should pass him. He placed himself in the line of cars and crept up slowly without stopping for the inspection. I tried to do the same thing, but the line was slower, and when I tried to pass by a man in civilian clothes put his rifle through the window of the car and said, "Why aren't you stopping?" I looked around. Manuel had escaped notice and it looked as though he would make it through the line. They had focused their attention to me. I trusted in my power of seduction. I smiled at the man to calm him down. "Don't scare me with that thing, all right?"

I stopped the car. The man kept pointing the gun at me through the window and another one asked for my papers and inspected them. A little leather case by my feet in the front seat had the documents in it. I was wearing shorts and a loose blouse. While the man was checking around, I undid one more button and flirtatiously put on the earrings I had in my pocket. I put my hand on my waist and unclipped the Walther. If they were going to frisk me, I would shoot first, even if the other guy killed me. I looked toward Manuel again. Just as he was pulling abreast of the last of the police officers, they noticed him.

"Stop!" they shouted.

There was a series of deafening beeps and one or two shots. Manuel sped up a little. The car didn't react, but after several attempts it finally moved. A group of police got in a patrol car, turned on their sirens, and took off after him like a bat out of hell.

"Open the hood!" the one inspecting my car ordered, while he picked up the leather case, tested its weight, and put it back on the floor. I looked at him stupefied; I didn't care about anything anymore. I wanted to run with Manuel.

"The hood!"

I didn't know how to open it, it was the first time I had driven a Renault cuatro.

"It's too hard," I told him.

He smiled, knelt down, and pulled on a button near the stick shift. His arm brushed against my leg and he looked at me square in the face. He got out of the car. The man with the rifle had gone from my side and was looking over the owner's papers, which were all in order. They looked at the motor and compared it with the papers.

"You can go."

I wasn't smiling anymore. I was terrified by the sound of the sirens in my head. I put the car in gear, and when I left the checkpoint I drove as fast as I could to catch up to Manuel and those chasing him. Tears clouded my vision. I felt terrible that I wasn't with him in this critical moment. I had left him alone! I cried and sped on but saw nothing—neither the patrol car nor Manuel's white Jeep. After about half an hour I went back and looked around carefully. I imagined that he had rolled the Jeep or that they had killed him—a thousand ugly possibilities sprang to mind. But I found nothing, no trace. It was as if he had been swallowed up by the earth. What could I do? I stopped the car on the side of the road and broke down and sobbed for a long time. Finally I regained my composure and realized that I had to make up for lost time and get to the meeting with the compañeros from the high command. I had to let them know about Manuel's capture or death. My soul hurt. I felt I'd failed in solidarity. I felt like an orphan.

I had never gone so fast on the highway, and I couldn't see very well through my tears. I got to the town where they were waiting for us only a little late. No one was there. Had I mixed up the automatic? I went to the other meeting place, about half an hour away. They weren't there, either. I was bewildered. I got out and had an ice-cold beer. I had to think calmly.

I went back to the first meeting place. Nothing! I decided to go back to Melgar. Whatever happened, Manuel was not going to turn me in. This place was the only one where the leaders knew how to reach me. They didn't have a car. As I drove, I thought, "I'll wait twenty-four hours. If no one comes for me, I'll leave the car with a doctor friend of Bateman's in Melgar and take a bus to Florencia. There I'll contact Ana María and I'll go with her to the Mobile."

I got home, bolted the door, and took a cold bath. I lay down with my face to the door and my pistol in my hand, just in case. I turned on the radio to listen to the news and lay still. The tears kept coursing down my face involuntarily. Around ten o'clock at night, my neighbor knocked on the door.

"Maricela, Maricela—telephone. It's Don Manuel."

My soul jumped back into my body. I ran to answer it. We yelled at the same time.

"How are you? What happened to you? Are you okay? But—are you okay?"

"I never knew I loved you so much!"

"I'm with your papá. Come tomorrow, really early. I'll be waiting for you in the first town at seven."

The tears kept falling; I don't even know why. Doña Carmenza consoled me. I told her my uncle had been in an accident but that it wasn't serious.

At seven I was at the appointed place. We hugged each other with intense emotion. My eyes were brimming with tears and they—Manuel, Bateman, Toledo, Fayad, and Almarales—were busting up.

"Manuel told us you'd been caught and he had to take off," said Toledo. "He said you'd probably been killed because you wouldn't let yourself be inspected."

But el Flaco said, "Did you see when they shot her?"

"No!"

"Well, then, I'm sure la Negra will get out of this one. Do you know where to get hold of her?"

We all laughed. And we began to compare the versions. The last thing Manuel saw was the man in civilian clothes putting his weapon through my window, and he decided to speed up. He got a few blocks ahead of the patrol car pursuing him, and after the first curve he went down a path he found half hidden in the brush, then turned around and sped back toward them. The patrol car raced past him but must have thought he was a different car. That's how he lost them. And that's why he got to the meeting before me and told his version of the story. By the time I arrived, of course they had left. Things like this happen in this kind of life—moments that plunge the world into chaos.

We celebrated our reunion with cold beers. How I loved them! I drew strength from this affection when feelings of loneliness and impotence came over me, when fear spied in my window, when resignation saddened me. I hated that abstract enemy of whom I knew only the olive-green, that monster that made us live in hiding, cover up our loves, distance ourselves from friends, give ourselves other names, wear borrowed clothes, and always, always pretend in front of strangers. Between love for my people and hate for the enemy, I found a passionate strength that kept me in militancy. Ideology alone could not achieve this feeling. It was the passionate love for my compañeros that was the motor of my life.

A Sea to Wash My Soul

One day I was called back to Bogotá. I had a meeting with Fayad to which he arrived very late. I waited for him for an hour out of pure love, breaking security rules, but when he got there all thought of reproaching him went out of my head. We had a tinto and he verified the status of my papers and the car papers. He made me give up my pistol in spite of my protests, and we went on a trip where our security depended solely on our cunning. We made up an alibi, chose the route, and calculated the time we'd need. I drove under the strict supervision of my *jefe* (boss).

When we got out of the city, I relaxed. I enjoyed these trips so much . . . I learned to love every piece of land by traveling over it. Etching the landscapes on my mind made them mine. Fayad heard me comment, overjoyed, on the beauty of the sunset or the color of the mountains, while we listened to Piazzola, Silvio Rodríguez, or Mercedes Sosa. I felt free as I rode down the highway. I would have liked that stretch of asphalt to continue to eternity. We got further from Bogotá and the warmth of the air caressed our skin.

Not everything on the trip was easy. El Turco was having problems with his ulcer, and the constant pain made him irascible. He couldn't stop smoking, lost his appetite, and was bothered by everything; he slept poorly and got up in a bad mood. He was like a spoiled little boy. I tried to be patient, aware of his pain. But one morning while we were eating breakfast, after one of his biting comments, two teardrops fell into my coffee.

"What's wrong?" he said softly.

"I'm tired of your aggressive answers and your bad mood. I never see you guys, and when I can finally be with a compañero I would like to receive affection and not only orders, reproaches, and critiques."

I dried my tears angrily. I had said enough. El Turco smiled and put his hand on my arm.

"You're right. We expect the best from our compañeros."

From that moment on he was calmer, his company became enjoyable, and the humor that accompanied our talks returned.

When we got to the sea, after we had completed our assignment, we gave ourselves two days on Tayrona Beach. For the first time I saw Fayad at rest; he watched the sea for hours without even moving. Immobility was so strange in him that I asked if he was sad.

"No, I'm not sad, I'm serene. The sea washes your soul."

We were back in Bogotá ten days later. I never saw Fayad again. Two months later, Manuel informed me that he had been arrested. I felt the blow of a gigantic gong, its boom echoing inside me. I didn't want to stay in Melgar; I needed work so I wouldn't think. I went back to Bogotá and rented an apartment with Lucho Otero. We passed ourselves off as a couple.

Sitting in a quiet corner of the house, I watched the seven o'clock news and saw the pictures of the first session of the military trial for the compañeros in the Picota prison. I recognized them one by one. They went into a room with their arms in the air, shouting slogans, making their fingers into the V for victory sign. You could feel the strength of the collective. We weren't witness to a failure but to a gesture of dignity. That was where my friends were, my loves, my compañeros, my compañeras. And I wanted to be with them.

I cursed my liberty—that liberty that tightened like a belt every day and was leaving me immobile, forcing me to avoid the houses of people I knew. Freedom to close myself up to think about my compañeros and be unable to go to them even in thought, freedom to cry over my solitude, to curse with clandestine hate and clenched teeth. I never thought that freedom could hurt me, but without my compañeros, it did.

Operation Colombia marked our option for war irreversibly. It put us on the path of large-scale armed confrontation. But also, in spite of the detentions, tortures, and military trials, it situated us as a symbol of opposition strength. The excessive military force used on civilians wore away institutional order and polarized the country. Many Colombians were unjustly accused of collaborating with the guerrillas and began to look sympathetically upon political proposals supported by insurgent groups. We had to do something to denounce to the world the arbitrary nature of a false democracy that penalized the illegal possession of thought.

7

We Risked It All

THE IDEA to rescue the prisoners became almost an obsession, as if we had to free part of our own hearts imprisoned with them. Each of us came up with a different proposal to get them out of prison.

A year passed. At Christmas Elvecio threw a party for clandestines in the organization who couldn't celebrate with our families. We got together in a café and decided to pretend we were drunk so as to make Elvecio and Jorge's job easier, which was to lead us by the arm to the party, so we could keep our eyes shut for reasons of compartmentalization.

When we got there, María, Jorge's compañera, Alfredo, and Omar el Tupa were waiting for us. As soon as we met, the comraderie was loosed; it was always like that. Belonging to the same group paved the road for friendship. It didn't seem odd to me that Alfredo greeted me with a light kiss on the mouth.

We danced, drank, and ate roasted chicken. We talked about Buñuel's films, Laclau's book on politics, Benedetti, García Márquez, Turbay's administration, and, of course, the military trials. We remembered the prisoners, drank to them, danced for them and, with our eyes closed, were with them. We spent the night on a makeshift bed created out of mattresses pulled close together. We had breakfast together and said good-bye, not imagining we would see each other again anytime soon.

On New Year's Eve, 1979, I did my last assignment with the logistical and communications structure. I went to the mobile led by Raúl on the Atlantic Coast, and 1980 snuck up on us on the streets of Montería, watching the municipal workers chasing away the swallows that landed on the electric wires.

I was ordered to leave the assignment I was involved in and take a break, go out of circulation for a while. My contacts were Elvecio and Lucho Otero. Elvecio seemed to have the time to dedicate to me. He tried to teach me to drive a motorcycle and, between falls, we had crazy fun.

You could predict nothing with Elvecio; one adventure followed another at his side. With him you could go from reading poems to a confrontation with the police in the blink of an eye. Those were moments of relaxation, and even though we didn't really have time to fall in love, we made up a fantasy romance. Elvecio is etched in my memory, with his pipe and his childlike laugh, with the sweetness of dusk in the company of a good book and a hot tea, with his swimmer's back speckled with stars. Between the games he took me to the place where "men drink sun from clay pots," as Nazim Hikmet describes the march to the sun in one of his poems. Everything about Elvecio was dreams and imagination. He was like Peter Pan.

I was almost never with Lucho in the apartment we pretended to be a couple in, but sometimes we met to keep up appearances and spent hours and hours talking. I loved to talk with him about diverse literary subjects, his taste for art, his knowledge in the kitchen, and, of course, our shared interest in anthropology. I don't know where this simple, shy man who went almost unnoticed kept so much knowledge. He treated me as if I were special; I remember him as one of the few men who brought me flowers.

In the middle of January I met the compañeros I would work with. I met Alfredo (the one who'd kissed me on the mouth) again, with María and Jorge, and they introduced Vicky, a doctor, to me. Everything about our future operational activity was speculation. Elvecio took care to build so much suspense that each one of us imagined something different. But we didn't dare say or ask anything. The only thing we could make out behind the mystery was that the action was related to the freedom of the political prisoners.

The instructions were precise: prepare ourselves physically for something like running the San Silvestre marathon. We needed stamina, agility, and speed in running. The first morning of training we met in Salitre park, and the workout was too much for us. María was a diehard smoker, Vicky had never run before, and I had no stamina. We finished our first lap at a walk, but our spirits did not wane. I was having trouble breathing. The cold air hurt my lungs, making each breath painful. I silently cursed the stiffness of my muscles, and I thought of the prisoners: Fayad, Afranio, Iván, Ana María, Pebles, Elmer, Vera, and the others. This helped me make the effort. I gave myself increasingly demanding goals, and I met them. Two laps today, tomorrow three, and that's how, after a month, I was an athlete.

Alfredo and I had decided to do more exercises. The others couldn't; Jorge and María had a son, Vicky worked. But we two walked from north to south until late in the afternoon. Breakfast of apple tart and coffee in the northern part of the city, fruit salad in the Restrepo neighborhood marketplace, lunch at the fish markets in the south. A nap in the Santa Clara woods. We liked being together and entertained ourselves walking around the city, but we were never in a rush or wedded to a particular direction. We enjoyed everything—the weather, the people, the windows, the busy areas and the quiet ones, the styles of houses and buildings, the billboards, all of it. Sometimes we sat on a bench or sidewalk curb to read some Hikmet poem or something from Castañeda. At the end of the day, when I got home, I missed him.

Crashing the Party

At the end of February Lucho, Elvecio, Rosemberg, el Tupa, Genaro, Alfredo, Otti, Manuel, and I attended a meeting. El Flaco Bateman was also to be there, but he was late. We feared for his safety because they had killed the leader of the PLA,[1] and the description matched his. But finally he drove up in his Renault, a smile on his face. The man most sought by security forces was walking around alone, a Browning pistol strapped to his right leg.

In Melgar, right under the noses of the elite counter-guerrilla school, we planned the takeover of the embassy of the Dominican Republic. Operation Democracy and Freedom's objective was to denounce the army's human rights violations, reject the military penal justice system being applied to civilians, and negotiate freedom for political prisoners. The name chosen for the operation questioned the meaning of Colombian democracy.

The political antecedents of the operation went back to the mobilization of the country's democratic forces around the first Forum on Human Rights, held at a very difficult time, when the prisons were full of political detainees. The people overcame their fear and publicly debated a subject that drew diverse segments of the population. The organization decided to reinforce the proposals and recommendations of the forum with a major operation.

1. The Pedro León Arboleda Commando, a faction of the Marxist-Leninist Communist Party of Colombia (PCC–ML).

The Melgar meeting went on for hours. Long after nightfall, we concluded that everything was ready. The operative proposal and the military plan design were Lucho's, but the plan was adjusted with input from everyone in the leadership. The leaders for this mission were Rosemberg, Genaro, El Tupa, and Alfredo.

The next morning we left as we had come. When I said good-bye to el Flaco, I hugged him hard. I was very excited about my participation in the operation that would free the detained compañeros. The mere idea of having them with us again was enough to make us jump for joy. Even Lucho, usually so serious, was euphoric. Lucho played a fundamental role in this operation, but he kept himself behind the scenes. He didn't like to be at the center of things and was always very modest. He was the one who suggested that I participate in the operation. Finally I felt that I could turn the pain I felt for my friends in prison into strength, into anger.

We played all our cards, and the stakes were high. We got all our weapons together and invested every last penny the organization had in this operation. The apartment I was renting with Lucho became the hideout for weapons, clothes, and other necessary things. Both of us ran around frantically buying sweatshirts, canvas bags, and soccer and volleyballs, and transporting weapons, ammunition, and grenades that we were given wrapped in newspapers on the street. But we had enough time for everything. I even had time to say good-bye to my son, write a letter to my mamá, visit friends and call my tía Myriam so she wouldn't worry. Of course I had to lie to her, so I made up some story about a scholarship I'd won to go study in Mexico.

We got together on the afternoon of 26 February in the same place we had had the Christmas party. The sixteen of us participating in the operation were there, as well as Lucho and Elvecio. That night the group leaders explained the mission to us and asked if we were willing to carry it out to the end. They let us know that if anyone wanted to, he or she could back out; we had replacements on the benches. No one stood down.

Then the leaders explained the plan in detail, with maps and pictures of the place. It seemed easy in military terms—we had the surprise factor in our favor. It required only decisiveness, speed, and a show of strength. The operation was called Jorge Marcos Zambrano, after a compañero killed in Cali. Our slogan was "Victory or Death." For the first time I thought seriously about that option.

More than excited, we were exalted. The political objective was crystal clear. The upcoming elections, scheduled for 19 March, would pressure the government to come up with a rapid solution. Turbay's administration would not want to go to the congressional elections with an international problem looming over it.

The meeting ended with a simple military ceremony. We fell into formation, with the central command in front, received the usual commands for close order, and then repeated the slogan "Victory or Death!" We then sat in a circle and talked about our feelings about the proposed task. It was a moment of crucial importance for the organization, just when the government was boasting of having eliminated our operational structures. Feelings of sacrifice or immolation were foreign to our discourse, not because we discarded the possibility of dying but because we chose to focus on our will to fight.

The meeting ended with a feeling of lightness for me, a feeling of coolness toward life. I had left no loose ends. I had only two great loves—my mother and my son—and they were already used to my absence.

The morning of 27 February dawned too soon for us. No one showed anxiety, but we all knew that it was there, squeezing at our necks. We wanted the action to begin quickly, but at the same time, deep down, we wanted the moment never to come. Fear? I think so. Or maybe we guessed that this act would change our lives definitively.

The house was bursting with activity. While some were practicing unholstering their pistols and taking the long arms out of the canvas bags on the patio, others were sewing last-minute things on their sweatshirts. They were all the same large size, so most of us, who were small and skinny, looked lost inside them. The sweatshirt sleeves were too long, the boots too big, the waists too wide.

We had a light breakfast. It is best to go into an operation with an empty stomach in case you are wounded. At twelve we were given the signal to leave. We went by taxi to Carrera 30 in front of the Universidad Nacional. There we grouped by commando units—four in each unit—that looked like groups of athletes talking about the last game. I was on the southern flank with Alfredo, Pedro, and Estela, the muchacha from Zipaquirá. I noted with concern that most of the guards and drivers were on that side, at the door of the Belalcázar café. Our unit was in its immediate line of fire. Just then Carlos Arturo, the youngest member of the team, approached me and tapped his forehead against mine tenderly.

"Ready?" he asked.

"Ready!" I answered. He went to his post. While we pretended to have an animated conversation, our eyes wandered along the space that made up the battleground. We took in the smoke shop, the location of the bodyguards, the parked cars, the lawn, and the sidewalk. Getting to the door of the embassy was the first objective. The instructions kept going through my head: Go in shooting! Yelling! Get to the door in seconds! Anyone who falls or drops to the ground to shoot is dead! Speed and surprise! SURPRISE AND SPEED!

Two elegantly dressed couples were approaching along the southern sidewalk. It was Rosemberg and María and Jorge and Vicky. It seemed they weren't getting any closer. The operation was to begin when they stepped over the threshold of the door. All I could hear was my heart beating like a big clock inside my chest. I brought my hands up to my pistol. When the four compañeros got to the stairs, I flipped off the safety. As soon as the fake ambassadors stepped over the threshold, we heard the first shot and the shouts of combat. I pointed my gun, pulled the trigger, and ran to the door. We were the first ones there. The guards had locked the door from the inside. Alfredo broke the glass with the butt of his rifle; I turned around to cover him and felt the bullets zing by me, smashing into the glass of the door. The guards had reacted quickly and I could see them stretched on the ground while they shot at us. Everything took place in slow motion. I could make out every detail. My pistol wouldn't shoot anymore, it was jammed.

In we went. Jorge held the door open and the compañeros ran inside and occupied their posts. I found Estela in the bathroom, cursing her jammed pistol. I took the clip out of mine and racked the slide to clear the jam. I did the same with Estela's and we ran to the second floor, which our unit was supposed to control. As I went toward the stairs I saw people lying on the floor covered with broken glass and the compañeros taking cover behind walls and shooting out the windows.

Alfredo and Pedro were already upstairs. Estela and I divided up the rooms; she would go to the left and I to the right. We had to get everyone together in the hall. In one of the rooms I found a very elegant woman with a glass of liqueur in her hands, repeating in terror, "Don't kill me! Don't kill me!" I took her by the hand. Her fear met mine, and I felt a strong current run through us. I was paralyzed, looking at her. Whichever of us took the initiative would win.

"Don't worry, nothing's going to happen to you!" I told her.

I took a deep breath and took her over to the others. I had to frisk them. I had never done this, and I didn't like fishing around in the pockets of the ambassadors from Egypt and Haiti, much less passing my hands over their genitals, as the police did at check points. But I had to do it, and I did.

From the second-floor hall I could see a doctor taking care of two wounded—a Bolivian man who took a bullet to the leg, and Renata, who had one knee and her head bound. There was a dead compañero on the floor, but I couldn't tell who it was because I didn't go downstairs for many days. They told me that he had caught a bullet in the back when he was entering the embassy; it turned out to be Carlos Arturo, the youngest among us.

At first I could only hear shouts and shots. Then silence fell like a heavy blanket over the scene. You could hear the jagged breathing of the people between shots. The air smelled like powder, like sweat. Like fear.

I took my defense post. Army snipers had arrived. If someone moved past a window, a shot immediately sounded, crashed through the glass and then whatever stood in its path. We made shields with bookcases and armchairs and fired from behind them. We had good visibility and controlled the house. We organized a chorus of ambassadors who asked the army to cease fire to protect their lives.

The combat had become more organized when the soldiers began to throw tear gas in. The canisters came in the windows on the second floor; we were able to throw some, but not all of them, back out. The tear gas was awful. It burned our eyes, noses, and throats and obscured our vision. It was suffocating. People panicked and some compañeros lost control. Those of us who knew its effects from student protests gave instructions to the others: put wet towels over your mouths and noses, water on your face, keep the faucets running, stay as close to the floor as possible, and don't lose your cool. There were desperate moments, but we overcame them.

In active combat, you aren't aware of the passage of time. The shooting lasted for hours and hours and we didn't even realize it. In an operation like this you become a spectator; you go outside yourself and look in from outside. You are in what you are in; there is no room for doubts or second thoughts; you can give no room to fear, because fear paralyzes.

Someone downstairs began to name the diplomats present: the United States, Venezuela, Brazil, Austria, Costa Rica, Haiti, the Dominican Republic, Switzerland, Guatemala, the Papal State, Uruguay, Mexico, Israel, Egypt. At that moment I felt like Ali Baba at the mouth of the cave of treasures. Every ambassador had a specific value in the exchange for political prisoners.

It was getting dark when Napo came in with a tray full of hors d'oeuvres and a glass of water. I wasn't hungry, but I was very thirsty.

"Eat, compañera, you need it. Chew slowly."

I obeyed. It hurt. My mouth was like a desert and salivating was intensely painful, as if needles were sticking the roof of my mouth. I sipped the water slowly. My throat was burning. I came into myself with the pain. At that moment Alfredo came over, put out his hand and caressed my cheek. He smiled.

"How do you feel?"

"Okay. Fine."

Alfredo's tenderness located my heart in my body for me. I squeezed his hand and looked into his eyes. They seemed brighter than ever. How beautiful Alfredo's eyes were, how clean.

Everyone was in place. The shooting let up a bit. Everyone moved to the second floor, to the library, for the night. The guard posts were at the windows and door. We made a general bed with mattresses, supplemented by armchair cushions. Some of the hostages refused to rest. There were a lot of people: cleaning people, waiters, guests, ambassadors, and groupies. We used only two mattresses for ourselves and took turns resting for an hour each.

My turn to rest came and I lay down on the mattress. My whole body ached and I needed a hug. That was my first combat operation. I closed my eyes and imagined that when I opened them I would be in my bed, remembering this dream. I had Carlos Arturo's childlike face and his last game stuck to my eyelids. René lay down at my side and pressed up against me; I felt calmer and was still, but I couldn't sleep. Downstairs the compañeros on guard watched over the dead. It was really cold that night, poor people. There weren't enough blankets; the Dominican Embassy wasn't rich.

The next day we let the cleaning people and the women go. It was a shame, because they are the best support in moments of crisis, always ready to help others. But we had to have a group we could control. In spite of the first releases, there were still a lot of people. We had to organize daily life to try to survive. Almost everyone helped. The diplomats rolled up their sleeves, put their ties in their pockets, and took turns cooking and cleaning. They laid out spaces for circulation and spaces for rest. Our role, above all, was to make sure that nothing, inside or out, put the operation in danger. We were even careful with the food because we thought the diplomats might try to drug us. During the first days one of us did the cooking. Then we decided to watch over the general cooks and eat after everyone else had eaten.

At first we were the bad guys, but the army soon took over that role. It became everyone's enemy. From the second day, the ambassadors knew that any attempt at rescue would be fatal. This aligned us in the same corner. The ambassador-hostages constantly pressured the Colombian government to negotiate a bloodless solution.

It was a difficult ordeal for everyone involved, including the government. Similar M-19 operations had resulted in state violence, and others were awaiting solutions. International tensions were running high, with displays of power alternating with diplomatic negotiations. A radical faction of Iranians had taken the U.S. Embassy in Iran and was holding hostages there. In Guatemala the army had killed peasants who had taken the Spanish

Embassy. Here in Colombia the congressional elections were approaching, and a violent solution would not be good for the government. Diverse interests came together—the government's, ours, and those of the different countries—that did not always coincide with the demands of the captive ambassadors. Dialogue was proposed in the midst of all sorts of pressures. A Red Cross van was chosen as neutral territory and was situated in front of the embassy. Delegates from the government, the M-19, and the ambassadors participated.

It was a good move for Rosemberg to choose la Chiqui to negotiate—first, because he could not leave the embassy, and second, because the presence of that tiny woman would ease the tensions. Showing the country a feminine image that broke the guerrillero stereotype and evoked sympathy helped create a favorable atmosphere for negotiation. Furthermore, there was an emotional link between Rosemberg and la Chiqui, as a couple, that facilitated understanding.

Yet la Chiqui had problems with her temperament. She came back from the conversations with the delegates of the Ministry of Foreign Affairs, exhausted from the effort to control her temper and not tell them to go to hell when they postponed the search for possible solutions. But she learned to negotiate, to listen, to respond, and to control her impatience. La Chiqui had an unbending will but also a special ability to communicate with people, always smiling, offering a tiny gesture, a kind word, and this made the ambassadors and negotiators value her.

Her relationship with the rest of the compañeros deteriorated as the days went by. Her fame went to her head, and she began to pull away from the group. The same thing happened with Rosemberg. They isolated themselves, coveted information about the negotiations, and gave themselves certain privileges, like sleeping together while the rest of the couples couldn't, or having jam and wine stored in their nightstand when the rest of our rations were divided up collectively. These were small things that in another context might have meant nothing, but in such a close group, under constant pressure and the dog discipline Genaro demanded of us, they became serious irritants. Rosemberg and la Chiqui swung back and forth between our love and indifference; we accepted their leadership, but we resented their attitude.

Almost everyone hated el Negro Genaro. He was in charge of military discipline and was like a drill sergeant, always ready to punish without asking first, without admitting excuses, with the same logic the regular army used. His attitude made us blow up. It hurt that a compañero would turn into our whip. But when he wasn't on duty, el Negro was a charmer. Rank definitely transformed him.

After a certain point most of us felt marginalized from political decisions; our task was limited to guard duty and keeping the hostages in line. Our unvaried routine was three hours of guard duty and six of rest. All we knew about the negotiations we learned from the comments of the ambassadors. This reduced our participation to military action, which had never happened before in the M-19.

In this operation I had to comply with a strict military order for the first time, and I had problems with the exercise of command conceived of simply as vertical and punitive. We had to function like clockwork, that was clear. The difference I had with my leaders was in my concept of discipline as the fruit of consciousness and self-control, not of Genaro's arbitrary orders. The military structure was like a plaster cast.

"Fall in!"

"Left!"

"Right!"

"Run in place! One, two, one, two! Knees up!"

"Stop!"

If you fell behind or made a mistake, ten sit-ups. If you tried to protest, twenty. And if you didn't follow Genaro's orders fast enough, thirty. Talking while on guard duty meant a double shift. We were punished for confronting Genaro, for not having our weapons clean, for this, for that, for everything. This made my insides revolt. Silent obedience punishes the spirit. Our group, like all groups, had its ups and downs, but if every one of us had a high level of consciousness and decision, why so much punishment?

It was like living on an island. Everything around us was calm and quiet. The army evacuated the buildings and neighboring houses so as to put their men there and interrupted traffic for several blocks around the area. They surrounded us so they could set traps day and night.

National and international journalists challenged military orders for weeks and were able to stay close to the embassy. They set up an observation camp there called Villa Chiva. They were the only civilians in the militarized zone. Their presence calmed us, in a way, even though the country had begun to censor the press and we only had access to international news via a six-band Sony radio Bateman gave us for the operation.

On guard duty, watching became our specialty. We knew the field of vision corresponding to each guard post like the backs of our hands; an obligatory curtain unfolded before our eyes during the three regimented hours. Any new element or the slightest change activated alarms. Sight and hearing worked like radar, and the brain processed the information. The result was a report that we communicated to the squad supervisor when he went on his rounds. He had a unified vision with the reports from each guard post. We could see that in a house on the southeastern side, five strong men with blond crew cuts and wearing overalls were talking around a table covered with scrolls of paper. They had to be gringo advisors or assault commandos. We also discovered that someone was watching us at night from a neighboring building with night vision equipment. We located the machine gun they installed in the university's College of Economics and every one of the soldiers whose guard posts were hidden behind the trees. We knew that the guards on the back patio got colds in April and that they were carrying out excavation work from the house next door.

When the congressional elections took place and the conflict still wasn't resolved, we saw that the takeover, originally calculated to last a week or two, would be prolonged indefinitely. Those most affected, obviously, were the hostages, who were most interested in a quick negotiated solution. Faced with a long delay, they reorganized their daily tasks to promote cohabitation with a minimum of problems. We had to do the same. We needed to keep ourselves physically and mentally fit and work to minimize tension between ourselves and the hostages. While we couldn't forget our internal differences, we decided to postpone our debate with Rosemberg, la Chiqui, and Genaro until after the fundamental issues were resolved.

Our mutual desire to survive led both sides to promote a spirit of co-operation with the other. Some sought to win our consideration by telling us whatever happened among the ambassadors. There were others of steadfast dignity. The hostages decided to name a group of representatives—the ambassadors of the United States, Brazil, Mexico, and Venezuela, the same ones who led the negotiations group—to communicate with us. Why these and not others? That was up to the hostages. They even organized ways of facing daily life that we accepted. The "important" ambassadors—those from the United States, Brazil, Switzerland, Austria, Mexico, Venezuela, the Papal State, Egypt, and Israel—lived in one room. In another were the Latin American ambassadors—from the Dominican Republic, Uruguay, and Paraguay—as well as those from Haiti and Jamaica and the consuls and some public servants from the Colombian Ministry of Foreign Affairs. The rest of the hostages were in a third room.

Relations inside the embassy were generally cordial. El Tupa and Genaro were the only guerrilleros who were tough on the hostages. In time, special affections took shape. The Venezuelan consul courted Estela in secret. He invited her to play backgammon or chess at rest time, talked to her in sweet tones, sought her out, and asked about her if he didn't see her. She didn't refuse him; I think she liked the gallant treatment, because the only one she really talked to was Pedro, who was from her hometown.

The ambassadors from Venezuela and Mexico took a special interest in la Chiqui, and she treated them well in return. Ambassador Barak of Egypt treated Jorge like a son. Brazil's Do Nascimiento and I cemented a very cordial relationship over tea, because we didn't like hot chocolate for breakfast like the others. I enjoyed talking to the gringo about science fiction, but he knew he was the least liked of all the hostages, because of ideological differences.

What happened to one person affected us all, so if someone got depressed we all, guerrilleros and hostages, took it upon ourselves to cheer him up, and we did so with genuine affection. Chiqui and Vicky pulled Ambassador Lovera of Venezuela out of a deep sadness that came upon him toward the end of his captivity. They even fed him like a baby.

There was no room for despair among us. It is an internal enemy that you have to exile categorically. Sometimes we were pursued by nostalgia for our loved ones, and thus Napo, a paisa worker, came up with a poem dedicated to his wife and his daughters, while Estela would wake up with her eyes swollen from crying. I had Alfredo to cry with on our mattress. María smoked more when she was worried or missed her son. But no one expressed these feelings of sadness openly. Collective living discourages demonstrations of individual unease. Whenever I felt longing or anger, I thought about the prisoners, about why we were there, and I swallowed my tears.

An Embassy for a Honeymoon

Alfredo and I told each other that we had taken over the embassy for our honeymoon. There was no love more intense than this one; it grew in the absolute present, between life and death.

Everything started a few days before the operation. The Beatles song "Yesterday" was playing on the old record player in the empty house where we went to rest after our exercise routine. The ochre light of the Bogotá afternoon and that song stirred in me the adolescent joy of the seventies. On the wall a huge poster masked the dampness and brought us a distant autumn. The smell of grass clung to our bodies, but it seemd to come out of the landscape. We were still talking when the golden color of the surroundings permeated Alfredo's eyes and left me entranced. The pleasure of being together mixed with desire and I had an incredible urge to know the pleasures of his body. There was no blocking this love. It crept up on us slowly, with no noisy announcements, and he came in and took my heart. His body, tense with emotion, contrasted with the tenderness of his kiss. In the vertigo of pleasure, the color of skin and autumn were the same, until his eyes completely swallowed up the afternoon light. As twilight fell, we still weren't done loving.

Thus I met the most beautiful of loves. With Alfredo, even in the midst of death, I always found life. With him, my body was aware of itself through sensation alone. Later, during the takeover, el Negro's prohibitions and separate beds could not keep us apart, we so needed to be close. René, who shared a room with us, was our Celestina. We insisted so vigorously that we be left alone together that the jefes finally got tired of nagging us and left us alone.

We had so much love it was coming out our ears. The only limit we had was when we were on guard duty. The rest of the time, we stole time from time to make love in the abandoned corners of the house, behind doors, and in the bathrooms. Without taking off our clothes, with grenades hanging from our waists and without dropping our weapons. Only in the contact with the other's skin could we feel life, only with our heads resting on the other's lap could we find tenderness. Only in our embrace did sadness dissipate. Affection generated strength for us. In circumstances like this, when the only security of existence was in the next minute, we learned to completely enjoy being in that place, even if love had equal doses of joy and anguish. Loving was a beautiful reality, everything else belonged to the realm of forgetting, or utopia. I repeat, never before, or after, was the present so extraordinary or love so intense.

Partial Victory

Life opens up paths even in adverse conditions. Hostages and guerrilleros alike used our imaginations to pass the time. We invented parties and sang the same songs together. We had potluck dinners with typical dishes from each country. One day María and I set up a fashion show with the dresses of the owner of the house. We also celebrated Passover with a rabbi who had come to visit.

Captivity made small pleasures a real treat for the hostages, such as receiving packages and letters from home, or spying on a muchacha showering in the early morning. Her sensual silhouette etched on the windows fed the erotic dreams of the diplomats.

There were also tense moments for everyone. The escape of the ambassador from Uruguay; Jorge's accidental shot, which almost blew his compañera's hand off; Napo and Pedro's fight over Renata; the loss of a kitchen knife that forced us to search everyone; news of a possible attack on the embassy by Israeli commandos; the military planes and helicopters flying above us—all of these things frayed our nerves. International events also caused general nervousness, among them the frustrated rescue attempt of the gringo hostages in Iran, when two U.S. assault helicopters were shot down, and the pressure from the OAS InterAmerican Commission for Human Rights to facilitate a definitive solution.

In spite of the pressures, the difficulty of the negotiations, and the fatigue, we didn't waver in our conviction that even if we didn't leave with the three hundred political prisoners, at least we would get the command compañeros. Our strength rested in our decisiveness. We didn't have enough explosives to make a roman candle, let alone to blow up the embassy in case of an attack. Our weapons were ridiculously few if we had to stop an attack by Israeli or gringo commandos. With Browning pistols, sawed-off shotguns, a few grenades, and scant ammunition, we would not last long in an all-out fight. We weren't capable of shooting hostages, either, or throwing them out the windows, as a lot of people thought we would.

Meanwhile, Bateman proposed in an interview with the press a 1 May meeting with the government, political sectors, unions, business groups, indigenous and popular organizations, and the Church to find a solution not only to the situation in the embassy but to the general problem of bloodshed in Colombia. It was convenient for us to postpone a definitive solution until that date, to press for a meeting with the country's forces of industry, commerce, and banking as well as political forces. But the OAS commission wanted an immediate accord. Negotiations entered the final stretch. The ambassadors played an important role in the advising, and Rosemberg found himself alone with the decision. Things started to go downhill.

None of us thought that we would leave the embassy alive without our compañeros. The slogan "Victory or Death" was the condition of our existence. We really internalized it, and we accepted the possibility of dying, knowing that the more real and beautiful option was to live. And so, when Jorge, in an informal talk, mentioned the alternative of ending the operation without an exchange and calling the political achievements reached up to that point a victory, we all vetoed it. The discussion got louder. It was one thing to negotiate and quite another to give up on the exchange. We were ready to stay as long as necessary to gain the freedom of the prisoners. The Sandinistas did it with Somoza; why couldn't we do it with Turbay?

That night, on my watch, I was so angry I cried. I hadn't come this far to leave with our compañeros still in prison. Without them, none of this was worth it. And yet this now seemed like a real possibility.

Rosemberg called a meeting to explain his decision to us. He summarized the negotiation process, the progress, and the impossibilities. Waiting longer meant losing the support of the people, who had grown tired of the standoff. Objectives changed with the circumstances, he said; politics had to be flexible. He said that we had achieved real victories in the political arena: the government had entered into dialogue with the M-19; the operation had drawn international attention to the human rights violations of the armed forces; the government had agreed to international observers to verify respect for procedural guarantees for civilians tried in military trials; and, finally, the government had agreed to sign accords with international organizations to oversee the fulfillment of international norms on human rights in Colombia.

These arguments were valid, but political reasons weren't enough, as far as I was concerned. I didn't quite know what I would do. I had lived in the "now," and suddenly I found myself faced with a future that I hadn't counted on.

We began to prepare to leave the embassy. The hostages were happy, needless to say, but we were far from ecstatic. We made the necessary arrangements. When the news of the accord was out, we took it calmly, as if it were a lie. The press published headlines, took their last photos, and prepared to exit. On the eve of the hostage release, the men who had watched us for sixty-one days opened the curtains of their observation post and came out into view to toast us with a glass of liqueur.

The morning of 27 April, fifteen guerrilleros and guerrilleras wearing berets and with kerchiefs tied over their faces, with false names and equally false safe passages from the Colombian Ministry of Foreign Affairs, leading a group of hostages, left the Dominican Embassy feeling that we had achieved a partial victory.

On the way to the airport, people lined up along the road to greet us waving white kerchiefs. Some of the soldiers guarding the route said goodbye by forming the V of victory with their fingers. It was a national triumph, just as the president said. But I would have liked to obtain freedom for my friends. When we boarded the Cuban plane we entered into friendly territory. Now others were responsible; as soon as we took off, the Cubans on board took our weapons. I don't know if I felt relief or insecurity when I put my Browning and grenade into their hands. I looked out the window at the territory we were leaving and I thought about Fayad, Iván Marino, Ana María, Afranio. What must they be thinking as their possibility for freedom receded? I wanted to stay near them, with my mother and Juan Diego. I imagined them there below, growing smaller with the plane's ascent. It hurt terribly.

Much later, the blue sea below us suddenly gave way to the browns and greens of an island. Someone shouted that it was Cuba, and all conversation stopped. I felt a weird floating sensation in my head. In my revolutionary dreams, Cuba was a paradise because it had el Che, Fidel, Caribbean music, Cuban socialism, Silvio Rodríguez and Pablo Milanés. I looked down and could hardly believe my eyes, which grew wet with tears. Cuba!

When they ordered us off the plane, we didn't really know what to do. A hoard of cameras, flashes, lenses, the press descended on us, shouting questions in several languages. Commander One and la Chiqui said hello and smiled; the rest of us were paralyzed with fear. They had come to get us and had brought us here, and we were still in a state of astonishment.

When Fidel visited us, it still seemed like a dream to me. I found him bigger, more thickly bearded, and much, much more accessible than what I had imagined. Watching him smoke his cigar, I actually thought he was a double, the ones they say they used to dodge CIA murder attempts. For me, it was impossible that such an important person would be sitting in our dining room having coffee. He asked, with the curiosity of any neighbor, for the simple details of the takeover. But what affected me most was his opinion on the resolution.

"I was afraid that you wouldn't know how to negotiate. You are an example of what it means to dialogue."

He left at about seven-thirty that night, when the sky was still lit up with the fiery clouds of sunset. On the island the summer afternoons were longer—just like our lives, from that moment on.

War Games

I learned how to be a good soldier for one year. I practiced military tactics on sand models with dwarf mountains and play weapons. I hardened my body with spartan discipline, and I prepared my spirit for the contingencies of war. I went back to the world of children and men, that of accepting all challenges. I programmed myself to obey the orders of a superior and I exercised my abilities in defense and offense; they were at times confused in combat. I learned to say firmly:

"As you order!"

"Yes, sir!"

"Immediately!"

"With your permission!"

"Ready!"

I memorized the fact that a soldier has limited firing range, functions, mission, and action on the battlefield. She can't shirk her duty, but she can't take the initiative either. I also learned to be a leader, which is very different: the leader is responsible for her soldiers; she thinks, makes use of, foresees, delegates, and orders.

This was a lot of work for me. I could not stand the invasion of privacy that constantly living in a military structure implied, nor could I renounce my individual self, and I chafed under the homogenization that comes with wearing a uniform. Obedience was not a part of my zodiac sign. Hundreds of times I wanted to run away or shoot myself with a cannon to erase myself from the face of the earth.

I was an excellent student according to the points I earned, but I discovered that I was not cut out for the military, in spite of wearing the uniform gracefully. The game of war means planning, dominating strategy and tactics, laying out every movement of the troops on models and topographical maps, assigning combat means, and foreseeing outcomes. Real war is another thing: it means pain and death.

Military school trained us for combat. It molded us into willing soldiers and got us used to psychological pressure. It developed tactical skills on land, gave us tools to calculate dimensions by sight, put in order our operative processes for fulfilling a mission, taught us operational planning techniques and how to use necessary instruments. But it also strengthened our combative morale with ideological arguments. We were clear on the why of our struggle and the use of weapons for politics. This training nourished values that are indispensible in battle—solidarity among compañeros, heroism, dignity, generosity in victory and compassion in defeat. We also discussed ethical issues with respect to the army. But no one told us what to do with the feelings of fear and pain we felt when confronted with the destruction caused by one's own self. No one told us that the machinery of war damages the soul, that sometimes it is better to die than to survive with such a heavy load. No one said anything about any of that.

8

An Army in Deep

O N 5 MARCH 1981 the inhabitants of the riverbank along the Mira, from Cape Manglares inland, woke up early, curious to see what the river had brought them. The sound of motors had invaded their sleep the night before, and this meant a bonanza in a territory known for smuggling. The inhabitants of a nameless hamlet could make out in the distance the four barges that had stopped at their docks. The bargemen were local and the passengers—six to ten per barge, all young—were accompanied by a man with white hair, perhaps their father, whose friendly gestures were belied by the weapons he was carrying.

Carlos Toledo was busy for a long time with a discussion. The bargemen didn't want to keep going. They were angry because the load of smuggled goods they had been hired to transport wasn't the norm: it weighed a lot, and there were too many armed people watching over it. They almost left us right there, but a bonus payment settled the difference, and the four barges took off again behind the other seven already downriver.

We had been traveling for five days, closed in the cabin of a boat, and the sun began to peek out when we got to La Honda, a sort of beach where we disembarked with the same eagerness Columbus's crew must have felt when they arrived in the New World.

Our boxes of "goods" were strewn along the beach and the bargemen got their 20,000 pesos—enough money to keep them partying for a month. We watched them hightail it out of there to get drunk and tell stories that were more legendary than real.

Once alone, we deployed our military structure and began following the rhythm of orders to establish the "Antonio Nariño" column with eighty-six men and women. Our mission was to begin the offensive in the south, to ignite insurrection in what had been the last bastion of royalism in Nueva Granada. We dreamed of glory days of battle in the political-military campaign that was going to bury the conditional amnesty, or "unconditional surrender," as we called the Turbay-Alaya administration's peace offering.

Jaime Bateman, el Flaco, was waiting for us in Putumayo with the military forces from Caquetá; we would join them to form one single army. Iván Marino and Toledo had decided in Panama that it was better to keep our entrance secret, to avoid fighting, because we did not know the area and lacked local support. Our contingency was part of an M-19 national operation plan to increase the level of guerrilla military operations in different geographical zones. We hoped to pressure the government for a less burdensome peace negotiation than the one offered by the president.

Two columns—close to 150 men and women—had arrived in less than a month through Chocó and Nariño. We took heart from the resurgence of the armed struggle elsewhere; the Sandinistas were in power in Nicaragua, and the Salvadoran and Guatemalan guerrillas were advancing. It was an era of war for the sake of peace.

We waged our first battle against inhospitable nature. The bank of the Mira River is an almost uninhabited zone of mangrove covered in dense thickets. The occasional sawmill or animal trap are the only signs of human presence. To find a path in that chunk of damp tropical jungle is a miracle. It was into this environment that we disembarked.

We all got complete supplies: a uniform and boots, a backpack with a change of clothes, a hammock, a blanket, plastic and rope for camping, a lantern, a knife, food, some medicines, a weapon assigned according to specialty and rank, and ammunition. Each backpack weighed forty to forty-five kilos, depending on the size and physical ability of its bearer. When you are barely a meter and a half tall and weigh fifty kilos, putting on a backpack is dressing like a turtle, no matter how much training you've had.

We chose a cleared area along the riverbank for our camp. We spread out along the area in defensive positions; each platoon and squad took its post. We set up watch posts and started to put up the lean-tos. It rained incessantly. The sky seemed to have broken and was dumping torrents of water. When we were finally able to hang the hammocks, it was already dark and the hot food was ready. I put on dry clothes with the intention of going to sleep immediately after eating my soup, and I wrapped myself in plastic so as to stay dry on my way over to the *rancho*,[1] where I stood in line and got my steaming portion.

The most enjoyable moments of a guerrillera's day come from eating hot food or resting. I think I smiled for the first time all day, while I balanced the *gacha* (bowl) in one hand, the gun draped diagonally across my shoulder, and held the plastic over my food with my free hand. I raised my eyes to orient myself and saw my lean-to a few steps away. Suddenly I was trapped in a mudhole that looked like *colada*.[2] I slipped and landed on my side; the soup spilled all over me, and the rain mocked me to my face. I had just enough dignity to get to my hammock and have an angry cry before falling asleep.

For the rest of the mission I never got completely dry. It was cold at night, a dank, sticky kind of cold, and during the day the heat was sticky too. The mud was sticky. We were sticky. There was no way to avoid the damned rain. That first night I woke up suddenly when Alfredo called to me, "Negra, get up, the river's taking us!"

The guards had heard a noise that was foreign to city people—"like a motor," they later said. They couldn't see a thing through the pounding rain. The warning was sounded when the boxes of ammunition and food started floating away; only then did they realize that we had camped in a dry tributary of the river that was now being flooded.

It was a nightmare. It didn't matter if our eyes were open or shut; we moved with the anguish and clumsiness of the newly blinded. We saved what we could from the river current, but the water fought us over every scrap. Uniforms, canteens, hammocks, lanterns, cardboard boxes, nearly every trace of our presence in the zone escaped downriver.

The leaders organized the move. I was completely disoriented and crawled along in the mud trying to go up a slope, but I couldn't understand what was happening with the water and the land. Since I couldn't see, I had no concept of space, distance, or dimension. Everything was black and thick; I moved my legs like an automaton in the direction of someone else I could hear moving. My sense of time was also diluted by the water. I didn't know if it took us one hour or ten to move to higher ground. My insides also felt like mud, because I was there without enthusiasm, fear, hope. I was simply in the world. The immediate future was survival, and to that end the

1. The mess hall. Also kitchen patrol, depending on the context.
2. A porridge-like food made of plantain, wheat, corn, or oat flour, often used as a baby food.

fundamental activity of my muscles was concentrated. My mind was a blank. Someone said, "Compañera, you can sit here."

I sat down, pulled up my knees, put my head between them, and rested. I canceled my thoughts to conserve energy. I had just lived through the nightmare of a dark world in which my imagination created strange realities without time or space, a world in which I couldn't manoeuvre, in which I was an automaton. I gave myself up to exhaustion. Outside myself I heard the activity of the compañeros who continued with the rescue. The water was still pouring down.

With the daylight I began to distinguish shapes. The world was again sketched in my brain and even my body seemed to wake up little by little, as if my sense of reality were connected to vision. I got up with difficulty and found that I was stiff. I looked at the path we had come up: a wall about 100 meters high. That's why we had crawled up. I was stupefied as I looked down and felt the desolation I had not had time to allow myself in the night. I wanted someone to save me, for my mamá or Superman to show up.

Suddenly I remembered what I was doing there and walked over to a group that was getting ready for the march. We had faces of the damned. We were masses of mud through which olive green splotches were visible; individual features were lost. If I'd had the strength I'd have laughed. Just then Alfredo appeared; I recognized him by his walk. We hugged. I felt the heat of his body through the mud penetrate my cold; when I was next to him everything seemed easy. I closed my eyes for a moment to keep this warm feeling inside and wished this were my only reality. I found my strength in his love.

When the exploratory squad chose a campsite, the train set off again, its wagons in order. First came the exploration group, the vanguard, then the main group and the rear guard with its security group. I was in the main group because I was part of the central command. Susana was in front of me, Estela behind. El Gordo Arteaga, and Rosemberg were close by.

My backpack weighed more than the day before, maybe because it was wet or because I was hungry and tired, or maybe all those things together. Fortunately we didn't have to walk too far. We set up camp again. I unpacked my hammock, the ropes, the plastic, and the blanket. I chose two trees and hung the hammock, then put my backpack on it. Suddenly I felt a sharp pain in my pinky finger. I shook my hand and saw an ant the size of a beetle biting down on my finger. I shook it off as best I could. Other ants were walking slowly from the tree along the hammock rope to my backpack. It didn't seem real. I hadn't seen the likes of those monsters even in Tarzan stories. I called to the closest compañero, and he called someone else until we had formed a small group. Someone said that these were the feared *tambocha*[3] ants that could eat a whole forest.

I got my things together and set up somewhere else, away from the ants. The pain in my finger soon spread to my arm; my hand swelled up as if it had been inflated. My arm was swollen up to my elbow. The compa in charge of health gave me an anti-allergy salve and something for the pain.

I picked up my G-3 gun as best I could and headed for the meeting of the central command that Toledo had called; he was the column commander. Six of us, four men and two women, made up the central command on this operation. Three platoon leaders also attended the meeting. We ten— Toledo, Rosemberg, el Gordo Arteaga, Susana, Pedro, Ismael, Alberto, Luis Alfredo,[4] and I sat in a circle.

We analyzed our situation and strategized about how to fulfill the objective of getting to Putumayo. We put our only map of Colombia, a river map that the barge crew had given us, in the center of the circle. Toledo solicited everyone's opinion. Rosemberg, Arteaga, and I all thought we should move for several reasons. The secrecy of the operation had been compromised since Panamá. It was impossible for eighty-six people to enter the airport clandestinely; besides, our moving along the Mira was too evident in a zone that was so sparsely inhabited, and there was still the possibility that the bargemen would lead the army to where we had landed, which was close to where we were. In my opinion, the troops wouldn't take more than a week to get there.

El Gordo Arteaga showed us on the map how we were trapped in a triangular strip of land between the Macizo Colombiano Mountains, the sea, and the Mira and Mataje Rivers bordering Ecuador. We evaluated our options. Several ideas for getting to Putumayo were floated. We could go over to the north bank of the Mira and try to move the column by truck to Mocoa, or cross the Nariño *minifundios*[5] on foot toward Putumayo, or go up the Mira as far as we could and enter Putumayo wherever we could.

Ismael and Alberto took inventory. Only two people knew the banks of the Mira up to where we had landed, and I knew the towns of Alto Putumayo and Nariño but only by highway, so I wouldn't have been able to guide in the country. We remembered our geography lessons in school about the Colombian Massif because of its great height and because that is where the majority of the country's rivers begin. No one even dreamed of crossing it.

3. Poisonous red-headed ants.
4. This is the pseudonym of a compañero who had fought in Nicaragua until the Sandinista victory and worked as a member of the revolutionary police. He joined the M-19 in 1980.
5. Small properties of one to ten cultivated hectares.

La Negra, five years old, on her balcony in Cali, 1956 (author's collection)

El Pato, 1957 (author's collection)

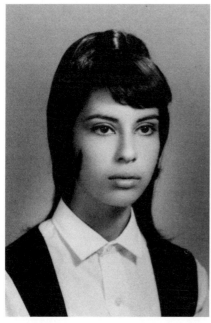

María Eugenia with her grand-parents, Mamá María and Papá Marcos, and her mother, Ruth, in 1962 (author's collection)

Maria Eugenia in 1968, in Pasto (author's collection)

La Negra with Ramiro Hernández, her first child's father, at the Universidad Nacional, 1972 (author's collection)

ABOVE*: Maria Eugenia in 1970 at the Pasto airport* (author's collection)

RIGHT: *M-19 propaganda, 1974* (courtesy of Magdalena Agüero)

Jaime Bateman, November 1982 (courtesy of Magdalena Agüero)

María Eugenia with Juan Diego after a school play in 1983 (author's collection)

María Eugenia during the signing of the first ceasefire and national talks in Corinto, department of the Cauca, in 1984 (Centro de Documentación Para la Paz)

Gladys López, member of the M-19 national leadership, dancing with a guerrillero at the Ninth National Conference in Los Robles, 1985 (courtesy of Magdalena Agüero)

LEFT TO RIGHT: *Gustavo Arias (a.k.a. "Boris"), Carlos Pizarro, Iván Marino Ospina, Antonio Navarro, Alvaro Fayad. The caption reads: The five of us, with infinite iron will, are going to the end—with enough joy to build our long-desired homeland. November 9, 1985* (courtesy of Magdalena Agüero)

Gladys López and her son, Kun, at the Ninth National Conference in Los Robles, 1985 (Centro de Documentación Para la Paz)

Rosemberg Pabón and Vera Grabe,
Ninth National Conference in
Los Robles, 1985
(Centro de Documentación Para la Paz)

María Eugenia during the Ninth
National Conference in Los Robles, in
the department of the Cauca, when she
was named member of the M-19
leadership, 1985. (Centro de
Documentación Para la Paz)

*Army tanks storming the
Palacio de la Justicia,
6 November 1985*
(courtesy of Magdalena Agüero)

*María Eugenia pregnant with
José Antonio in Havana, Cuba,
1986* (author's collection)

Juan Diego holding
José Antonio,
Havana, Cuba, 1987
(author's collection)

M-19 demonstration in Bogotá, 1989, before the peace accords
(Centro de Documentación Para la Paz)

La Negra in 1998 at the Testimonial Literature awards ceremony, with
Victor Cassaus (Cuban writer and poet) and Arturo Alape (Colombian writer)
(author's collection)

María Eugenia at an interview with the newspaper El Espectador in 2000
(used with permission of El Espectador, S.A.)

Other factors were added to our lack of topographical information. Since we didn't have the support of the region, the column took on the extra weight of weapons, ammunition, and food, which made any movement difficult. Furthermore, we were all weakened by the conditions of the trip and consuming medicine for malaria. Many suffered from diarrhea and dizziness. Most of us thought that, in spite of everything, we should make an effort to move immediately. Toledo disagreed. The criteria of the humanist doctor took priority over that of military leader. He decided that we would first get our strength back so we could move later. He made an agreement with some peasants next to the camp, who guaranteed us food for five days. He had already planned to send weapons in a truck to lighten the load, and some six days later the column would start marching, using area guides to get to the foot of Mount Macizo. Meanwhile, we would try to keep our presence a secret. We were used to obeying the leader's orders, and that was the end of the discussion. Toledo's word was the last.

On 6 March a truck full of coconut and *chontaduros*[6] that obscured the boxes of weapons left Mocoa in Putumayo. It made it through the hardest check points in Ipiales and Pasto, but when it was only six hours from its final destination, the guards in a department border customs mobile check point in San Francisco discovered the weapons. Coincidence or no, they then had the end of the skein in their hands and could more readily unravel our plan.

Meanwhile, in the camp we lived a routine that went against our security norms. It didn't seem to matter that noise would give our presence away, nor did we avoid smoke from fires or require everyone to whisper. Maybe we trusted too much in the desolate nature of the place. On the eve of the seventh day, the guerrillera guard posts informed us of noises and whistles coming from the landing beach. I sent an exploration squad to verify the information. The report informed us of tracks on the beach, which Toledo interpreted as curious natives. All his attention was focused, in vain, on stopping the bleeding of a compañero who had been hurt with a machete as he cut wood. What the doctor couldn't do, a muchacho from Putumayo did with a poultice of three herbs that stopped the bleeding.

While we adapted to the terrain and postponed the decision to continue the march, the army took the military initiative and began combat operations. On 8 March we wanted to celebrate International Woman's Day and we ordered a pig for the occasion. The air smelled of *chicharrón*[7] and the food was almost ready when the first shots were heard. The security squad from

6. A very nutritious fruit with a yellow and fibrous flesh, it is eaten cooked with salt.
7. A deep fried pork rind typical in Colombia.

the rear guard platoon faced them off, but the soldiers lying in ambush had already located the compañeros. Only one man and one wounded woman survived. The rest they killed.

At first everything was confusion. We thought a group of smugglers had come across our column, but the compas who came in from the first battle clearly identified the army. We organized quickly for the defense. While Toledo remained as commander of the vanguard to face the troops, the withdrawal was begun under the command of Rosemberg Pabón.

Ismael asked for volunteers to rescue the compañeros in the affected squad. I saw Alfredo take a step forward and I wanted to yell at him to stay with me, but I couldn't utter a sound. He received his orders and came to say good-bye. He hugged me, and when he left to command the group of volunteers, I stood in the same spot for a long time, feeling as empty as a locust shell. The voices from the command brought me back to reality; I had to leave with Rosemberg.

The Split

The Antonio Nariño column split in half. The first combat lasted five hours. Rosemberg took us far from the place and the pressure on us was lessened a bit. We stopped when night fell. We hadn't eaten since morning. The delicious pig was still in the camp we had abandoned. We split a can of sardines per squad. We didn't set up lean-tos but doubled the guard and stayed awake.

On the ninth Toledo's people met up with the army again and fought for hours. From that moment on, the two halves of our column lost contact with each other. We went ahead, mining our withdrawal paths to make enemy advance more difficult. Several exploratory forays brought back the information that we were surrounded. Troops on armed barges patrolled the Mira, and the rest of the forces pressured us to retreat to the mountains. We had to assume that they would lead us to a place where another group was waiting to annihilate us; this was a tactic known as "the anvil and the hammer."

We walked day and night. The last accord between the two groups was to go south to Ecuador, our only viable alternative. El Gordo Arteaga was in charge of guiding the march with a compass and the famous river map. He traced out our route, assigned a reference point for the peasant compañero who was with us, and led us to the indicated place. Then the steps were repeated.

Toledo's group bore the constant pressure of the army at their heels. They fought three or four times a day. We, on the other hand, sped up the march to get out of the zone by breaking through the ring.

As the days went by, our fatigue and hunger increased. The daily ration was one can of sardines split between six people, a little condensed milk, and pieces of panela. Each time I put a piece of panela in my mouth I wanted to vomit. I drank water so I could swallow it because I knew I needed to consume calories to keep walking. On the second day of marching I noticed that my period had stopped. It seemed that my vital functions were concentrated on walking. Walking was our only hope of survival, but even in these circumstances I trusted in the power of the group to get out of this trap, and I banished from my mind the thought that we were lost.

Sometimes we found a path or an abandoned sawmill and we could see the sun. With the light you could see the forest in all its colors. Every time that happened, happiness surged through me—the surroundings with huge trees and leaves of a thousand shapes around the trunks, the flowers, the ferns, the moss, and the mountain ear mushrooms were so beautiful. Where the sun's rays penetrated an explosion of life was heard in the melodies of birds and insects. Breathing in this scent of damp *monte*[8] and letting my senses fill with color and sound, I was taken back for a moment to an awareness of how beautiful existence could be.

We were increasingly silent. No one complained, not even the wounded compañera. When I felt myself running out of strength I looked at the other women; if they could keep on, so could I. At first Susana kidded around whenever she fell. It was really hard to get up with the weight of the backpack; we looked like beetles trying to turn over. But we fell so many times that Susana got tired of laughing.

On about the third day of this forced march, we ate bouillon dissolved in cold water during a rest stop, and it tasted wonderful after so much panela. My feet were on fire, as if I had burned them, and when I took off my socks to examine them I found that my soles looked like sponges from the constant dampness. They were thick, white, and porous with bloody furrows that revealed open flesh. If we had endured these conditions for much longer, we would have sprouted roots.

We had to be very alert on night marches, not so much out of fear of an enemy ambush as from fear of getting lost. We couldn't see two feet in front of us and had to feel our way, constantly seeking contact with the compañero

8. The *monte* is a zone of dense woods or jungle, very full of diverse vegetation, trees, vines, palms, etc.

in front. The fatigue was such that if we stopped for a moment we fell asleep on our feet. One of those nights we were warned that we were going to slide down a hill to the river and would have to wait for the signal to sit on the edge. When they gave me the signal I wanted to get used to what was coming, but someone pushed me down hard. The only thing I remember is something like a lance piercing my stomach and the giddy feeling of rolling down, falling endlessly, the pressure of a scream that I fought to keep inside. The blow of the water made me react with still more fear. I thought death must be like this, like a frozen vertigo that produces terror. Ismael's arm rescued me and brought me to the bank.

At some point we entered a swampy zone heavy with vegetation. We opened up a path with machetes. It was more and more difficult to advance, and the water came up to our waists. A soft fog clung to our bodies and we could see only half a meter around us, no further. I thought the swamp had swallowed us and I avoided the eyes of my compañeros so so as not to see there the same desperation I was feeling.

We finally got to a less dense part of the jungle, with giant trees whose ripe fruit had fallen to the ground. I knew they were *madroños*[9] by the smell, but on the ground there was only crushed flesh. Along the way I bent over several times to get the peels, which I savored. I was half-blind on this crossing. I had lost my two pairs of contact lenses in all the stumbling, and during the first confrontation, when I resorted to my glasses, the right lens fell out and was lost among the foliage.

During the night rest period, the compañera in charge of health asked me to help clean Lucía's wound, which had become infected. When I saw the state of her arm, I knew just how courageous the girl was. When we took off the bandage to clean the dried blood and remaining skin, we discovered that she still had the nose of the bullet in her wound. We took it out with a safety pin, leaving a hole that went clear through her forearm without touching the bone. This muchacha was lucky! We rubbed some gauze soaked with disinfectant back and forth over the wound until it bled again.

Another day we located a crop of plantains and sent three compañeros— Luis Alfredo, Gustavo, and Blas—to look for a house nearby, study the conditions, and see if we could get close. We gave them two hours to go and come back. After a while we heard some shots. Rosemberg ordered us to start marching immediately and left a post of two compañeros to get them in case they came back. It seemed to me that we were abandoning them, but

9. A small, yellow, soft-skinned tropical fruit with a large seed and white flesh. It is aromatic, soft, and sweet.

Rosemberg argued the need to preserve the group. No one said anything else. At dusk the guards arrived with Blas, whom Luis Alfredo had left at one point while he and Gustavo went closer to the house. Blas didn't see anything either, and when he heard the shots he waited. When they didn't come back, he decided to retreat. The army was close behind.

At this point we had to bury part of the equipment to lighten the load and make our movement quicker. We kept the indispensible food, medicine, and ammunition. The first symptom of unbearable fatigue was the refusal of two of the Panamanians to walk any further. Our efforts to lift their spirits did no good, nor did direct orders. They preferred death. Those muchachos, members of the Torrijista Juventud del Partido Democrático Revolucionario,[10] had joined our forces for military experience. They had no training, which explains their weakness. But it wasn't their cause either. After an endless hour and I don't know what arguments, the group leader succeeded in persuading them to keep moving. Their lapse injured our morale, and despair threatened to engulf us.

We reached another clearing in the monte and saw a hut of split bamboo. Rosemberg sent Mariano and me to contact the inhabitants and try to find a guide. We changed into civilian clothes and left our long arms behind. Mariano carried a pistol and I had my cyanide pill.

We approached slowly so they could see us and wouldn't be frightened. We greeted them with smiles. Two black women who were in the hall answered nervously and immediately an old man and a boy came out. The old man had a hunting rifle in his hands and kept it pointed at us the whole time. The tension was intense. Mariano and I were holding hands and said that we had gotten lost and needed directions to the nearest town. Mariano's hand in mine gave me confidence, but we were at the edge of fear. The family surrounded us to inspect us at their will, without getting too close; you could feel everyone's agitated breathing. We asked if they could guide us and they said no. We asked what they were afraid of, and they looked with frightened eyes toward the monte. We thanked them and left immediately. If we reached our compañeros without being shot it would be a miracle. But we made it.

We deduced from the attitude of the people that the army had to be near. We had to get out of there as soon as possible. The order was given immediately, and as I rushed to put on my uniform, I lost my cyanide. We went into the monte quickly, avoiding the paths, stepping in the footprints of the compañero ahead of us so we wouldn't leave too many tracks. The rear guard squad erased our prints with branches.

10. Followers of Panamá's Omar Torrijas, in the Youth of the Revolutionary Democratic Party.

During those days of pursuit I would remember Alfredo and feel a hole in my chest open up, knowing that he could be dead. Sometimes my eyes met Ivana's, the Costa Rican compañera of Luis Alfredo (the one they had killed). We communicated our mutual sorrow, but there was no time to speak of it.

We heard helicopters overhead, and though we knew that the foliage and our camouflage uniforms hid us, we couldn't shake the fear brought on by the sounds of those machines suspended in the air and felt exposed. We had to remind the group that helicopters are a fragile combat weapon in the monte and that we must not allow ourselves to be terrified by the sounds and must keep quiet. We continued to march, but when we heard them shooting rounds of machine gun fire, we knew that they were cleaning out the area for new troops, a tactic they called "the drop of oil."

"They're lost!" the compañeros said to calm themselves.

We reached an area with huge trees that were not too dense and vegetation with wide leaves through which we could walk without difficulty. Along the way we found several traps for small animals set in fallen trunks. Suddenly, an exploration group found an indigenous man half-hidden behind a thicket. We were ordered to stop and we froze like statues until we got instructions from Rosemberg to approach him.

The Indian was a providencial find. We moved closer carefully, talking to him so he wouldn't be afraid. Still, it was obvious he had found us, and not the other way around, as the majority thought. Had he wanted to hide, not even a witch could have found him. When we asked him for help, he said he could guide us to the Mataje River and show us where to wade across it at its shallowest point. The current was fast and there were waterfalls, but he knew a place where it would be easy to cross. Rosemberg offered him five thousand pesos and the knife he had on his belt, because the man hadn't taken his eyes off it the whole time they talked.

This was surely a smuggling route on which the man acted as guide, but even so we had to be careful of an ambush. We took every possible security measure to avoid surprises, walking not single file but in cradle formation. We walked all day without stopping. Along the way we found fallen plantains and ate some as we walked, against security norms that warn against eating food found on unknown lands because it might contain explosive mines or poison. Hunger won out over prudence.

We came to a small farm garden and passed an empty hut. Our guide knew more tricks than we did for not leaving tracks. He sent us downhill to avoid a bridge and led us not along paths but parallel to them.

Finally we neared the Mataje, on the other side of which lay Ecuador. I wanted to kiss the indigenous guide. He spoke very little but made himself understood with gestures. He showed us the ford, got his pay, and left. We had a moment of doubt. What if he had betrayed us? What if we crossed the river into an ambush, as Che's column in Bolivia had? What if this wasn't really the Mataje?

We didn't have many alternatives, though, and we had to make a decision. We followed every security norm in crossing the river, one of the most dangerous moments of any guerrilla march. One squadron occupied the defensive position on the Colombian riverbank. Then the exploration squad waded across the river and covered the other side, while two compas checked out the bordering land. When they were sure there was no ambush, they gave us the signal to cross carefully. The water came up to our waists and we could feel the current. Once on the other side of the river, I breathed a huge sigh of relief.

The idea of borders struck me as strange and arbitrary. That crossing an imaginary line could protect us was a bizarre concept, but it was the case. We found a place to rest about two kilometers from the river. Rosemberg and two compañeros went in search of a town called San Lorenzo that, according to our guide, wasn't far.

Although it may seem paradoxical, in the analysis that preceded the final decision, respect for international legislation was primary, and we decided to avoid any confrontation with Ecuadorian forces. That way our presence would not be interpreted as an aggression and we could take refuge in the right of protection from a neighboring country. Perhaps the outcome of our recent takeover of the Dominican Embassy influenced Rosemberg's decision. If we could break through a force like the one the army had set up, which according to their own data consisted of 12,000 men, and if we could couple that with a political event that would affect the Colombian government, then we might regain the initiative we had lost on military terrain.

In Rosemberg's absence we were under the command of el Gordo Arteaga, and we were getting ready to eat something when we heard shots. We didn't respond. Soldiers—we thought they were Ecuadorian—suddenly surrounded us. We learned later that this was a Colombian counter-guerrilla platoon under the command of Captain Morales, whose troops had crossed over to Ecuador and surprised us. Our confusion as to their nationality counted in their favor, for had we known their true identity we might well have fought back. Fortunately—and this was unusual—Morales respected war rights and gave us the treatment stipulated for prisoners.

We had made an unforgivable mistake. We had relaxed our vigilance before being sure that we were safe, and we were captured in the stupidest way. That day we knew defeat. By the time we realized our error, we were surrounded by three rings of army forces, ready to kill us if we made the least attempt to respond.

Again I thought that death would be better than capture. When I looked at the muchachos and muchachas, though, I thought they were so young and they deserved a chance that death wouldn't grant them.

The Colombian and Ecuadorian armies had made a pact, without consulting anyone else, to hand over the two units—ours and Toledo's—that had managed to get to San Lorenzo seeking asylum. We were moved onto Colombian soil by helicopter. From then on we had virtually no control over events. After more than fifty hours of combat, after evading the Colombian army for days on end, after losing eleven compañeros, the two halves of the Antonio Nariño column were reunited, this time as prisoners in a concentration camp improvised by the army. How long were we there? I can't tell even when I have a calendar in my hands.

Nightmare

I had contemplated death so many times it didn't worry me anymore. But the horror of detention under the Turbay administration was another story. Camacho Leyva was fresh in my memory because of the tortures to which so many Colombians were subjected and the atrocious nature of his techniques. No, I didn't think about being taken prisoner; to avoid it I carried the cyanide with me. But, as luck would have it, I had lost my capsule. I was forced to accept the reality of my detention.

Once my hands were tied behind my back and my eyes were blindfolded, I understood that dignity was the only thing that would keep me on my feet in spite of fear and powerlessness. If I could hold on to my dignity, I could face a life I hadn't counted on.

The days that followed were a nightmare, and it's hard for me to remember them. Torture, no matter how sophisticated, no matter the intensity of the pain or the terror it instills, is a practice aimed at breaking the dignity of human beings. There is nothing more aberrant than subduing a person by force; powerlessness wounds the deepest part of the being. I would prefer to leave the memories of this torture behind me. I want to forget those feelings, which I associate with crossing through a narrow tunnel, where time had stopped and there was no reality beyond the suffering of the body.

The army kept us, illegally, in a part of the jungle where day and night were divined by the effect of the equatorial sun on our exhausted bodies. In this concentration camp I understood that the difference between resisting and surviving is determined by the amount of dignity one can preserve. So I gathered up my strength to endure without any complaints, without giving up and without betraying my great loves. It was very clear to me that I could not live with myself or look my loved ones in the face again if I collaborated with my interrogators. I think that assuming the consequences of my acts prepared me to accept reality. What's more, I abandoned myself easily to whatever might happen, without hanging on to life or renouncing it. It is not easy to describe this feeling; maybe it's about not wasting yourself on useless efforts, but rather maintaining yourself in waiting.

Time passed and routines took shape. During what must have been the days we were blindfolded, tied up, and isolated in an large area in the sun. For what must have been the nights they took us to a pigpen and threw us all in together haphazardly. The mission of the guards was not to let us sleep. They led us away for individual interrogations. I trembled, not only from the cold of the nights but because with darkness comes fear. I felt it threatening from the croaking of the toads and the chirping of the crickets. Two contradictory things happened through direct contact with the soldiers: the enemy was made more concrete, and at the same time it was humanized. We knew that they could do with us whatever they wanted, and yet we saw them as flesh and blood, like ourselves.

One morning, very early, the soldiers dug a hole from which muddy water immediately gushed. They put soap on a stone and told us all to wash our faces and hands. We were so dirty that even though the water smelled rotten, the contact with soap gave us a feeling of cleanliness. It was nice to see our features again, free of mud. Then they gave us our first plate of hot food, while an official filmed the activities so there would be no doubt about the good treatment the army was giving its prisoners. They packed us off in trucks and, after a drive that seemed to last forever, they left us in the Mecanizado Cabal Group in Ipiales.

The cold there was frightful. When we arrived they exchanged the ropes on our wrists for handcuffs and put us in a large hall, men to the right and women to the left. The iron cots were lined up against the wall, each one covered by a grey blanket with the Colombian flag in the middle of it. The bathrooms for men and women were on opposite sides of the hall. Though our material conditions improved, we still had the feeling of absolute powerlessness. We were in their hands.

9

Bars on My Soul

I give my memories free rein
like shadows outlined
on the white wall.

Every centimeter of this cell has a name
a voice, a color, a word . . .
in the name of others my body harbors
hope.

I hide a little bundle of dreams in a corner,
the only way to survive
in this whitewashed corral.
—Buen Pastor Prison, Medellín, January 1982

Three months after our capture, eight of the sixty-six compañeros judged in the Ipiales military trials were taken to prison. Our trial was plagued with irregularities from the start. Under a pact between the Ecuadorian and Colombian armies, the prisoners were handed over, and the Colombian army ignored Ecuador's legislative processes and our right to asylum.

Torture, interrogation under pressure, and isolation kept us from defending our right to legal counsel during the investigative proceedings, and detention in military installations gave us no guarantee of due process. We were judged by military trial and our captors were the accusers and the judges. In the end, we were sentenced to nine years for rebellion, with no related charges.

The implementation of the penalty was in the hands of civilian legal institutions. We could appeal, but at that time, in spite of the efforts of defense lawyers and human rights organizations, little could be done against the military penal justice system. The majority of its irregularities or excesses were covered by immunity to civilian law.

So into the penitentiary van we went: Silvia, the pregnant compañera, her husband César, Susana, Marta, Marcos, Wilson, Guásimo, and me. They picked us up at the Medellín airport and took us to the Bellavista and Buen Pastor prisons. Some of us were facing nine years in the joint, others faced four.

The dull slam of the door as it swung shut behind us together with the semi-darkness inside the van added to our anxiety. A grid in the roof let in a little air. Silvia and César were huddled in a corner, both fighting tears. No one spoke. We were all scared.

The muchachos were left off at the Bellavista prison. "Good luck!" are the only words you can manage to sputter out, but they carry the fervent wish that everything will turn out as well as possible.

I had come to recognize fear in all its shapes and hues, but here I was, afraid of what the next nine years would hold. When we were left alone, our custodians started an animated chat detailing the violence of life in the women's prison. They spoke of the theft of any article considered of value, abuses by lesbians, the sick behavior of the guards during body searches, the knife fights, and the ferocity of feminine aggressivity.

I thought there could be nothing worse than being in the hands of the military, but the words of the guards made me bristle, though I knew that prisons at least were supervised by the judiciary and therefore could not be as bad as military justice. I looked at Silvia; tears were brimming in her eyes, so I grabbed and held her hand for a moment. Susana tried to shake the sadness out of her with funny comments. Her morale was the most important for everyone, not only because she was pregnant but because she was so young—she was barely eighteen. It's odd, but when you see someone else suffering, you find you have unanticipated reserves of strength.

The van stopped and the soldiers unloaded us and herded us into an impeccable waiting area with a wooden counter. The guards wore blue uniforms. They looked like chess pieces, standing erect upon the black-and-white floor tile. The soldiers clicked their heels, gave the report with artificial voices, put on a face of "mission accomplished," and left. I breathed a sigh of relief.

Then some very serious women, also dressed in blue uniforms, came for us. I waited for them to strip us down and give us their usual "welcome" body search, which the fools in the van had described in some detail. But contrary to what we thought, the guards didn't even touch us. They inspected us quickly. They took off our cuffs and fingerprinted us. Our hands had been cuffed behind our backs throughout the entire military trial. When the representative of the Red Cross International Committee, Erik Kobel, visited us and heard our complaint, he said keeping our hands behind our backs was good for our spines. The pain that tore through our muscles was inconsequential to him.

I saw no bars as we crossed to the yard. The tidiness of the halls and the walls reminded me of the boarding school I had studied in. I had never seen a prison before, but I had imagined a dirty, smelly place. Everything was shiny here, and instead of thick bars I saw wooden doors labeled with the names of the yards. I relaxed a little. I didn't yet know that the nuns put bars on your soul.

We approached a door in front of the yard that bore a sign reading "Recepción." The guards rang and the door opened. The women inside were quiet, their eyes fixed on those of us who were arriving. We kept very close together; we thought above all of Silvia and her pregnancy. The guards made us go past them and several women approached. It took us some time to figure out that they were being friendly.

"It's not so bad here."

"Don't worry, we all help each other."

"My name is Nubia and I'm here if you need anything."

"Where are you coming from?"

Their warmth disarmed us, and we relaxed a bit. The questions rained down and we answered them calmly. They thought it was odd when we said we were guerrilleras from the M-19 and had been charged with rebellion. Identifying ourselves as the political prisoners of a regime against which we had taken up arms was the first point we made with the muchachas. Admitting one's crime is not common in prison; more often prisoners profess their innocence and cast themselves as victims of circumstance. Only after making friends, and only then sometimes, do they tend confess their crimes amid guffaws and gloating.

A path opened up and one of the nuns in charge of the yard arrived. It was *Sor* (Sister) Irene, a tiny woman with a stern brow. She greeted us formally and informed us of the rules, meal schedules, hygiene requirements, and other regulations. Nothing seemed excessive to us; our daily lives in military school for more than a year had been similar to what she described. Later two nuns interviewed us, asking us for personal information and details about our families, education, and, finally, what had brought us to prison. Just like the muchachas, they were surprised that we didn't claim innocence. Then they asked if we were sorry for what we had done. Our answers were all similar:

"Rebellion is a right according to Saint Augustine."

"Rebelling against an unjust regime is a necessity."

"We cannot feel sorry for wanting change in this country."

In truth, the conditions of our detention and the scandal reported by the media made it impossible to claim innocence. We had been caught red-handed and all together. Seventy-five guerrilleros and guerrilleras, uniformed, armed, trained, and organized to fight against the establishment. How could we deny it? This was not a time to keep our militancy a secret, as we weren't like most political prisoners.

For us it was easy to claim political persecution, and this disconcerted our interlocutors. At the end of the interview the nuns peppered us with questions about whether we were communists or atheists, whether we hated religion and whether we liked to kill. We had to answer patiently that we professed the Catholic faith, were not communists, didn't like to kill, preferred peace to war, and that some of us had been educated by nuns. No, we weren't monsters. They looked at us, half-surprised and half-mistrustful. It took a long time to convince them that we weren't lying. From that day on they kept a close watch on us. They spied on us and sought us out to talk. As days went by they eased up some, but they never let their guard down, because they considered us dangerous.

Recepción was the name of the yard where the accused waited until their judicial situation was defined, and also where those who had been sentenced were acclimated before being sent to other places. It was a place of transition; some came in on Monday and left on Friday and were back again after two weeks. Generally the yard was occupied by *escaperas*—people who shoplifted by sneaking things out between their legs, *caimaneras*—who specialized in pickpocketing, skillfully moving their fingers like a caiman's jaws, and *raponeras*[1]—so named because of how fast they ran after snagging jewelry on the streets. It is hard to prove the charges in these types of theft because of the efficiency of the chain they operate. When they are caught

---

1. After *raponeo*, or theft of jewelry, particularly gold, by street thieves.

they have somehow managed to dispose of the loot; they've passed it on to partners who fade into the city.

The afternoon we arrived, the political prisoners from other yards found out about it and immediately communicated with us via a prisoner who worked in the workshops, sending us messages and the basic toiletries we needed. That's how we learned their names, the organization they belonged to, and the yard they were in. We were touched and excited by their greetings and felt a little less alone. Among them was a compañera from the Eme, María, whom we knew through others.

Two guards watched over our yard at night and two others during the day. Sofia, a stocky older lady who looked like a paisa grandma, was the guard the prisoners loved the most. We could get basic things like underwear, food, and crochet hooks and yarn from her. It's crucial to stay busy in prison. If you don't, either depression or aggression will invade you.

There was little activity, but getting to know a world so far away from my reality took all my attention and left no room for boredom. I talked with the other prisoners a lot, heard unimaginable stories, and found myself in a very peculiar and harsh feminine universe, in which the lives were so different from my own.

On the first visitation Saturday some poets from Medellín snuck in with Juan Manuel Roca, Susana's brother-in-law. We were happy to see them although we didn't know them. They brought us delicious *gloria* pastries.[2] It was the first time in four months we had had sweets. We were extremely happy, chattering like parrots and asking how the rest of the world was without us, when the director came in, looked at us, and stormed over. She asked each visitor how he was related to us, and when they said they were friends she told them, with a false smile, that we were allowed visits only from close relatives or legitimate husbands, which for her meant married by the Church. Then she threw them out.

The prison had its own rules on correspondence, visits, and books, which were made by the director to the best of her knowledge and understanding. For example, texts considered unconducive to the rehabilitation process were prohibited. The odd thing was that in the index of permitted reading you could find historians like Indalecio Liévano, poets like Pablo Neruda, writers like García Márquez, and Marx and his disciples. But the choices were few. Furthermore, the prison library had very few copies; most were old schoolbooks, biographies of saints, and *Reader's Digest* "selections" from the forties and fifties (in which I nevertheless found a goldmine of spy novels).

2. A pastry made of phyllo dough and filled with a caramel-type sweet called *arequipe* and guava paste.

The routine linked the days together like an endless train:

5:45 A.M. Get up and pray.

6:30 A.M. Obligatory cold-water showers, no lingering possible because of the number of women who had to share five bathrooms.

7:00 A.M. Voluntary mass, which we always attended so as to see the other compañeras.

7:30 A.M. Breakfast. Café con leche or hot chocolate with a roll.

8:00 A.M. Clean the premises, taking turns so all participated.

8:30 A.M. Go out to the workshops.

10:00 A.M. Snack. Bocadillo and bread, or bread and panela water.

12:00 noon Lunch. Soup, rice, potatoes or plantain, greens, and meat or egg; panela water was the after-dinner drink.

2:00 P.M. Return to the workshops.

3:30 P.M. Snack. Panela water and bread or bocadillo and bread.

5:00 P.M. Leave the workshops.

6:30 P.M. Dinner. Similar to lunch.

7:30 P.M. Pray the rosary or read the Bible with reflections led by the nun in charge of the yard.

8:00 P.M. Bed and general silence.

I felt like my soul was going to rot under such a restricted routine. In military school, we at least got Sundays off, with no set program.

There were about thirty or thirty-five of us in the yard. We had two collective dorms. One was big, with about twenty-five beds, each equipped with a nightstand. The other dorm was smaller. Susana and I were in the big one; Marta and Silvia were sent to the other one. At first I slept like a log, exhausted from the half-sleep of the military installations where I could never completely relax. After a while I got my light sleeping habits back, which allowed me to discover what went on in the dorm at night: some got up to steal, others to seek emotional or physical satisfaction, still others both at the same time. First, you'd hear the padding of bare feet and broken breathing. Then, under the quilts or the beds there would be a very strange party of bodies wrapped up in blankets, whispers, giggles, and panting that stopped, as if by magic, when the guard passed by on rounds, only to start up again a few seconds later. There were also those who got up to smoke a cigarette with the guard and talk, whether to distract themselves or the guard I don't know.

When the nuns explained to us that we had to study or work to lessen our sentences, we told them that we would work as teachers, but we were told this was impossible. So we offered ourselves as students, but the nuns didn't want that either. They were afraid we would contaminate the school ideologically.

But Mercedes, an (unconfessed) compañera from the Communist Party, was able to sneak in as a social studies teacher.

We signed up to work in the Fatelares workshop making cotton quilts.[3] Marta and I cut the cloth while Silvia and Susana learned to sew. They paid us for the work, but the sum was something like ten centavos per cut and fifteen per quilt, more symbolic than anything. The nuns managed our salaries in savings accounts, where they kept two-thirds of what each worker earned for when she was freed. They gave the remaining third to us. This barely covered toiletries in the prison store. None of those articles could be brought by relatives, according to the nuns, because of the risk that drugs might be smuggled in toothpaste or feminine pads.

Dolly held the quilt-making record. She sewed five dozen in a day and was like a frenetic machine. She had been in prison for fifteen years and still had a few left to go. She was a tiny woman, like one of those ballerinas with their pleated mini skirts hanging off rearview mirrors in buses. They got her for killing her husband and burying the body in a steel drum in her backyard.

"They didn't get me for the murder. They got me for the uniform because he was a cop," she told us, cracking up. She was never sorry that she'd killed him.

There were other workshops, like the Tejicondor, where they mended cloth on bolts, and there was Madre Eufrasia's embroidery workshop. Madre Eufrasia was eighty years old and took about four students at a time, teaching them to sew and talking to them about biblical passages. Everyone fought to go there because the little nun was almost blind. The muchachas took advantage of this and left her talking to herself while they went around the other workshops exchanging messages with friends and loves. In other yards they worked at packing raisins or making cardboard boxes.

Dreaming Has No Price … Escaping Does

During the two months we spent in Recepción, I again became aware that my hands could work separately. For example, one could scratch my head while the other could scratch my knee. I was so used to being cuffed that for quite a while I still kept my hands behind my back, or used them together as if they were still tied together.

After I got used to the yard routine, I let my imagination wander free by inventing escape plans. That's how I kept my spirit alive. If I had thought

3. Fatelares is the name of a factory that manufactured cloth.

for a moment that I would be in prison for nine years, I would have died from tedium or anguish. Every day my fantasies soared; all it took was the observation of a tiny detail. A roof, a cornice, a door, a window, or any movement of the personnel, guards, or nuns could serve to build a plan. I was always plotting, my muscles and brain churning toward escape. Thus I came to know every centimeter of the prison, the exact measurements of the walls, the area, the spaces, thickness, height. My military training enabled me to measure with my eyes, to calculate distances and systematically watch every centimeter of the land.

My plans varied according to my mood. Sometimes they were based on cunning and deceit aided by disguises. Other dreams oozed strength and daring. There was no lack of dreams in which a rescue force led by a compañero freed us, nor was there any shortage of romantic fantasies.

For me the dream became a real possibility when I found out that Elvecio Ruiz was in Medellín. He lacked neither the courage nor the romantic touch to be the prince of my rescue. So we sent him the map of the prison and a minutely detailed escape plan that was based on escaping from the church during mass. We made sure that he had received everything, and we began to prepare for the day when those on the outside would find conditions most favorable. We were ready every day. Every detail was foreseen. Our only worry was Silvia, who by then was about six months along, so we were always by her side to guarantee she'd get out with us.

The message with the chosen date would come via the compañeras from the Cultural yard, where the guard watched less. We had agreed that María would wear a green blouse to mass as a signal. Then the plan would be executed: at communion we would all sit near one of the doors where the rescue commando would be. Every day we went to mass and waited anxiously until María appeared, wearing any color but green. Time passed ... Silvia's tummy expanded ... and nothing. One day María forgot the signal and put on her green blouse. When she was about to go into the church she realized her mistake and faked a faint so they'd let her go back to her yard.

While we were dreaming of escape, Elvecio was having bigger problems. Following an M-19 commando kidnapping of Marta Nieves Ochoa, the daughter of Fabio Ochoa, the narcos had organized MAS,[4] and they decided to capture Elvecio to pressure the M-19 to release Ochoa. Fabio Ochoa was a paisa estate owner whose children were linked to narcotrafficking. Finally, after a game of cat and mouse, Elvecio was taken hostage by the mafia and turned over to the army. Our escape plan went with him. The fairy tale

4. Muerte a secuestradores (Death to Kidnappers), one of the first paramilitary organizations formed in the early 1980s.

didn't have a happy ending. The prince was thrown into the dungeon and we ladies kept throwing our handkerchiefs out the tower window, pleading for a knight in shining armor to come to our rescue.

While I thought about escaping, María entertained herself with fantasies of killing Sor Irene. While watering the plants on the second floor, she could let a pot fall on the nun's head, for example, and claim it was an accident. Of course María's fantasies about finishing off our jailer were just that—fantasies.

My own fanstasies of escape sent enough adreneline through my body to keep me from surrendering to apathy. One day a woman named Marta Muñetón came to the yard; she was accused of being a mafiosa. Her husband had begun the business, and when they killed him she took over the helm. I liked everything about her—the way she carried herself and the way she related to other people, her popular roots and the pride with which she talked about her background, her conception of life and her affection for her mother. She was unostentatious and very prudent, so I decided to befriend her, in spite of the reservations of the other compañeras, who disapproved of her drug selling. While she told me about her life, I watched and whispered to her my thoughts about escaping. One morning she told me that her trial would end soon, and I warned her that once they sentenced her she would be moved to a different yard. It would be easier to escape from Recepción, I told her, so her time was running out.

That very week they moved us four from the Mira to the Progreso and frustrated my first escape plan. About three days later my friend Muñetón gave me a seven-band Sony radio. The next day, when I went to send her a thank-you note, I was told she had escaped early that morning. I was happy for her. Later, piecing together the different versions of the story of her escape, I saw some of my own marvelous ideas incorporated in her plan. Of course she added something I hadn't thought about: 3 million pesos. Well, that may have taken away from her daring, but it assured the escape. Good for her . . . carajo!

"Classrooms" in Prison

In an effort to change prison lingo, the Buen Pastor authorities called the yards classrooms. Each yard had a certain status. The most prestigious, the one where the prisoners from the best families and no previous record went, was called the Cultural; there the muchachas could cook and order what they wanted to eat from outside. The uniforms they wore on visiting day were of better cloth and make. The Cultural was close to one of the prison exits, and the muchachas decorated the yard with plants, flowers, and colored curtains. The rest of the prisoners felt a certain enmity toward them because of their privileges.

The Progreso had the tightest security. It was located in the middle of the prison. Those who shared the fate of the political prisoners were mostly women from the provinces with long sentences for murder but no previous records. Others, including a policewoman, were accused of extortion, fraud against the nation, or kidnapping.

Then there was the Laboral, one of the most heavily populated yards. Everyone there was from popular sectors and worked in the workshops. It was a spacious yard and had a ping-pong table.

The Superación, an ugly place with a basketball court, housed the young, repeat-offender petty thieves; most were temporary lesbians while in prison. Those who resorted to this opportunistic practice were scornfully called *pirobas* by the rest of the prisoners.

The Familiar was spacious and very clean. It housed the tough cases. That's where repeat offenders of crimes such as aggravated theft, assault, murder, kidnapping, and other atrocious crimes went. It housed a sector that was very socially depressed and included the most renowned lesbians and most aggressive women.

Generally, when the nuns moved someone to a different yard, it was not to improve their conditions but to punish them for bad behavior. In complicated cases, such as those involving a fight that resulted in injury or a fight with the nuns and guards, or someone caught taking drugs or practicing lesbianism, the offender was confined to isolation far from the yards, in a tiny room with an iron door and only a small window high up in the wall. Isolation was the hardest thing, the muchachas said.

Single Stitch, Chain Stitch, Single Stitch

The years 1978 to 1983 were big ones for political arrests. Many women who were members of or collaborated with any guerrilla organization passed through the Buen Pastor. Because of the M-19's frenetic activity, we were still the most numerous group of political prisoners.

When we arrived, only Merceditas and Eunice, both members of the Communist Party accused of collaborating with the FARC, were there; Jannet, a peasant from Urabá, was in the same circumstances; Marta Inés was from the PLA; Fabiola was from the Brigadas Rojas anarchist group;

Mercedes and Beatriz from the ELN; and María from the M-19. All of them denied their militancy in the hope of getting the charges dropped. They were put in different yards, with no regard whatsoever for their status as political prisoners.

When our group arrived, things changed. We declared ourselves political prisoners, as did our compañeros in the Picota. And even though the nuns flatly denied the difference between common delinquency and political crimes, the entire country was debating the issue, especially after the takeover of the embassy of the Dominican Republic and the mobilization of the democratic forces around the Forums on Human Rights begun in 1980.

In the Buen Pastor, the authorities took security measures. They grouped us together in the Progreso. This had the positive effect of enabling us to communicate with each other and act as a group. But they simultaneously imposed special restrictions on us, watched us more closely than other prisoners, and allowed us visits only from close family members. Sometimes, even if the military brigade allowed certain visitors to enter, the director overruled the decision and we weren't permitted the visit. Arguing did no good. The internal regulations of the Buen Pastor overruled those contained in the "General Management of Prisons" rulebook.

Once Sor Margarita kept a letter from Silvia to a compañero in Bellavista, even after it had received the director's clearance, because she thought the word *preñez* (pregnancy) applied only to animals. Another time, a priest friend of my tía, the nun, got permission from the brigade to see me. To his surprise, the director, Sor Blanca Inés Velásquez, wouldn't let him in because he was very young and "didn't look like a priest"! We were truly cut off from the outside world.

The days of the week were meaningless, nothing but horizontal lines in a notebook. Twenty-one women were trapped within a small space confined by thirty-nine bars, almost all of us political prisoners. At first we all went to workshops, but our dissatisfaction about the pay and the unfair differential between our wages and the profits made by the factory itself caused a sort of malaise among us that we expressed in murmurs and reproachful glares at the nun in charge of the workshop. We were not allowed to talk while we worked, but this didn't stop us from making our views known through our eyes and body language. One day Dolly felt sick and asked to go back to her cell. Sor Margarita, who was in charge of our yard, wouldn't let her go, and so Dolly blew up, venting things she had kept inside for a long time. "Exploiting nuns," she fumed, "we aren't the thieves ... miserable nuns ... earning interest at our expense ... I don't buy any of this!" The result was predictable. She wound up in isolation, and they never let us return to the workshops again.

From that day on, our main activity was crocheting. The women who knew how taught the others the basics: single stich, chain stitch, single stitch. Before long we had designed our own backpacks. I crocheted some round monsters with big feet just for fun, and we gave them different expressions. Over time, the crocheting became compulsive. We took our yarn with us wherever we went and never stopped the single stitch, chain stitch, single stitch—as if life would end if our hands rested. We sat in a group while we crocheted and told personal stories endlessly. We talked a lot about the activities of the FARC, the EPL, the ELN, the PLA, and the M-19, re-created and compartmentalized at will. Ideological and political differences surfaced only when we secretly dictated a communiqué that would go out in some visitor's tooth filling or hem. Most of our differences were more semantic than fundamental. Maybe with a good dictionary they would have been easily resolved.

Thrown together by circumstance, we political prisoners united when it came to facing the nuns. Sor Margarita, who was in charge of our yard, really was out to get us. She was like a crow at our backs. Someone's chortle was enough to make her dash over and plant herself between us, scowling. A curtain of silence would fall until the nun went away.

To meet daily expenses we created a general fund with the profits from selling our crocheting work and what came in for solidarity from the politicals. We all got 70 percent of what we sold; the remaining 30 percent went to replenish the materials. We divided equally what was donated to us. Money from families went to individuals, but the M-19s split it up among ourselves so that no one would be without a peso.

Deborah, one of the guards, was second to Sor Margarita on the yard. She was a single woman with short gray hair in her fifties who practiced an uncommon strictness. She walked the yard in her blue uniform, her hands clasped behind her back, walking very straight, always supervising the prisoners. You could tell right away that she liked women. When Sara or Marta Lucía walked by her, Deborah looked up to the sky, sighed, and hummed in a childlike voice the same tune over and over—"*aquellos ojos verdes/de mirada serenca/dejaron en mi alma*"[5]—because the two muchachas had green and almond-colored eyes. In their presence her strict nature gave way to syrupy swaying, and her commanding voice dropped to a whisper.

5. Those green eyes/that serene gaze/left in my soul … "Aquellos ojos verdes" by Nilo Menéndez and Adolfo Utreras.

The other guard was much younger and worked at Buen Pastor because she had not made the grade as a police officer. Both worked twenty-four-hour shifts, and they had their own room in our yard. The nun slept in a room at the end of a hall. The night guard was almost always from outside the prison and was always a man. Actually, these male guards never had contact with the prisoners except when transferring a difficult prisoner to isolation. The Progreso's twenty-one cells were lined up in two halls. Each one had barely enough space for a cement slab with a single mattress, a night stand, and a wooden chair. A plastic pail under the bed served as a chamberpot. The bars closed with a big lock. The three bathrooms, three showers, and two wash basins were located on an open patio. The visiting room, TV, kitchenette, and dining room were on the second floor. The food came from the general kitchen, or *bongo*.[6] Once in a while we used the kitchenette to warm up food our families sent.

Them

The population in our yard was more or less stable. Only one or two women were released each month. For the most part we had long sentences, and the rest were cases with no foreseeable legal solution. I remember Ofelia and Lucrecia, two women accused of a kidnapping five years earlier. Every now and then it would seem that their trial was finally going to take place, but it never actually did, because the judges accepted millions in bribes from the victims' families.

Lucrecia was a little over thirty and had three children, the youngest born in the prison hospital. She got no early-release benefit for maternity. She supported her husband in good times and bad. You could tell she was as good as the bread she kneaded in the jail's bakery. She got up at four in the morning and came back to the yard at around six-thirty in the afternoon, exhausted and covered with flour. She talked lovingly about her husband, who was serving time in Bellavista. They had to write in secret after the nuns found out they had not been married by the Church. Once a month Lucre fixed herself up with painstaking care to go to the visit with her kids. That day we saw her with no flour on her rosy cheeks but only a radiant smile. After the visit she closed herself up in her cell to cry. We heard the weeping well into the night.

6. A kitchen, kitchen patrol, food, or the large pot in which the food is cooked, depending on the context.

Ofelia was young and full of life and would not accept her fate. She had barely tasted the pleasures of a comfortable life with a lawyer fifteen years her senior who had decided to dedicate himself to a business more lucrative than litigation: kidnapping. He set up the company and started to run it successfully. He said the kidnappings were political to throw the authorities off his trail. Everything was going well until one day a narc turned them in and their luck ran out. The police came in shooting and then asked who was who. They arrested Ofelia in spite of the fact that she wasn't yet eighteen, and her daughter was left as the only heir to a fortune that others ended up enjoying. Ofelia knew that her trial would be postponed until the Jewish kidnap victim got tired of bribing the judge.

Sara had been in prison for four years and had quite a few left to go. She was a farm girl and had never been out of Segovia, in Antioquia. She was as good at work as she was passionate for men, until the day she fell in love with one. When she told her story, her almond-shaped green eyes still shone with anger. Someone had told her that he had a girlfriend, so one Sunday she went into town. She thought about the baby she was expecting, measured her love, and decided to fight it out with the other woman. She fortified her courage with some *guaros*,[7] went into the bar, looked at the woman who was pointed out to her, and walked defiantly over to her. It was as if the other one had been waiting for her, for she unstopped a bottle and poured it over her. Sara's knife was first, but each woman impaled her enemy's belly. She watched her rival fall in the glow of red neon light. Only then did she realize that her rival was pregnant too, and then she fainted from loss of blood. She lost the baby in the Segovia jail and never saw her man again. Her trial and sentence were mere formalities. She is still paying for her crime, but she has no regrets. She was an angry cat with enough courage to bear anything and everything.

Beatriz Villa turned eighteen during her trial. A tiny woman, but with strength that didn't fit in her clothes, Beatra was the second of six living children of don Nino, a huge gordo, a *paisa de raca mandaca*.[8] He was a troublemaker who lived off selling anything that would get him money to support his family and keep up his supply of guaro. Beatriz went everywhere with him. She said one of her brothers was good for nothing, another had decided to go to school, and the others were little, so she answered for the old man when he went out drinking. One day, at a cockfight, a guy picked

7. Liquor in general, often more specifically *aguardiente*, or cane spirits.
8. A paisa through and through, to the core.

a fight with don Nino. When he and his pals left the fight, Beatriz was sure they were waiting outside to attack her father, so she left before he did. When one of the men threatened her father, her knife was already in hand, and she attacked him from behind, stabbing him in the neck.

For this she was sentenced to ten years. Every Saturday Nino visited her, and every Thursday a package arrived from home. Beatra was rebellious and forthright and knew nothing of reverence to the nuns or the guards. But she knew about solidarity and loyalty. She had three great loves in her life: her father, her good brother, who, according to her was like us in his mania for the news, and her *feíto* (little ugly one)—that's what she called her black *cumbambón* with crossed eyes,[9] the boyfriend who stood by her the whole time she was in the slammer. Her family became ours. Nino visited us on Saturdays because it made him sad that we were like gringas who had no visitors.

The Widow Gaviria, Alba was her name, was one of the women in the Progreso we liked the most. She was a tall blond with a beautiful face and an elegant carriage. She hid the gap of a missing tooth with a Mona Lisa smile. She acted shy, humble, and innocent, but her temperament often made her burst into laughter, shouts, or insults. Few had the chance to hear her brazen sex stories or see her weakness for money. She was one of those women who is on either God's side or the Devil's, but with us she was great fun.

Raised in a traditional Antioquian family who went to Sunday mass and held collective readings of *El Colombiano*[10] at breakfast, Alba studied under nuns at La Presentación School. As a girl she devoured Corín Tellado's novels and harbored the dreams of every teenage girl—to marry a rich man. Her father made a paltry salary as a bank guard salary, and her mother never stopped praying to San Antonio for good husbands for her four daughters.

At that time people in Medellín could become rich instantly, and a few muchachos from the neighborhood would show up in a new car, with a gold chain or an expensive watch, becoming the economic support and the pride of his family and the neighborhood. No wonder that Doña Susana requested a mass for her patron saint when she found out that Alba was going out with Pacho, a mechanic in whom she saw great promise. The señora pretended not to notice when her daughter started coming home later and later, and she stopped her husband from interfering as well. The good señora looked at the gifts this muchacho gave his girlfriend and her family and judged that his intentions were good.

9. A person with a jutting jaw, like a pelican's or a boxer's.
10. A local newspaper circulating in Antioquia, especially in Medellín.

The day Alba went to live with Pacho, her mother ignored the Church's commandment about marriage, and not one critique was allowed in her home. As Alba carried out her last suitcase, her mamá told her, "Sometimes a man needs a child to get married." Alba gave her vieja a kiss and left.

At first everything went well. It wasn't long before Alba became pregnant. Meanwhile, she learned the ins and outs of her husband's business and helped him out little by little until she became indispensible. When she got pregnant for the second time, one tear was enough to convince Pacho of the need to get married.

To help her family financially, Alba made use of some tricks.

"I manipulated him in bed because I have a natural advantage that few women possess. It's the ability to contract my vagina, and I knew that this drove him wild. So while he made love to me, I'd put my hand under the pillow where he kept his wallet and take out some dollars for my mamá. He never found me out," she told us as she let escape a tiny giggle while she covered her mouth with her hand.

There were several versions of the story of her arrest. She worked with the IV Army Brigade in the military books section and they had caught her in some mafia deal. Or when she filed the real estate taxes they found discrepancies between the true and the declared value. Or she couldn't explain where a considerable amount of money in her bank account came from. Pacho was never caught and never was seen in the prison.

Every week Alba received a visit from her mother or her sisters, and they doubled over with laughter when they told of how, whenever anyone asked about Alba, they said she was on vacation in Miami.

A policewoman shared the yard with us. She had been in the control and vigilance corps of the metropolitan police. Her girlhood dream was to become one of Charlie's Angels. One day she dyed her hair platinum blond, like the TV detective, and filed an application for acceptance to the police force. She worked there for years, learning the tricks that allowed her to earn extra money, until she was arrested for extorting someone who "had connections higher up." She was the yard narc, always spying to find out something that would interest the nuns. She had no friends among the old *caneras* (prisoners), and she took advantage of the newcomers to make friends until they got to know her and avoided her.

We shared the daily prison routine with all of these women and discovered new worlds through our acquaintance with them. We learned from them. But our strongest connections were naturally forged among the politically involved.

Us

The group identity of the political prisoners trumped the differences between us when it came to confronting the rest of the prisoners or the nuns. This group identity strengthened us and generated the affections and solidarities characteristic of all groups confronting a hostile environment. I remember all of them with special tenderness, but I will tell you only of the ones I was closest to, the ones who were with me in the same corral, the Progreso yard.

Susana looked as if she had just stepped out of an almanac from the thirties. Everything about her had the sepia tone of old photos. Tall and slender, with huge eyes, shoulder-length hair, and gestures like Greta Garbo, she had caused quite a commotion among the soldiers but, inflexible in her convictions, she rarely spoke to them. Even her interrogator showed her particular reverence. Not even in the worst moments did you ever hear a complaint from her. On the contrary, in the Mira, when we were isolated, when fear and solitude combined to make us believe we were lost, I knew she was there because she sang boleros to encourage herself, and that gave me an unusual calm.

Susana had studied sociology at the Nacional in Bogotá, but her vocation was theater. I met her there in one of those crossings of clandestine life. She maintained her theatrical ability in prison and she could make us laugh till we burst or scare us when she lost her temper, because when she was furious she was a like a wild storm. Her face could be deeply expressive or it could turn to stone. Without a doubt her gifts in acting helped her to maintain an implacable or imperturbable exterior when she wanted to. Watching her walk around the yard was like watching Ingrid Bergman in *Joan of Arc*. The lesbians liked her beauty and several fell in love with her silently and discreetly.

We called Marta "Angel Hair" because her thick, jet-black hair wouldn't stay in place without a hair dryer. Fixing it so that it wouldn't look like a hedgehog became one of the tasks she assumed with the same rigor she brought to everything. She had studied chemical engineering at the Nacional, and during her time in the military she had kept up her reputation as a good girl. She walked slowly, and the weight of her body helped us recognize her steps by the vibrations they made. When she lowered her head and blinked slowly, we knew she was about to utter a balanced, impartial opinion like a chemical engineer, but she had a sense of humor and would often follow these pronouncements with a long peal of laughter.

Marta was reserved; her passion only came to light in confrontations with the nuns and guards. To control the anger she felt for them, she spent long days exercising, doing yoga and breathing exercises, and maintaining a vegetarian diet. Most days she wore a sweatshirt and tennies, changing into a skirt only on visiting day, when she had to wear a uniform.

Silvia was with us until her daughter, Libertad, was born. She was no fragile muchacha, but her pregnancy made all of us protect her. Still, behind her youth and sweet manner was a strong personality. The daughter of a man who owned a medium-sized coffee plantation, she studied her first semester of law in the Universidad Externado of Colombia and still lived at home with her brothers and sisters when she was invited to train as a guerrillera. The soldiers interrogated her insistently, perhaps trying to take advantage of her age, but all they found was the strength of her convictions.

Susana, Marta, Silvia, and I were the four from the Mira, but there were other Eme compañeras with us temporarily who were linked to the kidnapping of Marta Nieves Ochoa, whom the MAS wanted to exchange for Elvecio.

Beatriz Rivera was with us the longest. She was twenty-one and had the face of a schoolgirl and the vocabulary of an arriera. She was all noise, activity, and laughter. Her dark braid danced wherever she went. The military and the MAS arrested her while searching her house for Marta Nieves Ochoa. Those inside—her compañero el Mono Candelo, another muchacho, and Beatriz—responded with bullets. It was her job to cover the attempted withdrawal from the yard; when the ammunition was gone, the soldiers surrounded her. She didn't know it then, but they had killed the others.

Beatriz endured torture without a word. It was not until ten days later that the judge in the investigation told her that her comrades were dead. Beatriz thought about killing herself, but she opened her eyes and decided to remain strong and live for el Mono and herself both. The soldiers interpreted her strength during the interrogation as harshness and a thirst for vengeance, but nothing was further from the truth. She was motivated by hope and perseverance, and a sort of faith in life against all odds. She mourned the death of her first love in silence. When she heard songs by Alberto Cortés her look darkened, as if she were entirely eclipsed. Her pain penetrated my soul. I loved her in a special way. She wanted to learn and became my student. I felt that my operational experience was in the best hands.

Another Beatriz, whose last name was Betancur, had been a student at the Universidad de Antioquia and doubled as our hostess when we got to the Progreso. She had been there for a year, accused of being part of the ELN. She was a total paisa; everything about her was exhuberant—her happiness, her laughter, her anger, and her voice. She had a blasting voice that delighted everyone when she sang. She told us the stories of her life to keep herself busy, because if she didn't she was overcome by a melancholy love. On the days when secret letters from her compañero, a prisoner in Bellavista, got through, she blossomed. When we were together she supported us generously with all her organizational infrastructure and the contacts she maintained from prison with the Universidad. Beatriz possessed limitless solidarity.

Fabiola, who studied chemistry at the Universidad de Antioquia, was moved to our yard as punishment for insulting a nun in the Laboral, where she had been kept for more than a year. She was arrested because the police had searched her house and found dynamite. She belonged to an anarchist group called the Brigadas Rojas and placed special importance on explosives in the struggle against the system. The anarchist was tempermental, and the nuns drove her nuts. She had only to feel them close to prepare herself for the attack. She couldn't let them pass by without tossing out some insult, which we all thought was funny. But she didn't laugh; her anger was nestled deep inside and eventually even gave her an ulcer. With us, however, she expressed her joy for living, overflowing with happiness and tenderness. Her love, Juancho, compañero in life and fortune, peered through her eyes on nostalgic afternoons.

Tínez, as Fabiola called her father, supported her unconditionally since he knew of the torture she had endured silently. It didn't matter if she was right or wrong, she had stood up for what she believed in, and that was enough for him. She and her sister, born in a free union of her father with a woman who was mentally ill, were brought up by Tínez's legal wife with more love than if they had been born of her womb.

Fabiola learned to play the guitar in prison. She mistook the direction of the notes in all the songs, but she didn't stop trying new rhythms. You could say that she only enjoyed the company of her compañeras. The constant, petty asphyxiation of spirit the nuns subjected us to was intolerable for her. When she reached her limit she would weep, shaking her curly head while uttering all the bad words that she could think of.

Soeli was accused of belonging to the EPL and, though she never denied it, she lived as much apart from others as she could. She spoke little but supported us in all we did, even if it got her in hot water. She dealt with the nuns and guards only when forced to, preferring to ignore them.

Marta Lucía and Angela, the teen cousins recently graduated from high school, belonged to the same EPL commando unit, as did their boyfriends. They were arrested days before the 1981 civil strike with molotov cocktails and *niples*.[11] Marta Lucía had an innocent face and the exotic beauty of a

---

11. Plastic tubes used to carry water to houses, cut and filled with dynamite and then lit with matches or chemicals.

cat. Angela had a precocious seriousness and a clear intelligence. Since she was the elder, the responsibility for her cousin rested on her. The young ones in our group kept joy alive for the group, and they did their one year of time without too much anguish. This experience even gave them a certain halo of heroism.

Others also spent time with us in the same yard, among them Denisse, a morenita who looked like a secretary, accused of being in the FARC, and Olga, Marta Correa, and Clara, of the M-19, linked to Marta Nieves Ochoa's kidnapping. We were the political prisoners on the Progreso yard, the sisters, the compañeras, the friends.

The Others

The nuns were a group unto themselves, of course. Sor Blanca Inés Velásquez personified the angel of vengeance; God and society punished violators by her hand. Big and imposing, she walked with a haughtiness that was unusual in a nun. She had come to be prison director not only because of her professional ability and her firm principles of authority but also because she belonged to one of the big-money Medellín families. She was about thirty-six years old and she completely fulfilled her mission as the whip of the sinners, convinced that as she punished bodies she purified the soul. We prisoners called her la Paloma because of her bleached white habit and the way her head moved, something between startled and alert. Everyone was afraid of her, and she liked it that way.

The male and female guards didn't dare try to profit from the needs of the detained, as in other jails where everything had its price—changing yards or cells, moving to other places in the jail, or extra visits—and where you could get anything: drugs, alcohol, weapons, porn magazines, cards, dice, or just about anything else. They couldn't be bribed, either; the nuns were very strict about that. Just as the guards watched us, the nuns watched them. The guards who came to the Buen Pastor were screwed, because they had to live off their salaries alone.

Blanca Inés was, in a way, a sacred figure, because she had legal and religious authority. People with those otherworldly connections had a double power, one given by law and one that came from God. The punishment inflicted by the nuns likewise had the double purpose of enforcing social sanctions and atoning for sin. Once the sentence was filled, we had supposedly paid our debt to society and taken steps toward the salvation of our souls. Such excess found no great resistance in such a Catholic environment as Antioquia.

We were the only ones who thought a prison run by nuns was cruel. We politicals didn't accept the nuns' religious authority, we didn't render them homage, and we never let our impotence seem evident. Without ever losing sight of the fact that we were before the penal director, we fought face to face.

After our first denunciations of the system during the monthly visits of the judges, Sor Blanca Inés decided it was better to avoid exhausting confrontations. She couldn't bear our public questioning of the arbitrary nature of the prison rules, or that we doubted her respect for human rights; still less could she abide our questioning of her Christian practice in daily life. Several times our complaints made her lose control, but we finally learned to live together, if not peacefully then at least with clear rules.

Once this truce of sorts had been established, we began to negotiate such things as getting newspapers and accepting the censure the director herself enforced over political news, violence, and sex. When newpapers made it to our yard, we took turns reading them, cursing when we turned a page and found a window the size of our heads. We were also able to convince her of the prestige that would accrue to the institution if she linked a group of prisoners to the Distance University at the Universidad de Antioquia. When we politicals were the only ones to register for classes, she had two guards register as well to guarantee that she was kept informed of what went on.

When Elvecio was caught and our plan to escape from the church was discovered, the director wouldn't let us attend mass, but we threatened to write to the bishop and even the pope and accuse her of denying us the spiritual consolation to which we had a right as Christians. Within a few days, she allowed us to return. The politicals from all the yards organized a negotiating committee. Merceditas, Elizabeth, Susana, and I were part of the diplomatic delegation that talked with the director. Little by little, she agreed to authorize fundamental things to which we had a right, things like appointments with the prison psychiatrist. She also agreed to consider requests for medical exams with specialists outside the jail and to give us our mail.

Sor María Margarita, who was in charge of the Progreso yard, was a tiny, dry woman with an invariably stern face and a great ignorance about everything. She didn't need much education for her job, either. At around age fifty she remained convinced that a guerrillera was the devil without a tail. To make matters worse for us, at about that time, in the shadow of some protest over a hike in bus fares, a group of hooded people set fire to a car and two nuns burned to death. This macabre incident, which the media attributed to the ELN, motivated Sor Margarita's sermons. Every morning she woke us up by offering the day to Jesus Christ, so that by his Holy Mother's pain he would soften these atheist and impious souls that filled our homeland with violence and blood, killing soldiers and nuns. Our Father who art in heaven...

We knew that if it were up to her, Sor Margarita would accuse the guerrilleras of Christ's crucifixion. The nun acted by an elementary logic whereby her mission was to save our souls at any price. The prison was the proper instrument for inflicting the saving punishment.

We did not demonstrate remorse; on the contrary, we affirmed our status as rebels, and this disconcerted her a great deal. She considered us demonic elements and was correspondingly aggressive. If we were happy and whistled, she told us to be quiet; if we sang in the shower, she called us to order. She prohibited the song with the lyrics *"como un pájaro libre... de libre vuelo... así te quiero."*[12] If we listened to the radio with earphones, she followed us to find out what we were listening to. She snatched our personal notebooks away from us to look them over. She wouldn't let us drink coffee, laugh out loud, or run in the halls—the list goes on and on.

Sor Margarita blamed us for everything. One day the baby Jesus whom Saint Anthony was holding was blindfolded. Sor Margarita called for us and furiously accused us of witchcraft, of atheism, of mocking religion and a dozen other offenses. We were stunned; we had no idea what was going on. When she ended her diatribe, another one of the yard nuns explained with veritable anguish that she had blindfolded the baby because that was how Saint Anthony had helped her find what she had lost. The nun didn't know what to say and merely turned on her heels, grumbling. Margarita, in her immense ignorance and simplicity of spirit, became an executioner, poor thing, instead of consecrating her sisterhood to prayer.

The most notorious nuns were those in charge of the yards: Irene in the Recepción, Raquel in the Cultural, Carmen in the Laboral, Inés in the Familiar, and Teresa in the Superación. We did not feel the presence of the ones in other services; they lived in the kitchen, the bakery, or administration. When a woman opts for the convent there are several possibilities: she can be a teacher, a nurse, a caretaker of the elderly or of orphans, a gardener, or a seamstress, or she can go into seclusion to pray. But the task of straightening paths with whip in hand and closed up in the prison is the worst of all. For that task you needed a good dose of perversion.

The rigor of the nuns in budget management and the concentration of all authority in the director, from whose watchful eye nothing escaped, made

12. Like a free bird/in flight/that's how I want you. "Como un pájaro libre," by Adela Gleijer and Diana Reches, recorded by Mercedes Sosa, Polygram (1982). The verb *querer* can mean both "to want" and "to love" in Spanish.

Medellín's Buen Pastor a prison that was free of the plundering for survival so common in other places. With the nuns we had good food, we were clean, there was a garden for plants and flowers, drugs were very controlled, lesbianism was masked. Apparently everything went along well. They called the prisoners "boarders," the prison "boarding school," and the yards "classes," as if by the magic of words we would suddenly find ourselves in an educational institution, receiving useful knowledge.

Their method of dominating our will was subtle. Violations of human rights were not as evident with them as with the soldiers; their violence was muted, directed at the spirit, at conquering rebellion, at subduing us bit by bit, at wearing away our strength. Thus they tried to deny us our essential identity as political offenders. They prohibited mention of our organizations, their abbreviations, symbols, and songs of freedom. They limited reading, supervised all studies, read our personal notes, prohibited certain radio programs, limited our visits, kept our letters. They isolated us. They also did us constant violence when they punished us for no reason, denied us fundamental rights like going to the bathroom, pregnancy leave, visits from lawyers, and medical attention.

There were no serious fights; none of us politicals went to isolation. The nuns concentrated their efforts on making the little pleasures of daily life difficult by reminding us that we were in prison and by not allowing us to be ourselves, by slowly domesticating us. This constant campaign to wear us down was exhausting.

Some afternoons you could hear the monologues shouted from the punishment cells in our yard:

"Let me out of here so I can kill that bitch narc who turned me in!"

"Get me out ... this is killing me ... get me out!!"

"You're all going to pay! You'll see how you'll pay, you pack of *gonorreas*[13] ... I'll make you all pay with pleasure ... I'll run you over!"

"I'm not afraid of you! Cowards! Let me out ... I want to see that bitch Paloma. I'm not afraid of her!"

"I've been in here for a month ... you want to kill me in this hole!"

And they banged on the iron door until they were spent. Then came the sobs. I hung on their words until their voices grew hoarse; I felt their shouts as an expression of the same thing that burned inside me: rage and impotence. But my dignity kept me from unrestrained outbursts. Sometimes I wondered if it was worth it to keep it all inside. The explosion of words

13. Disgusting people, plagues.

had to be a relief. Then I closed my eyes and I told the others in my heart, "Yell, yell louder! Because you can! Yell for me!"

There is a moment when you reach the limits of your endurance, and then you lunge with all the rage pent up inside you against whatever is in your path. Even if you know it's suicide, it's your last act of freedom. I finally understood this in prison.

Resistance

Our obsession with conspiring gave us access to poems by Nazim Hikmet and books like Julius Fucik's *Notes from the Gallows*, and other prohibited texts. We hid them inside the covers of the books we were allowed to have. We also hid letters from our compañeros in La Picota and elsewhere in odd places—in a Quaker Oats jar, wrapped in plastic and stuck inside the cell toilet tank or under the toilet bowl. More than once the words were blurred and ran together, but we had memorized them anyway.

We laid out survival strategies and ways to achieve the greatest freedom among ourselves. When we were able to attend appointments with the prison psychiatrist, we prepared our scripts in advance. Fabiola would concentrate on the aggression Sor Margarita ignited in her with the prayers she directed against us, as if we were the devil. Marta would talk about the desire to kill born of so much isolation, as if we were lepers. I would again and again state that I couldn't bear the thirty-nine bars on the yard, that I was on the verge of going crazy seeing so many walls and bars. But the psychiatrist was a Freudian: he talked to Fabiola and me about Oedipus and to Marta about the castration complex.

We worked to get closer to the Buen Pastor priest, who was Basque. I took the lead on this because the other compañeras didn't know how to use their confessions to block the nuns. I think deep down they were afraid of abusing the sacred, because the priest only asked us to confess and repent. It wasn't easy for me, either, but I knew more about nuns and priests than the others. It was not in vain that I had studied with the Franciscan nuns since the second grade. So I went to confess with the mindset that I was going to an interrogation. I asked the priest to ask me things, because I had forgotten the procedures. I tried not to lie; I only told half-truths that wouldn't hurt anyone, including myself. The odd thing is that I wasn't sorry, because this was the key to a rapprochement. From then on it was easy to talk to the chaplain, even for the other compañeras.

I confessed every so often, especially when I wanted the priest to know about Sor Margarita's harassment. My sins were against her; she provoked them. And this had an effect. Margarita softened up a bit because of the chaplain's influence. At that stage I had a spiritual awakening, not with the priest but with the idea of God. I liked to feel that someone was looking out for me.

Little by little, living together became less tense: we were allowed an hour a day in the sun on the basketball court, where we could also take a bath in the tub, two hours a week in the library, and permission to attend whatever class was given on first aid, sewing, or baking, generally taught by the SENA.[14]

On the court I exercised till I was exhausted. Physical exhaustion meant gratification for the muscular movement that meant life, and I clung to any feeling that affirmed life. Lying with my face to the sun, an open horizon with the blue sky above or a tree branch gaining ground against the wall; these things enabled me to take flight in my imagination. To fly above the bars, dreaming of other spaces in the company of the people I loved, to seek that other world in movement that was beyond imprisonment.

I invented many things to fight against falling apart behind the prison walls. When I listened to music I closed my eyes and imagined I was dancing in the air. Dance is freedom. With a little effort I could also see the moon from my cell or the yard, and then I felt that life was new. The bars didn't stop me from dreaming, or breathing, much less from remembering. These things cannot be caged by bars.

At night and on Sunday afternoons during the required siesta, I began to reconstruct the most beautiful moments of my life, the places and the people who endured in my memory. Quietly, in a corner, I joined fragments together until I achieved the clarity of memory, and in this tiny square place I reproduced yesterday with the same voices, the words, and the warmth until I was almost there again. My entire body possessed the imprints of love and my mind kept images intact, as if I were blind. I was able to live past joys. Returning to the present, however, was painful. I could remember warmth, but all I had was cold solitude. Still, the pain of longing also lets us know we're alive. Many a time I did not know what to do with the love that welled

14. El SENA: Servicio Nacional de Aprendizaje (National Training Service), a technical vocational school.

up inside me, my body ripe with desire, and I felt rage crash through my skin
and my bones in endless sobs. Feeling! Feeling was being alive!

Happy is this body that misses you
to still feel life
slowly coursing through
the tiny tunnels that are my veins
                              —Buen Pastor, Medellín, March 1982

The worst punishment for all of us was to be deprived of visitors, because
the sanction also affected our relatives, who had to spend hours waiting in
line, only to be told that their daughter or sister or wife or mother had lost
the right to a visit because of bad behavior.

Men and women had to visit on different days—men on Saturdays at
noon, and women all day on Sundays, so they could "attend to" their
compañeros. This rule clearly favors men. In women's prisons there was
less time on Saturday to be with their boyfriends or husbands, and there
was no way to be intimate. This was to prevent pregnancies the nuns feared
could lead to early release. But finally the nuns adjusted the penitentiary
rules. Saturday at noon both men and women could visit prisoners for up to
four hours, though of course we were watched over by nuns and guards.

Saturdays broke the routine. It was a rest for those of us who didn't have
visitors. In the morning we worked as usual, and lunch, as always, was served
at noon. But from then on the muchachas got ready to receive their visits.
The yard seemed smaller from the continuous comings and goings of women
lending and borrowing mascara and lipstick, taking turns with eye shadow,
undoing paper curlers amid cries of pain and hurried hands. We were still
required to wear our uniforms, but everyone tried to wear some accessory
that would make her uniform more beautiful.

"Does this look okay around my waist?"

"Do these earrings go with the color of the blouse?"

"Help me fix my hair."

"Lend me your shoes."

One hour of primping to about three of romping with the family. The
door of the prison opened at one o'clock, but it could take an hour to
get through the search and make it to the yard. At five the whistle blew,
announcing the end of visiting hours.

Our mothers and a few of our sisters made the effort to travel from
Bogotá, Pasto, Armenia, or Ibagué to spend three hours with us every two or

three months. Having them with us was marvelous, but we never imagined how hard it was for them to subject themselves to the rigors of the search. They had to take off their underwear and show their vaginas to the curious guard, who used a kerchief to search their private parts for drugs and then handled their breasts. This is a frightful degradation, especially for older women. Sometimes by the time they got to the visit they were in tears from the harshness of the search. Only love could spur them on to risk visiting us again.

The embraces when we met erased any bad memories. These relatives were a bridge with the outside world that we dreamed about, the one we had already started to forget. The mothers came with love that had been bottled up inside them for months, fresh news, requests, greetings from everyone, and a growing solidarity with us in our plight. From the first visit they became everyone's mother, everyone's sisters. With them we invented the chain of affection, and the luck that accompanied us from then on blossomed.

After their visits a double feeling lingered: we were comforted by their affection but pained by their anguish. They had no choice but to leave us again and await the possible news of our deaths in the papers or on the radio, or hear about our capture, pray for our strength, and get the temporary consolation of seeing us. From this common pain, this mutual awareness among mothers, associations among families and solidarity groups were born, and they stayed with us for as long as we were there.

When a prisoner had no visitors, she was locked up in her cell. To avoid this we volunteered for activities so we could see people. We offered to help the missions by selling empanadas during visiting hours; Lucrecia made them in the bakery and we paid for the ingredients, while the money we made went to the nuns. That way we could chat with some people. Margarita and Deborah never took their eyes off us, and after about three weeks they decided to sell the empanadas themselves. So we went back to spending Saturdays locked up reading or writing letters that never reached their destination.

During the visits we were euphoric, in spite of how little one could be intimate in that public interview. When a boyfriend or common-law husband was able to sneak in by saying he was related in some way, his expressions of affection had to be limited to gazes and half words that got tangled up in conversations with other relatives, under the jealous watch of the old maid Sor Margarita. With luck and a little ingenuity, they got in a tight hug under the stairs, or a quick kiss as they went through the door.

The visits did not always bring good news about relatives, loves, and friends. Sometimes our families forgot to tell the standard lie: "The lawyer says that everything is coming along well in the case, you'll be out soon."

Sometimes their answers to our questions failed to conceal the waning interest or the unfaithfulness of boyfriends and husbands, the problems that plague every family, including sometimes a death: after such visits the muchachas closed themselves up in their cells alone with their torrent of tears.

I'll never forget the day Ramiro brought my son Juan, who was eight, to visit me. He needed my permission to go out of the country and wanted the child to say good-bye. He was there for an hour, and I made an effort to show that the situation wasn't difficult, that I was doing fine. I hugged him, aware of the fact that I wouldn't see him for years, and I smiled and waved bye to him until he was out of sight. Then I turned on my heel and fell completely apart. I walked down the hall but I couldn't see, wracked by silent, uncontrollable sobs; it was the first time I had cried in a long time. Sor Blanca Inés caught up with me and put her hand on my shoulder; at that moment I was grateful for her contact, my pain was so great. I got to the yard and sat down with my head between my legs. The compañeras surrounded me in silence and stayed by me until my tears were spent. Sobbing in prison is like a flood; when it happens you cannot contain it.

Life is like a seesaw seeking balance, on one side sadness, the other, joy. Around 28 December 1981, we held a parade with costumes we made with what we had on hand. Everyone took part enthusiastically and creatively in the preparations. We laid our hands on anything we could find: clothes, paper, sheets, makeup, and we tried to preserve the originality of every character. Within three hours we were dressed up and the parade began. Alba wore stark black, stuck a photo of Pacho in her lapel, covered her head with a black shawl, and wept her widowhood in the halls. We called her Widow Gaviria, because we were sure that Pacho, the mafioso, had disappeared from her life. Marta dressed up like Bateman as he looked at the first interview he gave after the robbery of the weapons from El Cantón, with an afro and a hairdryer in her hand.

Beatriz Betancur dressed up like a prostitute, wearing a short skirt with a slit up the side, black stockings, and a red rose behind her ear. The cousins dressed up like little girls, with pyjamas and pacifiers. Sara was a *llanera*.[15] The policewoman became a pirate, and Beatriz Rivera an arriera. Susana was a vampire and I was an Arab, covered up with a sheet that showed only my eyes. There were cats, knitting grandmas, weird bugs, and other curiosities. Then we danced until dinnertime.

We dressed up for New Year's with the idea of being the way we wanted 1982 to be. We politicals had the dark idea of playing with the changes in

15. A woman born and raised in the *llanos*, the plains.

our looks that we had relied on so heavily during our clandestine lives. I had a short afro, a long dress, and high heels. Susana pulled her hair back in a bun and wore a tight skirt and high heels. Marta put on makeup and a skirt. The cousins looked like a couple of princesses, Beatriz Rivera like a doctor, with her glasses and her tailored suit. What is sure is that in prison there are tons of clothes: clothes left behind by the ones who get out and clothes the *damas grises*[16] or other volunteers leave for the inmates.

We went to evening mass and had the effect we had hoped for. Sor Blanca Inés, the director, couldn't take her eyes off us. She paid no attention to the liturgy, and when we left she came directly to our yard and made no pretense of hiding her alarm. We pretended not to notice and began the party with music, empanadas, and Coke. She left for a minute and came back to spend the rest of the night with us. At midnight we wished each other Happy New Year and were sent to bed. Blanca Inés breathed a sigh of relief when she saw us all locked in our cells. The next day we learned that the nuns had declared the prison in a state of emergency and called for a police patrol. She thought we were going to attempt an escape.

It became a tradition to celebrate our birthdays with a serenade on the evening before. The night before mine, when I was in my cell and the lights were out, I heard guitars being tuned on the second floor. I wasn't in the mood for celebrations just then, and I decided to surprise them with a joke. I got my inspiration from an Agatha Christie novel I was reading and decided to pretend I was dead. I wore a white nightgown, covered my face with powder to make me look pale, and made some dark circles under my eyes with a black pencil, giving me a touch of the macabre. I put a sheet on the floor, a pillow under my head, and lit two candles on either side of the headboard. On the bars of the cell I hung a sign saying, "Let the dead rest in peace."

I heard my prison mates come down the stairs to surprise me in the dark with the serenade. Deborah, the guard, was with them. They approached the bars. You could hear a scream of terror down the halls. I held in my laughter. Deborah was the most scared; she sprinkled blessings over me and crossed herself, transfigured from fear. The Widow Gaviria couldn't stop screaming. The cousins told me to stop fooling around. The one who brought me back to reality was Beatriz Rivera. She was hanging on to a bar crying, saying over and over, "Don't do this to me, Juana. Don't die."

It took a minute for me to understand such suffering. Beatra had lost her compañero during the raid when she was arrested, and she still hadn't

16. "The Gray Ladies," a Catholic charity organization made up of high-society ladies.

gotten over that loss. For her it wasn't a joke but like sticking my finger in her wound. I jumped up and tried to make her laugh, but she just kept on crying. Later she finally looked at me and wiped her tears with the back of her hand, smiled through her tears, and started to cuss me out. The serenade had begun.

We did anything we could to shake off the monotony. They were running an English series on TV on Sunday afternoons called "Captain Poldark." It was the story of a handsome Englishman in a peaceful agrarian society in the 1800s. The happy captain, a social reformer, reached our souls; he won an audience so faithful that there were acts of insubordination when the TV on our yard went out and we were going to miss that week's episode. We threatened to destroy the place if they didn't move us to another yard to see that show. Sor Margarita agreed reluctantly. With Captain Poldark we indulged our repressed libido; each of us imagined the end of his next adventure, pretending we were his costars.

During the talks in front of the TV, I learned to flirt and tease men. The other women were full of sexual comments about every man who appeared on the screen. I wasn't used to women showing their desire for a man openly and directly; at first it embarassed me a little, but then I found their remarks very funny. In spite of the camphor in the aguapanela, our bodies didn't stop producing hormones. Why shouldn't we show these emotions? It was a healthy, playful exercise and it was fun, a chorus of erotic humor.

A few of us also went a little way down the spiritual path. We read Lobsand Rampa, the Tibetan lama, and we were very impressed by his experience. It occurred to me to practice some exercises in concentration described by the master to achieve astral journeys. One night, while I was relaxing before starting my exercises, I heard a moan from Susana's cell next door. I sharpened my ear and heard another.

"Susana ... Susana ... what's going on?"

Surprised, she answered me, "Nothing. I'm saying a mantra to go on an astral journey," and she giggled so much it ended the concentration of anyone else who was trying to do the same.

We failed in this attempt at escape. Marta was afraid that if she succeeded in leaving her body she might not be able to come back. I fell asleep. Susana, too, slipped easily from deep breathing into snoring. The rest made fun of our Tibetan practices.

We tried to alleviate the boredom by playing the ouija board as well. One night during study hour we got a table ready by drawing the ABCs on it and getting a light glass to put our fingers in while we called the spirits. The idea was that the spirits would communicate by moving the glass toward the letters to answer our questions. Marta and I were the mediums and we began the session with great concentration. When the glass moved, we thought the spirit had come and we asked him to present himself.

"Who is here with us tonight? Identify yourself."

"Tell us, who are you?"

Suddenly we heard a thick voice that made our hair stand on end:

"It's me, Pedro Rodríguez, ID number 2-8-5-3-2-4-9, from Medellín." It turned out to be Susana, who had hidden nearby in order to make fun of us.

These pastimes, the classes on whatever the nuns could think up, and the visits from the catechists who made us hold hands and sing rounds, were welcome distractions. I had never before done so many useless activities, but they were a way to have contact with people from the outside and to preserve our sense of the dimensions of the world. They were happy moments, in spite of everything, respites from the prohibitions, impediments, and punishments.

Signs and Devotions

In the slammer you look for signs of liberty everywhere. If you find a scorpion, you keep it in a glass jar until it dies for someone's freedom. If a bird flies into a closed place, it also foretells freedom. When we were taken before the judges, we put saliva behind our ears for good luck. And once you finally got out, you never wore the clothes you'd worn in prison; they were sullied. Signs of bad luck made us cringe. A black butterfly announces death. Breaking a mirror is the harbinger of something awful.

In prison people professed really weird devotions, such as the Lord of Good Hope or the Just Judge, protector of those pursued by justice. The prayer goes like this:

Worship the Just Judge. My dear Jesus, have mercy on me. The Just Judge watches over me and defends me from all my enemies and misfortunes; it is time, come to my defense, Lord let my enemies have eyes that do not see me, let them have mouths that do not talk to me, let them have hands that do not catch me, let them have feet that do not follow me.

Lord, let my courage make me like John and Saint Paul and for my deeds I may go free wherever I like. Be a tiger, be a lion, be a man, be a woman, all will come humbled as my Jesus came to the cross on Holy Friday. I ask you not to allow me to be a prisoner, or wounded, or pursued by justice.

The image of the Just Judge adorned the walls of many a cell. Dressed in white and green, he sits on a throne. In his hands are a cross and a cane. At his feet kneels a chained man in supplication. In a corner, a disembodied hand holds the scales of justice.

With Saint Judas Tadeo you have to be careful. He's very effective in gaining freedom but charges a very high price. He does his work and then inflicts deep moral suffering, almost always the loss of a loved one. It's best to think twice before asking him to perform a miracle.

Many of the women in the yards prayed to Servant José Gregorio and Domingo the Pious, brother of the prison chaplain, because on their road to sainthood both answered the prayers of those willing to pay the price. The muchachas, in spite of the risk of fire, left candles burning in their cells to illuminate the saints. But almost no one went to daily mass. Only on Sunday did everyone go.

La Virgen de Las Mercedes is the patron saint of prisoners, and her celebration is a great event every 24 September. The night before, a serenade was arranged for us that provoked nostalgia and tears in almost every cell. The next day there was a playful atmosphere to accompany the breakfast spread. We went to the rec room to enjoy a series of plays improvised by local artists. Later, amateur musicians livened up the party by giving us their art in an outburst of generosity. It was never a "great" show. The repertoire invariably contained "El Preso," "La hija del Penal" and "La cama vacía,"[17] songs that brought exclamations of joy from the women.

At the end of the day the troubadours came and performed improvisations about prisons and loves. Suddenly the tone changed, when they performed numbers critical of the guards and the nuns. The scene became chaotic as we all applauded frenetically, but the director threw them right out on their butts.

Then the *mariachis* came in, singing one of the audience's favorite songs, "La Cuchilla."

Si no me querés
te corto la cara
con una cuchilla
de esas de afeitar . . .[18]

17. "The Prisoner," "The Daughter of the Prisoner," and "The Empty Bed."
18. If you don't love me / I'll cut your face/with a razor/one of those shaving razors. "La Cuchilla," by Jaime Rincón Parra, sung by Las Hermanas Calle.

Finally they put on music so we could dance with the mariachis. Couples were formed until we ran out of men. The rest of the women pressed their foreheads against one another and followed the rhythm—physical contact among us was forbidden. I was really happy when one of mariachis asked me to dance, but a few minutes later I understood that of the fifteen musicians dressed as macho mariachis, the one I got was gay!

Then we had raffles led by volunteer señoras. These women were clean and perfumed and had forced smiles and fake postures. We called them "La Feria del Exito" (the fair of success) because the sales from that store ended up in our cells: cheap tchotchkes that inspired the same joy in us as the grab bags. All day long they came and went, with one surprise after the other, watching so we wouldn't mingle too much with the people from the outside.

We went to bed that night tired, happy, and sated. The polite, proper volunteer señoras, the ladies of paisa high society, you could be sure they were sleeping beneath the smiling gazes of their guardian angels, after washing their hands with alcohol, just in case.

A Little Liberty in Prison

One November night Silvia started having contractions and told me so from her cell. I calmed her down and told her that a birth took a long time and that it probably wouldn't come until the next day. Meanwhile, I recommended that she walk and breathe deeply. But she was nervous—being locked up tortured her—and so she decided to ask the guard on duty to let her walk in the hall in front of our cells so we could talk to her and keep her company. The guard wouldn't unlock her cell, and Silvia started to cry until the contractions stopped. She had borne the soldiers' interrogations courageously, contained her horror before the bodies of our dead compañeros, and yet was terrified of having a baby locked up in a cell.

Beginning at dawn we started demanding that our compañera be given the proper attention. Around eight o'clock they moved her to the IV Brigade infirmary. The soldiers wouldn't allow her to be hospitalized for security reasons. Episodes like this fed our rage and impotence, two feelings that wound deeply and leave their trace.

Eight days later Silvia was back; the contractions had stopped and hadn't returned. That very afternoon, while she was talking with us, they began again. We politicals closed ranks; we weren't going to let her be locked up again. When she was almost ready to give birth, they moved her back to the infirmary, and she was back six hours later with her little girl.

We called her Libertad (Liberty). The yard turned into a teeming day-care center; we all functioned in coordination like an army with the mission of taking care of the mother and the *nena*. One washed diapers, another cooked for the mother. I was a nurse, taking care of the umbilical cord, supervising the nursing, and advising the first-time mother. The new task broke the routine and filled us with enthusiasm. When Sor Margarita tried to forbid something, we growled at her like new mothers in the wild.

One month later they gave Silvia a sixty-day suspension of her sentence and put her under house arrest instead of jail. We were very saddened by the departure of her and her little one, but we knew that everything was ready for her asylum in the Mexican Embassy. Libertad came into the world bearing a ticket to freedom for her mamá.

We went back to the routine, happy in the knowledge that at least one of us was safe. We thought of César, Silvia's compañero, and decided to write him more often. Corresponding with our compañeros who were also in jail was a vital exercise. We communicated weekly with our compañeros from the Mira; from the Picota we got letters from M-19 leaders under different names. Fayad wrote me under the name Orlando Sánchez, a compañero from the Valle. I exchanged many messages of love with Alfredo. But Afranio Parra was the most ingenious and constant with his friends; even during the military trial I got his notes and drawings; people with no links to our organization would bring them. He sent paintings, necklaces, stories, poems, and songs that would set my imagination soaring like a bird.

They say friends really get to know each other when times are tough. It is true that affection helped us live. Any little gesture of solidarity was celebrated. But the indifference of those whom we thought would be close was a deep disappointment. Many loves withered during my years in prison because I got tired of waiting for a sign. I understood that people were afraid they'd be accused of insurrection, but there were clandestine ways, indirect ways, to remind us that we had a friend out there.

Sometimes strangers played a fundamental role. Fernando Rendón, one of the poets who snuck in to visit us soon after we arrived, sent me a poem he wrote for me, along with a selection of Nazim Hikmet's work. It was one of my treasures. I couldn't remember Fernando's face, but the words of his poem remained in my memory.

Another person I particularly remember is Eduardo Umaña Mendoza. One day, out of the blue, I was called to the receiving room. Sor Blanca Inés was waiting for me. I recognized the size of her white silhouette even without my glasses.

"María Eugenia, your lawyer is here."

I pretended that I knew him. You never know—someone can come for important reasons. He seemed rather tall to me, and when he smiled two dimples formed in his cheeks. I hadn't seen him before, but his hug instilled trust in me.

"I'm Eduardo Umaña Mendoza."

I recognized his name. He was linked with the most famous defenses of political prisoners. He explained that Vasco had sought him out so he'd take on my appeal. This made me smile. El Maestro was a grouchy old man with his students, but he was also a very important ethical and human influence and reference for me. I never knew what he thought of my academic abilities, but he was always there.

The trial of the political prisoners who had taken over the Dominican Embassy was coming up, and though I had not been called by the court, the soldiers could request my presence at any time.

"I've already read your case file," the lawyer told me. "The statement is good. It leaves no room for accusations like those formulated before. From now on, any addition to the statement, any judicial requirement, we do together."

I told him that a lawyer meant nothing with the military; I had already experienced the farce of the public defender in Ipiales, an air force lieutenant who did virtually nothing to defend me. All he did was sign some papers confirming his presence at my statement. And then I had a defense lawyer who opted to attack the military trial in open court and wound up requesting— shouting even—that we should assume the sentence for rebellion as the highest honor bestowed on a group of patriots. In a strange twist of fate, that lawyer was el Loco, from my theater days as a teen.

"I'll be in touch," he laughed. "I'll see you rather frequently. Here are my numbers in Bogotá."

Then he sat down and began to talk about everything: the amnesty law, the people in the Picota, the Mira case, and how he had structured their appeal. After a four-hour visit he departed, but not before saying good-bye to the director. The nun melted before the gentlemanly manner of my lawyer.

I left the interview and headed toward the infirmary. I felt sick. Maybe because I had smoked a pack and a half of Marlboros with Eduardo, after a year without smoking at all, or perhaps because his visit had been an emotional shock.

I saw Eduardo once a month. He seemed to bring offers of life at fixed rates in his lawyer portfolios. He blew into the prison with the last breeze off the street, his hair tousled, and held out his hand while he leaned in to offer his cheek for a kiss. His visit was an emotional event because of his warmth, the strength of his presence, and most of all because he talked about my compañeros who were prisoners elsewhere. I don't know if he exaggerated the greetings or made them up, but I do know that he understood precisely a prisoner's need for a friendly word.

Through Eduardo, el Turco came alive again, complete with his affectionate manner. I was told of Miguel's love, about la Mona, Afranio, and el Gordo Pebles. Through Eduardo I could see clearly that world you see only through a fog from inside, interrupted by bars and grates. Political news, debates about amnesty, public debate, and the position of the M-19 management in la Picota. Talking with Umaña was like going for a walk.

At the other end of the receiving room, the tick-tock of the clock imposed its relentless norms. At five o'clock the visit was over. How much was still left unsaid! Eduardo was leaving and I was staying there, standing before the last door, praying for him to come back and bring a bit of clean air to that cemetery of souls, where we refused to bury our dreams. Today I wonder if all of his defendants loved him at one time or another—or, like me, forever.

The Law of the Jungle

In July 1982 we awoke one morning to the nun's prayer, as we did every day. But on this morning she didn't unlock the cells. She told Susana and Marta to get ready because they were needed in the guard station. Something weird was happening. Was it the soldiers again?

Susana's eyes were even bigger than usual as she passed by my locked cell door.

"Hermana, it must be a search—take this." And she handed me the paper containing the summary of our tactical lessons and some letters from Carlos Pizarro in la Picota. I put them in my robe pocket. Then Marta did the same with another roll of papers. I fingered them. There were a lot, in spite of the fact that we wrote super small. I looked for my own copy of the summary and put it together with the rest of the papers. There were formulas for making explosives, complete chapters on tactical movements, types of ambushes, principles of topography, drawings of hideouts, and anything else we could think of to systematize as an exercise for our memory.

"What should I do? What if they call me?"

I had a bottle of orange pop on the nightstand and I decided to eat the military secrets before they fell into the hands of the enemy, just like in the spy novels. When the compañeras said good-bye I was chewing and swallowing the papers with difficulty. The pop couldn't make the bitter taste of the ink, or my fear, any easier to bear.

They took Marta and Susana to Bogotá. The director had requested the move after the nuns found the escape plans on Elvecio.

It was a bad day, but I didn't cry until they locked me in my cell that night. I felt like an orphan in a hostile world, more alone than ever without those two. We had made a good team: Susana was the radical wing, I was the conciliator, and Marta kept the balance with yoga and fruit juices. To this spiritual unease was added the fearful weight of my stomach. I don't know if it was the mixture of the explosive formulas and tactical exercises, or the bond paper and ink with the orange pop.

A week later I got a letter from my two friends. They said they felt like they were in Miami in the Buen Pastor in Bogotá, a prison led by civilians. The political prisoners were a considerable force, and they had well-organized daily activities, a library, a collective kitchen, daily exercises, movies, shifts for watching TV in their cells, unrestricted visits on Sunday, and other benefits.

I sighed with relief for them. At the same time, however, my hierarchical responsibilities with the M-19 had put me in a difficult situation. Three of those accused in the kidnapping of Marta Nieves Ochoa had been moved from Bogotá. Conflicts arose among them because some had confessed and because the wife and the lover of the same man encountered each other. But it was not so easy to condemn a person for confessing when you understood the human circumstances of women like Marta Correa, kidnapped by the MAS with her two-year-old daughter. While they interrogated Marta, they drenched her little girl in gasoline and held a lit match close to her. Could we blame Marta for confessing? Should we isolate her from the group, as the others asked?

I remained firm in the position I had taken since the military trial. There was no time for divisions or discriminations; we could not allow jail to become another trial. There, under negative conditions, we should unite to confront the difficulties we faced. An external threat contributed to the cohesion of the group: we were told that someone had paid a million pesos to kill Beatriz Rivera in prison. We didn't know if it was true, but we had to take protective measures. In 1981 anything was possible. There was no clear division between the narcotraffickers and the soldiers with respect to counterinsurgency actions.

All the political prisoners supported each other, but we couldn't hope for help from anyone else, and we didn't ask for it; we didn't trust anyone. We no longer accepted food from outside. Before we went to the reception room for visits, we asked for the names of the visitors. We didn't walk in the yard alone, and at group events we formed a tight circle, with Beatriz in the middle. I became her bodyguard.

It was a difficult time. The generalized repression of Turbay's administration and the instrumentalization of torture as an interrogation technique made many politicals lose morale. Some gave in to fear and isolated themselves. Others maintained their status as rebels by being part of a collective that defended them, but they weren't active. Few kept their desire to work hard for political and social change or politics, whatever the cost. We had to make collective efforts to maintain a positive spirit in the face of imprisonment, to preserve the cohesion of the group, to avoid internal confrontations. In this I could count on Beatriz; despite her youth, she was the most mature of the muchachas.

The military trial for the kidnapping case of Marta Nieves Ochoa concluded with an absolution for Beatriz and an eight-month sentence, already served, for the other three defendants. August was beginning and almost a month went by before she was freed. Anxiety broke everyone's routine, but Beatriz couldn't sit still for a minute. She did exercises all day long, stopped the calming practice of crocheting, and constantly asked me about the things I had taught her, wanting to remember the lessons.

The news of their release had a tremendous impact in the yard; four people almost never got out at once. In ten minutes they were ready. We said good-bye with overwhelming emotion. When I hugged Beatriz, I felt two intensely powerful emotions: joy for her and pain for myself in the loss of her. With her a part of me was also freed—but what would happen to her? I was afraid for her life. My student, my sister, in some ways my daughter was leaving for good. She was the first to shed tears, and my own tears welled up in spite of my desire to be strong.

"Take care. Good luck!"

She was the last one of the four to leave. She looked like an ugly duckling, with her nose all red, her mascara running, her braid undone from all our hugging. When they closed the yard door I sat down to cry. Alone again.

In the middle of September, the process was repeated: one morning Fabiola Martínez and I were called to the guard station. Paloma was there, smiling.

"Your transfer came," she told us.

I felt my stomach go cold. Medellín's Buen Pastor wasn't a paradise, but what was in store for me?

"Where are we going?" I asked.

"I can't tell you, by orders of the brigade. For the security of the transfer."
It seemed to me she was afraid of the soldiers who were waiting for us on
the other side of the door.

"Don't worry, you're not going alone." I looked at Fabiola, who was
calm.

"It's going to be hard for Tínez and la Mamita," she said.

Fortunately, by long training, we had everything we needed in our pockets. That's how we left; the rest of our things were packed by the guards. We
waited in the receiving room. Eventually María, another compañera from the
M-19, appeared, and then nine more muchachas from different yards. The
guards made us line up and called roll. When they opened the door we saw
before us a mass of uniforms and the familiar sound of boots and weapons
moving quickly to comply with an order.

"Who is María Eugenia Vásquez?" barked out the captain. I was silent.
A stupid question was echoing inside me: "Why me?" No one seemed to
have heard. The captain asked again, "Is María Eugenia Vásquez here?"

"Here I am, it's me," I responded in the firmest voice I could muster.

He approached and looked at me incredulously. He turned on his heels
military style and said, "Okay!" They indicated for us to get on the bus. The
captain seated us.

"You here," he signaled a place on the right side, almost in the middle.
Fabiola sat next to me; in front of us was Elizabeth.

They cuffed us. A lieutenant situated himself behind us. The muchachas
were shouting with happiness. Only one was crying uncontrollably.

"It's okay, you'll find someone better there, shhhh," the one sitting next
to her said.

"The nuns will take care of your amor," said another.

Prison loves are intense and the muchacha couldn't control herself. She
sobbed inconsolably. The women began to joke around with the lieutenant.

"Sit here, I don't bite," one said to him.

"I can't move from here. Can't you see they assigned me to her?" and he
nodded toward me.

"Ooooiiii, Juana, oooooiiiiii," they said, laughing. I blushed.

"You're dangerous," the lieutenant said, laughing. I burst out laughing.

"Me, dangerous? Stories of soldiers who see shadows everywhere. Me,
dangerous?" I relaxed. We started to joke around. Fabiola was jubilant.

"Any place is better than that yard of witches. Finally I'm free of Margarita
and la Paloma. Finally! Otherwise I would have gone nuts. Band of witches,
devils, old maids!"

"Women without men. Nothing more," I said, remembering a speech from the García Lorca play *La casa de Bernarda Alba*.

The muchachas yelled their good-byes to the guards. Blanca Inés came and went, talking with the captain. The caravan was pulling out when Deborah came running up with a bag of fruit in her hand. She gave them to Fabiola.

"I had left this for them but they sent it on because there's . . . " She put her hand in the bag and her eyes were shining. "Yes, there's a coconut in here," she lowered her voice, "a spiked coconut the muchachos sent us in the package."

I felt a void in the pit of my stomach. Spiked with dynamite? Of course, I thought, of course, the anarchists probably put dynamite in it.

With that, the driver started the engine. In front of us there was an army jeep carrying a sergeant and three soldiers, then a police truck with ten men, the driver, and a corporal. Then came the bus with its twelve prisoners and fifteen police officers, men and women both, under a lieutenant. The army captain brought up the rear with his jeep, a driver, and one soldier.

We looked out the window. Sor Blanca Inés stayed behind blessing us and waving good-bye. They were moving us because of our attempted escape, as if it weren't legitimate to attempt it or at least dream about it obsessively. Resigning oneself to serving a whole sentence is like accepting death. It's giving up, and whoever gives up drowns.

I decided to look at it as an outing. We were leaving Medellín, a city I didn't know in spite of having been there for more than a year. I had been outside only once, when they took me to the San Vicente de Paul hospital for a biopsy. I was cuffed and guarded by fifteen soldiers—an incredible spectacle. But the people expressed their sympathy to me in dozens of ways; they attended to me like a queen. The doctor wouldn't let any soldiers be present during my exam and made them leave the office after uncuffing me. It was a gynecological exam.

I looked at Fabi, who was holding the bag of fruit and the coconut. What should we do? Were we to use it to escape? Now? After we arrived at the new prison?

"What should we do with the coconut?" I asked.

"That's up to you—here it is," she replied, handing me the bag.

I grabbed it with my free hand. I scratched the outer part of the fruit with my nail and found the plastic wrap they had used to seal it up after they spiked it. I shook it a bit and heard liquid inside. As far as I knew, explosives could be like a gelatin, but liquid?

"What's in it?"

"I don't know. The nuts probably filled it with rum or brandy."

I closed my eyes and settled down in the seat. I didn't even laugh. I had thought it was explosives. Brandy! I couldn't even remember the taste of it. We never thought to have them bring us liquor in prison.

On the first stop of the trip it was really hot, and the muchachas asked the police to buy them an ice-cold Clausen. We did the same, and the police didn't object at all. For them it may have been a small thing, but for us a cold beer was a huge treat.

The first gulp tasted glorious, the icy, bitter liquid refreshing our throats. We toasted the compañeras in the Buen Pastor who couldn't enjoy a beer. Later, while we admired the panorama along the way and chattered away like parrots, the three of us enjoyed the coconut milk the anarchist friends had sent with us.

I had always liked to travel. The landscape that day was wearing its Sunday best. Everything looked recently bathed, fresh and new to our hungry eyes and anxious souls. It would sustain us in the months ahead, when we were locked up again. At every bend in the road the soldiers took tactical measures to avoid an ambush. They also stopped to drop off women in the prisons along the way, which made our trip three times longer than normal. We could hear the song of the crickets as night fell, while the vehicle still rolled along the asphalt. For a while we forgot that our hands were cuffed to the seat and that we still had sentences to serve.

We reached our destination in the wee hours of the morning. The Buga prison, in the Valle del Cauca—a high-security national penitentiary—had a women's wing that held about thirty prisoners. The guards who greeted us didn't waive the nude search, in spite of recognizing our status as political prisoners.

They located us temporarily, each of us in a room where other women were sleeping. When they closed the door, I was afraid, alone with people I didn't know. I thought about trying to stay awake to avoid any abuses, but the exhaustion from the trip and the anarchist brandy were stronger than my mistrust.

At 5:30 in the morning the guards woke us up with three knocks on the door. Two women jumped up from the bed, and while they gathered up their toiletries they spoke to me.

"Welcome. Where are you coming from?"

"Transferred from Medellín."

"Do you have a lot left?"

"I was sentenced to nine years; I've served one and a half."

"*Jueputa!*[19] What did you do?"

"I'm from the M-19." The two smiled as if I had said a magic word.

"You'll be fine here. You'll see. With Eva, the fat guard, you can get what you want; of course, she charges more than it's worth, but she's not a bad person. The other is more serious, but she's not mean. Here the *bongo* is disgusting, but you can order food out with the orderlies."

I told them I had come with two other friends, that we were gringas and had no choice but to eat the bongo.

"You can get a hot plate from Eva and you can do something to soften the blow."

We went to the bathroom together. There were six collective showers from which I could hear voices. I got goosebumps.

"These over here are empty," one of my new roommates told me, pointing to two private bathrooms.

I found Fabiola and María in the hall. They looked rested.

"Take everything you need with you for the day. You won't come back here until it's time for bed," the guard said.

Once on the yard, we lined up shoulder to shoulder. A guard, a list in his hand, ordered us to number off.

One, two ... I remembered military formations, and so when the numbering reached me I said, "Eighteen, and last!" The guard looked at me and nodded.

"Three new," he said, and left.

We inspected the place. It was about sixty square meters, half in the patio under the roof, the other half on uncovered ground. There were six individual showers in the middle of the yard, without roofs, two sinks, a small kitchen, and three toilets. For furniture there were only two long benches and a seat for the guard. We put our things on the ground and sat down to wait for breakfast.

"The bongooooo's here!"

There was much commotion as the muchachas rushed to get their bread and coffee. The guard brought us a pitcher with our ration.

Fortunately we still had some money. We had to buy plates, cups, spoons, and a bowl at scandalous prices. In Buga we were initiated into the culture of national prisons, where everything has a price. The guards seemed to be bottomless collection boxes.

---

19. Son of a bitch.

The first days were hard. Someone stole some money I had left in my shirt pocket while I showered. But that day the other muchachas also learned what we thought of rats who stole from compañeras.

"This is a good beginning!" I shouted on the yard. "But listen up! We aren't to be trifled with! And remember that we didn't get here because we're pretty and sweet. If you don't believe it, ask the army." They were all quiet. Such was our introduction.

Little by little we found out that the law of the *cana* (slammer) was the law of the jungle. Male and female guards alike pretended they didn't know what was going on with whatever brought them no money or could bring them problems. Everyone did whatever they wanted if they could negotiate it with those in control, and these weren't always the guards. There are very strong powers inside prison.

After two days we knew who the political prisoners were. So we paid a guard to set up a meeting with compañero Hermes Rodríguez, who had been there since the military trial. He was the muchacho the army had captured wounded and made him confess about a school in Cuba, which later served Colombia as the pretext for breaking relations with Cuba. We knew that he had cooperated with the army, but we understood his loneliness and how painful his confession must have been for him.

There were only two politicals in this prison—Hermes and a peasant man with one arm who was about fifty years old and was in charge of taking care of the prison's pigs. He had been there three years and they hadn't yet called him to trial. He was charged with kidnapping and belonging to the FARC. All together we made up a group of five political prisoners, and we quickly began to make contacts with the outside so as to gain some solidarity. Meanwhile, we negotiated a room for the three of us women at a low price. Our *cambuche*[20] was a paradise. From the top bunk we could see the mountains and thickets through the heavy glass blocks that were our windows.

Unlike the Buen Pastor, here the only fixed schedule consisted of wake-up call, meals, and bedtime. The rest of the time was ours and we savored it. In the morning, after we did our exercises, we began a solemn beauty session while listening to the radio, sunbathing, or reading. No one made us do anything, and soon we put our leisure to good use. The only approved activity for lessening one's sentence was laundry duty, and we didn't like that idea. So we started thinking of other jobs we could do.

The Buga prison was designed for men; we women were a last-minute addition. We had no workshops, infirmary, athletic courts, or grass. We had

20. Tent, bunk, or dorm, depending on the context.

only our rooms, the yard, and two enormous baths. We asked for a meeting with the prison director. A man who looked like a bureaucrat received us, and he loved our ideas for improving the conditions of the women prisoners. He left it up to us to gain support from the Buga population.

After a month, everyone in Buga knew that some muchachas from the M-19 had arrived, and everyone wanted to visit us. Human rights groups, business interest groups, lawyers, and teachers all wanted to talk to us. We became the Saturday outing for a lot of people who were bored at home. And we started to work from prison. We secured a lawyer for the FARC peasant, got an interview on the local radio and talked about the amnesty that was being discussed after the state of siege was lifted, after Turbay's term had ended. The M-19 had achieved an undeniable leading role in this process.

We took advantage of our connections to get the Damas Rosadas[21] to donate a sewing machine and material so we could make dolls and crochet backpacks and use the profits from selling these things to create a savings fund for all the prisoners. The majority of them were gringas like us, and their only income came from washing clothes—and even there they had to compete with the male prisoners for jobs.

In a short time we had converted the dirt patch in the yard into a garden planted with vegetables that supplemented our deficient diet, generally made up of soup and rice. Everyone could use the garden. At first the care and watering were left up to us, but when the other prisoners saw the first harvests, everyone began to help.

We also got the guards to take us to the athletic courts on the men's yards twice a week. We had to file past the men's yards and were showered with comments as we did so, from the tender to the vulgar and disgusting. While we played we could hear the men shouting all kinds of things, and when we filed back past them they stuck their hands through the bars to wave at us and sometimes even exhibited their penises. But friendships were also forged with a simple smile or a gallant phrase.

A few courtships evolved from these interchanges. The lovers had only the opportunity for a brush of hands twice a week, but these fledging liaisons were maintained for months by notes and details sent via the orderlies. A pack of cigarettes, a bar of scented soap, or a plate of food from the daily bongo cemented the love.

The cutest mafioso in the prison fell in love with Fabiola. First he sent her love letters. She did not respond. Then he sent little gifts for all three of

21. "Pink Ladies," an organization of high-society women dedicated to volunteer work with the poor and handicapped.

us—books, records, chocolates, and even flowers. Fabi was noncommital, but she thanked him for the gifts and walked with a bounce in her step.

We called María "María of the guards" because all the guards looked at her with eyes as big as gumdrops. She had a way with men in uniform, but she always remained serious. The only one she allowed to flirt with her was Henry, one of the defense lawyers for the political prisoners in Buga. María loved her negro Genaro on the outside. He was a thick-skinned mechanic of hearty peasant stock and in him she had discovered the love of her life. Her heart beat for him alone through the years.

I fell in love with Guillermo Bolívar, a professor from the Universidad del Valle, a human rights defender. These loves, while platonic, at least had a closer source than the happy Captain Poldark from the television series, and they allowed us to dream of an upcoming visit, to imagine a romance even if we knew that it could never really go anywhere.

My compañero Alfredo served out his sentence for the embassy takeover without his trial ever coming up. Finally he was released, and I received word that we was coming to see me. The news threw me off base for several days. It had been a year and a half since I'd seen him, but he was still inside me, feeding my memory. Yet I was afraid to find out if our love had survived all this time apart in prison.

When he arrived for the visit I held him close and wished that time could stop. But I didn't know what to say to him in the three hours we had together. It was like starting over, getting to know each other again from scratch. After he left I went back to my room, threw myself on the bed, and was quiet. I was filled with conflicting feelings. He had re-entered me with his smell, his stature, his warm embrace. He had recovered his place in my bodily memory only to leave me empty again. I felt a burning in my skin as if my protective wrapping had come off. I cried for his closeness as much as I did his absence.

Juancho also came to Buga, and Fabi went through the same thing I did. That night we heard her singing "La Zamba para Olvidar" with her whole heart:

> No sé para qué volviste
> si ya empezaba a olvidar
> te fuiste, mi amor, te fuiste
> que mal me hace recordar . . . [22]

22. I don't know why you came back/I was starting to forget/you left, my love, you left/how it hurts to remember. "La Zamba para Olvidar," by Daniel Toro, sung by Cuco Valoy.

The civilian prison was different from Buen Pastor. It wasn't easier, but it was less schizophrenic. In the Buga prison we lost weight because of the awful food, but our spirits soared. In Buen Pastor we had been like butterflies in a matchbox. But in the civilian jail we recovered our identities, we were ourselves again, we said what we wanted without anyone prohibiting it, we could read what we wanted, sing freely, be lazy, spend the night working if we had to, leave our light on all night without risk of the guard passing and blowing out the candle. In the Buen Pastor we were isolated from the rest of the women in the prison. In Buga, everyone, politicals and regulars alike, all moved in the same place. We knew each other and started to live together.

There were few women from Buga and Tulúa. Most had been transferred from prisons in other cities for bad behavior. The most frequent crimes were robbery and personal injury. Our first friend was la Negra Mery, a very beautiful *chocoana*[23] we called "Muñeca" (doll) whom we met as a repeat offender in Buen Pastor. The jealousy of a lover had left its mark in a scar that crossed her face from her cheek to her neck. She sang almost all the time. She hummed *vallenatos* and pulled a rhythm out of anything, a spoon, a lid, a wooden bench. When they closed us up at five in the afternoon, she started a song to which other muchachas would chime in on an endless, melancholy serenade that almost always ended up with the same Daniel Santos song:

Preso estoy
estoy cumpliendo la condena
la condena que me da la sociedad
me arrepiento, me averguenzo y me da pena . . .[24]

Then came silence. Being locked up feeds nostalgia for the outside world.

Mery related to everyone without getting close to anyone. She had a sort of haughtiness. She came closer to our group little by little, trying to find the support of a combo, which was vital to surviving in prison. The strong protect, and those protected submit. We liked Mery, so we accepted her, but as an equal. We all did the same jobs. If she washed our clothes one day, we washed hers the next. We all shared the food, and she never took any more than what was hers.

Our friendship flowed without complications. We told her about ourselves and she told us her life story. She had left Tadó very young in search of

23. Someone from the department of Chocó.
24. I am a prisoner/I'm doing my time/the time society gives me/I'm sorry, and ashamed, and it makes me sad. "El Preso," by Daniel Santos.

a bigger world where she could live as she liked. At eleven she let herself be "laid" by an older man who gave her money, but she never liked the caresses of men. Once in Medellín she got domestic jobs in family homes, but she couldn't take it. She started to hang out with paisanos and acquaintances and got into the world of drugs and robbery. She dedicated herself above all to raponeo because she was a fast runner and because she knew her gold, and never made mistakes as she lifted chains, earrings, watches.

"It's just that, look—I was going down the street with nothing in my head, when I saw all that gold jewelry coming toward me and my heart started racing. Gold called me—I tried, but I couldn't resist the temptation, you know?"

They got her because she was high and had no reflexes. They took her to the Buen Pastor as usual, but each time she was there she got more and more rebellious and would take no crap from the nuns or anyone else. And so she ended up in Buga with a two-year sentence, because during her last crime someone had been injured. She told us it was the *suco*'s[25] fault she was *embalada*.[26]

The Muñeca's loves were many and intense. We loved to listen to the fluidity of her stories with that almost musical rhythm in her words. Through her we began to understand the sweet and sad complexity of love among women. A form of human feeling surrounded by taboo that you can't talk or ask about and that most people just reject.

In our yard there were only four heterosexuals: we three politicals and a real bacana prostitute named Nubia. But the fact that we weren't lesbians didn't keep us from becoming their confidants in their love problems and even the mediators in their lovers' quarrels.

Almost all of them had a personal history of violent emotional and sexual relationships. Some began with a rape or abuse by adult men in their own families, or with abuse from the men they married or got involved with, who beat them or cut their bodies. The violence was often mingled with alcohol and drugs. Love between women didn't change the basic relationship dynamic: the feelings of possession, jealousy, suffering, and ecstasy were just as much a part of it.

There were also power plays among the lesbian couples, the same kind of thing that goes on between men and women. There was a woman about twenty-six years old everyone called el Mono. She was the man of the yard.

---

25. Short for *basuco*, slang for a drug similar to crack but of lower quality and more harmful.
26. Here this means "in such a mess," but it can also mean high or drugged.

Everything about her was very masculine, her body frame, her angular face, the way she walked, her haircut, the way she dressed. El Mono had several lovers and used the bait-and-hook method with them. She threatened them, beat them, loved them, and protected them from any abuse from the guards or other prisoners. Her women attended to her every need. They got her food, did her hair, washed and ironed her clothes, and gave her money.

Many of the muchachas opted for lesbianism while in prison but also had occasional relations with men—even prisoners from the same prison—for cigarettes, soap, or money that they sent as gifts. Once el Mono fell for a prisoner who was in isolation. Or rather, she fell in love with his arms, when he put them out to make signs to her through the bars. They wrote notes to each other and the guards delivered them. I stood by el Mono when she was communicating with her love, from our yard to the punishment cells about a hundred meters away.

"Mono, what do you see?"

"His hands and his arms."

"Nothing else?"

"Why something else?"

"What's he saying to you?"

"Can't you see? That he loves me."

"How do you know that's what he's saying?"

"Because he's putting his arms together as if he were hugging me."

Her only love for the opposite sex lasted about a month.

We had a rather distant relationship with el Mono; she felt that we were a force that was different from her own. Once we had a confrontation. "Fresh meat"—what they called casual prisoners who spent only a few days in jail—had arrived in the form of two weepy kids who were coming from a town jail. El Mono threw herself at them, not to conquer them but to attack them. When they were alone she pinched their breasts and they screamed, terrified. The guards pretended they didn't know what was going on, so I yelled at her for being a coward. If she was so berraca, she should win them over, not mess with them by taking advantage of their fear.

She came at me in a rage and challenged me to a fight. Immediately Fabiola, María, Mery, and Nubia were at my side, and Mono's women were at hers. We were face to face, and the verbal confrontation began. Words have power, and insolence implies a great strength that, if handled well, can prevent physical violence. We yelled everything at each other, each bragging about her strength and her ability to finish the other off, and in the end we didn't have to use our hands.

Words cut, wound, humiliate, beat, kill. Tossing out an insult like piroba at the right moment wounds. The tone of voice is key. You surprise with shouting, chew obscenities. The gestures sustain the words; they intimidate. Legs apart and hands on the hips mean challenge. You grab your genitals to attack. Gesticulating adds tremendous force.

We had to win respect on the same plane that the other prisoners mapped out; we had to play by their rules or the devil would take us. There is no unearned compassion in prison. Aggression becomes magnified when it is locked up, as do impotence and fear. There's so little to lose.

At first the harsh words of Buga embarrassed me. I was used to swearing, but not to stringing so many barbarities together. Yet I ended up learning them one by one. I appropriated them, and when I used them they came out of me willingly, like a release.

In civilian prison you have to demonstrate strength. Even the guards are careful with their arbitrary acts if they know there's someone backing you. They're afraid of revenge. After all, the same rules apply to them. Prison is a very harsh environment; the weak can't take it. Once a woman of about forty-five came in. She looked like she had some money and was charged with assaulting a man. From the beginning we noticed something odd in her behavior, because she came in crossing herself and praying in a low voice. A mystic madness, we thought. At dinner time she told pieces of the story. They had put her in isolation because a man tried to rape her and she had defended herself and cut open his head with her heel. After dinner, several of the prisoners took her over to one end of the yard and stole her earrings from her. The woman screamed, but the guards were deaf as always. When we got there, she was crying, terrified, and was holding on to her ears. We asked who had done it, but no one had seen anything.

The woman entered into a growing state of nervous glorification and became enraged to the point of losing control. In five days she went from mystic madness to an extreme state of aggression, with a vocabulary that was worse than ours. The guards couldn't even handle her, and she beat herself against the bars of isolation if anyone came near. Once she accepted a bowl of soup we offered her, but when she saw the guard she threw it at her. Finally she fell into a stupor and lay on her bed as if dead, her eyes fixed on the ceiling. The director ignored our requests that she be put in an asylum; the judges had declared her sane. One day they took her out on a stretcher. We heard she had been seen begging in the streets two weeks later. That is the sort of sorrow you never forget.

Freedom Is a Wide Open Space

We did as we pleased in the Buga prison when the amnesty law that automatically covered all political crimes was declared. Our freedom was only days away. It was Christmas 1982.

Fabiola had been opposed to peace negotiations with the government, to amnesty, and to the participation of guerrilla groups in legal politics. Her position was very radical and we took advantage of it to tease her about being freed by the action of those negotiations.

"Fabi, you're the anarchist, you shouldn't accept freedom by amnesty. If I were in your shoes, I'd finish my sentence with dignity."

"I'm an anarchist, not an idiot," she told us, laughing.

Anxiety penetrated down to the bone. During the wait we tried to keep our sanity, but we could hardly sleep. One fine day they told me I was free. I didn't believe it.

The papers took some time as the authorities went over each piece of evidence, each official stamp, each judgment and statement. Outside a lawyer and my mother were waiting for me. When I walked out of that prison, I looked out toward the horizon to the wide open space before me. Freedom made me dizzy; I felt unsure walking without the walls that had surrounded me.

10

Singing to the Sun Like
a Cricket

THE FIRST THING I did when I got out of jail was to recover my body for freedom and love. I stayed in Buga for a few days, living out a romance invented in prison with a friend of lost causes. I danced salsa to shake off the lethargy of jail and I talked about politics until I was hoarse. I gave interviews to the local media with other compañeros from the Mira and I let myself be babied by people close to me.

The M-19 formed the Frente Amplio (Broad Front) with some of the people who had been released from la Picota, to further the work for peace. It was clear that amnesty was a first step, but it wasn't our goal. The M-19's goal was to broaden democracy, and to fashion a social pact that would put the country on the road to solving the main social problems. As far as we were concerned, peace involved not only the guerrilla but the whole country.

Since I had ignored the M-19 management's call to present myself in Bogotá the day I got out of jail, when I did arrive they had already left for a meeting overseas. *¡Qué vaina!*[1] But every cloud has a silver lining. I found Alfredo and we resumed our long-interrupted honeymoon. We rested for two months while the national M-19 leadership deliberated.

---

1. What a pity! (or) What a pain!

It was clear in the course of the M-19's meeting abroad that Belisario Betancur's administration lacked the will to make peace state policy, and the M-19 decided to recover the political initiative the president had gained with amnesty. To do this, we were forced to raise the level of armed confrontation as a tactic to pressure for a national dialogue for peace, in which industry, commerce, and banks would participate. We tried to involve more people in the search for peace with social justice. Bateman had come up with the idea, during our takeover of the Dominican Embassy, to call on the political class, the church, popular sectors, and unions to talk in Panamá about the country's problems.

The M-19 went back to war with all its weapons. The cards for the next hand were dealt: Alfredo would leave with the forces of the eastern front under Antonio Navarro, while Susana and I would take the coffee regional. Neither Alfredo nor I defended the private plans we had made as a couple before the organization decisions. We were ashamed to give love priority over our availability for combat.

We loved each other madly and tried to slow time down with caresses. I was at his side until he left. I saw him leave and watched his figure grow smaller and smaller among the traffic and the people until he became a tiny dot. When I lost him from sight, I consulted for a moment the measure of his absence, and a dull pain in every fiber of my being revealed the dimension of the emptiness. I wanted to shout, cry, and run until I couldn't run anymore. I wanted somehow to deaden the pain, to flee from it, but I stayed right there, outwardly calm, with a commitment that went beyond love.

It came time for my trip to Armenia. When the leader of the PMO, the Politico-military Organization of the M-19, informed Susana and me that our mission was to gather together the 300 militants of the organization in four departments and organize with them a political-military assignment, they couldn't quite explain why they had chosen two women to replace one man.

I thought that Beatriz Rivera would be a good person to complete our team and went to Medellín that same night. I was afraid, because the leader-ship had warned me that the military brigade in that city knew all about me. Still, I wanted to bring Beatra with me; it felt inexplicably urgent to me. As soon as I got there I went to the Universidad de Antioquia, where she was studying economics. I found two other compañeras from jail in the cafeteria and they took me to the classroom. I peeked in and waved. Beatriz raised a ruckus that was typical of her. We hugged. It was the first time we had been together in the outside world.

I had always thought that if Beatriz stayed in Medellín, even if she worked legally, the army would end up killing her. I presented my proposal that she come with us to Armenia. At first she argued that she didn't want to leave her family or her studies, but she finally accepted my arguments, adding that Lieutenant Beltrán from the IV Brigade was harassing her. She agreed to leave Medellín and work with Susana, Martha, and me. We made a date for ten days later. That night I convinced her mother that Beatriz needed to change her location. I returned to Armenia the next day with the good news.

Almost a week had gone by when we heard on the radio and read in the newspapers that Beatriz had been disappeared. I called Medellín and talked to her mother. She knew only that Beatriz and a friend had been kidnapped on their way home from the university. I hung up the phone with a feeling of anger and pain. Why? Why her? The younger sister, the untamable muchacha who laughed in the face of death. I lived a nightmare. I thought of Beatriz everyday, imagining the suffering they would be submitting her to, and my flesh ached. I was exhausted by the pain of these visions. She appeared in my dreams, looking lost, walking without hearing my call, or looking at me with an infinite, voiceless sadness. Her image always faded before she could tell me where she was. Uncertainty makes grieving endless.

"Where are you, where, hermana?" That question still echoes inside me. There is nothing more monstrous than disappearings for those of us who are left waiting. Sometimes I yelled for death to come and relieve her, because I imagined she was being tortured. I wanted her body to show up, to put an end to her mother's pain. At the same time I never stopped imploring life for a chance to find her alive. Many times I have seen someone that looks like Beatriz and my heart has leapt up. But it has never been her.

It sounds absurd, but that pain gave me strength. I made myself work harder. I traveled for a while, filled with melancholy, as I built clandestine structures for operative work. So much coming and going made me confuse the cities, but it didn't much matter; the work was the same.

Once, when I returned to our apartment in Armenia, I found a note from Susana telling me that she had decided to get out of activism to take care of her pregnancy. I felt abandoned; I didn't understand her choice at that time. It didn't matter to me that she was leaving the assignment but that she had left me alone, with no one to talk to about anything.

I made a new team with Martha and Guayabita, who were located in two different towns. I kept traveling from city to city as if I were on an endless merry-go-round, till I completely lost all sense of direction. When we had put together a team of five, all that was left of that army of four departments they'd led us to believe existed, we were finally ready to start operating. The M-19 called me from Bogotá to say that they wanted me to help with the work in the capital.

I returned to Bogotá without much sadness, leaving the coffee regional in the hands of Marta and Guayabita. At the first meeting I met Violeta, a member of national management with whom I would form a team.

The M-19's Military Forces—FM, an urban operative structure—and the PMO, which was more linked to work with the masses, were working separately in the city, with poor results, failing to recruit workers to our cause. While the FM worked to obtain resources that would allow them to pay rent and eat, the PMO worked with almost no resources in the popular sectors. We decided to fuse them in order to achieve a greater political impact. A good number of middle cadres were in preparatory courses overseas. We brought together as many people and teams as we could—twelve people with experience and some muchachos who came and went from commando unit to commando unit seeking activity and decompartmentalizing the work.

We organized as a regional central command with a central command of columns under it. Most of the leaders were women. The muchachos called us the "Doñas." It wasn't easy to win their respect because women in the political and military fields were underestimated. We constantly had to demonstrate to the men that we could do everything we demanded of them and more. We were famous for being hard and authoritarian, but it was the only way to command respect from the men. In spite of it all we achieved teamwork that was really productive. When the structures were all fused together, we were all PMO officials, with ranks of first, major, or superior. Our task was to design the regional policies according to the strategic orientations from management, and to plan military operatives according to political tasks. At that time urban military operatives consisted primarily of actions of armed propaganda.

When militants worked full-time for the organization, they were considered professionals. By 1983 the number of professionals had risen significantly because almost everyone who had been arrested in the previous years had been forced into hiding. To maintain us, the organization designated a stipend that was equal to a minimum salary. People with responsibilities and more demanding work got higher salaries. Our salaries enabled us to pay a modest rent and cover transportation costs; food was mostly covered by personal or structural support networks. Money was provided by the high command via the regional representatives, and for that we had special financial structures.

I had lived more than half my life in Bogotá, and I had never felt completely at home there. But now that I was well acquainted with the entire city, I found it very different: it was a friendly city, it let us hide in the middle of the street, it offered us several alternatives for existence. I understood Bogotá's beauty, even after six in the evening, when the neon lights eat at the soul like teeth. I felt it was mine, ours, an accomplice. It became pleasant to work there, even when I would occasionally be struck down by loneliness in the middle of a crowded street. Bogotá. Everything I had was there, and yet I had never been more alone in my life.

Complicit City

The regional central command was made up of Violeta, Facundo, Abraham, and me. We had two hierarchical superiors, Pacho and Alvear, whom we saw at monthly planning meetings or when they gave us a special task. Pacho, an outstanding chemistry student at the Universidad del Valle, had to go into hiding because of an operative error, and from that time on he took charge of the organization's newspaper. Alvear was also from Cali, and since they couldn't take him down a rank, they put him over us like a hat, as decoration. Fayad was in the high command as the national leader of the PMO.

Two column leaders were under each one of us. Manuel, Dúmar, and Palomo worked with me. Under them were Pilar, Iván, Pedro, el Karateca (the karate expert), Máximo, Marcela, Ariosto, Ernesto, Rosa la Primorosa, Arturo, el Gamín (the street kid), Félix, Adriana, and other muchachos and muchachas, almost all of them university students, teachers, or professional clandestines.

From the regional central command we imposed a style of teamwork for all positions. Even though we respected hierarchies, the responsibilities were divied up equally so that everyone could command and learn to plan and lead the actions. The rest supported whoever was commanding. There were no power struggles because there were no privileges. Those of us in charge of the regional carried out or supervised the groundwork for every one of the actions the muchachos had to do. We worked shoulder to shoulder and taught by example, just as we had when the M-19 was first formed. We loved each other and were united by our cause and by fighting to survive. The lowest-ranked compañero became student and son at the same time. His learning and personal development for the revolution was our responsibility.

I loved all of them. Actually, desire was present in these relationships, even if, for ethical reasons, I never took them to bed. Seduction can be used to dominate. I seduced them so they'd obey my orders, because I liked the fact that they looked at me as a woman, or perhaps because there was no other space for flirting in such a limited universe.

After the takeover of Florencia, the capital of Caquetá, in March 1984, the Frente Sur came into its own under the command of Boris. Some of the urbans had asked to be moved to the rural sector. That day I was to tell la Gordita her good news: they had accepted her request to go with Boris.

I got to the meeting scheduled for that day, and before it began León and Claudia said that la Gordita and Arturo, nicknamed el Enano (the dwarf) and the youngest in the group, had taken up together. They blushed. They had loved each other for a long time without saying anything. It was her first love. She looked happy.

"And didn't you ask to be moved to Caquetá?" I asked her.

"But not now," she responded, holding her compañero's hand. I kept the news to myself. Why should I mess up the kids' honeymoon?

It was a unit with a lot of experience. Our operation was to recover a revolver. I looked over the proposal the commando had written. It didn't look tough: the guardpost was in the parking lot in the south of the city. The place had good access points, the surprise factor was in our favor, we had four armed people and a getaway car. I approved the action and arranged the control appointments.

That night I had an argument with Violeta; she thought my decision not to send la Gordita to the Frente Sur was irrational. I explained that I only wanted to let them live out their love. After all, la Gordita wasn't indispensible in the Caquetá; if she stayed behind, the revolution wouldn't be held back. On the other hand, her urban experience at that time was very useful. But it was my decision, and I stood behind it. Violeta reproached me for giving so much importance to people's personal issues.

The next day the operation went down. I verified that the situation was normal in the area and left to wait for León and the rest. At the appointed time, Arturo appeared. He was walking slowly, with his head down. I approached him impatiently. He looked at me without saying a word, his red eyes full of tears.

"What's up?"

"They killed la Gordita," he said in a tiny voice.

My God! The light in my brain went out. I shut my eyes a moment to locate myself and when I opened them Arturo's were still there, full of tears. I wanted the earth to swallow me up. What could I say to him? There was so much pain in his little face. Damn! What should I do?

Being the leader at a time like that is horribly difficult. A leader must be tough, must assume responsibilities and take care of the others, come what may. I came back to myself quickly. I went with León, who felt responsible because he was the leader of the operation. He and his compañera also lived with la Gordita, and they loved her like a sister. Claudia hadn't even been able to get to the control site, she was so upset.

"Hermano, are you sure she was dead?" I asked.

"Very! I was the one who caught her with the two shots in her chest, and she was only able to say she was dying before she passed out. I dragged her a bit, but she didn't respond to anything. I took her pulse in her neck and nothing." León was crying and angrily dried his tears.

We took care of telling her family, moving her things, hiding the muchachos who participated in the operation. While we did all those things I found out what happened. It seems they had made a lot of noise around the place. When la Gordita approached the guard, the surprise factor had already been lost and the man reacted first. They struggled. The compañero who was covering her fired and got the man in the shoulder. La Gordita stood up and the man shot her twice. She ran to León, who was running to help her. He caught her. The guard kept shooting. With the compañera in his arms, León ordered everyone to retreat. The car picked them up. La Gordita was dead.

I sought out Moritz at dusk. I didn't want to be alone, but I couldn't let myself fall apart in front of the muchachos. I needed to break down with someone with whom I didn't have to maintain the image of strength, someone who loved me. When he took me in his arms I began to cry and couldn't stop. He caressed my head and I let all my sorrow flow out with my tears. I was so upset I couldn't even speak about what had happened.

I felt responsible for having decided that she could stay in Bogotá, for not being able to be with the muchachos in the operative, for not having foreseen it. It was the first death of a person in my charge. I didn't know what to do with León's anguish, Claudia's grief, or Arturo's adolescent widowerhood.

In a different mission, a muchacho named Manuel was the leader of an assignment to distribute free milk in Ciudad Bolívar. For a month we gathered intelligence, did a detailed observation of the milk truck's delivery routes, decided where we would hold up the truck, where we would take the driver and his helper while we carried out the mission, and where we would distribute the milk. This type of armed propaganda operation was an attempt to introduce the movement to segments of the population in great need. After such a mission we could begin organizing militia structures, conceived to meet the basic needs of the people but supported by the armed branch of the M-19.

To get the necessary information, we designed a commando unit that watched all day long, in tough shifts. Then the first officer, leader of the column, and the second officer, in charge of the unit, planned the operation, mapping out the routes, locating the security blocks, distributing the goods, designating the meeting point. They delegated work and assigned arms. I reviewed the plan meticulously and made necessary corrections, discussing them with the authors and those responsible.

I went with the unit to the neighborhood where they would take over the truck after they subdued the driver and the helper, to take it to Ciudad Bolívar. Everything was in order. I set a meeting time for an hour later, to make sure that the first part had gone smoothly. I was in the café waiting when Manuel came in, transfigured. He looked thinner and deathly pale. He sat down but said nothing and merely moved his head nervously from one side to the other.

"What happened?"

"We killed a man!"

He hastily recounted how el Patrón, a very good compañero for the mission, had tried to subdue the driver with his weapon in his hand while he opened the door. The man got scared and started the truck, so that the compañero was caught on the running board. He yelled at the driver to open the door, to stop, but the frightened man accelerated. So he shot the weapon and the driver slumped down into the seat. Manuel ordered them to leave immediately. The door of the truck was open and the driver was bleeding.

"We killed him! We killed him! And he was a muchacho, a worker . . . he was unarmed," he repeated in anguish.

I didn't know what to say. This absurd death made me angry. I was angry at the careless one who had fired needlessly, at Manuel as the one responsible for the operation, at myself for not being there. Manuel ran his hand through his hair as if he wanted to push the scene out of his head. He saddened me. I thought about how el Patrón must feel. I couldn't yell at them; it was a critical moment in their lives. I could only try to make it less difficult. I was their leader; I couldn't hug him and cry with him. I put my hand on his arm.

"I understand. But calm down. We can't do anything now. It was careless, but it was a product of the pressure. When you have a weapon in your hand, you may be killed or kill another. Those are the rules of the game. Now, tell me, where is el Patrón so we can talk to him?"

We were together all day long. The entire unit was inside for security reasons, and though we said nothing more about this issue, we were all worried. We sent someone to verify the story and found out that they had taken the driver to the hospital and that he was conscious. That calmed us down a bit. That night, by myself, I cried for my kids. The face of death is a serious thing and it had surprised them before their time. The responsibility weighed on me painfully.

Armed propaganda operations awoke sympathy for the M-19 among the population. We thought to take advantage of it in the regional for political work and in this way link with a new concept armed and mass work, putting weapons they themselves held at the service of the needs of the people. A lot of our focus had to do with the idea of forming popular armies or preparing insurrection in the cities, as the Sandinistas in Nicaragua had done during their final offensive.

We chose a population in great need, in marginalized areas of the city. We determined the needs of the people in those neighborhoods and then carried out an armed operation to hand out food, clothes, and even construction materials. The muchachos would perform this operation with their faces unmasked. We reasoned that clandestine operations were for the enemy, not the people. We had to be careful with our identity, but we would show our faces, so they could see us in flesh and blood solving their daily problems with them.

Thus was born the concept of popular militias, organizations of people around concrete needs, supported by weapons when necessary. It was no longer the armed apparatus that supported the requests of popular organizations, as when the M-19 kidnapped Ferreira Neira, the manager of INDUPALMA, to gain footing for the union's demands. Now the same people, with minimal knowledge of tactics and weapons, planned and executed simple actions such as guarding the hoses that took water to a neighborhood so the owners couldn't cut it off, as had happened with the pirate land sellers who wanted to avoid reselling lots,[2] or the expulsion of *gamonales*[3] who scared the people.

Our compañeros in the PMO were responsible for overseeing our work in organizing neighborhoods and preparing the people for insurrection, achieving increasingly more political content in the struggles for daily survival of those people excluded from all the benefits of the city and forced into the hardest jobs and the worst living conditions.

The majority of the efforts in the Bogotá regional in 1984 were dedicated to these assignments. There were also worker assignments and student assignments, and assignments with professionals and journalists. We also had an intelligence apparatus, though it gathered more gossip than information.

2. This is a practice through which unscrupulous profiteers take over land an owner has not used, divide it up, and sell it to the poor at low prices. They do not give them title to the land but only a receipt indicating the amount paid, by whom, and for what lot. When a neighborhood is later built on land thus sold, it gains value, and the government must pay the legitimate owner, who then pays the pirates. If the land is not legalized by the government, the pirates still come out ahead, even if the legitimate owner does not.
3. Large landowners or local bosses.

From the twelve that started in the middle of 1983, we grew to 100 militants by August 1984, not counting sympathizers and collaborators.

The organization was at a peak when el Flaco Bateman disappeared one day while flying between Santa Marta and Panamá. Many of us imagined that he was simply waiting for an opportune moment to jump out of the clouds and surprise us with a new proposal. One year later they found a destroyed plane in the Panamanian jungle, along with the bones of Bateman, la Negra, and Conrado Marín. For a year we had prepared ourselves to accept his death, though we had entertained all kinds of fantasies that he would miraculously return one day.

I believed that the organization would not survive without Bateman, but there it was. Iván Marino succeeded el Flaco as general commander, and Fayad was dedicated to working out a truce for negotiations. The rural fronts of Caquetá and Cauca fought with new tactics of regular warfare, increasingly close to the cities. The plan was the same as always: to take actions that would pressure the authorities for advantageous negotiations with the guerrillas. From the military trials, prisons, and amnesty, we armed groups had gained an audience. Political exclusion itself had legitimized us. In Colombia you had to shoot to be heard.

Around that time Carlos Toledo was killed while demonstrating his vocation for peace by practicing medicine in Santander. Negotiating a truce in this country of hatred and political intolerance, a country accustomed to seeing constitutional change come about only through war, was not easy. But in this attempt to achieve an accord for dialogues, Fayad was not alone. Many citizens, friends of peace, with no regard to their political affiliation or social condition, supported this effort, whether openly or from the sidelines.

We called assemblies in the neighborhoods to discuss peace with social justice and to promote the political participation of the people. But we still kept a lot of faith in weapons, even if they were silenced, as a backing to the voices that began to open a path toward dialogue. The guns had to be quieted for us Colombians to talk about the country; that was the point of the truce and the dialogue.

Stop the War for a Moment

I often thought of Alfredo, my compañero, and sometimes a sob welled up in me in the middle of a memory. One day I heard of his death on a radio news program. I called for confirmation.

"Yes, it happened about a month ago," said someone at the other end of the line.

I couldn't coordinate my thoughts or move a muscle. The noise of the street became deafening and I felt as if my body were melting. Suddenly I became aware that I was standing on the edge of a street filled with traffic. I have no idea how, but I crossed that street and made it to the meeting with the regional central command. Violeta looked at me with surprise and asked me in a whisper what had happened. I must have been pale. She took my hand under the table and squeezed it in solidarity. No one there knew what had happened. Throughout the meeting the tears fell silently and I dried them discreetly. Violeta from time to time draped her hand over my arm. The compañeros asked no questions.

I gave no time to my pain. I refused to give space to mourning. Work had multiplied and I scared away my sadness with the tasks I had to complete. Sometimes the tears flowed freely while I traveled by *buseta*[4] or walked along the street. The only thing that really made me happy were the meetings with my muchachos, who were increasingly smart and creative.

Alfredo was my emotional axis. As long as he had lived I had felt the certainty of love: it was both of us against the world. Now he had left me alone. At first the feeling of abandonment assaulted me, and I was angry at the way he'd let himself be killed. Then I accepted his death as an inevitable part of war. We were subject to that contingency, and he had bet his life on a dream of peace that often veered dangerously close to death. It had happened the way he'd have wanted it to: during battle, after the takeover of the municipality of Miranda. He was shot in the forehead. He never saw it coming and so was spared the antechamber of pain, the anguish. It was the death of a guerrillero.

For months my pulse was low, as if my energy had evaporated along with my lover, and for all the ideology I put into it, life without passion was exhausting. Only the announcement of the truce shook me out of lethargy.

In August 1984 the ceasefire accords were held with President Belisario Betancur and the dialogue tables were begun. Two towns in the country— Corinto in Cauca and El Hobo in Huila—were the seat of the public acts. There the two army fronts met with M-19 fronts, some urban commandos, some delegates of the government, and the press. The people spilled out of the towns. They came in droves to meet the most famous guerrilleros of the time, to ask for their autographs as if they were movie stars and have their pictures taken with them.

4. A small bus, more like a van, that is cheaper than a taxi but more expensive than an average bus.

Fayad ordered me to go to Corinto. He told the message carrier to make it clear that it was urgent and pressing: "Otherwise, don't come back," he had said. We chose the most outstanding compañeros and compañeras and made a squad that was representative of the Bogotá regional. We traveled with all the security measures to Cali, and in the terminal we asked shyly for transportation to Corinto.

"You're going to have to wait in line—look, everyone wants to go see the guerrilleros. They say Commander One is there, and even la Chiqui. Shall I get you an express?"

We paid double the usual price for the transportation. On the road the driver asked if we knew the guerrilleros and we told him we did not. We passed ourselves off as journalists.

From about two kilometers before the town there were guerrilla checkpoints, the last one on the plaza. They wouldn't let us pass without the permission of the guard. I asked them to call him over to us. The official in charge, Mariano, came to greet us—he was the muchacho we had had the scare with in the Mira. First came the clamor of our greetings and then a hug that lifted me off the ground. With him were Efren and Platanote, two other compañeros from the adventure in the Pacific. The driver watched in amazement while I greeted the compas I hadn't seen since we'd been released from prison.

There was a carnivalesque atmosphere in Corinto. People had come from Cali to visit their guerrilla relatives, indigenous people had come down from the mountains to talk with the comanches; the curious, neighboring villagers, local authorities, and tails were all in attendance. We put on a fair, with barbequed meats, dancing, flower sellers, fruit sellers, candies, Colombian flags and M-19 flags, photographers, and the ubiquitous fortune-tellers foretelling peace in the lines of the palms of all the guerrilleros.

It was one of the happiest events of my life. In the midst of that festive atmosphere, I again saw Iván Marino, his wife, Fanny, and their kids, who were already men. I met compañeros from the Mira like Ismael and el Gordo Arteaga—I must have met half of the organization, and would have met the other half, but they were in El Hobo.

At dusk, my body hurting from so many tight embraces, the euphoria gave way to nostalgia, and I wept in the corner of the school where I was staying. I was tired of waiting for Alfredo's face to appear alongside his compañeros' from the eastern front. Only three short months had passed since his death, in one of the last battles fought before this truce we were celebrating.

When the accords were signed, when the last shots were fired into the air to bid farewell to war, I remembered Julius Fucik's lines: "how tragic it would be to be the last soldier to be shot through the heart by the last bullet in the last second of a war."[5] But someone has to be that soldier. The greatest absences were of Jaime Bateman and Alfredo. I would have loved to see them enjoying the moment of truce, something we had thought impossible only hours before the signing, when police at a checkpoint nearly killed Carlos Pizarro and did blow Laura's fingers off when she tried to protect him from the shots.

My memories of the truce celebration are as clear as photographs. At the table where the accords were signed sat Bernardo Ramírez, the delegate from Belisario Betancur's administration, the journalist Enrique Santos, Alvaro Fayad, Iván Marino Ospina, Israel Santamaría, Almarales, and Pizarro, wounded, with his arm in a sling. They were surrounded by the happy faces of people who believed that the end of hostilities had finally arrived. After the flashbulbs stopped popping, we resumed the celebration. There were many slogans about peace, carnations in the barrels of the guns, music, dance, and crowds who showed us in their faces their faith in the change we had mediated. A little inner voice warned me not to take what I was seeing as the only reality. Perhaps it was the premonition of the fortune-teller who had warned me of the attempt on my life. She said I would come out of it wounded. Even in the midst of euphoria, one could not forget death.

Signing the truce meant silencing the weapons, not throwing them away. Both sides of the truce believed only halfway. Our instincts told us that confrontation on the political front would end up talking through weapons once again, sooner or later. Most of the military forces were concentrated in two camps, one in Yarumales, Cauca, and the other near el Hobo in Huila. Around them the army established checkpoints and located the troops. Was this a seige of peace?

Dialogues of the Deaf

The day of the ceasefire, the M-19 told us that Antonio Navarro, Israel Santamaría, Andrés Almarales, Vera Grabe, and Alfonso Jacquin would participate in the dialogues; the rest would be people from the regional processes. We applauded them heartily and wished them luck, but deep down we thought of the enormous risk they were running—they would probably be among the next to die. But it was one thing to declare willingness to work together and quite another to implement it. Peace talks were delayed for weeks while those indispensable to them were persuaded to participate.

5. Julius Fuchik, *Notes from the Gallows* (New York: New Century Publishers, 1948), 53.

A few weeks after the signing, Fayad visited me in Bogotá. He loved to eat home cooking, so Violeta and I cooked. We talked well into the night; only then did he propose that I participate in the dialogue. I told him no. I preferred to remain clandestine and keep working in the neighborhoods, because I didn't trust the state's intelligence services. Besides, in order to appear publicly I would have to acknowledge my participation in the embassy takeover, and it wasn't worth it. I argued that I didn't know how to talk in public, so no . . . no! But he teased me the whole time and finally argued that the organization needed a "bouquet" of berraca women to show off. I was never any good at saying no, and I finally yielded to the needs of the organization. I made one last attempt to decline, however, and told Fayad that a fortune-teller in Corinto, the one he had also consulted, had warned about an attempt on my life. Fayad cracked up and said, "That's so you won't let down your guard."

The decision was made. I didn't want to leave the regional; I liked work-ing with the teams. But I had to go. I said good-bye to Violeta, rented an apartment with my boyfriend of the time, a professor at the Nacional, and started to come out into public life little by little, but warily, as if I had been pushed out onto the catwalk to do a striptease show.

"My name is María Vásquez, I'm a member of the M-19, I was involved in the takeover of the embassy—for as much as I denied it—and I think that we will only achieve peace for the country through dialogue." I repeated this chorus before leaving home so I wouldn't forget the script.

We met in a suite at the Hotel Tequendama, the headquarters for the dialogue team. The group grew larger with the addition of regional delegates, community leaders, students, and professionals who had never participated in military structures. Many people wanted to express their opinions. The apartment was like an anthill teeming with people from all walks of life: senators, union leaders, community workers, vendors, rebel members of the oligarchy, intellectuals, and artists. The feeling that we were surrounded by supporters gave us a little confidence in spite of the push and pull of the conversations with the government and the political class.

The M-19's work with the masses progressed. The people felt that the support of weapons allowed us to mediate their demands with greater strength. They called on us to talk to the lot pirates and to stop abuses in the neighborhoods. We met with business owners to support the labor demands of the employees, with the owners of the Central de Abastos (Corabastos) to negotiate a space in the plaza in the name of hundreds of small-scale retailers, with owners of bullfighters in defense of the national *toreros*, with television programmers, pro-actor unions–the list was a long one.

Government intelligence organizations didn't rest, either. They bugged our phones, wrote down the names of our friends and the addresses of the houses we visited, listened to our conversations, and planted spies within the organization. We perceived all of this, but sometimes we wondered if we were being paranoid. I told myself to protect my security to the hilt, along with that of those around me. I didn't give out my telephone number, didn't call from friends' houses, never gave anyone my address, kept no document containing information about the structures of the PMO. Nor did I talk about my operational past with anyone.

Meanwhile, in the rural zones close to the guerrilla camps, the military forces grew tired of watching checkpoints where food supplies entered for the guerrilla, and tired of filling notebooks with the names and ID numbers of any paisano who entered the peace territory. The most recalcitrant segments of the population still suffered shocks every time some guerrillero talked on TV or appeared at the cocktail parties of the political, social, or diplomatic world.

Four months later, between Christmas 1984 and New Year's Eve, the army attacked with mortar fire the Yarumales camp where Pizarro's forces were concentrated. They said the guerrilla had kidnapped a hacienda owner from the region and was hiding him in the camp. The peace commission and the government's delegates who verified that this was not true were worth nothing. Their word made no impression on the armed forces.

The atmosphere of mutual mistrust had prompted us to carry out military engineering work in the previous months, and we had dug trenches, erected shelters, and even amassed water reserves that would sustain us in the event of a seige. And a siege there was—a two-week offensive—and we were glad we had taken these precautions. The considerable disadvantage in weapons was compensated by the courage of the compañeros. Pizarro designed and led the defense and attack plans. From the trenches, in the line of fire, he demonstrated a military skill that surprised everyone, especially the army, who swore they would defeat the guerrilla during the Christmas holidays.

Sixty men and women, with about thirty weapons between them, held their positions and repelled the army forces. The war had resumed. The army declared its right to territorial control and the guerrilla demanded respect for the accords. Measures before the peace commission were worthless, as were verification commissions and denunciations to the press. The ministers weren't even in their offices, nor was President Betancur. No one went out in defense of peace.

On 6 January, as those of us involved in the dialogue were gathering up our people in the cities and heading for the monte to back up the battle, the government seemed to wake up and started to try to fix the issue. We continued our march to the monte. On the way we found our people from the southern front doing the same.

The government and our representatives had to negotiate again, but we had the advantage in public opinion. The score was 1–0. The army had broken the truce. So we proposed to hold an M-19 national conference to decide the direction of peace, with the aid of representatives from industry, commerce, and the banks, as well as government officials and international guests. Meanwhile, we gathered in the monte with everyone who came up from the cities to offer support for peace.

How Could We Believe in Peace Forged with Bullets?

Negotiations for holding the conference began. While the troops surrounded us, we guerrilleros took positions and dug trenches at night barely eighty meters from their watchposts.

My first mission was to command a vanguard squad, whose position was as close as possible to the army. All of them were peasants and getting them to trust me was really tough. They had advantages over me in knowing the land, and I lacked the skill to move at night, to locate myself geographically and lead a march. I had learned these things in school, but I had never put that knowledge into practice. I think the peasants also resisted having a city woman in the lead. They did only what I ordered and exactly as I ordered it; they took absolutely no initiative. And they smiled slyly every time I made a mistake.

After three days I realized that I had to confront the situation head on. Over lunch I acknowledged their skill on the land and their courage and acknowledged my limitations and lack of practice in the monte. I also told them about urban operations I had participated in, operations that had helped the M-19 achieve its political goals. Those actions held as much weight as their recent experience in Yarumales, so we were tied. My strategy worked. From that day forward they stopped putting up obstacles and we became a team.

As the date of the Robles conference approached, the debate in the organization became increasingly intense and polarized between the urban and the rural, the political and the military, dialogue and war. The army attack on Yarumales and the triumph of our military force magnified the weight of the war and increased mistrust in the conversations with the government.

In the midst of all this, many wanted to go to the conference to participate in the peace deliberations. The army arrested them in nearby towns and so they resorted to taking over churches and capital cities in protest. The majority of those who came to the camp did so by dodging the seige with the help of those who knew the region. Sometimes the three-hour trip took two days, but they took the risk. All told, more than 500 guests arrived.

We had to accommodate the visitors somehow, so we made collective cambuches with *paceras*[6] to accommodate the guests, beat out paths, organized showers and latrines, set up KP duty to feed everyone, and built a conference room and a hospital. We did all this using military tactics, making sure that gathering spaces were shielded from enemy fire. We also built trenches and shelters in case of an artillery offensive like the one on Yarumales. We were aware of the great contradiction at the heart of our activity: as we worked publicly to continue the peace and dialogue process, we were preparing for war. That was a problem for the whole country. How could we believe in peace that was forged with bullets?

In Los Robles we felt invincible. We were gathered there to decide for war or peace. There we saw all the old compañeros again; I hadn't seen them all since the days when the organization was a family. In attendance were Iván Marino, Fayad, Afranio, Boris, Elvecio, Raúl, Gladys, and Eddy, la Negra María and Jorge from the embassy, el Gordo Arteaga, Ismael, and compañeros from the Mira, Violeta, Manuel, and my muchachos from the regional, and friends and collaborators like Olga, Camilo, el Gato (the cat), Omar, and other people from the Nacional. I was able for the first time to talk with compañeros like Arjaid, famous for his crude vocabulary and the sensitivity of his pen, whose existence I knew of from the stories that circulated in the organization, and Ester Morón, a legendary woman recognized not only in the M-19 but also in the JUCO, in Girardot, and now throughout the country and beyond. I had heard talk of her from the first years of militancy. Some remembered her in the freshness and ardor of her communist teen years, others in the more secret tasks she performed with Bateman, others in the tasks of insurgent diplomacy. Many more talked about her heroic spirit; I think she was the only one among us who managed an undertaking that was profitable for the organization. But Ester seemed unaware of the halo over her head; she didn't try to seem anything or to be anything, she was simply herself with a great deal of conclusiveness. I dare say that Los Robles was the first and last time that almost all of us from the M-19 congregated with our people. We could get together so rarely. During the conference I

---

6. Wooden slats measuring between twenty centimeters and a meter, used as bed frames. *Paceras* are used in more permanent camps, and are considered a luxury in the monte, which is why they were given to the guests.

felt that we could achieve utopia if only we stayed together, and so the idea of "being a government" didn't seem like a trick we were pushed into. I felt so strong at Los Robles.

I had a compañero around then, *el sardino* (the kid) Lucio, one of the negotiators with the government. I think I accepted him because the audacity of his advances unnerved me. I was seduced by his intelligence and his age. There is nothing more rejuvenating than the love of a young man awakening to life.

Corinto and Los Robles were two landmarks of rapprochement with the real country. But in spite of touching the dream with our fingertips, we could not forget the void created by our dead. In the middle of the conference, when we learned that Clementina, Bateman's mamá, was coming, we all ran out to greet her, with as much enthusiasm as if she had brought her son with her. She rode in on a horse that a guerrillero led by the bridle, and we greeted her with cheer after cheer, for her and for our disappeared commander. I had a camera and I recorded on film her emotional face, her embraces with everyone, and the tears that rolled down her cheeks, until my own tears clouded my vision. El Flaco Bateman *was* with her. He was there in her honey-colored eyes, in her gestures, in the strength of her seventy years.

Children of War

Among the armed men and the guests child guerrilleros ran around in play. About twelve kids wanted to emulate the guerrilleros, and, in spite of being sent back because of their age, they returned and would not be sent away. Many people, moved by their commitment, took these children under their wings. They made up a squad under the command of a thirteen-year-old girl, the daughter of a prostitute from Miranda. They helped in the camp tasks and served as couriers between the settlements of the various platoons. But above all they played. They almost always played at war, using sticks for guns and ambushing each other.

The kids enjoyed many privileges. They were the the first to eat, got the biggest pieces of meat—when there was meat—and no one made them do anything, no one yelled at them, and they slept cuddled up next to their tutors. Their only responsibility was to attend the school that Laura improvised in a corner of the propaganda cambuche, at least four hours a day. They resisted this a little because it kept them from play, but they complied.

Miguelito was the most spoiled of them all, maybe because of his tiny, old man's face, a sign of chronic malnutrition, or because he won over the women with tenderness and wheedling. He said he was thirteen, but he looked eight. His mamá came to visit him at camp and he ran around introducing her to all his friends. She was a tiny, bony woman whose difficult life showed in her face. She hadn't come to take Miguelito away, as a lot of us thought, but to bring us her youngest son, because her salary as a washerwoman wasn't enough to support them and the kids had to find food in the streets. With us, she said, they learned "good things" and were cared for. The guerrillero's life was preferable to the dangers of the streets. That night I lay awake for hours. More than flattering me, what Miguelito's mamá said made me sad. The country was really in a terrible situation when the life of a guerrillero was a good alternative for a poor child.

Some muchachos in their teens, among them a boy named Mao, had grown up in the southern front of Caquetá. Mao told of how, one day when the compas were passing by his house, he offered himself as a guide and stayed for three days. They sent him back because he was so young. He went home, got clothes, and went back to the camp. He offered himself as a courier, a guide, whatever they needed, and this time they let him stay.

By the time he was eleven Mao already had a gun, an M-19 rifle he had recovered after a battle. Once he was playing ambush with an older boy who had also joined the guerrilla, when he saw an army patrol coming up the hill. At first he thought that it was part of the game, but as he watched they began to advance. Silently, he put in the clip and charged his carbine. As the patrol approached, he aimed at the first soldier in the column, but then saw the officer just behind him and took careful aim at him. When the officer was about thirty meters away, he fired and watched the man fall. The column was plunged into fear and chaos. The two muchachos retreated at a run to warn the compañeros. Mao told this story like a veteran. He was only eleven when he killed an army lieutenant, as if it were part of the game.

When I met Mao in Los Robles he was about fifteen and was lovesick and tired of war. He had participated in the takeovers of Florencia and Paujil, had been at Yarumales, and now his girlfriend had left him for a city boy. Mao asked to be moved from his platoon to the propaganda structure. He liked to use the mimeograph machine, take pictures, and chat with the guests. But he confessed to me that it was time for him to study. He wanted to get into the SENA, and after the conference he thought about "going down to the city to learn things," because he couldn't understand how a city boy could steal his woman.

We arrived at the conference in Los Robles with illusions, frustrations, faults, glories, defeats, sorrows, and dreams. The traces of the battle could already be seen on some of our bodies, and they were imprinted in our souls. More than half of us had been tortured or imprisoned; others carried pieces of bullets under their skin or scars that became the pretext for heroic stories. Some found more certainty in their acquaintance with death than in their relationship with life. There was a great mix of people, from dreamy poets and peace diplomats to men who wanted war. This was the M-19: a complex multiplicity of beings willing to think in the company of others, to deliberate publicly. Perhaps it's more accurate to say that we tried to inspire our disenfranchised country with our dreams of power and glory.

11

Mortal Wounds

L
OS ROBLES WAS like a family vacation, but after the conference we spread out. We all defined our missions with the organizational commission and headed for the corresponding region to do our work. By the end of February, I wanted to go back to the city. Vacation in the countryside had been really nice, but I didn't want to stay in the military forces. I preferred urban work. I accepted an assignment to form the peace camps in Cali with Afranio, Jacquin, Laureano, and Carlos Lucio.

Working with Afranio was great. I had full confidence in him, and besides, I was involved with el sardino Lucio. I told Pizarro, who was in charge of the eastern region, of my decision.

"It's cool that you want to stay in our military region," he said. "But did you talk to Fayad?"

Up until the conference I had been under Fayad's command. Now he was commander general. This time I took advantage of my promotion to the national command to take initiatives regarding my work. When I told him of my decision, he already had a mission for me; still, he didn't object. It made me sad to separate from him; if he had insisted a little, I'd have stayed under his command. That was my first act of autonomy.

Peace Camps

Our goal was to "be a government," so we threw ourselves on the cities in the hope of conquering the masses. We wanted to duplicate the experience of Los Robles in the urban arena. We believed that the recent triumph of the Nicaraguan revolution and the Salvadoran struggle marked a trend of insurrection. Our idea was to educate and motivate the poorest sectors of the cities till they became an alternative force. We were aware of the threat that this would pose to the established powers, which is why we wanted to prepare the people themselves for insurrection. We believed firmly that popular organization was a sure way to achieve their demands in the short and medium term, but with armed backing.

At first we sought out friends and acquaintances who could help us get closer to the neighborhoods we had chosen for their needs and strategic location. One of our criteria was that in case of a massive uprising of these neighborhoods, we had access to the mountain range, where our military forces were.

The getting-closer phase was quite clandestine. We walked all over the Terrón Colorado neighborhood with Afranio, asking people here and there about their most serious problems; at the same time we were doing territorial recognizance. On the one hand we analyzed political strategy, on the other, military possibilities. Other compañeros did the same in Siloé, Aguablanca, and Petecuy. We rented a house in each neighborhood and moved some compas there to start the job. At this stage, in spite of our giving priority to our work with the masses, clandestine and military habits were still deeply entrenched in us. We paid more attention to finding land that was good for digging trenches or building a shelter than to the political education of the people.

El sardino Lucio changed this. He was tired of making declarations on TV and radio, and one day he decided we should visit Petecuy, a neighborhood on the edge of Cauca. He invited the people there to talk with the M-19 using megaphones. He planted two flags on an empty lot, the national flag of Colombia and the flag of the M-19. A lot of people turned up, and el sardino delivered a fiery speech. By five in the afternoon he had formed a commando unit with the neighborhood people, as in the ANAPO days. We thought it was a bit rushed, but while we got five members, he got forty, and he set up a headquarters under any patch of trees around. From there civic activity unfolded around bettering the living conditions of the inhabitants. The feeling of belonging to a political force made the muchachos who had written off the neighborhood into its staunchest promoters. We liked el sardino's success, and we adopted his model in several other neighborhoods.

Thus were the peace camps born in the cities, and they became places where people who wanted to change their daily lives could converge. They were brought into the process by talking with their neighbors in a public area, under the shadow of some flags that gave them confidence and strength. They found the solutions themselves in those informal meetings; we played the role of local referees.

The guerrillero was still something of a mythical figure in the popular imagination; we backed up the promise of change with the power of our weapons. "With you, we can really do it," they said.

We talked a lot about how to make this casual sense of belonging, this spontaneous militancy, into something more formal. Someone had the idea that the closed order of the militia—hierarchy, military rituals, a hymn and a flag—could work as identity referents for the masses. We started to incorporate symbols and rituals into the camps. We had a "weapons yard," where every morning there were formations that raised the flag. We sang hymns and composed slogans. The strategy was a hit. The muchachos came in droves. War brought them faster than peace did, even if it was symbolic.

In the beginning the peace camps were groups of unarmed youths in charge of mediating disputes, combatting robbery, repairing roads, improving the neighborhood, encouraging general assemblies to resolve more serious problems, lending service to the neighbors, and organizing soup kitchens. Some afternoons they got elementary military instruction in land maneouvres and coordination of command voices. In a short time these neighborhood muchachos were disciplined, and the people gained confidence in their own ability to organize. But that had its own dynamic, which was independent of our will.

The first confrontations with the police came about in sectors that had recently been invaded, because when people found out that the M-19 had headquarters in marginalized neighborhoods, the number of squatters in those neighborhoods increased. In Petecuy, for example, a new group of huts appeared on the edge of Cauca every day. The compañeros from the regional dialogue command tried to negotiate solutions to this problem with a popular housing corporation called Invicali, but the police began evicting the squatters anyway. These were the first pitched battles of police against organized neighborhood forces. They lasted up to two days and militias from other camps appeared as backup; even the youth gangs came to offer their services to fight. While some fought at the site of the huts, others made statements to the local press and negotiated with the governor or the mayor for temporary solutions. These organized confrontations brought results and opened the door to negotiations.

Later on we reached agreements worked out by our spokespersons in the dialogue, along with the department administration, universities, and the community, to stabilize the new settlements and protect the environment, improve some public areas, and develop projects for community gardens. We even did joint campaigns with the metropolitan police for health and community work. We had been working in this area for only three months, and we had achieved a new negotiation style based on the concrete needs of the people, with the backing of mobilized popular forces. The experience of Cali began to repeat itself in several cities along the Atlantic Coast, in Medellín and Bogotá. People from other regionals consulted with us to learn about direct work with the camps.

El Valle presented us with special conditions. Our military forces had achieved visible successes in the previous stage, they remained concentrated close by, the departmental and municipal authorities had demonstrated good will in the peace negotiations, and, above all, the people had a common cultural identity that facilitated their mobilization. The peace camps expanded rapidly from three to fifteen, each with about fifty members. Unfortunately though not surprisingly, our success in El Valle del Cauca did not please the ruling class there, which became increasingly impatient with our presence.

We had formed a regional central command that had one militia structure and one dialogue structure. In the militia were Afranio, Eduardo Chávez, Laureano el Mocho, Gisella, Liliana, Hipólito, and me. Carlos Lucio was in charge of the dialogue, the work tables, and some negotiations and declarations. Our official headquarters were located in a hotel facing the Hotel Intercontinental, in a residential area in Cali. We held some meetings there that couldn't be held in the camps. One morning a journalist friend came to warn me that a military intelligence official from the III Brigade had threatened to prevent our further growth in Cali. I thanked him for his concern and told Carlos Lucio and the others.

We knew that some militia and right-wing sectors would try to push us out of the ring. We had plenty of experience of this kind of opposition—the ambush of Iván Marino on his way to an interview with the peace commissioners, days before the signing of the accords; the shooting of Pizarro and the compañeros en route to Corinto to sign the ceasefire; the Christmas military offensive against the Yarumales camp; and the attack on a commission of compañeros after the Los Robles conference.

We had lived with risk for many years. The possibility of death always lurked in the background, and we knew that one day it would be our turn. But when? I often felt as though a hunter were stalking me and this intuition may have saved me from many a danger. I moved quickly, left one location or avoided another, propelled by a negative energy, as skittish as a rabbit in the mountains. But on this occasion we took no measures to avoid risks. We at least had the advantage in El Valle that our movements were not planned.

The army stalkers nevertheless kept up their surveillance, waiting for the right moment to strike. Navarro moved to the Los Robles camp, and they arrested him for a day in the Codazzi Battalion in Palmira. He was freed because of a radio interception from the compañeros to the army and the immediate notification of the press. In the wee morning hours of 23 May he arrived at our headquarters. That morning around eight a group calling itself "Democracy" tossed two grenades onto a bus full of army employees. Navarro condemned the act and told the press that the M-19 had nothing to do with that type of action.

It was nearly ten when we went out to breakfast at the only cheap place around, El Oeste café. We met other compañeros there, and the six of us sat at the center table. As we were finishing up, a deafening explosion hit. In a flash the world spun around and the place filled with smoke. Stray pieces of wood, mud, and machine gun penetrated my body. In a daze I made for the door. Armed men, who looked at me as if I were a ghost, were retreating. Where were my compañeros?

Navarro was lying on the floor amid overturned tables and chairs, covered in blood. Carlos Lucio was dragging himself along the floor, looking for cover. Eduardo Chávez was screaming for help, and people in the streets were running toward us. I tried to move, but my legs wouldn't respond. I watch blood spurt out of tiny holes. I was aware that I was injured and allowed myself to slide down the door frame. An ambulance came and loaded the wounded one at a time. Someone carried me out and put me in the ambulance, closing the door behind me. My impressions were of the smell of blood, moans from Antonio in agony, sharp pain in my legs. I remembered the fortune-teller in Corinto: "They're going to try to kill you. Poor thing, your legs are hurt, and there's a lot of blood. But don't worry, no one dies." Incredible! She had seen the event.

I clung to her words: no one dies. Silvio Rodriguez's song came into my head: *"Nadie se va a morir, menos ahora."*[1] Carlos's head rested in my lap; I encouraged him and tried to keep him awake. Antonio's bloody moccasin was

1. No one's going to die, much less now. "Preludio de Girón," by Silvio Rodríguez.

hanging near my chest. I thought it weighed heavily on him and I took it off. A mass of flesh and blood came away with it. My God! Antonio was really hurt; he was moaning and spitting mouthfuls of blood. No, he couldn't die. The ambulance siren screamed out our anguish as it sped toward the Universidad del Valle Hospital. As we were carried into the hospital, journalists swarmed over us like flies, asking questions and taking pictures. Army soldiers were waiting for us in the emergency room. They descended on us as if we'd been arrested. I felt fear and impotence. Eduardo Chávez protested from his cot and got a gun butt in his face. They took my wallet away. The doctors and nurses rescued us from their hands.

Evidently they were paying us back for the morning attack on the official bus. Hell of a coincidence!

Carlos, Eduardo, and I were put in the same room and examined. The doctors ripped off my bra to look at a blood stain on my left breast; the wound was small. They ripped my pants up to my knee, which was very painful. There was a lot of commotion; Carlos Alonso's vital signs were falling fast.

"We're losing him!" a doctor yelled.

"There's almost no pulse."

They rushed him out of the room. I had no idea what to do. I was blocked, my jaw rigid, my tongue asleep, my hands numb. Someone asked me a question and I couldn't answer. I thought about my pregnancy; no one had confirmed it but I knew. I made an effort and was able to stutter that I was pregnant, but no one paid any attention to me.

"I'm pregnant," I repeated over and over again. Finally a nurse laid a lead apron over my stomach.

Then they took me to a room. People came and went; everyone was very nice and asked me how I felt. A girl mentioned my cousin, the medical student, and I said she was fine and asked the nurses please to notify my mother, but I gave no more information; I trusted no one. In the evening they brought Carlos Alonso in, still under the effects of the anesthesia.

The next day I tried to stand up but my legs wouldn't obey. I didn't like feeling limited in my movement; it made me feel unsafe. Militia people from the camps watched over us. The previous night a woman from the DAS, whom my compas saw with the man who had thrown the grenade in the attack, had gone into Navarro's room, maybe to speed up his death. Luckily Chávez recognized her and raised a huge ruckus.

When Carlos Alonso woke up later that day, we were already surrounded by his family. He almost didn't notice me. In his weakened state he could barely handle seeing his family, and I felt very alone with the responsibility of the child I was carrying. Would I have to abort?

Three days later we left the hospital because no one would answer for our safety. If a member of the DAS was connected to the attack, what could we expect? The attorney general moved me and Chávez to the airport for transport to Bogotá. The other two compañeros, Alberto Caicedo and el Gordo Alvarado, had left the day before. Navarro and Carlos Alonso remained hospitalized.

Toniño, a painter friend of the M-19, and his girlfriend, were waiting for us at the airport. We were expecting at the very least a security detail; after all, Eduardo had witnessed the DAS woman's link to the attack. But the compañeros from the dialogue group granted no importance to our arrival. We took a taxi to the long-term hotel at the Plaza de Toros, where our headquarters was located at the time. When the compañeros there found out what had happened, they decided to find us safe lodging.

Fayad met us there. He was very worried about the difficulties of maintaining the truce and all the problems in fulfilling the recommendations of the work table of the dialogue. We talked a while, and before he left we asked him to put us under the responsibility of the military structure. We felt safer in the hands of the organization, especially given our physical defenselessness. Eduardo's leg was in a cast up to the knee, and both my legs were wounded and my right arm almost immobilized.

For some incomprehensible reason, we ended up in an apartment the police had raided a few months before, where some Ecuadorian compañeros from the Alfaro movement were now hiding. I felt very content, but we were moved again two weeks later, and this time I was separated from Eduardo. I was in the house of a nurse who, in spite of her good intentions, couldn't care for me or feed me as my convalescent situation required. I was desperate. I spent the whole day alone, and since I couldn't walk, getting up to go to the bathroom meant dragging myself along on my bottom, which depressed me terribly. I thought of my pregnancy, that I needed to drink milk and didn't have any. It made me sad not to hear anything from Carlos Alonso, who was in Bogotá.

I decided to leave the place in spite of the risks. I couldn't handle the isolation anymore; I needed to be with friends. I told the organization my decision and three days later was given the address of a compañera from the university who had offered to take care of me. I managed to go out to a public phone and call Carlos Alonso. We did not have much of a conversation, however, for I didn't have enough love in me to forgive him for his lack of interest in my pregnancy. It never occurred to him that I needed special attention and that his family could provide it. I felt very fragile then, not just because of my injuries but because of the pregnancy. I was especially anxious because the neurologist at the hospital had told me I should have an abortion because of possible damage to the baby's nervous system caused by the explosion and my injuries. I needed emotional support more than ever. It had been Carlos Alonso's idea to have the baby, so why did he leave me alone with the tough decision of whether to continue it or not?

I was rescued by María Elvira Carvajal. We met at the Nacional when she and el Negro Vélez were going out. She was a cheerful, rosy-cheeked girl who wore a Scottish skirt and moccasins. They called her manzanita (little apple), and she studied educational sciences. She and Vélez received me in their home and took care of me with love and patience. Their little girl, Marcela, who was about seven then, became my greatest companion. María Elvira was like a fairy godmother. She helped cure the anguish that had been draining me. Under her protection I recovered the hope that my pregnancy could be successful, and I pondered saving a love that, like my body, was healing. That's why I agreed to go to Mexico with Antonio Navarro and Carlos Alonso Lucio.

Dreams of Insurrection Buried in the Mud

The news of the attack profoundly affected my son, Juan. When we saw each other, I was moved to hear him confess his fear that something bad had happened to me. He gave me a tiny rag monster with a sign that said *"Suspiro por verte"* (I can't wait to see you). As a precaution I told him nothing about my pregnancy; even I didn't yet know if it would have a happy ending. The morning before I left for Mexico I went to say good-bye to him. I visited him at his father's house and explained why I was going out of the country for a while. He agreed, was even a bit happy. After all, it was safer for me to be out of Colombia until I was completely healed. I called my mom to tell her good-bye and then my son went with me to get a taxi to Lucio's house. My little boy had to help me get into the car because I still couldn't do much, and he gave me money to pay for the ride because I didn't have a single peso.

I saw Carlos Alonso again. He greeted me as if we hadn't been separated for a moment. Delegates from the attorney general were at his house. Around twelve noon they drove us to the airport, taking complex security measures. Antonio came in on a flight from Cali; one of his relatives, a doctor, was with him. One month after the attack, his health was still very delicate, and Betancur's administration wouldn't guarantee his safety, not even after another attempt to kill him in the Valle Hospital. The peace commission, and even more so the measures taken by Laura Restrepo and Gabriel García Márquez, had resulted in Mexico's offer to welcome us for six weeks for humanitarian purposes.

In Mexico City security was tight; the Mexicans kept our arrival out of the papers. The Guaruras, or state security staff, watched over us day and night. We left our compañera's house only to go to the hospital where Antonio was staying. We couldn't do much else, either; none of us could move very well. In this hospital, finally tired of fighting for his life, Navarro asked the doctors to amputate his leg as the only way to beat the infection that threatened to consume him.

The day of the operation I felt most for Laura, who looked after Antonio with loving care. Pedrito, her little boy, didn't want to leave his mother's side, and she, with infinite patience, helped them both. Antonio, still unconscious, was moaning pathetically. He had to be enduring all the pain in the world, even after all the pain killers. For a man as active and energetic as he, the loss was going to be especially difficult. If it was, he never showed it. After the amputation his recovery was almost miraculous: the fever disappeared, he didn't need oxygen any more, he began to eat normally and to talk. Most of all, he played with Pedrito again. Antonio then allowed us to see his sensitivity and emotion, which he normally worked at hiding behind a strictly rational appearance. Undoubtedly, the miracle that made all this possible was named Laura Restrepo. Without her, Antonio's heart wouldn't have sprouted from that stump of a leg.

After forty-five days we were thrown out of Mexico. The Mexican government's reasons for the humanitarian gesture had expired. For a moment we didn't know what to do or where to go, with Navarro still recovering in a wheelchair. They had taken Carlos's cast off and he could use crutches, but the bone in his leg wasn't knitting, and I was walking with difficulty and an increasingly large tummy. The compañeros in charge of international relations used all their contacts to find us somewhere to recover.

When I found out they weren't going to renew our visas, I went to Teotihuacán, knowing that if I left Mexico before seeing that place I would never forgive myself. I crawled up to the Sun Pyramid and sat there for a long time, filled with reverent awe. Sitting before that group of monuments, the silence echoing timelessly through the plains, I felt a warm current of life surging to my insides, to my baby, for the first time since the attack. The ancestral magic of Teotihuacán gave me strength.

While the compañeros were trying to arrange our immediate future, we received an invitation that was a lifesaver. The Cubans wanted us to attend the continental meeting on foreign debt, to be held in Havana on 26 July 1985. The trip was arranged in a week. I loved Cuba and had never imagined

I'd go back. I cried when we landed. In many ways the island brought back memories of Alfredo and the love we had shared there. The Cubans put us up in the Hotel Habana Riviera, overlooking the sea. In the halls of the convention center we ran into well-known Colombians, among them the ex-president, López-Michelson, Gabriel García Márquez, General Matallana, and Andrés Pastrana.

Antonio was given ten minutes to speak at the event. When he wheeled himself onto the platform, a complete silence fell over the room, where hundreds of people from all over the Americas had gathered. It was the first time he had sat for more than half an hour without fainting. I never thought he'd be heard. But his voice resounded all the way to the back of the room. Even as his body still had not completely won the battle, he spoke of peace. The standing ovation he received shook the auditorium. In that moment Navarro resumed his political being, and from then on his recovery proceeded at a much more rapid pace. One month later he was playing motocross in his wheelchair under Pedro's supervision. By September he was walking with crutches, and less than a year later he was dancing salsa with a prosthesis.

After the first Cuba meeting there were others, also on foreign debt, for intellectuals, journalists, and students. Friends and acquaintances from Colombia attended them and brought us news of our homeland. The peace treaty had been broken, and we found ourselves once again facing war that would affect the urban population with whom we had established the peace camps. The government's military tactics were backed by terror. The muchachos from the citizens' militias resisted in Siloé, Aguablanca, and Ciudad Bolívar, but the army killed, captured, or disappeared dozens of people as a warning. In the Cauca and Valle, our military forces under Pizarro and Boris brought the combat ever closer to the city.

The rhythm of the war imposed itself, and the popular urban movement that had gestated at the peace camps suffocated in fear. The survivors had to go underground into clandestine lives. This time the hits were more accurate, because we had shown our faces and let our friends talk. Or maybe because we didn't completely believe in peace either, and we decided to prepare an insurrection legally, trusting in popular enthusiasm.

The only thing the people remembered were the popular assemblies at which they had decided what needed to be done in the neighborhoods and held courts to punish thieves and violators without resorting to violence. They also remembered legends like Afranio Parra, whom the soldiers couldn't see even if he were right in front of them, because he smeared his face with tiger grease and wore a jaguar fang and a piece of quartz hanging from his neck.

The rest was frustration and despair. Many youths paid for the dreams with their lives. The Aguablanca mud, the Siloé red dirt, and the Malvinas cold in Ciudad Bolívar formed the basis of the utopia of popular power we imagined. The whole country had played at "peace" without ever removing their fingers from the trigger, and the dreamers wound up dead.

A Palace of Ashes

Cuba. Every revolutionary's homeland. Only there could we feel better than at home, be with friends, live without fear. The Cubans treated us like human beings who deserved to live.

As soon as the meetings were over, we were put through all sorts of medical tests. The Cuban doctors put us back together piece by piece, an operation here, another there. Rest and recover—that was all we did. Carlos Alonso needed an operation to reconstruct the bone in his leg and another to do a graft on his eardrum. He was in the hospital the longest.

The genetics experts kept close a watch on my pregnancy. In addition to the risks from the attack, they had detected a tropical virus that, if active, could cause deformities in the baby. I wasn't convinced my pregnancy was viable until the fifth month. It was decided by points, much like a baseball game: a favorable genetic concept, an unfavorable viral concept, one OB-GYN exam in favor, another exam that sowed doubts. Finally the points in favor of a normal pregnancy won out. The decision to have a child with risks of abnormality caused me anguish. It was, above all, my responsibility, though Carlos Alonso, the eternal optimist, thought nothing would go wrong.

We were at the Hotel Riviera for the duration of our stay in Havana, in a room overlooking the sea. We had a car and driver to ferry us to the hospital and wherever we needed to go. We spent the time in a lazy daily routine. We had the best food and could swim in the sea or the pool, walk in the evening down El Vedado, and top it all off with an ice-cream in Copelia. We enjoyed the world of art and shows led by Frank Fernández, the marvelous pianist who had been Bateman's friend. We made friends and got invitations and kindnesses of all sorts. The atmosphere only changed around the end of the year, when a hurricane hit. But the storm was so well forecast that it was more like a show than a tragedy. We spent hours watching from our window as the wind whipped the sea against the walls of the embankment.

On 5 November the press faxes brought us news of the M-19 takeover of the Palace of Justice in Bogotá. We met with some compañeros in Navarro's room to watch the news. We didn't say much, though there were optimistic voices. I wanted to trust that everything would turn out okay, but I couldn't quite believe it.

The next day, when the screen showed the palace in flames, I understood how the compañeros who were trapped inside with the kidnapped must have felt. I listened to the news on Radio Reloj all night, imagining Elvecio, el Negro Jaquin, Andrés, and Lucho trying to fight the fire. How I hurt for them and the rest, all the ones in the palace!

The next day Antonio, Laura, Pedrito, and I went to the beach. We were alone, contemplating the sea in silence for hours on end. We didn't even look each other in the eye. I told myself, as Fayad had taught me, that the sea washes the soul clean. But this time, all the water in the Caribbean wasn't enough to return us to tranquillity. We returned to the hotel in silence, and several days passed in the same way. What could we say?

Life and Death

While my child was winning a battle of life, compañeros as close as Iván, Elvecio, Jacquin, and Lucho were dying in various confrontations. I felt the struggle between life and death in my womb, and I wanted with all my heart for the energy from those who were leaving to be caught up in the little being growing inside me. This thought was my only solace.

On 17 January, the twelfth anniversary of our theft of Bolívar's sword, my son was born. Because of this, and because he was conceived on 19 April, we named him Simón José Antonio, after the Liberator.

It was not an easy birth, but I was much more aware than I had been when I had Juan, which made the suffering bearable. The conditions and the treatment from the doctors and the nurses were radically different from my first experience. After fourteen hours of labor, still not sufficiently dilated, when I felt I couldn't handle the pain any longer, I asked the doctor, a sweet Nicaraguan, to help me once and for all. At the next contraction, he facilitated the dilation by opening the cervical neck with his fingers. I felt like I was being split in two, and I didn't even have any strength to scream, but the head of the baby peeked out. The birth came quickly after that. I slept the sleep of the truly exhausted.

José Antonio was surrounded by love from the moment of his birth. Besides his mother and father, he had Antonio. But he also had Frank and his family, Ester, his grandma and the muchachos, my friends Aideé and Clarisa, the compañeros from the America department, who officially tended to us, and others who were around us. The Cubans love children; they privilege them, they take them into account. Children's rhythms and needs are under-stood in the best way, and no one gets impatient or angry when a baby cries. In the hotel the baby was in the arms of the waitresses, the bellhops, and the drivers. Everyone offered to take care of him.

My little one was two months old when they killed Fayad. I received this news in a midnight phone call. I thanked the Cuban civil servant, who was unable to provide much detail but offered me his condolences. I was alone; the baby was asleep in his crib. I went out to the balcony overlooking the sea, and curled up in a corner there, where I cried until I was completely empty. The next day not even one drop of milk came out of my breasts for my son. The pain of this loss had left me a desert.

The memory I have of that time is that I took care of José and Carlos in the hotel room. The Cubans took care of me. I had never been in a setting more conducive to happiness, yet the events that were shaking Colombia and the M-19 put happiness out of reach. My pampered existence made me feel guilty. I felt that my duty was to be by my people in this difficult situation, and the peace I was enjoying in Cuba made me ashamed.

By December 1986 the list of the dead had grown. El Gordo Arteaga, Ismael, Boris, Gladys, Alfredo's brother, Manuel, Rosa, Ernesto, and twelve more muchachos from the Bogotá regional were just the ones I knew.

Pizarro stayed on as general commander after Fayad's death, and he decided to call a new, broader meeting of the national command, the first one since Los Robles, to see how far we'd come and to define new strategies. In less than a month, almost all the invited were together.

At this meeting, the weight of the military aspect put the analyses out of balance, and the hierarchies were determined more by tactical success than by political strategies. This, at least, was my assessment of the situation. I think that at that point the militarization of the M-19 was already clear. Even the idea of a military force with international combatants that could act in several countries was part of the military delirium the war had plunged us into.

After this meeting there was another, with the ELN, the EPL, and the M-19, attended by all the commanders of all the organizations. There they lowered the profile on the Battalion America proposal, the name given to this dream of internationalizing the revolutionary war. In any case, the strength-ening of our own military forces was maintained as a priority, as well as the insistance on the development of the joint experiences with the EPL in Antioquia and the ELN in Santander.

My task as mother came to an end. Pizarro proposed that I accompany Carlos Lucio in his military preparations, helping him as the second in com-mand in a school that would be established in Libya. I tried to make him see that investing my time in an activity that I was already sufficiently pre-pared for would sacrifice my personal development, and that it was, above all, a useless investment when I could be on another front acting effectively. But Pizarro gave priority to Carlos Alonso's training; he really believed in el sardino, and he knew that only I could agree to subordinate myself to a freshman militant in spite of my higher rank. Let's say that he took ad-vantage of the love that was still left in me, and so I accepted the proposal. Going with Carlos Alonso meant leaving my second son, as I had the first, and renouncing the possibility of being with him a bit longer. My militant conscience left no room for personal options, so I didn't even think about it as a choice.

In the first days of January Simón José Antonio went to Colombia with his paternal grandparents and his brother, Juan Diego, who had come to meet him. I handed my son over to the Lucios with all the documents so they would have full custody. I went with them to the airport, and when I kissed my sons for the last time, my heart stopped.

I sat for a long time and watched the plane take off. I felt as if my body wasn't real anymore, as if my tears made me invisible. That night, when Carlos Alonso went out dancing with other compañeros and compañeras, I knew that I was no longer tied to him in any way.

I renounced motherhood for the second time. I left the lives of my boys in the hands of others, trusting that we would have time together under better conditions in the future. War was not compatible with motherhood. Once more I put my mission as a soldier above my personal life. I did this with sadness, but without regret.

Before leaving for Africa, I went to Nicaragua. The enthusiasm with which the people had greeted the Sandinista revolution captured my at-tention. No one had a monoploy on truth there, plans were amended to accommodate realities, and the Sandinistas invented a new way to confront difficulties every day.

Managua was a huge, sprawling city, like an endless puzzle not yet put together. The earthquakes and the war had left neighborhoods united by avenues and memories whose nomenclature referred to places that no longer existed. People would give directions like "go two blocks toward the lake, and one to the right, where the MacDonald's was, in front of the big tree." You could see the happiness of those who no longer had to address their "betters" as señor or patrón, or ask for permission to enter the city's only five-star hotel. Everyone's clothes—even the children's—included some piece of military apparel that indicated their relation, direct or indirect, to the war. I also noticed the irregularities of dress even in the uniforms of the army and militia.

I liked the people, with their chocolate skin and Indian eyes, the food, so similar to ours in the coffee region, and the easy hospitality. Much as I loved Cuba, its rigid socialism made me feel like I had a starched shirt on, while in Managua I wore a tee-shirt.

Commander Bayardo Arce had dinner with us and spoke without pedantry of the successes and absolute screwups of the past seven years. Later we attended a mass event to celebrate the triumph of the revolution. The full plaza in the mid-day sun and the fiery speech of Commander Ortega inspired many *vivas* and much passionate applause. How happy I felt in those days in Managua, with Pizarro, Navarro, Pedro Pacho, la Negra Flor, and Tico! While we swam in the Xiloá Lake at dusk to refresh ourselves, my commitment to our struggle was renewed. The Nicaraguan people didn't live much better than they had before, but they had hope, and that made all the difference. They had faith that the Sandinistas would be able to pull the country out of its morass.

Back in Havana, we made our final preparations for the trip to Africa. Most of our friends thought that setting up a school in Libya was crazy, but the M-19 had always done crazy things. We hoped to move about seventy soldiers from Colombia to train them in combat tactics and the use of war technology. To me, it simply seemed a very costly effort, and I suggested that it would be better for us to support a school in Colombia or another country in Latin America. But the accords between the organization and the Libyans had been signed.

We traveled in April 1987. I saw bits of Europe in springtime along the way, but our movement was limited by security concerns and the need to maintain the secrecy of our destination. Even then I found a way to visit museums and historical sites. I spoke only Spanish, but I armed myself with an English-Spanish dictionary and went out as I pleased, while Carlos Alonso slept in the hotel.

The Europe I had read about in books had awakened my interest in history, which I studied in college with Professor Castillejo. But the books had not prepared me for the elaborate architecture, the sculpted works of marble and bronze, the majestic cathedrals. I walked the streets and admired the monuments and bridges, visited churches, inspected towers, climbed endless stairs. I finally understood the magnitude of royal power, the coarseness of war, the importance of merchants and artisans in the configuration of cities during the Middle Ages, and above all the striking disparities between socioeconomic classes.

I was fascinated to see that Europeans did exactly what they planned, as if there were no time to waste. They moved quickly, almost mechanically, as if they had all been wound up at the same time. Sometimes I stood looking out the door of the hotel and felt I had been left completely alone in the world, it was so quiet. Only in the parks did the people seem unprogrammed and able to relax at their leisure. Even the youth, all dressed in black and adorned with metal jewelry and colored hair, went about with dignified faces. What serious people!

On my last day in Europe I sat down on a park bench to have a beer and enjoy the warm sun that made the trees and flowers shine. What an orderly world, I thought. Everything seemed important, transcendental, while we Colombians went through life as if borne by an April wind. Maybe Isadora Duncan was right when she said that the possibility for the future, for new creation, was in America.

Distance

We arrived in Tripoli in May, the month of Ramadan, the time of fasting and praying in the Islamic world. The car that carried us away from the airport sped so fast that the city was a blur of sepia and gray, white and green. My first impressions were of sand, dust, and emerald green as the official color. The people wore white and spoke in gutteral sounds impossible to mimic; their street signs looked like drawings, impossible to read. The streets were empty except for some kids running in the wind in their tunics.

The public gardens were all abloom. We entered a neighborhood by way of a paved street. Once inside the neighborhood there were dusty side streets, sheep eating garbage, and cats discreetly hanging around windows and roofs. In the yards, old, leafy olive trees stretched out their cooling shadows. An unmistakeable aroma of coffee with cardamom wafted to us on the breeze. Modern buildings, houses embellished with arches, round domes, and mosques adorned the sandy landscape.

We stopped at a building and the driver opened the door. Compañero Abdala, who was in charge of us, told us in fluent Spanish that this would be our home. A sleepy man inside greeted us and put us up on the third floor in a big carpeted apartment with two bedrooms, a dining room, and a huge living room that contained only a mattress and cushions. The kitchen had the basic appliances, a washing machine, and a dryer, all of them manufactured abroad. Everything was brand new.

Abdala introduced us to Mohamed, the administrador of the building, which belonged to Mathaba, a worldwide organization of the Jamahiriyah (i.e., the Republic, or State, of the Masses). Mohamed spoke French. He walked us through the place and introduced us to the other guests, a Burmese, a South African, an Ethiopian, a Tanzanian, and a Chilean—all men. We also met the service personnel, a Moroccan and a Tunisian, in charge of the food. The porter and the driver were Libyan. In the next days we saw the offices where the political representatives would work, with Carlos Alonso at the lead, and the camp where we would have the school.

The Libyans were so courteous and warm in their greetings—bringing their hands up to their chest and bowing their heads—that I felt like a princess. But when we sat down to talk and I expressed an opinion, they looked right through me and continued the conversation as if I hadn't said a thing. The accords with the organization were defined exclusively by Carlos Alonso. As far as they were concerned, I was only the wife of the M-19 representative in Tripoli. This irritated me to no end. I could live with making concessions to Pizarro, but for these people to erase me like this was maddening in the extreme.

At Mathaba headquarters I felt like I was in the Tower of Babel. Everyone spoke a different language, and the common tongues, English and French, were spoken so poorly that even I managed to understand. I tried striking up a conversation with the Chilean compañero from the MIR,[2] but as luck would have it he was a mathematician who thought sociology lacked conceptual rigor, and therefore, he said, had a difficult time relating to me. I was done for! Most of the time I just smiled.

I learned some Arabic from the driver and the cook. *Salam aleicom; shucram; aleicom salam* (peace be with you; thank you; and also with you). I also learned the names of the neighborhood and the street, and watched TV to accustom my ear to the language.

A week later twelve compañeros arrived for the class. Among them was Iván, whom I had known for years. I felt as if a relative had joined me in exile. Two women also came, which was a relief; up until then I had been the only one. Now our military routine resumed. We got up early, performed our daily exercises, talked about political documents, and programmed recreational time. We had to wait a month for the thirty other students to arrive.

I explored this new cultural universe almost always alone. I had no one to share my curiosity with. I watched the rituals of Ramadan unfold. Ramadan reminds the Arab people of their ancestors' difficult marches through the desert, and this strengthens the spirit. A little before four in the morning, the people got up and washed their faces, arms, and legs and were ready at four o'clock sharp, when the imam, or priest, intoned his praise from the tower

2. Movimiento de Izquierda Revolucionario (Revolutionary Leftist Movement).

of the mosque: *Allah, akba* (God is great). The faithful then poured from their homes, praying on their knees on a straw mat and bowing deeply, over and over again, toward Mecca. Everyone except mothers and children under twelve fasted all day, abstaining even from water, smoking, and making love until after dark. No one had strength for anything, and the heat made matters worse by making them sleepy. Movement in the entire country was reduced by 90 percent during Ramadan.

At night everything came alive, as if by magic. At about eight o'clock the parties began in the old part of the walled city. The men, dressed in *abbas* and *farmalás* with *kashabías* covering their heads, and the women in their long *farrashias*,[3] bought fruit and other food in the markets. The alleys turned into theaters. Crafts, incense, and clothes were sold; the commerce on the port was reactivated; and the music of flutes, bagpipes, and drums filled the air. It was like the awakening in *Sleeping Beauty*. People talked in loud voices, there were flashes of color everywhere, and the sweet smell of burning resin filled the air.

In Tripoli, the last night of Ramadan is like something out of *A Thousand and One Nights* or the novel *The Arab*, which tells of love-kidnappings in the desert and tents in the streets. Beautiful men with eyes as black as olives stroll by, letting the wind reveal their virility as it licks at their abbas. Beautiful, mysterious women hide under white fabrics. The tea is strong and sweet and sticks to your tongue, the coffee with cardamom smells like incense, and the dates are like honey.

The Arabs stretch out on straw mats with cushions to rest and play dominos. They smoke from the same narghile and drink tea constantly. After midnight, quiet returns. Along the narrow side streets the two-story houses rest against each other, as if to hold each other up in their old age. Garbage blankets the ground, the cats go on the prowl. A warm wind blows over the scene.

Libya is a strange country of beautiful men and women, Khaddafi's revolution, the Koran, and Islam. For the first time I felt like a true alien, like a green cat that doesn't know how to meow. Theirs was a different logic; their common sense had nothing to do with mine. In politics, arguments were interwoven with religion, and if I asked for an explanation they surprised me with anecdotes. They conspired out loud and in public, yet there was nothing more secret than the delights of the women wrapped up in farrashias.

---

3. The *abba* is a long, sometimes two-piece, tunic. Worn with the *farmalá* (vest), it forms a suit. The *kashabía* is a headpiece similar to but larger than a skullcap. The *farrashia* is the traditional women's long chemise, which may have more than one piece.

I didn't understand their kind of politics, or the methodology of their military schools, or the way they treated women, or even their hierarchical-religious relation with their leader, General Khaddafi. Then there was affection and the support of brotherhood; belonging to the Jamahiriyah created special solidarity. The Libyan people took care of us and loved us as if we were members of their own family, but they also expected reciprocity. We were tied hand and foot in this relationship.

Twenty-four men and women were able to come for the class. The effort of traveling by various routes to keep the final destination a secret, obtaining the proper documents, and the secrecy of the mission weren't compatible with the Libyan concept that military schools demonstrate political alliances that gave them power over their enemies. While we were aware of the security dangers in relations with those marked by the West as terrorists and warmongers, and thus maintained secrecy, they published our pictures in their newspapers with a sort of social note that welcomed us. Their intention after the completion of the class was that our muchachos' final exam should consist in fighting in Chad as Libyan allies in a territorial war that we never completely understood.

Carlos Alonso and I consulted quickly with the compañeros and decided to request that the M-19 leadership send no one else to the class. It made a mockery of security. Libya was the CIA's bogeyman, and our presence there put us on the side of international terrorism. All this when, in reality, they had very little to teach with respect to guerrilla warfare in the countryside or in the cities, because their experience was carried out in specific political and cultural contexts that weren't very useful to us.

The first class, on weapons, was pathetic. To teach us how to arm and disarm the AK-47, a Libyan professor gave instructions, another interpreted in English, and Carlos, who knew the least about weapons, interpreted in Spanish. Furthermore, everyone attending the class, except the Central American allies who were part of the Battalion America, had at least three years of combat experience. The first class lasted one week. It couldn't go on like this. The sophisticated weapons they had promised we would learn how to use we saw only in magazine articles about the war with Chad.

Taking advantage of the presence of Otto, an Ecuadorian radio technician who had been in charge of our communications with Pizarro for three years, we set up a school that specialized in communications. At first I wanted to attend the radio classes and learn how to use the latest equipment on the market, but I found that Otto's pedagogical philosophy wasn't compatible with mine. He was convinced that you had to pressure combatants as heavily as possible so that they would respond under pressure. I, on the other hand, thought that discipline went hand in hand with humanism and fraternity; after all, we were part of a project of new men and women. I couldn't condone his authoritarian treatment nor could I forbid it, so I decided to participate only in the political and ideological discussions. This decision isolated me from the rest of the compañeros most of the time.

The City and Men

A chorus of sheep bleating woke me up at dawn on 2 July, the day the Muslims sacrifice one or more sheep per family. The sheep massacre in Tripoli was considerable; the whole city smelled of blood. Days later you could still see pieces of lamb hanging from balconies and windows or on clotheslines, curing, and an an odor that is somehow both acrid and sweet filled the air.

Animals are an important part of this urban-rural world; it was not unusual to see sheep in the front yards of houses, even in the median strips dividing the streets. The first time I saw one of those animals in the back seat of a brand-new Mazda I thought the heat had finally gotten to me; but later I got used to seeing them all over the place. Their meat is as desirable as the camel's. After a while it stopped being strange to see sheep being transported by Mercedes Benz or Mazda. The drivers were simply bringing home the groceries home, but alive.

There were very few stray dogs in Tripoli, just an occasional dog barking in someone's yard. But cats were everywhere, strolling around as if they owned the country. They were like kings as they crossed the street without a care in the world; cars stopped to let them go by. One day I saw a camel in the market and stood watching him in wonder until his owner signaled to me to let him eat in peace.

Tripoli is a commercial city. People sell anything anywhere. All you have to do is set up your wares on a sidewalk or in boxes inside a doorway. The aesthetics of the shop windows don't matter much. Business is done out loud, dinars jumping from hand to hand. All the latest makes and models of cars are driven quickly down wide avenues that go on and on like reels of gray tape. Tripoli is half-urban, half-rural. The kids play in the street, raising a ruckus. The elderly, dressed in white tunics and turbans, with canes and mules, raise the dust as they share the street with sheep. The hospital is staffed by foreign doctors. At the huge supermarket the cashiers decorate their hands with traditional henna designs. Men walk down the sidewalks followed by matrons wrapped up in white cloth, moving with difficulty after their husbands. A white Mercedes Benz convertible, the latest model, zooms up the street. A dark man is at the wheel, wearing a white headdress, the ends of which flap in the air. He's a modern verson of the desert rider. For a moment I relive the novel *The Arab*, which I read as a child, and I want that man to kidnap me and hide me in the folds of his abba, to later possess me on the sands of a dune. It's a fleeting dream.

Walking through the old city was like walking through the past. In the craft workshops, cloth was woven with threads of silver and gold. The craftsmen made jewels to capture the sun, dresses with tulles, satins and sequins that copied styles of no particular time. They painted oases and caravans of camels, feminine faces with lilac eye paint. Merchants sold tin, wood, perfume, and ground coffee with cardamom.

I took lots of long walks. Sometimes a man would frighten me with his advances and I'd run home to hide. I took to carrying a wooden cane with which to fend off the wandering hands that surprised me in the streets, or the erections, hidden beneath the abbas, that rubbed up against me in the shops, or to confront the one who jumped out to touch me in a bend of a park lane. Arab men do not seduce women. They take what they think belongs to them. I must have seemed accessible because I walked alone, even though I followed the rules and didn't expose so much as a one centimeter of my skin beyond what was permitted. On the park benches young men rested their heads on the legs of their compañeros and caressed each other's hair; others walked hand in hand. They never did the same with a woman, whom they touched only in private.

I started having recurring nightmares. I dreamed that I was alone in a place; a man would enter, wanting to touch me. I tried to scream but no sound came out. No one helped me. But suddenly I would overcome my terror and jump on the man, beating him with my own hands. Sometimes I strangled him, sometimes I beat him against the floor, sometimes I hit him with a stick until the blood splattered on me. The awful thing was that I couldn't stop, though I knew I was destroying him. Then I would wake up in a fright.

Neither fear nor heat kept me from going out; being closed in was unbearable. Most of the time I read, but my books in Spanish ran out. I went by the offices of Mathaba daily to have coffee and exchange greetings with my compañeros, but it wasn't enough. I would go to the window, look over the yards of the houses and the people passing by. Bored, I would go out, walk a bit, and start to feel like the world was melting away. The sun drank up my liquids before they even got to the surface of my skin. Sitting in a café I watched the men and women go by, wrapped up in meters and meters of white cloth. They were covered up and I wanted to go naked in a tub with wheels. I would go home and get in a tub of icy water. I waited till four in the afternoon, when the wind was blowing, and then I could walk in the streets that went down to the port by the sea.

I was in Libya because of political accords, and this forced me to move around in a masculine world. I had no relationship with any Arab woman; the ones I met were relatives of the compañeros from Mathaba. It was hard for me to understand the way they treated me. For example, when I was with one of them and we greeted each other or talked a little, they wouldn't look at me in the eyes. If I asked for something, they threw it at me without even looking at me. The same thing happened to me in the markets: the clerk turned his face a bit as he gave me the goods, so he wouldn't look at me directly, and threw them on the counter. I interpreted this as rejection, and it bothered me. The impossibility of relating to them on equal footing was very frustrating indeed.

Feminine Mystique

I was able to convince Nury, one of the Libyan men who had lived in Latin America, to invite me to a wedding. He introduced me to his wife, who had lived in Venezuela for two years but spoke no Spanish. We greeted each other with a smile and parted.

A large awning dressed up the street for the party. The ground was covered with carpets and cushions to rest on. About sixty women of all ages were there, and maybe twice as many young children. The air smelled of incense, sandalwood, and perfumes. A band of blind men played Arab music. The bride, dressed like a fairy in tulles and colored sequins, presided over the party from her velvet throne. Some infinitely fine sandals revealed the henna drawings on her feet; her hands had the same design and over the design were rings and chains that held her golden bracelets in place. Around her neck were gold necklaces that met in a belt. Her long reddish hair was done up with a gold diadem, and dark makeup adorned her eyes.

Under the awning no one wore a farrashia. The young women, their beauty exposed, were transformed. The elderly had left their beauty in the children they had borne, and now had time etched on their faces and gold caps on some of their teeth. They all wore brightly colored outfits: the elderly wore traditional cloth of golden or silver threads and the young wore the latest Western fashions. The scene looked as if it had been touched with golden frost, so brightly did the jewels sparkle.

The women took turns dancing for the bride, each wearing a scarf at her hip to emphasize still more the sensual, undulating movement that seemed to start at their waists and slither down to their ankles. While one danced, the rest kept time by clapping. When it was my turn, I did a *cumbia*. I couldn't move the way they did.

Older women passed out sweets made of honey and nuts, dates, colorful juices, cheese fingers, figs, damasks, almonds, and other delicacies. The kids jumped like goats among their mothers. They were everyone's children, rocked, nursed, and scolded by all the adults alike. The names sounded musical to my ear: Fatma, Yamila, Yadira, Ludmila, Zamira. At dusk we said good-bye and *ma'salam* (go in peace), with more embraces than I could count.

The women always greeted me with great care. When I visited someone's house, always accompanied by men, the father of the family came out to greet us but then escorted me to the other women of the house, who took care of me. They talked, smiled, took me by the hand, and led me through the feminine spaces of the household, the kitchen, the bedrooms, the yards. In this way I learned that appreciation was expressed with gifts and love with jewels; they all had several sets of gems and adorned me with these and then positioned me in front of a mirror. They also perfumed me and sometimes even covered me up with a farrashia. I could tell from their loving gestures as they touched my head that they were sad because of my very short hair. They wore theirs long and treated it with henna, which gave it a copperish tone. But these women had no contact with the men who visited the house. The single ones served the food and then went back to the kitchen.

Food was always abundant: fruit, juice, lamb, couscous, and the ubiquitous mint tea. We had to eat and eat, and our plates were constantly refilled. Before we left, they gave us gifts.

When I saw the Leptis Magna Roman ruins, a city on the shore of the Mediterranean, I almost cried from joy. I wandered through the enormous grassy spaces drinking in the pink, green, and gray marble columns. In the rooms, which are open to the sky, there were benches and sculptures, also of marble. The baths were spacious and designed for pleasure, with a hot water supply system and collective toilets that drained. The city was carpeted with stone paths, and the scale of everything dazzled me. I ran my hands over the marble, caressing each carefully chiseled grape, leaf, body, and fold of material. The rest of our party rushed through the ruins, and our guides explained little, so I took the time on my own to enjoy this marvel.

Our guides also took us to a public beach. Tents of all sizes sheltered entire families. The men and the women, dressed in abbas and farrashias, played in the water with the little ones. Under the burning sun the cold water of the Mediterranean was deliciously inviting. We wore tee-shirts over our bathing suits, and the kids ran away at the sight of our bodies. Some teens swam under the water to catch a glimpse of our legs. When they emerged from the sea, the cloth of their abbas or farrashias clung to their bodies, but when we emerged, the people moved away so as not to have to see our "nudity." Some older men scolded us as we walked to our tent, where one of our hosts cooked goat meat with paprika.

Lost in the World

After several months in Libya, an uneasiness settled in my soul with such intensity that I begged Carlos Alonso to get in touch with Ester in Havana and ask her for news of my family in Colombia. We called from the office, breaking all security rules. That was how I found out that my first-born child, Juan Diego, had died a month before, at thirteen years of age.

A dull ache nestled itself inside me. I wanted to shout so I wouldn't explode, but I couldn't even do that. I understood nothing. Suddenly I was standing in the middle of the world with no point of reference beyond my own pain. I heard Carlos Alonso's voice far away; then silence descended on me like a black veil, and I thought I'd close my eyes and die. I abandoned myself to this feeling; why fight death? I didn't resist, and the worst kind of sadness filled me to my core.

The next day Carlos Alonso left for Ghana. I couldn't even cry. I just lay in bed staring at the ceiling, my mind a blank, numb except for a dull ache inside. The Chilean compañero made me get out a bit, and the mathematician, out of pure solidarity, became my only companion day and night. He knocked on my door early in the morning and made breakfast for us; then he invited me to go for a walk, and we ate lunch together. Faced with my silence, he decided to tell me his life story, to pique my interest. But I remember absolutely nothing, only that he talked and talked. At night he prepared a pitcher of maize blossom and valerian tea, and he drank it with me slowly. At midnight he left for his apartment, returning early the next day. If not for him, I think madness would have won out. I don't even remember his name.

The days went by. No consolation was possible. But time forced me to accept the pain as part of my life; life held on to me stubbornly. Death and destiny are cowards. I was tired of challenging them with no response, while they took the most defenseless victim. Anguish filled my heart; I lost interest in everything. Why should I survive Juan Diego's death?

A devastating earthquake raged inside me. For many years I had worked far from my son, convinced that this was how I could guarantee a better future for him, always hoping for the reunion, the time to love each other, and ways to fill the abyss of absence with tenderness. That hopeful tomorrow was suddenly destroyed. I had no real referent anymore, all my sacrifice had been in vain. It seemed impossible that so much love could have no future, but there was nothing left, only an immense emptiness. Death settled down inside me. Not even Carlos Alonso's return, or his affection, could dislodge it. I began my existence as a ghost.

The death of my son was the culmination of all the suffering I had ever experienced, the sum and multiplication of every stab my heart had ever absorbed, as, one by one, my friends, sisters, loves were lost. As long as I had my son, I had hope. With his death, I was left utterly alone, lost in the world.

I tried to summon up the reserves of strength that had enabled me to survive all the other losses, but my strength failed me. I acknowledged that I was a coward and that somehow I had to exhaust this pain until it had no more breath left. At night I went out on the terrace to contemplate the darkness, and I measured the distance separating me from my country and my people by looking at the celestial dome. My loneliness emptied my soul out through my eyes, and I was powerless to stop it. So I decided to go back home, to die less alone.

12

Reinventing Life

THE DEATH OF my son Juan at the dawn of his teen years broke me in two. I was sufficiently prepared for my own death, and I had borne the deaths of my beloved compañeros in battle. I was even able to understand the murders that in recent years had ended the lives of compañeros and collaborators as part of the cruel dynamic of confrontation. But the sudden death of my muchacho—no! It wasn't part of the calculations, there was no reason for it. It was no wonder at all that the world fell away from under me.

I knew how hard it would be to return to Colombia, but I didn't care, maybe because I was seeking death more than life. It took me almost six months to do it, six months that were like an endless nightmare. The person I had been up to that moment had exploded into a million pieces. The hope and faith in the revolutionary project that I had kept alive through the years no longer made sense to me.

For many years my identity had been formed by my politics, my belonging to the M-19, my ideals. My growing awareness of the dissonance between what we wanted to be and what we were had not destroyed my faith. Even as I witnessed increasing divergences within the organization, I had hoped to correct them from within. Now all of that was not enough. Nor was the love that, along with the passion of ideas, had kept the flame of my existence burning. For half of my life, I had felt accompanied by men and women I didn't even know, people with whom I identified as part of a common project. I felt incarnate in an organization, part of a militant worldwide cause. The idea of that collectivity fed me; I found my strength in that common sense of purpose. But with a worse and more urgent pain and sadness than I had ever felt before, I found that I was utterly alone.

I returned to Colombia in December 1987 in pieces. Manuel, my accomplice, felt my agony when we met outside Colombia, and he offered me all of his help. Taking all sorts of risks and acting on his own, he pulled the strings necessary to sneak me in through the back door of migration. What was I here for? The whole country was littered with tombs. Why had I come back? Maybe, deep down inside, I trusted that someone would have an answer for me, that someone would invent some formula to rekindle my desire to live.

First I sought out my usual hermanos, compañeros, and friends of the organization. They took turns trying to make me feel that things could be the way they had been before. For a while I didn't want to think and merely sleepwalked from one place to another, avoiding Bogotá. Manuel and his kids took care of me, lovingly and without any time limits, and I could have stayed with him. But everything must come to an end, and the time came when I had to confront reality.

A kind of claustrophobic fear made relating to people difficult for me. I had knocked on several doors, and many had closed in my face with a smile. Even my cousins in Cali breathed easier when I left after a four-day visit. Almost all my acquaintances saw me as a bringer of death, a bearer of this danger because of my status as a wanted woman. I understood their fear but their rejection hurt me. No one seemed to notice my inner fragility. At times like those I wanted with all my heart to try another path in life, but I was labeled a guerrillera and had the mark of death on my forehead.

My poor mother, more worried than happy about my return, was always close, not knowing what to do. Her mere presence forced me into life. I stayed with her for a while, but as soon as I could I resumed my wandering.

I went back to the capital at last. A couple of friends, María Elvira Carvajal and el Negro Vélez, in whose home I had recovered after the attack in the restaurant, took me in again. At their side I found the oasis of calm I needed to take up some activities that helped keep me busy. María Elvira herself hooked me up with Camilo González Posso, who needed help with some booklets on democracy. The exercise of reading and writing became a pleasant task that gave some meaning to eight or more hours every day. But I was still empty, and not even love for José, my baby, could shake the cold from my insides. In fact, he stayed at the Lucios' and didn't even recognize me after a year of absence. This was another open wound. I grappled with conflicting desires: should I make his life the center of mine? Did I dare to risk another loss?

When I had a little more strength, I decided to visit the cemetery. I had avoided it for months. One sunny February afternoon, as I walked among the tombs, a gray sadness enveloped me in thick waves, like lava from a volcano. I read Juan's name on the tombstone and reality struck me in the chest. We were both alone against death. How that memory still hurts! I imagined his body under the grass and wanted to penetrate the earth to warm him in an endless hug. For hours I did nothing but sit with that pain, but torrents of tears failed to empty me of it. When I left the cemetery I knew that the feeling would be with me forever.

The City: A Map of Absences

Between love and dreams, I had built a whole life next to my compañeros in Bogotá. Walking around the city now only reminded me of their absence. On that corner I had met with Pablo. In those dorms I had stayed with Alfredo. I met Manuel and Rosa in that cafeteria. We ate with Fayad here. I lived with Violeta in this building. This was Lucho's favorite bakery. Someone would walked by whose gait or voice evoked my lost loves, and I would come undone.

My world was populated with ghosts; I saw them everywhere in Bogotá. In dreams I brought them all together in a loving embrace. The burnt ruins of the Palace of Justice and my son's tomb stood out as the symbols of my reality. The silence of the dead was my own inner emptiness. Existence hurt.

In spite of constantly wishing for death, I had to invent my life chapter by chapter. The first small step was my work with Camilo. When we finished the booklets on democracy, he suggested that I continue with some research on Colombia's international relations policies in the Frente Nacional. I had to gather documents on Colombia's severing of diplomatic relations with Cuba in 1980. Camilo's intentions produced results. In reviewing the subject, I found a way to enrich my own experience as a participant in the events that had brought about the episode, and to understand our actions in historical context. This buoyed me, and I wrote a chronicle of the M-19 deployment in the south and its repercussions by weaving together versions from the press and my own experience. I understood then that I was the bearer of a history that didn't belong entirely to me, and this meant that I must exercise a measure of responsibility with respect to others. I couldn't die with such impunity, at least not until I had consigned this part of memory that belonged to the history of the country.

I looked for a way to do it and turned to the profession I had chosen when I had started at the Universidad, the major that got wrapped up in political events. I thought about writing my thesis for anthropology as an analysis of my experience, to contribute to the reflections being written at that time to arrange the disarmament of groups like the M-19.

I went to Luis Guillermo Vasco, who suggested I speak with Jaime Arocha, who had served on the Commission for the Study of Violence. I went to his office but almost left without telling him why I had come. It was hard for me to talk to someone I didn't know about the secrets of my past. Fortunately Vasco had already filled him in, and he went right to the heart of things. He proposed that I do a self-analysis paper using Ira Progoff's intensive diary technique as a way of recovering and recording elements of guerrilla culture. The result could be very interesting, he thought, ethnographically speaking.

In March 1989 I began the difficult and painstaking process of seeking the logical conducting threads of behavior that would allow me to understand myself. The idea of death loomed large in this process from the very beginning. Jaime Arocha's questions about what I was writing unleashed processes that led me to scrutinize my insides, sometimes with great anguish. I wanted to overcome the recurring idea of death, but I constantly returned to it. Finally I stopped resisting, and death began to be the object of analysis. I decided to face it by studying how different cultures ritually work through death, and thus be able to deal with my own experience of it.

In April, days before the anniversary of the M-19's founding, news came of Afranio Parra's assassination by the police. Afranio was the best of my friends, always there, it didn't matter where I was, someone whose solidarity had no limits. Losing him placed me in a situation that could easily submerge me in the black hole I was trying to get out of.

If I Didn't Bury This Sadness, I'd Die

Afranio and I saw each other outside organizational structures relatively frequently. After my return we saw each other several times, to talk about his latest stories and life itself. It wasn't possible to remove politics, but our friendship had other points of coincidence. With him my identity blossomed effortlessly. The same things moved us. Afranio saw my distancing myself from the organization with a sort of sadness, but he respected the decision, and our relationship didn't change at all. He never pressured me to take up my militancy again.

One weekend he called me, wanting to get together, but I couldn't make it. The following week I went in search of him, not sure I could find his house. I asked Iván, one of the muchachos whom I trusted, to come with me to look for el viejo. I didn't catch him at home, but I got some books and a card he had left me, and I left a note with his cousin. I left around nine that night. Afranio got my message, but he had been drinking and decided to stay in Ciudad Bolívar where he was partying with some friends. That same night the police picked him up and killed Afranio Parra and the other two militant compañeros.

The next day someone called me to tell me el viejo had been killed. An intense cold between my chest and my stomach made me feel like another part of me was dying. I walked alone in the street and cried, helpless. I damned the peace process that mentally disarms the guerrilleros but not the killers. Once again life hurt, and solitude weighed down on me. Then I wanted to hear music and so I went to a tavern. I needed to fill myself up with sounds; I couldn't handle the silence of my dead anymore.

I couldn't sleep that night. I held a piece of quartz Afranio had given me, invaded by images of life and death. By dawn I had made a decision. I had a strange strength within me, as if it had risen from my own ashes. The pain demanded that I call on life to exorcise the death that had me at my limit, to break out of the circle of blood that had surrounded the country for so long. For the first time, I wanted to see the face of death to find life there somehow. I was going to go to Afranio's wake, to mourn him and understand his absence. I'd go through a complete mourning process, and not leave this new pain stretching on into infinity.

I sought out Iván and together we went to the wake, held at the Casa Gaitán. Among the crowd I found his kids and Chacha, his most steady woman, his parents, our friends, the people from the town, his people. I couldn't look at him at first; it was impossible because everyone was crowded around the coffin. When I could get close, I looked at him slowly, afraid to confront his silence for the first time. And I talked to him: "Afra, viejo. I'm here. I'm going to cry for you. I'm going to stay at this wake to understand that you are dead by seeing you immobile in this box. To learn not to wait for your hug anymore. Because if I don't bury this sadness with you, if I don't bury all my unburied dead with you, I'll die."

There, at the foot of the coffin, I felt more serene. I contemplated him for a long time, still talking to him as if he could hear me. Finally I saw that they had laid him out in a friar's robe and I had to laugh at the thought that his guerrillero soul wouldn't like that holy covering.

His hands made an impression on me. His essence was imprisoned in them, not only because they held the jaguar fang, the quartz, a rose, and the tortoise shell spurs I brought him for his chicken fights in heaven, but also because they had always accompanied the magic of his words with their tireless gestures. And now they rested immobile on his chest, an unmistakable sign that he was really gone.

I left only when the mariachis came. My viejo loved music, and he had given his daughter the voice of a goldfinch, along with the memory of his songs. Milay sang at her father's wake, to please him before he left forever.

For the next nine nights we sang and told stories and anecdotes around a bonfire. The old friends all got together, his family, the paisanos, his women and friends. We sat with his presence among us until we all—including him—got over the surprise of his death and accepted it. Then Afranio could go peacefully beyond life.

I thought a lot about his last moments and the rage he must have felt at having his time cut short when there was still so much left for him to do. He must have known that this time it was inevitable because they had him tied up when the weapon canon sang its *Te Deum* in his ear, but at least, surely, he was happy to die without having to "hand over his weapon."

El viejo was a legend in the neighborhoods, even before his death. He had an unforgettable personality. He was a man in whom the line dividing reality and dreams was erased, because by dreaming he turned things into reality. For that he used his pen, a paintbrush, or words, and sometimes weapons. He talked, painted, and shot with the same efficiency. He knew how to choose the moment. Afranio pulled miracles out of his sleeve for the most unexpected people, the common people, to lead them to their most heroic acts. He was deterred by nothing, and the only thing he dodged was power. He died the way he was: a man that only his own fate could surprise. I suffered this sadness differently, deep within, without giving myself over to it, in a constant struggle.

One day, as if Afranio were telling me, I heard: "It's time for the flowers to bloom." With this sentence I knew that I was emerging from the abyss and rising to the surface, because the quartz heart of the guerrero was with me. I began to trust life again. Only then could my friend close his eyes and lie back on emptiness in infinite rest.

Unwalking Steps

Again I took up the paths of memory. I returned to the places where I had constructed the identity I was trying so desperately to recover. I found pieces of myself in my friends; each one gave me a sketch of myself, stored in and fed by their own hearts. No one noticed the need I had for their affection, but I took it, truly grateful. Places, the ones that endured like old photographs in my memory, were a source of life. When I penetrated them, I wanted to steal the experiences that belonged to me from them. I found them generous in evocation, in feelings. From them I could rebuild myself. Perhaps by remembering who I had been I would find the one I wanted to be.

I went to Cali at the beginning of my search, to find emotional support and recover parts of my childhood. From Cali I went to Pasto, trying to recover my adolescence and the point on the path that had led me to militancy. With those trips I also wanted to go back to my cousins and my friends from school, and find out the direction of their lives, so I could compare them to mine. When I met them again, I realized that I had lived in another world and that we had little in common anymore. Everything had changed so much.

I was so confused! Not being a guerrillera left me in limbo. Where did I belong? Many a time I had harbored the hope that if I dressed up in the elegant clothes my son's grandma gave me, I could be a señora like the owner of the clothes, and I did make an effort to look like it, only to have to admit that high heels and fake gestures exhausted me. I wanted to be like most women and have a family, a house, and a secure job; and sometimes, tired of everything, I dreamed only of finding an ordinary man in the street who'd offer to take care of me, of handing over the responsibility for my existence to someone else.

I no longer really knew who I was. My life was a series of comings and goings, partial identities and unknowns; but slowly, in the midst of such contradictions, I rebuilt myself.

For one month I delved into my distant past. I asked my mom for all the old pictures and I sat down and studied them. I realized that at least fifteen years were erased from my visual memory because I hadn't let anyone take my picture since Juan Diego's birth. There was only one photo of me from this era, from a moment when a compañero's camera had surprised me in Corinto at the signing of the truce in 1984.

I went for a walk in downtown San Juan de los Pastos, because from there I could appreciate the architecture skirted by landscapes, the same landscapes that had accompanied my youthful Sunday walks with my girl-friends. I wound up sitting in the Maridíaz Chapel, at my old school, talking with the Niño Jesús de Praga, who in my absence had become miraculous. On the way back home the movie of the boarding school under the supervision of Madre Rudolfina played in my head, along with the happiness that the pranks we pulled on the nuns produced in us.

I also visited the offices of old friends and suggested that they help me find a job. All but one professed that they could not help me. After all, since the military trials in Ipiales, my background was common knowledge in the city, and no one wanted to get burned through associating with me.

I closed the Cali-Pasto chapter. There was no room for me there. Only my mother linked me to those two cities. I returned to Bogotá with nostalgia and a kind of lightness. The death of expectations is a relief in a way, but it also closes paths.

Many times I wondered where love was. And I found that it was in my memory, as if avoiding the present. So I sought it out in the past. I visited Moritz, that half-love of my teen years. He seemed the same as always, with his free and easy laugh and the sob that snuck up on him in the middle of a confession of affection. His warm hug and brimming love made me happy. Neither of us could avoid the urgent need to measure the passing of our own time in the other. We loved each other again, holding hands and watching the afternoon go as we sat together on a park bench. I felt accompanied in my heart while he was close, and when we said good-bye I knew I wouldn't see him again. The Moritz who was my compañero of ideals had lost his way in business. Between the two of us nothing was left undone. Past loves are but unrepeatable images.

I thought that parts of us are tied to others when I ran into one of my muchachos from the militias, as he was seeking a future in several jobs. Militancy had caused our paths to cross more than once, and that was enough to make us love each other. Discovering that every feeling of mine had an echo in him granted me more happiness than surprise. We communicated without words, our shared understanding forged in the daily exercise of clandestine life. It was easy to move from camaraderie to love. We communicated with gestures, with looks, without fear of mistaking the reciprocity of affection. Caresses were a natural, an appropriate language for us. It was as if desire were reclaiming us from the past, when we bet our dreams on the same roulette table. Together it was possible to retake the dimension of the "now," present only in the proximity of death, and with it we rescued the intensity of every act—an intensity that is lost when you think of life or love as future projects. We loved each other for a few days, desperately, as though it was all the time we had left in the world, clinging to the strength we gave each other, trying together to feel our way out of the solitude in which we found ourselves after renouncing our militancy. We both needed to find alternatives and a way to support ourselves financially, and we had to fight down the desire to break the law in order to claw our way out of what seemed like a bottomless pit. Because together we could easily have robbed a store and kept our financial woes at bay.

Certainties, wordless pacts, and old loyalties linked us. Above all we were still hermanos, even if we were as far from each other as a pair of shipwrecked sailors. In the end, life separated us again, but we were used to that.

I missed love; I wanted some warm hands to make me feel I wasn't abandoned and to bring me back to life in full. And one afternoon William, my lifelong friend, appeared. With his first tender embrace he gave me new life, and I felt the need to talk to him as never before, to learn from his words and silences again, to lose myself in the adventure of knowledge that is his life. We began at once to try and find words for the avalanche of events and feelings that had accumulated in our separation. We talked for hours.

We sought each other out almost every day. The way we perceived each other began to change, and he suggested without urgency the possibility of a late love. Little by little, the rational connections that block the madness of love began to break. I closed my eyes and heard the pressure of desire that subordinated my body and I thought that I wanted not just to hear him but to be in him. To confirm that his sensitivity was measurable with my touch, to try to vanquish the fear of falling in love. He was my friend; what did I have I fear?

William unlocked me with his hands, and fresh air penetrated to the depths of my soul. It was a time of calm, of sharing daily life and shuffling life again and again, trying to reflect on many things. He is by vocation an orderer of worlds, a task that almost no one takes on anymore, and I had the luck of meeting him at the very moment when my interior chaos threatened to suffocate me. His words helped reorder my feelings. I had begun with Professor Arocha the exercise of activating my memory, but this caused me much pain. William helped me to pursue that path with less anguish. Beyond that, he restored to me the sense of love as an inevitable urgency. I still have a note he wrote me during this period:

> I had tired of waiting for you, but today you came again. In the past you came from time to time, you brought your face full of a childlike surprise. Today you came and you were different, in your eyes I discovered the path of a thousand battles and I felt that you suffered life hopefully. She said she wanted to learn to think. I smiled, she had always thought well. I felt the need to tell you that I wanted to learn your body and feel your pain in my skin. I didn't say anything, I was quiet and looking far away; I only wanted to fill your life with surprise, that childlike surprise that favors love.

From that day on, my infinitely patient friend entertained himself by scaring away the anguish that surrounded me like a vulture. He became my spiritual country, my territory. With him my identity was re-created from shared interests and likes, common pasts, and the same utopia.

Before we had been together long enough for the usual petty irritations to arise, William went back to his rivers in el Chocó, waters on which he had built and unbuilt himself so many times. I packed up my things, and with them the memories of the good times at his side. We went our own ways. Freedom doesn't hurt, it shouldn't hurt.

Love was not enough to calm my inner restlessness. It couldn't become in itself reason enough to live. For me, love was unbreakably linked to the idea of sharing the greatest utopia, the dream of a more just society. To love for love's sake, like living for life's sake, was not enough for me.

Confronting the Past

On the street, at friends' houses, even at work, people who one way or another had something to do with my past confronted me. I couldn't help constantly comparing the past and present, even when this was the last thing I wanted to do. Sometimes this brought back attitudes and experiences that I didn't want to repeat, and other times it filled me with nostalgia. When I left the Eme, I felt I had left a secure territory to enter an uncertain future.

I was not the only one who had left the M-19, of course. There were others, and the hostility of the environment led me to maintain contact with them, because we were all searching, trying to find meaning and remake our lives. I needed to regain contact with the people who inhabited my heart for the simple reason that we shared a common history. We got together and the memories began to flow. In this way we helped each other analyze the past and begin to create new identities for ourselves. Laughing at ourselves and our sorrows became the best therapy. Little by little, through listening to each other talk about the difficulties with the day-to-day, a picture of our common problem began to emerge. We knew that we had to proceed from here on out on our own; the group didn't shelter us anymore. But at least we had each other, and these talks helped us feel less alone. We knew that we were no better or worse than our compas who remained within the M-19, just different. Some of our differences caused us problems. One of the most common was the difficulty in creating affective or work relationships and making the long-term commitments they required. Another had to do with our habit of taking a radical approach to resolving any conflict. One of the most difficult things to overcome was the feeling that we could and must work to change, as quickly as possible, a reality as complex as

Colombia's. But the biggest problem we faced was learning to live without "the cause."

At the same time, though, other differences gave us some advantages. Our social vocation and spirit of loyalty and solidarity, our interest in public affairs, our facility in responding to changes, our capacity to take on challenges, and the ability to make decisions at critical moments—all served us well, no matter what path in life we might choose to follow now. The sad thing was that each of us was alone in the face of our individual realities and the possible ways out of a past that exercised an extremely powerful pull and intensified our loneliness.

I could also contemplate the other side of the coin and understand how the ones who had suffered from our actions saw us. They were people like ourselves, who had experienced the kidnapping of their loved ones as a huge trauma with no possible justification, relatives of dead and disappeared compañeros who couldn't understand their absence. They were all unforeseeable victims of our actions, as were the people of the neighborhoods who had to try and swallow their fear during the massive raids until they cursed our names. When the pain of these others reached me, I wondered painfully why life had chosen me to observe from many perspectives the effects of our actions. I had joined one side in the war, while most people had remained defenseless in the middle. This responsibility was hard to bear.

Around this time I found a job in a construction company. I promoted the participation of the owners in community management. I was the anthropologist on the staff, and I had to wear nylons, high heels, and a silk blouse. They called me "doctor." I could afford a family-size apartment and had been granted the right to have my son on weekends. But I felt terribly ill adapted to the world of professionals, the world of my workmates, or of the woman whom I sat next to on the bus that took me to work each day.

I was obsessed by Jaime Arocha's questions about how I had learned to be who I was. I was still working on the monograph in my free time, convinced that if I were to understand the lessons of the war, I could unlearn what I had to so I wouldn't feel this anguish of being neither there, where I had come from, nor here, where I was trying to be. I still felt my country, its happiness and its joy, as part of my body, yet the guerrilla's mission was no longer enough for me. I was a mass of contradictions. I chose freedom and didn't know what to do with my solitude; for half of my life I had fought against the establishment and now I couldn't completely assimilate it; I was a mother and I didn't know how to be one, or didn't want to play that role; I was a being who suffered marginalization and powerlessness at the same time that I wanted to break out of that role. Yet I couldn't completely abandon myself and remain adrift. The inner strength of a collective history for which I was partly responsible kept me going.

I slowly discovered that it was nice to be outside the organization even though it hurt me, if only in the sense that I now felt in control of my own life. I no longer had to live for others; I had to make my own decisions and I didn't know where I was going. Fear of the unknown paralyzed me. Sad is the destiny of a leader in the middle of the battlefield with no troops and no battle. That's how I felt: free and empty. What my life was and would be depended on me; it was in my hands, no one would resolve anything for me. In spite of everything, I fell in love with that freedom; little by little I got used to being with myself, even though I realized the dimensions of my contradictions and the contrasts of light and dark in my uncertainties, or precisely because of that, because I admitted my weaknesses. I took back the reins of my life, even though I didn't know which way to go.

Being a Woman

I was a soldier. The fact that I was a woman by biological definition didn't bother me, but I wasn't very aware of what it meant, either, in a world that made us all the same in ideology. Our sameness weighed more than our difference.

From a very young age and with the support of my mother, I rejected the roles and characteristics traditionally assigned to women. At home I was granted the freedoms of any muchacho, with the complicity of my grandpa and my stepfather, though for different reasons in each case. I learned to ride a horse at a very early age, and my interests leaned more toward hunting and the countryside than dolls. In my childhood years there was no masculine challenge that I couldn't meet successfully. My sense of being at home in a man's world facilitated my entry into the world of a guerrilla group. Politics and the military are traditionally considered men's domain, but it was easy for me to find a place in that male universe.

As a militant revolutionary, I use my femininity to good advantage. My gender was useful for throwing people off track, dodging searches, and getting information. The most macho men, the ones who underestimated us, wouldn't grant us the status of enemy, and we took advantage of that. But when they discovered that we had penetrated their territory, war territory, they became implacable foes. They punished us twice as hard, once for being subversives and again for being women. This is why, when guerrilla women are tortured, rape or sexual assault in one form or another is almost always part of the treatment.

When I left the militant life, one of the first surprises I had was the discovery of my feminine being. I encountered it slowly, through other women, sharing with my friends and entering into confidences while I built my daily life. I began to find things in common with María Elvira Carvajal and la Nana, Catalina and Clara Inés, Pilar, Tutuy and Claudia Mejía. We talked about personal things, something in which I had almost never engaged in militant life.

Instead of making me feel that men were the enemy, discovering myself as a woman led me into understanding other dimensions of myself that I still didn't know. I understood the straitjacketed gender roles and how, in spite of my rebellion, I had played them, not really rebelling in this respect in spite of political militancy. Being a female soldier had meant renouncing power and recognition for the benefit of others, sacrificing my personal interests to the collective, as mothers do. It also meant loving and loving until I was emptied, and offering my body up to the desire of those I loved.

Understanding myself as a woman helped me become aware of the changes I wanted for myself. Paradoxically, this is how I was able to begin to come to terms with the uneasiness I felt about being a different kind of mother. And I understood that the social pressure I felt to get my son back submerged me in a false contradiction. I had to be able to build a mother-son relationship that was different from the traditional one, without violating myself as I tried to be the mamá I couldn't be in my economic and existential life. With somewhat more certainty, I began to open up a space for myself in my son's heart. He still lived with his paternal grandparents. And given the sociocultural context the Lucios lived in, creating that space was a titanic task.

One of the fundamental bases for the reconstruction of my identity lay in the recognition of my gender difference, which largely explained my behavior, both in the military structure and in my love relationships. It wasn't easy in those days to identify inequality or discrimination, much less the power men exercised over us. All this and the fact that the M-19, perhaps because it was made up of students, the urban middle class, and intellectuals, was more open to feminine participation in some command positions than some guerrilla groups. This is not to say that there was no machismo; of course there was, as there is in any army. But for us women as well as for the men, many of the inequalities between the sexes were somewhat neutralized by our culture; they were not as visible as they are in the mainstream world, so we didn't feel them so much and we didn't emphasize them. As our thinking gained more clarity, we began to demand organizational spaces in which to resolve women's issues, which gave rise to all types of jokes among the compañeros. But they didn't stop us. Vera Grabe, for example, called a women's meeting at the Eighth National Conference, when we were still in the Buen Pastor prison. But at that time I think the agenda was equal opportunity for women.

Love and emotional relationships were areas in which there were fewer masculine transformations. Perhaps in the areas of politics and participation, even in the recognition of the operational abilities of some of the compañeras, progress was made. But in the intimate arena of couple relationships, our compañeros were like all other Colombian men. We, the compañeras, the guerrilleras, paid a high price for innovating and transgressing the norms of matrimony, affection and sex. We were left alone; not even the organization compañeros thought of us as wives. I don't know if this was better or worse than the traditional arrangement and attitude. We were seen as the perfect lovers, but not women to whom these men would commit themselves in marriage, especially if we were in positions of responsibility.

Maybe we guerrilleras ourselves somehow broke through the myth of eternal love and viewed it in a more traditionally masculine way, as something instrumental, a mechanism to help ourselves get through life more than a reason for living. Our courage to experience a relationship depends on our own strength; for many of us I think it meant cultivating the art of solitude in order to live a bit more freely.

I don't consider myself submissive, but for me the contradictions between discourse and practice are best expressed in the area of love. I think the same thing was true for a lot of us. On the one hand, we had the courage to break with the reigning social norms, while on the other we found ourselves still trapped by those norms. We granted autonomy to the men that was not granted to us; in addition to being soldiers, we assumed the domestic and childcare duties that have always been the primary responsibility of women. We thought the compañero's tasks were more important than ours, and we sacrificed our growth to support them. In short, we renounced our own personal projects, what we wanted, what we expected from life, first to the organization and then to them—our beloved compañeros. This shows how love and submission go hand in hand for women. Still, our roles within the organization did expand the meaning of womanhood, not radically or permanently, perhaps, but measurably.

If I wanted to take control of my life as a civilian, I could not search for a new partner right away. I knew that I had a great weakness in giving myself entirely to another, and this was an obstacle to rebuilding myself and gaining individual autonomy, one I had to work hard to channel. To love a man at that time would have been to refuse myself again, and now I was trying to find myself.

It was a painful process because I had always been in love. Love represented a fundamental complement to my great revolutionary ideal. Now that I sought independence, I had to renounce love until I could learn how to love in freedom. Of course I didn't know how to live without the love of another, either. It was as if I loved myself through the men who loved me. I needed to love without depending on it, and at the time this was impossible.

A Path with a Heart

I renewed my acquaintance with the organization when Antonio Navarro arrived to sign the peace accords. In October 1989 I received word that he was coming to Colombia. I wrote to him in Santo Domingo, in Cauca, that his presence in the negotiations for disarming the movement made me happy. He responded by inviting me to the camp to talk.

Until then I had avoided going to Santo Domingo because the emotional ties I had with the organization still weighed heavily on me. I was afraid to go back, more for reasons of the heart than for political ones. Now I decided to take advantage of the opportunity to greet Antonio and confront my break with the organizational structures—for I had not yet formally renounced my post in the national command or my militancy.

Rubén Carvajalino arranged the trip. We took several guests with us. Setting out on this journey was a huge event for me. I had not been back to the monte since the Los Robles conference. I was exalted, euphoric, and nervous. I wanted to get there as quickly as possible, but the whole way there I wondered what Antonio and the others would say, and what I would answer. What if they wanted me to stay?

We arrived in Santo Domingo as dusk was falling. I tried to hide my emotion, but every embrace with a compañero made it obvious. Antonio received me with particular warmth. At first nothing seemed odd; we talked over each other in excitement, as one always does at a reunion with brothers and sisters after a long separation. I hadn't seen many of them since Los Robles in 1985.

That night there was a welcome party for the guests and we ended up dancing amid the usual guns and uniforms. From hug to hug I felt that the links in the emotional chain were closing again. I left the dance for a moment and stood for a while watching the starlit sky. I wanted to be alone with my feelings, to take stock of where I was and what I was doing.

Apart from the compañeros from the command group and some survivors from the beginning, all the faces were new. These newcomers, understandably, had a different way of talking about the past wars, which were remote from them in a way they could never be to us old-timers. Even their way of carrying their weapons was different. They seemed tired. I had the impression that everything was unimportant, as if the scores of war dead had caused the organization to lose the initial meaning of armed struggle as the continuation of the political struggle.

But there in the mountains the old hermanos were also there, lost among dreams, delirium, and hopes, and with them my heart. Yet I knew I needed to find a different path. If someday I went back, it would be because I had recovered my faith in the guerrilla movement as a political option, and not because that was the only way open to me in the world. That was the universe I had known for years, but I had to distance myself. I cried because it hurt to leave them when I loved them so much, and I was thankful to the ones I was closest to for not asking me to stay.

I talked with Pizarro the next day. I didn't like some of the ways they were handling the negotiations or some of the dark figures that surrounded him as advisors. Pizarro listened to me, agreeing about some things and explaining many of the difficulties and the internal and external pressures. When our chat was over, and in spite of the discrepencies, I was convinced that the M-19, led by Pizarro, was waging a definitive battle for peace.

Surely none of the compañeros guessed the importance of that event for me. With that visit I made up my mind at last to leave the guerrilla and closed a chapter in my life. I had joined the M-19 when I thought it was time to do so, I gambled with the political project until I couldn't anymore, and now I was leaving in order to explore other paths. My life stretched out before me like a blank page.

Death can be drawn with a single line, a single shot. Life, by contrast, must be reinvented every day.

Epilogue

MY PERSONAL AND professional lives meld together. I dedicate most of my time to work with the same intensity I once dedicated to militancy. After rejoining civilian life I have consulted on a number of projects involving women and children displaced by the violence that persists in Colombia. For the past 15 years, I have been working for the defense of women's rights, especially with respect to the armed conflict and how it relates to women, and former combatants in particular. I have also worked with groups to support women who have been affected by social and political violence (those widowed and/or displaced). Currently I am participating in an NGO project focused on displaced women, in collaboration with a UN organization. The project seeks to strengthen the rights of groups of women who migrate to urban areas, victims of forced displacement, and also groups of women who have returned to the places from which they were forcibly displaced because of massacres.

I still have a very close relationship with my mother, Ruth. At eighty-three she leads a simple and peaceful life in Bogotá, and we spend extended periods of time together. My son, José Antonio, is now eighteen years old and still lives with his paternal grandparents in Bogotá. Building a solid, loving relationship while exploring the possibility of being a nontraditional mother is an ongoing task with him. It is a challenge we both assume with love and patience.

As for a compañero, I don't need one anymore. I have loved many and much, but over the years my solitude has helped me construct a life that offers me a great deal of autonomy. I question the notion that a woman without a partner is a lonely woman. We are often more lonely when we have a partner. I have many friends, both male and female, whom I love and who love me.

Like most everyone, I like to spend Sundays lazing around in my jammies, reading in bed while enjoying some tasty fruit. But I also love going to work on Monday with a clear head. I always get up with the sun; it's a necessity for people born under the astrological sign of Leo. There is nothing I like more than traveling, meeting new people, and experiencing new cultures. One of the things I would do again if I could is to study anthropology, but in much more depth. I love airports, all kinds of terminals, and hotels—all those "non-places" Marc Augé talks about, maybe because they are places that ensure some kind of autonomy and some link with my "clandestine" past.

I dream of a peaceful life out in the country where I can grow aromatic herbs, vegetables, and flowers on a small plot of land. I have accepted the fact that I have to stand on my own two feet in this life. When I am fifty-five—retirement age—I won't be receiving any pension, so I'll have to work as long as I have the strength do to so. But I'm an optimistic realist: things aren't the way they should be, not in Colombia or in the rest of the world, but change can be achieved, with persistence and joint effort.

Chronology of Major M-19 Actions

Note: This section includes other events that help to explain the national political situation in Colombia.

1974

January The Movimiento 19 de Abril, born of electoral fraud, is introduced to the public by the taking of the sword of Bolívar and the takeover of the Council of Bogotá.

1975

February An M-19 commando reads a political declaration upon María Eugenia Rojas's taking command of the ANAPO.

1976

February José Raquel Mercado, president of the CTC, is kidnapped.

April José Raquel Mercado is condemned to death and executed after the López Michelsen administration's refusal to accept the M-19's conditions for his freedom, i.e., the resolution of the Rio Paila strike.

November Weapons are taken from the Thomas de la Rue Company.

1977

April The M-19's Seventh National Conference is held.

August Hugo Ferreira Neira, INDUPALMA manager, is kidnapped by the M-19 to pressure for a favorable resolution to the strike of its workers.

September A favorable agreement is reached in INDUPALMA and Ferreira Neira is freed the same day the National Civic Strike takes place.

1978

April The Jorge Eliécer Gaitán Museum is taken and a floral offering is presented.

May In an act of solidarity with the struggle of the Nicaraguan people, an M-19 commando unit takes over the Nicaraguan Embassy in Bogotá.

November The M-19 takes over a radio station in Bogotá.

December More than 5,000 weapons are taken from the army in the north of Bogotá.

1979

March Democratic sectors of the country hold the first Forum for Human Rights.

April An M-19 commando unit attacks *El Caleño* newspaper in the capital of Valle and prints a supplementary section denouncing the human rights situation.

June The M-19 Seventh National Conference is held, focusing on the struggle for democracy.

August The M-19 takes over San Pedro Alejandrino Quinta in Santa Marta and steals the Liberator's command baton.

November The Picota military trials begin against 219 people accused of belonging to the M-19.

1980

February The M-19's Jorge Marcos Zambrano commando unit takes over the embassy of the Dominican Republic.

March The government names its representatives to negotiate with the M-19.

April Journalist Germán Castro Caicedo is detained and freed after interviewing Jaime Bateman Cayón, general commander of the M-19. Castro Caicedo delivers a message to President Turbay outlining the insurgents' proposed 1 May dialogues with the forces in the country.

After seventy-one days, the commando unit that took the Dominican Embassy arrives at an agreement with the government to free the hostages.

June The M-19 demonstrates its willingness to sign a treaty as the product of accords with representative sectors of the country, to broaden democracy.

The leaders of the M-19 escape from Picota Prison.

July The government presents Congress with a proposal for amnesty for insurgents. The M-19 takes over Radio Super and publicly demonstrates its rejection of the government's restricted amnesty proposal.

August The M-19 base coordinator detains Liberal member of parliament Simón Bosa, proponent of the amnesty proposal, and four journalists. They are freed after they express the M-19 position on the amnesty.

September The army frustrates an M-19 summit and captures several leaders. Bateman escapes.

Programs on the RTV M-19 station are begun, interrupting national television channels.

November RTV M-19 announces the presidential candidacy of Jaime Bateman Cayón and again rejects the amnesty proposal presented by the government.

December The M-19 hijacks a plane in Santa Marta to block a meeting of heads of state to commemorate the 600th anniversary of Bolívar's death.

1981

January Confrontations with the M-19 begin in the south.

March A truck full of weapons for the M-19 falls to the army in the south.

An M-19 column under Jaime Bateman takes over Mocoa, the capital of Putumayo. Another column takes a village in Huila.

Confrontations held with the army in Chocó.

Combat between the army and the M-19 on the Ecuador-Colombia border.

Guerrilleros seeking political asylum in Ecuador are handed over to the Colombian army.

April Combat in Chocó, Huila, Caquetá, and Putumayo continues. Armed actions take place in Barranquilla, Manizales, Bogotá, Santander de Quilichao, and other cities.

May More M-19 actions are carried out against the army, the police, and the Colombian air force in Zipaquirá, Bogotá, and Florencia.

Guerrilleros detained in the Ipiales Battalion go on a hunger strike to protest lack of trial guarantees during the military trials.

June Guerrilleros in the Picota Prison go on hunger strike to protest restrictions on visits to political prisoners and to request access to the media in the public part of the military trials.

July M-19 actions continue in Calarcá, Quindío; Manizales, Caldas; Belén de los Andiaquíes, San Vicente del Caguán, San José de la Fragua, and Puerto Solano in Caquetá; Bogotá; Puerto Umbria and La Tebaida in Putumayo; Las Mesas in Nariño, and Florencia, Caquetá.

In joint actions the M-19, the FARC, and the EPL attack or combat the armed forces in Manizales, San Vicente del Caguán, and Belén de los Andiaquíes. The town of Puerto Solano in Caquetá is also taken.

Television host Fernando González Pacheco and journalist Alejandra Pineda are detained in Bogotá. Pacheco bears a peace proposal from Jaime Bateman to the president and the country.

October The M-19 hijacks a helicopter with dynamite.

The M-19 hijacks an Aeropesca plane to transport weapons cargo to the southern front. The plane makes an emergency landing on the Orteguaza River.

November After a battle with the armada, the M-19 sinks a ship laden with weapons.

The M-19 kidnaps Marta Nieves Ochoa in Medellín.

The group Muerte a Secuestradores (MAS), a private justice group financed by narco-traffickers, is formed in Medellín.

December Two members of the M-19 are killed in Medellín in actions related to the kidnapping of Fabio Ochoa's daughter.

1982

January The M-19 hijacks an Aerotal plane with 128 passengers and denounces the army's collaboration in the creation of the MAS.

M-19 guerrilleros travel to Cuba.

March The M-19 carries out electoral sabotage in the biggest cities of the country and battles the army in Caquetá. Southern towns in Cauca and Putumayo are taken.

The peace commission formed by the government at the end of 1981 issues its first report and recommends a negotiation process with the insurgency.

May Members of the peace commission resign when the government and the Conservative Party refuse to negotiate with the guerrillas.

The work of the M-19's secretary of international relations is consolidated. Beyond relations with guerrilla groups on the continent, contacts with international socialist parties and the Conferencia Permanente de Partidos Políticos de América Latina (COPPAL, Permanent Conference of Latin American Political Parties) are established.

The government's amnesty law fails.

June The M-19 again proposes a national dialogue on the country's problems.

July The M-19 attacks the government palace with mortar. Other actions are carried out in Cali, Neiva, Bucaramanga, and Yumba to pressure for dialogue.

The M-19 sends a letter to Congress on the first day of its new session, reiterating interest in dialogue with the new government.

A group of senators presents to Congress a new amnesty project that takes into account the recommendations of the previous peace commission, the parties, and the M-19.

August The M-19's Eighth National Conference is held in Caquetá. Sends a message to President-elect Belisario Betancur.

September The M-19 attacks the Israeli Embassy to protest the massacre of Palestinians in Sabra and Shatila in Beirut.

The first Picota prisoners are freed and join the legal political commando to push for progress in national dialogues.

October M-19 military forces continue with actions to pressure for passage of the amnesty law. The town of Chía is taken and the administrative offices of the army in CAN in Bogotá are attacked.

November The unconditional amnesty law is passed. The M-19 clarifies that amnesty does not mean peace and that a truce is needed before progress can be made with dialogue about needed political reforms.

Death squads and other paramilitaries murder amnesty beneficiaries in the cities and countryside.

December The M-19 national management meets in Panamá and decides to resume combat to push for peace.

1983

April Jaime Bateman Cayón dies in a plane crash between Santa Marta and Panamá. The plane, flown by former Conservative member of parliament Antonio Escobar and carrying Nelly Vivas and Conrado Marín, both members of the M-19, never reaches its destination.

May M-19 military actions are resumed. The group takes the town of Pujil in Caquetá as well as the villages of Danubio, Las Iglesias, Las Doradas, and La Sonora.

Between May and August several urban operations are carried out in Bogotá, Yumbo, Cali, Jamundí, Barranquilla, and Bucaramanga.

August The southern front, led by Boris, continues the campaign in Caquetá, Huila, and Putumayo. Garzón, the second-largest city in Huila, is taken for an hour, while M-19 members talk to the population.

October M-19 leaders Iván Marino Ospina and Alvaro Fayad meet with President Belisario Betancur in Madrid.

The M-19's military actions are continued until December.

An accord is signed between the FARC and the M-19 to enter into joint negotiations with the Betancur administration.

1984

March The EPL and the M-19 sign a joint declaration of unity.

The southern front military force takes Florencia, the capital of Caquetá.

April The M-19 takes Corinto within the framework of the "Jaime Bateman campaign for truce and national dialogue." The movement insists on making known its criteria for the ceasefire and the mechanisms for popular participation in national dialogues.

More skirmishes take place in the countryside and the city as the M-19 tries to promote the proposal. In Florencia the M-19 attacks an army bus; in Bogotá it sets off a bomb in the armed forces payment office and attacks the chief of the operations divisions of the national armada. The M-19 attacks the Pichincha battalion in Cali and the Ingenieros Cadazzi battalion in Palmira; a tourist train carrying 500 passengers is taken near the capital; in Bogotá the M-19 takes over the newspaper *El Bogotano* and issues 80,000 copies of an edition containing the movement's position on the contents of a peace that includes political, economic, and social democracy.

May The FARC and the government's peace commission sign a ceasefire; a verification commission is formed for the accords, and a period of one year is set to organize a political front. The M-19 rejects the accord as an obstacle to unifying the guerrilla forces, weakening the possibility of a negotiation with President Betancur and excluding the nation in the process.

The M-19's western front takes Miranda.

July The M-19 takes Algeciras in Huila in Zipacón to the west of Bogotá, and steals weapons from a businessman in Bogotá.

August Carlos Toledo Plata, a member of the M-19 central command and pioneer of a negotiated peace, is killed in Bucaramanga while working as a doctor in a hospital.

An M-19 column takes over the town of Yumbo in the Valle del Cauca, eleven kilometers from Cali, emphasizing the need for broad popular participation in the peace dialogues.

A truce is signed and the national dialogues, started during the takeover of the Dominican Embassy, resume. The acts to formalize peace are held in Corinto, Cauca, and El Hobo, Huila.

M-19 guerrilla columns are concentrated in camps and the M-19 national dialogue command is formed to coordinate the participatory process.

December Colombian army attacks the freedom camp in Yarumales, Cauca. For a month the guerrilla forces resist the military siege and the artillery attack, and simultaneously the army is pushed from its dominant position at the high point of the camp.

1985

January The verification commission mediates new negotiations between the government and the guerrilla, who achieve a ceasefire pact to maintain the accords signed the year before. The M-19 military forces move to Los Robles, a few kilometers from Yarumales.

The M-19 decides to turn its Ninth National Conference into a conference for peace and democracy and invites all forces and people to an open forum to debate the developments of the peace process and the political proposals of the movement.

February Two days before the beginning of the conference, the government forbids it and tightens the military siege on the new camp. More than 500 people nevertheless meet in the mountains of Cauca. Journalists, priests, representatives of political parties, indigenous people, union members, intellectuals, representatives of social groups, and other guerrilla forces and international delegates arrive.

March The first four M-19 urban camps for peace and democracy are formed in the popular neighborhoods of Cali.

May Peace and democracy camps are set up in Bogotá, Barranquilla, Medellín, Zipaquirá, Manizales, and Bucaramanga.

Army annihilates urban camps in various cities.

Attempted assassination of members of the M-19 in Cali.

Army and M-19 forces skirmish in Cauca and Valle.

June The government declares illegal the National Civic Strike agreed upon by the workers for 20 June.

In light of the army's violations of the peace accords and the government's lack of definitions, M-19 commander Alvaro Fayad declares the truce broken and the M-19 resumes offensive actions.

Takeover of the village of Génova in Quindío by the M-19's Mariscal Antonio José de Sucre column, commanded by Oscar.

July Takeover of the village of Herrera in Tolima by the M-19's Héroes de Yarumales company, led by Carlos Pizarro.

Takeover of the municipality of Riofrío in the Valle del Cauca by the M-19's Héroes de Florencia company, led by Boris.

Confrontations between M-19 militia units and the army in the Petecuy, Marroquín, Siloé, Terrón Colorado, Mariano Ramos, Las Brisas, and La Floresta neighborhoods of Cali. M-19 distributes milk and food to the people of these neighborhoods.

The Héroes de Florencia company takes the villages of Naranjal and Primavera in the municipality of Bolívar, Cauca, and the Héroes de Yarumales company takes the municipalities of Rioblanco and Campoalegre in Tolima.

August In a joint M-19–Alfaro Vive action, banker Nahím Isaías Barquet is kidnapped in Guayaquil; he is one of the richest men in the neighboring country. Social works and a large sum of money are demanded as ransom.

Specialized M-19 commandos place dynamite in Cascabel and Urutú tanks in the Ipiales battalion. The M-19 attacks a communications station in the Cerro del Cable, the mountains surrounding Bogotá, and security agency Sevis in Bogotá.

Iván Marino Ospina dies fighting the III Brigade troops who attack his house in Cali.

September   The Mariscal Sucre Company ambushes the army between the departments of Quindío and Valle. The "Colombia Stands" campaign is begun in the departments of Cauca and Valle. Battles last seventeen days.

M-19 stages militia actions in the cities to hand out construction materials and food among the population. Eleven unarmed militia members die at the hands of the police.

An M-19 urban commando kidnaps Camila Michelsen, daughter of Jaime Michelsen Uribe, a banker responsible for fraud against bank customers through the Grupo Gran Colombiano; he flees.

October   M-19 attacks army troops of the Caicedo de Chaparral Battalion in their camp at the foot of the central mountain range, between the departments of Valle and Tolima. The M-19 command requests humanitarian aid for the wounded, and only five days later receives the aid.

Military prisoners are freed before the press and the attorney general.

Special M-19 commandos destroy the Cisneros No. 8 Ingenieros Battalion of the army's 111 Division, headquartered in Armenia. The VIII Brigade and the central police command are attacked in this city.

In Bogotá there is an attack against General Rafael Zamudio Molina, army commander, who is slightly wounded.

November   The M-19's Iván Marino Ospina company takes over the Palace of Justice on the Plaza de Bolívar in the heart of the capital. The action is called the Antonio Nariño for Human Rights operation, and its goal is to sue the government in the Supreme Court for its failure to honor the peace accords.

December   Battalion America is formed with Ecuador's Alfaro Vive group, Peru's Tupac Amaru Revolutionary Movement, and Colombia's Quintín Lame (an indigenous organization). The project is considered the seed of the Bolivarian army, which seeks a true continental democracy.

1986

January   Battalion America begins the "Conqueror's Path" campaign. In the Jambaló Plaza in Cauca, Pizarro proposes calling a national Congress to form a new government. Pizarro's forces ambush an army patrol and later take the town of Silvia in the department of Cauca.

The M-19's national guerrilla coordinator meets and proposes a popular national assembly to create a new political block to pressure for true national dialogues among Colombians who want to build a new country. At the same time joint schools are formed to advance a new concept of the military. A joint military campaign is launched.

February   The M-19's Héroes de Yarumales company ambushes a Rifles Battalion convoy near the Panamericana Highway linking the departments of Valle and Cauca.

Battalion America takes the town of Morales in Cauca.

Army troops and the Mariscal Sucre company face off in the Valle del Cauca.

March   The "Conqueror's Path" campaign gains ground in the midst of combat between guerrillas and the armed forces near the capital of Valle. Battles break out in Totoro and Paniquita in Cauca and advance along the Panamericana Highway to

Morales. The "Conqueror's Path" ambushes the Colombia Battalion in Timba, fights in Jamundi and then in Pance and Villacarmelo, on the outskirts of Cali. Afterward it arrives at the Universidad del Valle and the Ciudad Jardin neighborhood in the south of the capital. At the same time, militias attack the army in the Olímpico, Siloe, and Aguablanca neighborhoods.

Alvaro Fayad, commander of the M-19, dies in Bogotá during a raid in which the armed forces sacrifice Maria Cristina Marta, who is unarmed and pregnant.

The Héroes de Yarumales company takes the town of Toribio in Cauca and ambushes an army convoy of reinforcements.

April The M-19 decides to support guerrilla unity in the CNG, to move from being opposition to being a government, to call a national popular assembly such as the one the EPL proposed, and to consolidate urban work. The stage is defined as the "War on Oligarchy."

May In Bogotá M-19 militia forces carry out mortar attacks on the U.S. Embassy and the Coca-Cola buildings to protest the signing of the Declaration of Tokyo by the United States, West Germany, France, Italy, Great Britain, Canada, and Japan.

In the presidential elections the Unión Patriótica (UP) becomes the third political force of the country, though the number of its dead at the hands of paramilitaries reaches 300.

June In Bogotá the M-19 makes an attempt on the life of minister Jaime Castro because of his lack of commitment to the peace process and his passive attitude toward the murders of popular and leftist leaders.

The M-19 declares a unilateral ceasefire because of the pope's visit. A social pact for peace is proposed in which the pope could play a large role.

Battalion America steals eighty boxes of dynamite from a company in the Valle del Cauca.

July M-19 commander Boris is assassinated.

August CNG meets and issues a joint statement entitled "Popular Alternative for a New Colombia."

M-19 forces take the town of Nemocón, about sixty kilometers from the capital. Battalion America occupies Belálcazar in Cauca within the "America, Inheritance and Destiny" campaign to protest the Barco administration's taking of office.

October The joint forces of the EPL and the M-19 battle in Antioquia against two battalions of the army.

1987

January The M-19's national management proposes a "national pact for a transition government" as a way of linking the initiatives of the masses and the political-military movement, recently sketched out.

February The Battalion America submits to the Consejo Regional Indígena del Cauca (CRIC, the Regional Indigenous Council of the Cauca) a proposal entitled "From Cauca and for Colombia: Life and Peace," with three fundamental points: (1) the indigenous should assume the planning and administration of the Plan Nacional de Rehabilitación (PNR, National Rehabilitation Plan) resources to change it from a counterinsurgency strategy to one of peace; (2) all armed protagonists, including the army, should be withdrawn from the indigenous reservations; (3) a development plan for the zone should begin with the participation of all social classes and institutions.

March The second assembly of commanders of the national guerrilla coordinator proposes a "convergence for a great national accord"; all are called to dialogue and integrate the proposals of all social classes worried about the country.

During the first half of the year social protests peak. There are two regional strikes, three departmental strikes, and forty-three municipal strikes. Roughly 442 municipalities are affected by local mobilizing.

September M-19 urban forces take over the *Diario 5 pm* in Bogotá and print an issue denouncing the assassination of human rights activist Hector Abad Gómez and proposing a "national pact for a government of peace," which begins with a "convention for life," to seek a negotiated solution to the social and military conflict, with the participation of the entire country.

The M-19 presents in the UN General Assembly a folder with documents about the dirty war in Colombia.

The different insurgent forces meet in Sumapaz and agree to build the Simón Bolívar Guerrilla Coordinator (CGSB). The coordinator rejects the Barco administration's ultimatum for demobilization.

1988

January The movement holds a meeting camp and decides to declare a unilateral truce with the army to support an anti-oligarchical policy of civil disobedience.

April The CGSB meets and decides to convoke a national consultation so the people can be heard on the issue of reform. There is talk of the need for a new constitution that would take into account the primary constitution and reflect the new social and political forces.

June The M-19 kidnaps Hurtado as an act of war against the oligarchy that is destroying the nation. It proposes a broad dialogue beyond the guerrillas and the government.

July A mini-summit of national leaders and the Catholic Church is held in Panamá to negotiate a national summit to be held later in the month in Colombia and to negotiate the release of Alvaro Gómez Hurtado.

The national government backs out of the summit. The Catholic Church proceeds with the event on its own and stresses the need to continue the dialogue process.

September The government publicizes its initiative for peace, which proposes changes in the policy of reconciliation, rehabilitation, and normalization, while recognizing the importance of dialogue.

December The regional and sectional dialogues continue with great difficulty. The CGSB studies the response to the governmental gestures toward constitutional reform. In Cauca an "admirable meeting for peace," which explores viable approaches to achieving peace in the zone, is widely attended.

1989

January M-19 commander Carlos Pizarro and presidential advisor Rafael Pardo issue a joint declaration that calls on other guerrilla groups, political parties, and social organizations to find a negotiated solution to the conflict.

February An M-19 meeting is held to evaluate the conversations with the government. Educators Isidro Caballero and María del Carmen Santana are disappeared in the department of Cesar.

A national meeting for peace is held in Ibagué to create a favorable environment for progress with the accords.

The FARC proposes the formation of a commission of notables to work for peace.

March M-19 leaders meet in Mexico with the presidential advisor. UP leader José Antequera is killed in Bogotá.

The M-19 issues the "Santo Domingo Declaration," which proposes concrete steps toward institutional normalization for the insurgents. A group of spokespersons is formed to represent the M-19 in political dialogues.

Troops of the IX Brigade attack the Gloria Amanda Rincón company, led by Chalita, in Huila.

April A roundtable for peace and national reconciliation is established in the Nariño Palace to guarantee participation in the construction of the "great social pact," which is intended to lead to a new constitutional charter as a peace treaty.

Afranio Parra, member of the M-19 high command, and two other compañeros are assassinated by three police officers in a neighborhood in the south of Bogotá.

May A roundtable for analysis and accords is established to make proposals for the work table, from which the constitutional charter reforms will come.

June The commission of notables meets with the FARC to agree, according to the disposition of the Fourth Conference of the CGSB, on mechanisms for direct dialogue with the government.

July Four M-19 militants are killed by troops of the V Brigade, along with a two-year-old minor, the son of one of the militants.

A woman from the Santo Domingo community is assassinated where the military forces of the M-19 are concentrated, as is an M-19 member on the Cali highway.

The roundtable concludes and the proposed laws discussed and accorded at the "analysis tables" as parts of the constitutional reform are presented.

Luis Carlos Galán Sarmiento, presidential favorite of the Liberal Party, is assassinated in Bogotá. The government adopts strong measures against drug trafficking and the group called "the Extraditables" responds by loosing a terrorist wave in the main cities of the country. Carlos Pizarro proposes a "pact for national salvation."

September A new declaration by the government and the M-19 announces the accords discussed in the "analysis tables," and proposes a demobilization plan that will legalize the insurgent movement.

October The Tenth National Conference of the M-19 is held in Santo Domingo, and the members vote (227 out of a total of 230) to lay down their arms, reintegrate themselves into civilian life, and build a legal political movement.

A meeting is held in the department of Meta with the CGSB and the government to talk about a possible signing of accords.

November The "political pact for peace and democracy" is entered into protocol, including twenty-seven proposals from the "analysis tables" on coexistence, strengthening justice and normalizing public order, socioeconomic issues, political democratization, and electoral issues.

The M-19 launches its proposal as a political movement: "More Than a Party."

December Congress issues a pardon for insurgents who "unmistakably" demonstrate their will to lay down their weapons, but the constitutional reforms contained in the political pact and presented to Congress are not passed in their entirety in the second round. Thus the status of the pact remains unresolved, but the M-19 maintains its determination to move ahead with the proposal.

1990

January Carlos Pizarro and Antonio Navarro meet in Bogotá with different social and political forces to try to establish a proposal for a vote to move ahead with the reforms. They succeed only in agreeing to primaries with the Liberal Party presidential candidates.

March The M-19 hands over its weapons in Santo Domingo in the presence of international observers and joins the legal political process.

Index